The

Publications

of

The Harleian Society

ESTABLISHED A.D. MDCCCLXIX

Volumes CXIII and CXIV

FOR THE YEARS MCMLXI AND MCMLXII

ASPILOGIA

BEING MATERIALS OF HERALDRY

GENERAL EDITOR

SIR ANTHONY WAGNER, K.C.V.O., F.S.A.

Garter King of Arms

II

ROLLS OF ARMS

HENRY III

THE MATTHEW PARIS SHIELDS

GLOVER'S ROLL

WALFORD'S ROLL

ADDITIONS AND CORRECTIONS
TO THE *CATALOGUE*

PLATE I

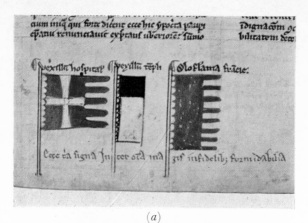

(a)

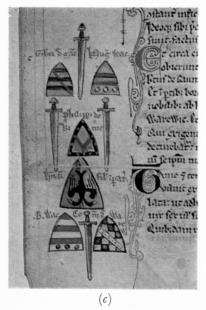

(b)

(c)   (d)

Illustrations from Matthew Paris. Corpus Christi College, Cambridge,
MS. 16
(a) MP IV. 41–3; (b) MP IV. 5; (c) MP IV. 49–54; (d) MP IV. 32 and VIII. 16

Rolls of Arms
Henry III

THE MATTHEW PARIS SHIELDS
c. 1244–59
Edited by THOMAS DANIEL TREMLETT, F.S.A.

———

GLOVER'S ROLL, *c.* 1253–8
AND
WALFORD'S ROLL, *c.* 1273
Edited by the late HUGH STANFORD LONDON, F.S.A.
Norfolk Herald Extraordinary

———

ADDITIONS AND CORRECTIONS TO
A CATALOGUE OF
ENGLISH MEDIAEVAL ROLLS OF ARMS
By SIR ANTHONY WAGNER, K.C.V.O., F.S.A.
Garter King of Arms

PRINTED AT
THE UNIVERSITY PRESS, OXFORD FOR
THE HARLEIAN SOCIETY
MCMLXVII

PRINTED IN GREAT BRITAIN

CONTENTS

PLATES

PREFACE

THE *Catalogue of English Mediaeval Rolls of Arms*, which appeared in 1950, was designed from the first to be followed by editions of the Rolls therein described and it was thought desirable that these should appear in chronological sequence. Work on the projected new *Dictionary of British Arms* and on texts of later rolls for use in its compilation (see p. 257 below) had, however, to be given precedence, and it was not until 1954 that the late H. S. London was able to start work on the editions of Glover's and Walford's Rolls, nor until 1958 that Mr. Tremlett undertook the editing of the Matthew Paris Shields.

These being the three oldest English rolls of arms and the oldest documents of English heraldry, apart from some few seals, literary references, and a very few arms on monuments and the like, it was thought that they should have more detailed annotation and analysis than would be necessary or possible for later rolls. It should not therefore be taken that editions which may follow these in the *Aspilogia* series will necessarily be comparable in scale. Furthermore, there are important distinctions between the Rolls in this volume, which are reflected in different editorial treatment. The Matthew Paris Shields are the work of a clerk, a keen, and accurate observer, but one who looked at heraldry from the outside. Glover's and Walford's Rolls, on the other hand, look like the work of heralds, or just possibly of knights, at all events of men personally and professionally involved in the subject. This appears first and foremost in the use of blazon, the technical language of heraldry.

Glover's Roll and its contemporary the French Bigot Roll mark an epoch in the development of heraldry because they are not only (putting Matthew Paris on one side) the earliest rolls of arms but are also the earliest texts in blazon and show this technical language at a crucial stage of development. Conventional forms and terminology had been attained, but these were in some ways fluid and still primitive compared with what we find fifty years later. On mediaeval blazon in general Mr. London was the best authority we have had, and it is therefore a great piece of good fortune that he was able to complete this study of its first stage. His observations on the subject in his introduction to Glover's and Walford's Rolls are a major contribution to our knowledge.

Certain names and arms are to be found in all three Rolls. Accordingly, a certain number of notes originally written by Mr. London for an occurrence in Glover or Walford has been transferred to an earlier occurrence in Matthew Paris. As if to balance this a number of the genealogical notes on Glover and Walford have been substantially revised by Mr. Tremlett. We have all, indeed, collaborated throughout, and no section of the book is the sole work of its nominal author. It is, however, but just to say that, since Mr. London died some eight years before the book went to press, the final touches and cross references were added to his section by Mr. Tremlett. The same so greatly regretted loss gives me an opportunity to point out once more how great a student of pure heraldry, its art, grammar, and development, we have lost in Hugh London. We have thus great reason to be thankful that his notes on Glover and Walford embody essays on a much wider range of topics than we had any right to demand, and in fact contain most of the material for an essay on the English heraldry of the first three-quarters of the thirteenth century. In the process he has set a new standard for the editing of heraldic documents.

My own section of the book has been read and criticized by Dr. C. E. Wright of the British Museum for whose constant help and advice in the interpretation of heraldic manuscripts and their history Mr. London, were he living, would, I know, wish to join me in expressing gratitude.

ANTHONY WAGNER

ABBREVIATIONS

THE late Mr. H. Stanford London transcribed for the projected *New Dictionary of British Arms* the greater number of the English mediaeval rolls of arms. Typescripts of these are in the library of the Society of Antiquaries and it is to these that reference is made. Only in a few instances was a printed text accepted as satisfactory and in these references the edition is indicated. For information about the rolls of arms the reader should consult *Aspilogia I, A Catalogue of English Mediaeval Rolls of Arms*, by A. R. Wagner, Society of Antiquaries, 1950.

A	Dering Roll.
AHS	*Archives Héraldiques Suisses*, i– .
AN	Antiquaries Roll.
Anselme	*Le Palais d'Honneur*, by P. G. Anselme. Paris, 1663.
Ant. Journ.	*The Antiquaries Journal.*
Arch.	*Archaeologia.*
Arch. Ael.	*Archaeologia Aeliana.*
Arch. Camb.	*Archaeologia Cambrensis.*
Arch. Cant.	*Archaeologia Cantiana.*
Arm. Équestre	*Armorial Équestre.*
AVD	*L'Art de Vérifier les Dates*, by M. F. d'Antine, C. Clémencet, and U. Durand.
B	Glover's Roll.
Baker, *Northants*	*The History and Antiquities of the County of Northampton*, by G. Baker. 2 vols. London: J. B. Nichols, 1822–30, 1836–41.
Barons Letter	*Some Feudal Lords and their Seals.* The De Walden Library, 1904.
Beds. Hist. Rec. Soc.	Bedfordshire Historical Records Society.
Berry	Armorial du Héraut Berry.
Bibl. nat.	Bibliothèque nationale.
Bigot	*Armorial Bigot*, ed. P. Adam-Even. *Archives Héraldiques Suisses*, xiii, 1949.
Birch	*Catalogue of British Museum Seals*, ed. W. de Gray Birch. 6 vols. London: British Museum, 1887–1900.
BM	British Museum.
Book of Fees	*Liber Feodorum. The Book of Fees*, commonly called *Testa de Nevill*. 3 vols. London: Stationery Office, 1920–31.

Book of Seals	*Sir Christopher Hatton's Book of Seals*, ed. L. C. Loyd and D. M. Stenton, Oxford: Clarendon Press, 1950.
BW	Bowyers Book.
Brit. Arch. Assoc.	*The Journal of the British Archaeological Association*, i– .
C	Walford's Roll.
Cal. Charter Rolls	*Calendar of Charter Rolls preserved in the Public Record Office*. 6 vols. London: Stationery Office, 1903–31.
Cal. Close Rolls	*Calendar of Close Rolls preserved in the Public Record Office*, London: Stationery Office, 1902–63.
Cal. Fine Rolls	*Calendar of the Fine Rolls preserved in the Public Record Office*, x–xxii. London: Stationery Office, 1911–62.
Cal. Gen.	*Calendarium Genealogicum. Henry III and Edward I*, ed. C. Roberts. 2 vols. London: Longmans, Green & Co., 1865.
Cal. Inq.	*Calendar of Inquisitions Post Mortem and other analogous documents preserved in the Public Record Office*, i–xiv. London: Stationery Office, 1904–52.
Cal. Pat. Rolls	*Calendar of Patent Rolls preserved in the Public Record Office*, i– . London: Stationery Office, 1901– .
Camb. Ant. Soc.	*Proceedings of the Cambridge Antiquarian Society*, i– .
CB	Coulon. *Inventaire des sceaux de la Bourgogne.*
CBB	'Notes on some of the Foreign Coats in the Roll of Arms of the Thirteenth Century comprised in the ms. no. 6589 of the Harleian Collection', by C.B.B. *Herald and Genealogist*, iv, 1867, pp. 425–34.
CEMRA	*Catalogue of English Medieval Rolls of Arms. Aspilogia I*, by A. R. Wagner. Society of Antiquaries, 1950.
CG	Cotgrave's Ordinary.
CKO	Cooke's Ordinary.
ChP	'Armorial Chifflet-Prinet', *Moyen Age*, 2ᵉ s. xxii, 1920.
Clay, *Extinct and Dormant Peerages*	*The Extinct and Dormant Peerages of the Northern Counties of England*, by J. W. Clay. London: J. Nisbet, 1913.
Clipearius	*Clipearius Teutonicorum*, ed. P. Ganz, *Histoire de l'art héraldique en Suisse*, 1899, p. 172.
CM	*Matthaei Parisiensis monachi Sancti Albani Chronica Majora*, ed. H. R. Luard. 7 vols. Rolls Series. London: Longman, 1872–83.
coh	coheir, coheiress.
Coll. Top. and Gen.	*Collectanea Topographica et Genealogica.*
CP	*The Complete Peerage.* 12 vols. London: the St. Catherine Press, 1910–59.
Cumb. and Westmorland Arch. Soc.	*Transactions of the Cumberland and Westmorland Antiquarian and Archaeological Society*, i– .
Corn. Gailliard	Corneille Gailliard, *L'Anchienne Noblesse de la contée de Flandres*. Maldeghem, 1866.
CVL	Calveley's Book.

D	Camden Roll.
d.	died.
dau	daughter.
DCL	Duchy of Lancaster, Coucher Book.
Ddq.	*Collection des sceaux de l'Empire* par Douet d'Arcq. 3 vols. Paris: Imprimerie Impériale, 1863–8.
D.L.	*David Lyndsay's Armorial.* Published as facsimile of an ancient Heraldic Manuscript emblazoned by Sir David Lyndsay of the Mount Lyon King of Arms 1542, ed. by David Laing. Edinburgh: William Paterson, 1878.
de Raadt	J.-Th. de Raadt, *Sceaux, armoiries des Pays-Bas et des pays avoisinants, recueil historique et héraldique.* Brussels: Société Belge de Librairie, 1898–1903. 4 vols.
Derbys. Arch. Journ.	*Journal of the Derbyshire Archaeological and Natural History Society*, 1879– .
DNB	*Dictionary of National Biography.*
d.s.p.	died *sine prole.*
Dugd. *Bar.*	Sir William Dugdale, *The Baronage of England.* 2 vols. London, 1675.
Durham Seals	Catalogue of the Seals in the Treasury of the Dean and Chapter of Durham from a manuscript made by the Revd. W. Greenwell collated by C. H. Hunter Blair. Society of Antiquaries of Newcastle-upon-Tyne, 1911–21.
d.v.p.	died *vita patris.*
E	St. George's Roll.
EYC	W. Farrer and C. T. Clay, *Early Yorkshire Charters.* 12 vols. Edinburgh: Ballantyne, Hanson & Co., and Yorkshire Archaeological Society, 1914–63.
Eyton, *Shropshire*	R. W. Eyton, *Antiquities of Shropshire.* 12 vols. London: John Russell Smith, 1854–60.
F	Charles Roll.
Feudal Cambs.	W. Farrer, *Feudal Cambridgeshire.* Cambridge University Press, 1920.
FW	Fitzwilliam Roll.
G	Segar's Roll.
Ganz	Paul Ganz, *Geschichte der heraldischen Kunz in der Schweiz in XII. und XIII. Jahrhundert.* Frauenfeld: J. Huber, 1899.
GB	Gandilhon, *Les Sceaux de Berry.*
GWW	Notes by G. W. Watson on the Fitzwilliam Roll in the *Genealogist*, N. s. vi–viii.

H	Falkirk Roll.
HA	Matthaei Parisiensis, *Historia Anglorum*, ed. F. Madden. 3 vols. Rolls Series, London, 1866–9.
Harl. Soc.	Harleian Society.
Haus zum Loch	'Wappen aus dem Haus zum Loch', published in *Die Wappenrolle von Zürich*, ed. W. Mery and F. Hegi. Zürich: Orell Füssli, 1930.
HE	Herald's Roll.
HKF	W. Farrer, *Honors and Knights Fees.* 3 vols. London: Spottiswoode, Ballantyne, 1923–5.
HMC	Historical Manuscripts Commission.
Hodgson, *Northumberland*	J. Hodgson, *History of Northumberland.* 7 vols. Newcastle-upon-Tyne, 1820–58.
J	Guillims Roll.
K	Caerlaverock Roll: *The Roll of Arms of the Princes, Barons and Knights who attended King Edward I to the siege of Caerlaverock in 1300*, edited from the manuscript in the British Museum with translation and notes by Thomas Wright, Esq., M.A., F.S.A., etc. London: John Camden Hotten, 1864.
L	First Dunstable Roll.
La Chenaye	La Chenaye des Bois, *Dictionnaire de la noblesse.* 1863–1876.
Lawrance	H. Lawrance, *Heraldry from Military Monuments before 1350 in England and Wales.* London, Harleian Society, 1940.
Lespinoy	P. Lespinoy, *Recherche des antiquitez et noblesse de Flandres.* Brussels, 1631.
Lipscomb, *Bucks.*	G. Lipscomb, *The History and Antiquities of the County of Buckingham*, 4 vols. London, 1847.
LMRO	Lord Marshal's Roll Old.
London, *Royal Beasts*	H. S. London, *Royal Beasts*, Heraldry Society, East Knoyle, 1956.
m	married.
Macdonald	W. R. Macdonald, *Scottish Armorial Seals.* Edinburgh, 1902.
MP	Matthew Paris.
Misc. Gen. et Her.	*Miscellanea Genealogica et Heraldica.* London: Hamilton Adams & Co., and Mitchell, Hughes & Clarke, 1868–1937.
Moor	C. Moor, *Knights of Edward I.* 5 vols. London, Harleian Society, 1929–32.
Morant	P. Morant. *History and Antiquities of Essex.* 2 vols. Chelmsford, 1816.

N	Great Parliamentary or Bannerets Roll.
Nav.	*Armorial du héraut Navarre.*
NCH.	*History of Northumberland.* 15 vols. Newcastle-upon-Tyne: Andrew Reid, 1893–1940.
Nichols, *Leics.*	J. Nichols, *The History and Antiquities of the County of Leicester.* 4 vols. London: J. Nichols, 1795–1811.
Northants Rec. Soc.	Northamptonshire Record Society.
P	Grimaldi's Roll.
P.A-E	Paul Adam-Even.
PCL	Portcullis' Book.
PE	Peterborough Roll.
Pinoteau	H. Pinoteau, *Héraldique Capétienne.* Paris, 1955.
PLN	Peter le Neve's book.
P*MA*	Prinet, *Moyen Age,* 2ᵉ s. xxv, Paris, 1923, pp. 223–56.
Po	Powell Roll.
PRO	Public Record Office.
Q	Collins' Roll.
RCHM	*Royal Commision on Historical Monuments.*
RD	Raine-Dunn Roll.
RH	Randle Holmes Book.
S	Willements Roll.
s	son.
Sandford	F. Sandford, *Genealogical History.* London, 1707.
Saunders, *English Illumination*	*English Illumination,* by O. E. Saunders, 2 vols. Florence, 1928.
SD	Second Dunstable Roll.
Soc. Ant.	Society of Antiquaries of London.
SP	*The Scots Peerage,* ed. J. B. Paul. Edinburgh, 1904-14.
Spener	Spenerus, *Historia Insignium Illustrium.* Frankfurt o. M., 1680.
Suffolk Inst. of Arch. Proc.	*Proceedings of the Suffolk Institute of Archaeology and Natural History,* 1849– .
Surtees, *Durham*	R. Surtees, *History and Antiquities of the County Palatine of Durham.* 4 vols. London: Nichols, Son and Bentley, 1816–40.
Suss. Arch. Coll.	*Sussex Archaeological Society's Collections.*
T. de C.	*Tournoi de Chauvenci.*
TJ	Thomas Jenyn's Roll.
VCH	*Victoria County History.*
Vetusta Monumenta	*Vetusta Monumenta.* 7 vols. Society of Antiquaries, 1747–1966.
v.p.	*vita patris.*

WB	Wrythe's Book.
Wijn	Wynbergen Roll, ed. P. Adam-Even, Jéquier, 1955.
WJ	William Jenyn's Roll.
WNR	Sir William le Neve's Roll.
WS	Walpole Society.
Yorks. Arch. Journal	*Yorkshire Archaeological Journal*, 1870– .
ZWR	*Die Wappenrolle von Zürich*, ed. W. Mery and F. Hegi, Zürich: Orell Füssli, 1930.

THE MATTHEW PARIS
SHIELDS

INTRODUCTION

MATTHEW PARIS illustrated his histories with paintings in the margin of the manuscripts. Many of these paintings are shields charged with the arms of the persons referred to in the text. They are placed upside down when the death of the owner was recorded. Others in a normal upright position accompany the notice of a coronation or other ceremonial event. In addition there is a sheet in the Liber Additamentorum (BM MS. Cotton Nero MS. D 1, f. 170, 170b) with painted and unpainted shields. In the same manuscript there is a sheet with twenty-seven roughly sketched shields.

These drawings and paintings may justly be considered to constitute the earliest English roll of arms and as such appear first in Sir Anthony Wagner's *A Catalogue of English Mediaeval Rolls of Arms, Aspilogia I*. In this edition the arms have been blazoned and each entry is accompanied by a note on the heraldry and on the persons concerned. The work is divided into eight parts.

I. BM Royal MS. 14 C VII, Matthew Paris, *Historia Anglorum*, the author's autograph copy to f. 154b, written on 232 vellum leaves measuring $14\frac{1}{4}$ by $9\frac{1}{2}$ in. The folios where the shields occur and the editions and notices are described in *Aspilogia I*. To this may be added *Matthew Paris*, by Dr. Vaughan (Cambridge, 1958), where there is a full discussion on all the manuscripts, particularly in chapters 2–8 and on the heraldry in pp. 250–3.

II. BM MS. Cotton Nero D I, f. 170, 170b (BM 171, 171b) f. 185 (BM 186), f. 198, 198b (BM 200, 200b).

Vellum leaf $8\frac{1}{2}$ by 14 in., painted and written. (a) On the face with 33 shields in 5 rows of 5, with 3 more below and 5 in the lower part of the right-hand margin, with names over and Latin blazons over them or below. Eleven of the shields are coloured and 1 partially so. (b) On the back are 42 shields in 7 rows of 6 all coloured, with 1 uncoloured beside the first row and torn fragments of 2 at the ends of the last 2 rows, with names over and Latin blazons over them and below. The editions and notices of this sheet are described in *Aspilogia I*.

There is little doubt that 170b, where all except one shield are coloured, was really the front sheet which at some date has been bound in back to front. In this edition the verso 170b is described first.

There are two shields on f. 185. There are 27 shields roughly drawn on f. 198 and 5 items on the dorse. This is a small piece of parchment $7\frac{1}{2}$ by 5 in. which was used by Matthew Paris for sketches and notes.

III. Corpus Christi College, Cambridge, MS. 26. Matthew Paris, *Chronica Majora*, vol. i, written at St. Albans and presented by him to the abbey. 2+6+140+2+1 vellum leaves measuring $14\frac{1}{5}$ by $9\frac{3}{5}$ in. The pages where the shields occur and the editions and notices are described in *Aspilogia I*.

IV. Corpus Christi College, Cambridge, MS. 16. Matthew Paris, *Chronica Majora*, vol. ii, written at St. Albans and presented by him to the abbey. 5+281 vellum leaves measuring 14⅕ by 9⅗ in. The pages where the shields occur, and editions and notices, are described in *Aspilogia I*.

V. MS. Chetham's Library (Manchester) 6712, Matthew Paris, *Flores Historiarum*. Quarto, written in double columns, containing in all 299 leaves including fly-leaves and Calendar prefixed to the volume after its removal from St. Albans to Westminster. On ff. 184ᵛ, 185ᵛ, 186ᵛ are painted four coats of arms. These are described in *Flores Historiarum*, edited by H. R. Luard (Rolls Series 95), in vol. ii, pp. 304, 305, 308, 312.

VI. BM MS. Cotton Claudius D VI, Matthew Paris, *Abbreviatio Chronicorum*. Author's original copy bound up with other historical works. 215 vellum leaves measuring 12¼ by 8¼ in. of which the *Abbreviatio* occupies 86. In the margins of ff. 16*b*, 20*b*, 36*b*, 90*b*, 91, 92, 94 are 11 shields. The work was edited by Sir Frederic Madden and printed in vol. iii of the *Historia Anglorum*, pp. 153–348 (Rolls Series 44). The shields are described on pp. 177, 186, 218, 219, 333, 336, 338, 339, 346.

VII. BM Royal MS. 14 C VII, Matthew Paris, *Chronica Majora*. This is the portion of the *Chronica Majora* from 1254 to 1259 bound at the end of the *Historia Anglorum*. It runs from f. 157 to f. 218*b*. In the margins of ff. 159*a*, 162*a*, 164*b*, 165*a*, 165*b*, 170*b*, 174*a*, 182*b*, 195*b*, 217*b*, are 11 shields of which 2 are left blank. This was edited by H. R. Luard in *Chronica Majora*, v. 421–748 (Rolls Series 57), and the shields are described on pp. 431, 448, 459, 463, 487, 504, 549, 741, with the exception of the two blank shields on f. 195*b*.

VIII. Heraldic details from drawings of scenes by Matthew Paris in sections 1, 2, 3, 4, and in Cambridge University Library MS. Ee iii 59 (Edward), *La estoire de Seint Aedward le Rei*. The drawings occur at the following places:

    1. BM Royal MS. 14 C VII, ff. 42*b*, 116*b*; they are described by Madden in *Historia Anglorum*, i. 223, and by M. R. James, *The Drawings of Matthew Paris*, Walpole Society, xiv. 19 and pl. XIX.

    2. BM MS. Cotton Nero D I, f. 3*b*, described by M. R. James, op. cit., p. 22 and pl. XXIII and in *Ancestor*, v. 108–9.

    3. Corpus Christi College, Cambridge, MS. 26, pp. 160, 220, 279, and are described by H. R. Luard in *Chronica Majora*, i. 498, ii. 144, 328, and by M. R. James, op. cit., pp. 5–6 and pls. II and III.

    4. Corpus Christi College, Cambridge, MS. 16, ff. 37, 44*b*, 51*b*, 75*b*, 88*b*, 133*b*, 170*b*, 194*b*, and are described by H. R. Luard in *Chronica Majora*, ii. 580, 640; iii. 23, 28, 87, 194, 254, 277; iv. 26, 306, 486; and by M. R. James, op. cit., pp. 8–16 and pls. VII, VIII, IX, XII, XIII, XIV, XVII.

    5. Cambridge University Library MS. Ee iii 59 (Edward): La Estoire de Seint Aedward le Rei. Drawings on pp. 3, 5, 6, 19, 20, 57, 60, 64, edited and described by M. R. James, Roxburghe Club, 1920.

    6. Trinity College, Dublin, MS. E i 40. Reproduced by W. R. L. Lowe and E. F. Jacob, with description by M. R. James, Oxford, 1924.

The arms from these pictures have been placed in a separate section. While some, as the shield and banner of the Knights Templar (VIII. 1.) are undoubtedly heraldic, there are many where the details, tinctures, and charges do not conform to heraldic practice. They are of a quasi-heraldic nature. Thus the shield of Reginald de Boulogne in the picture of the battle of Bouvines is *Argent, semy of annulets gules*. This we might take for his arms were it not that such a pattern occurs constantly. French knights and the Saracen king at the battle of Damascus have surcoats *semy of annulets*. Another frequent device is a small cross with a circle in the middle. A large number of such devices have been excluded from this work, but there remain a few which are on the border-line between heraldry and decoration.

The order of the first four sections is not the chronological order, but the order in which the manuscripts were listed in *Aspilogia I* and which it would be confusing to change.

The chronology of the manuscripts and the relationship of the drawings to each other is a matter of some complexity. The chronology has been examined by Dr. Vaughan in *Matthew Paris*, and it is chiefly on his conclusions that the following notes are based.

The earliest may be the sheet of arms in the Liber Additamentorum (BM MS. Cotton Nero D I), which was placed in *Aspilogia I* as No. 2. In the margin of f. 170*a* is a statement of the preparations of Henry III for war with Scotland in 1244:

Nota quod Rex Henricus III quando ivit hostiliter super regem Scotie Alexandrinum habet M et ducentos milites eleganter ad unguem armatos. Rex vero Scotie quingentos milites et sexaginta pedites milia. Pedites vero erant expediti et armis decenter communiti scilicet securibus peracutis, lanceis et arcubus, et animosi valde parati pro domino constanter vivere vel mori, vincere vel vinci, reputantes mortem martirum et salvationem.

As this is in the margin of the sheet, it suggests that the shields had already been painted in or before 1244.

Internal evidence supports a date of about 1244. There are at least twenty-one shields on the sheet which can be assigned without any doubt to individuals the dates of whose deaths are known. Thus the entry for Comitis Huntundene can only refer to John le Scot, Earl of Huntingdon who d.s.p. 1237. The earliest death of one of the twenty-one individuals is that of William de Mandeville, Earl of Essex, who d.s.p. 1227, and the latest that of Richard, Earl of Cornwall, who d. 1272. Four of these persons died between 1234 and 1237, seven between 1241 and 1249, five between 1250 and 1257, and three between 1265 and 1268. Certainty cannot be attained, but a date of 1244/5 seems likely.

Whether this collection of shields was made to illustrate a particular group of people or whether it is merely a collection of those arms that Matthew knew, is a question that is still unresolved. Major Göschen considered that they were the shields of benefactors to churches but was unable to prove that they were benefactors of St. Albans (Major Oscar Göschen ('Pusikan'), *Wappen aus den Werken des Matthias von Paris* (†1259) in *Vierteljahrsschrift für Heraldik, Sphragistik und Genealogie. Herausgegeben vom Verein* ('Herold') zu Berlin, IX. Jahrgangs,

Berlin, 1881). Nor is the argument at all convincing that they are the shields of the benefactors of Westminster Abbey, whose forty shields were placed in the north and south aisles. In the first place, there is no proof of any connexion between Matthew and Westminster Abbey. Secondly, the coincidence between the arms in the Liber Additamentorum and those in Westminster Abbey is no more than would be expected of two series of arms of the principal men of that date. Of the forty shields listed by Neale (*Westminster Abbey*, ii. 26–27) fifteen at least do not appear in the Liber Additamentorum sheet. If this sheet were intended to record the arms of the Westminster benefactors, the coincidence would have to be far more complete. We are driven to conclude that this collection was made for Matthew's own interest. Possibly, it was an exercise in blazon and painting to be used as a reference for the arms he was to draw in the margin of his histories.

Though not of the importance of f. 170, 170*b*, the small manuscript of rough drawings of shields, f. 198, 198*b* (BM 200, 200*b*), at the end of the Liber Additamentorum, may be slightly earlier in date. Close by the first entry is written 'xxxvj milia marcas cepit rex de episcopatu Wintoniense vacat'. This must relate to the vacancy between the death of Peter des Roches in June 1238 and the admission by the king of the election of William de Ralegh in April 1244 (Le Neve, *Fasti Ecclesiae Anglicanae*, iii. 8–9). Under the year 1239 Matthew writes of the oppression of the See of Winchester by the king (*CM* iii. 622). The note may have been added before the shields were drawn but it is probably contemporary. It seems natural that Matthew should use scraps of parchment for sketches and notes of heraldry, which he used before painting the finished shield.

The earliest manuscripts of the histories appear to be those at Corpus Christi College, Cambridge, Mss. 26 and 16. They were begun about 1245 and continued until 1251. The chronicle was then continued until 1259, the last shield being on f. 279, in MS. 16, in the annal for the year 1253.

The *Historia Anglorum* (BM Royal MS. 14 C VII) is an abridgement of the *Chronica Majora* which was begun in 1250 and continued until 1259.

The *Flores Historiarum* (Chetham's Library, Manchester, MS. 6712) was written shortly after 1250.

The Abbreviatio (BM MS. Cotton Claudius D VI) was compiled probably after 1255.

The *Chronica Majora* (BM Royal MS. 14 C VII) runs from 1254 to 1259.

The early date of the Paris shields gives them an exceptional importance. In these manuscripts there are 143[1] different coats for about 400 different persons. The difference between the two figures is explained by the repeated use of such coats as those of England, France, Marshal for several members of those families. Only the first appearance of a coat is included in the first figure. Only seals can claim an equal importance, and although some seals give earlier examples of arms none, of course, show the tinctures. Moreover, of the British coats which number 72, 27 appear for the first time in these manuscripts, and this figure does not include any of the coats that appear on seals of approximately the same dates as the manuscripts, nor arms which differ in some minor way from those belonging to a family which appeared on a seal of earlier date (see Appendix).

[1] In all statistics the heraldic details from sketches in MP VIII are not included.

The arms of nearly all the most important lay magnates of the time make their appearance. Berkeley, Mohun, Mortimer are omitted, but none of them were of the first importance at that time. Moreover, arms of persons of far less importance as John de Lexington, Geoffrey and William de Mareys are included. Matthew also painted the arms of foreign rulers as the emperor, the kings of France, Jerusalem, and Norway.

In the Nero sheet the descriptions of the arms are written above each shield. The terms are usually but not wholly in Latin as *scutum de gules leones aurei* for 'gules, three lions passant gardant or', and *scutum de gules, cuppe argentee* for 'gules, three covered cups argent'. *Albus, aureus, rubeus, niger,* and *viridis* are used for 'argent', 'or', 'gules', 'sable', and 'vert'. *Argenteus, d'argent, de blanc* are also used for 'argent'; *azur, de azuro, d'azur,* and *azurineus* are used also for 'azure'; *gules* for 'gules', and *de purpura* for 'purpure'. *Leo, aquila, avis,* and *uter* are used for 'lion', 'eagle', 'bird', and 'bouget'. *Superius* and *in capite* are used for 'in chief', *in pede* for 'in base', *campus* for 'field', *utrobique* and *lineata* for 'cotised'. The French terms as *rampanz, benda, fesse, papegai* (latinized as *papaginibus*), *cheverun, manche, devant* (dexter), *unde* also occur. *Fesse* is used indiscriminately for any transverse stripe; thus it is used for fess in II. 57, 70, 109, for bar in II. 68, and for bend in II. 28. *Benda* is used for bar in II. 56.

In the introduction to the Glover and Walford rolls, Mr. London has discussed at some length the nature of blazon in the thirteenth century. Matthew's descriptions are certainly not the technical blazon of the other two rolls. '*Scutum superius de gules, leo aureus, inferius scutum de albo fesse de gules aves de gules*' is not an adequate blazon of '*Argent, a bend between five martlets gules, on a chief gules a lion passant gardant or*' (Bassingbourne). The 'blazons' of Burgh (II. 16) and Percy (II. 52) are incomprehensible. In eleven cases Matthew omits the number of a charge. On the other hand, in some respects his descriptions correspond to blazons in the technical sense. The tincture of the field is given first. The number of charges is given nineteen times out of a possible thirty. The position of the charges is not, however, indicated except in Bassingbourne cited above and '*Quarterium ubi stella alba de gules aliud cum suo [pari] aureum*' for Vere. Prepositions as *cum* for 'with' and *a* are used, e.g. '*Scutum de or cheveruns cum bordura de gules*' for Daubeney and '*Scutum de or bende or a iij gasteus de blanc*' for Huntingfield.

The usual six tinctures and two furs are used. The fields are gules (30), or (30), argent (20), azure (17), sable (5), vert (1). Vairy occurs twice, ermine once. There are 10 quarterly fields, 9 per pale, one of them per pale gules and azure étincelé or, 5 barry, 3 party per fess, 3 checky, 1 lozengy, 1 paly and 1 gyronny.

The most common charge is a lion (27) usually rampant. The next commonest is the cross (20), plain (4), patonce (4), formy (4), recercly (3), moline (3), voided (1), Toulouse (1)). Bends (12), bars (13), fess (16), and chevrons (7), are the next most frequent charges.

Marks of cadency occur four times, the label of Lusignan-Valence (I. 83), Artois (I. 94), the crescent and roundel of Conrad, king of Sicily (VI. 8), and the fess of Manfred, illegitimate son of Frederick II (VI. 9). Of differencing in the larger sense by adding a charge to a coat to form a different coat, there is the example of the sable bend of Lacy making '*Quarterly or and gules, a bend sable*' for John de Lacy, Earl of Lincoln, whose arms belong to the Mandeville group of allied coats. It is difficult to determine whether the following are intentional differences or merely variations without significance:

Geoffrey de Mandeville: *Quarterly gules and or* (I. 25)

William de Mandeville, his brother: *Quarterly or and gules* (I. 43)

Eustace de Vescy: *Gules, a cross patonce argent* (I. 26)

William de Vescy, his son: *Gules, a cross moline argent* (I. 102)

William D'Aubigny, Earl of Arundel: *Gules, a lion queue fourchée or* (I. 36)

Hugh D'Aubigny, Earl of Arundel, his brother: *Gules, a lion rampant or* (I. 72)

There are several different versions or variations of the Marshal arms:

William Marshal, d. 1219.
Party per pale or and vert, a lion rampant queue fourchée gules (I. 29).
Party per pale or and vert, a lion rampant gules (IV. 14, 30).

William Marshal, d. 1231.	Richard Marshal, d. 1234.	Gilbert Marshal, d. 1241.	Walter Marshal, d. 1245.	Anselm Marshal, d. 1245.
Party per pale or and vert, a lion rampant gules (I. 47).	*Party per pale or and vert, a lion rampant queue fourchée gules* (I. 50; IV. 32).	*Party per pale or and vert, a lion rampant queue fourchée gules* (I. 51). *Party per pale or and vert, a lion rampant gules* (I. 65; II. 18). *Party per pale or and vert, a lion rampant argent* (IV. 47).	*Party per pale gules and vert, a lion rampant queue fourchée argent* (I. 78). *Party per pale or and vert, a lion rampant gules* (IV. 66; V. 2).	*Party per pale gules and vert, a lion rampant queue fourchée argent* (I. 79). *Party per pale or and vert, a lion rampant gules* (IV. 67; V. 2).

It does not seem possible to discern any system of differencing in these variations.

Only one coat is attributed to two different families, that is 'Ermine, three bars gules' (II. 56) for Giffard and Hussey of Hastings.

Dimidiation occurs three times: England dimidiating the Empire for Otto, Emperor of Germany (I. 21, 24; IV. 5); Henry, son of Frederick II (VI. 7; VII. 2); and the Empire dimidiating *a cross recercly argent* for Henry, son of Frederick II (I. 69). There is also a shield of England dimidiating *sable* as a sign of mourning for Henry, son of Henry II (III. 13).

The only quartered coat, apart from those whose fields were always quarterly (i.e. Mandeville, Beauchamp, and Neville), is that of Castile quartering Leon. There are six examples of canting coats: two barbels for Bar (I. 60): three herrings for Herring (II. 40): three sparrow hawks or muschets for Muschet (II. 41): three kennets or hunting dogs for Kennet (II. 50): a fess of five fusils for Percy (II. 52): a cross voided for Crevequer (II. 66). 'Gules, three bars wavy argent' may possibly be a canting coat for Sandford (IV. 81).

In VIII. 8, 15, 16 there are charges that may be regarded as crest and as badges. In VIII. 8 one of King John's minions wears a surcoat powdered with hammers, in VIII. 15 William, Earl Marshal, bears a hammer on his shield, and in VIII. 16 Richard, Earl Marshal, has a surcoat or, powdered with hammers gules, with a hammer on his helmet and a hammer on the back of the pommel of his saddle. Hammers also occur in VIII. 31 in a shield and on saddle of the soldiers of Verulam. In the absence of any other evidence it seems unlikely that this device was ever borne by the Earls Marshal and it is probably an invention of Matthew's who saw its appropriateness for the Marshals. The horn above the shield of John de Neville, Chief Forester, (IV. 69), may be an official badge.

Matthew attributes arms to people who never bore them as Harold, William I, and William II. It is not necessary to assume that he really thought that they used arms. The illustrations in the margin were not inserted in any scientific sense, but he drew arms for those he mentioned in the text, as today the arms of saints may be placed on screens in churches without any suggestion that such arms were ever borne in practice.

Dr. Vaughan has discussed in detail the problem of how far the illustrations in the manuscripts are Matthew's own work. Only a few he considers may be attributed to another hand. At the end of his life he had an assistant who probably painted the shields in the end leaves of the *Chronica Majora*, the *Historia Anglorum*, and the *Abbreviatio Chronicorum*. Dr. Vaughan also feels doubtful about the attribution to Matthew of the pictures of the seated kings and their shields in the *Abbreviatio Chronicorum*.

As Matthew was a person of wide interests it is not surprising that he should have taken a lively interest in heraldry. It appealed to him as an artist and a chronicler. He shows a wide range of knowledge of both English and foreign arms. There does not seem to be any need to suggest that he derived his knowledge from a roll of arms that has since been lost. He collected his information from visitors to the abbey and on his travels. The blazon of Fitz Matthew (II. 71) and the Valence note (II. 64) suggest that he had seen pictured representations of the arms, but *secundum dictum* (II. 27) points rather to verbal information. No very recondite knowledge was needed to compile his collection. St. Albans was a day's journey from London on the main road to the north. Dr. Vaughan has printed a list of visitors to the abbey mentioned by Matthew and by Roger Wendover between 1220 and 1259, which shows that Henry III stayed at the abbey nine times, and was doubtless on these occasions accompanied by the Court. As Dr. Vaughan has said, a visitor's book would have contained the names of most of the eminent men of the time. Among Matthew's known friends and those whom he consulted were Henry III, Richard, Earl of Cornwall, Hubert de Burgh, Richard de Clare, and John of Lexington—all of whose arms he depicted. Heraldry was in the thirteenth century a part of everyday life. Matthew learnt his heraldry as he learnt the events he chronicled.

In the text the name of the family is given in capital letters. Then follows the caption or extract from the text of the manuscript to which the shield refers, the blazon in italics, and identification. In MP II the conventional blazon is given in the line below the description given by Matthew Paris. This is followed by the folio references and references to the printed texts of the manuscripts. Each entry is numbered. Cross-references are given but not completely for those arms which occur with great frequency. A reader wishing to consult all the examples of the arms of England, France, or coats of such frequency, should use the index. The cross-references are given for the first appearance of the arms in the text and for other examples where some variation may be of interest. Beneath each entry is a brief comment on the arms if such a comment appears useful, and a note on the person who bore them. Dates are given in new style and the year is assumed to begin on 1 January.

Acknowledgements

The work on the Matthew Paris Shields for this edition was first undertaken by Mr. W. H. Humphreys, F.S.A., whose notes have been of great value. I must thank Miss Hilda Lofthouse for kindly answering questions about the Chetham Library manuscript, Mr. W. O'Sullivan, Keeper of Manuscripts, Trinity College, Dublin, for allowing me to examine the paintings in the Book of St. Albans on exhibition at Burlington House. Miss Eileen Edwards, Miss Sheila Furnell, gave help and advice at many stages. Dr. Richard Vaughan, Professor Francis Wormald, F.B.A., Mr. Michael Maclagan, F.S.A., and Dr. C. E. Wright, F.S.A., have given generous help. I owe a debt, and I think Mr. London would acknowledge a greater one, to Dr. Paul Adam-Even who has been constantly consulted about foreign coats and who commented on the notes to Walford's Roll. I have to thank the Syndics and Librarian of the Cambridge University Library for allowing me to examine *La Estoire de Seint Aedward le Rei*. I have to thank the Master and Fellows of Corpus Christi College, Cambridge, for leave to reproduce paintings. Mr. N. H. MacMichael, F.S.A., read the book in proof and gave much valuable help. I must thank Sir Anthony Wagner, K.C.V.O., Garter King of Arms, the general editor of this series, for constant and invaluable help at every stage. Finally, whatever merits this edition may possess are mainly due to Mr. London: for the errors and defects I am responsible.

T. D. TREMLETT
Society of Antiquaries

APPENDIX

As far as is known arms of the following British families occur for the first time in Matthew Paris. For the others there is known to be a seal of an earlier or contemporary date.

Bassingbourne	Oddingseles of Maxstoke
Beauchamp of Bedford	Peyvre of Toddington
Beauchamp	Reviers, Earl of Devon
Berners of Dunmow	Ros of Helmsley
Breauté	Sandford of Aston Sandford
Despenser	Scotland, King of
FitzNichol	Segrave of Segrave
Giffard	Siward
Kennet	Thweng
Lexington	Tong
Mareys	Turberville of Bradninch
Marshal, Earls	Umfraville of Prudhoe
Mounteney	Wales, Prince of
Muschet	

MATTHEW PARIS SHIELDS

MP I

British Museum Royal MS. 14 C VII

Historia Anglorum, ed. Madden, Rolls Series 44

HAROLD, King of England

1. Clipeus Haraldi.

Azure, a lion rampant queue fourchée or. (Shield and crown reversed.)

Death of Harold, 1066.

> f. 10a.   HA i. 7. Cf. MP III. 1, 2; VIII. 29 (*p*).
>
> There is no evidence that Harold ever bore arms, nor has this lion been found except in MP. In MP III the tail is forked. Later rolls from *c.* 1380 (WJ 808) give him two bars between six leopards' faces, sometimes with a crusuly field.

ENGLAND

2. Clipeus Willelmi ducis Normannorum et jam novi Anglorum regis.

Gules, three lions passant gardant or. (Shield with crown above.)

Coronation of William I.

> f. 10a   HA i. 7. Cf. MP I. 19.
>
> Although Matthew attributes this coat to the Conqueror and all his successors, there is no evidence that it was used before its appearance in 1195 on the second great seal of Richard I (MP I. 19). There is, indeed, no evidence that any armorial bearings were ever used by William I or William II, though it is probable that Henry I (MP I. 5) used a lion in some way or other, and there are grounds for thinking that Henry II bore two lions passant gardant. (London, *Royal Beasts*, ch. iii.)

ENGLAND, William I

3. Willelmus primus.

Gules, three lions passant gardant or. (Shield, crown, and sceptre reversed.)

Death of William I, 1087.

> f. 13b.   HA i. 35. Cf. MP I. 19.

ENGLAND, William II

4. Willelmus cognomento Rufus.

Gules, three lions passant gardant or. (Shield with crown below.)

Coronation of William Rufus, 1087.

> f. 13b.   HA i. 35. Cf. MP I. 19.

Second s. of William I, d. 1100.

ENGLAND, Henry I

5. De coronatione Henrici Primi Anglorum regis.

Gules, three lions passant gardant or. (Shield with crown and sceptre.)

Coronation of Henry I, 1100.

> f. 36a.   HA i. 176. Cf. MP I. 19.

> Youngest s. of William I. Although there is no direct evidence that Henry I used arms, the fact that when knighting Geoffrey of Anjou he gave him a shield powdered with golden lions leaves little doubt that Henry himself used a lion, or lions, in some way or other. (London, *Royal Beasts*, ch. iii.)

JERUSALEM, Godfrey de Bouillon

6. Rex Godefridus Jerosolimorum.

Or, a cross argent. (Shield reversed with crown below.)

Death of Godfrey de Bouillon, King of Jerusalem, 1100.

> f. 37a.   HA i. 185. Cf. MP I. 101; II. 1 : C 14.

> Second s. of Count Eustace II of Boulogne; Duke of Lorraine 1082; elected king of Jerusalem 1099, but refused the title of king and was styled *Advocatus Sancti Sepulchri*. (Runciman, *The History of the Crusades*, i. 145–6, 292–3.)
>
>   These arms are assigned by Matthew to the kings of Jerusalem on five occasions, but the *Clipearius Teutonicorum, c.* 1242, line 9, gives *Argent, a cross gules*. Some support for one or the other of these is afforded by the seal of Amaury I of Anjou, d. 1175, which has a representation of the city of Jerusalem, with a banner charged with a cross. MP I. 101 and MP II. 1 give *Or crusuly argent, a cross argent*, but D 1 and FW 2, both *c.* 1280, reverse the tinctures, and *Wijn*, 1259, of a similar date, substitutes a crosslet for the plain cross. The cross potent, which soon became the established pattern in the arms of Jerusalem, first appears in C 14, *c.* 1275, 'Le roy d'Acre d'argent poudre a croysille d'or a une croys d'or byllette'. The seal of Louis de Beaumont, Bishop of Durham 1318–33 (Birch 2459), gds. of John de Brienne (MP I. 101), still has the field crusuly, but soon after that the crosslets were reduced to four (*Nav.* 1256). (P. Adam-Even, *Études d'Héraldique Médiévale, Contribution a l'Héraldique de l'Orient Latin; Coat of Arms*, i. 25–26.)

JERUSALEM, Baldwin I

7. Coronatione regis Jerosolimitani Baldewine.

Or, a cross argent. (Shield with crown above.)

Coronation of Baldwin, King of Jerusalem, 1100.

> f. 37.   HA i. 186. Cf. MP I. 6.

> A younger brother of Godfrey de Bouillon (MP I. 6); Count of Edessa 1089; elected King of Jerusalem in succession to his brother 1100; d. 1118. (Runciman, *History of the Crusades*, i. 324–6,; ii. 105–6.)

FRANCE, Philip I

8. Obiit rex Francorum.

Azure, semy de lis or (4, 3, 3, 2, 1). (Shield with crown below, both reversed.)

Death of Philip I, King of France, 1060–1108, s. of Henry I.

> f. 40b.   HA i. 209.

> S. of Henry I. On the great seals of Henry I (d. 1060) and of Philip I (d. 1108) the king is represented with a fleur-de-lis in his right hand. This charge appears on coins under Louis VI (d. 1137) and in quasi-heraldic guise on a seal of Louis VII (d. 1180). It is practically certain that this last used the above coat. Old France, as it is commonly called, was certainly borne by his son Philip II (d. 1223) and by his successors. At first the number of fleurs-de-lis varied. Philip III, for example, shows 10 on his royal counterseal, but the seal of the regents in 1285 has only 3, and that number was seen as early as 1228. In MP the number is usually 6, but 3, 7,

9, 10, and 13 occur. In 1376 under Charles V, New France, *azure, three fleurs-de-lis or*, was officially adopted as the royal arms in deference to the insistence of the intellectuals that these should symbolize the Blessed Trinity. Nevertheless, Old France continued in use for some time side by side with New France. (Pinoteau, *Héraldique Capétienne, I.*: Ddq. 32, 33.)

The Temple (*see* MP VIII. 1).

FRANCE, Philip, associate king

9. De morte Philippi regis Francorum.
Azure, semy de lis or (3, 3, 1). (Shield uncoloured with crown below, both reversed.)
Death of Philip.

> f. 45a.   *HA* i. 243. Cf. MP I. 8.
>
> S. of Louis VI; associate king 1129; d. 1131. Matthew enters his death under the year 1129. (*AVD* v. 516).

ENGLAND, Henry I

10. Obiit rex Henricus Primus.
Gules, three lions passant gardant or. (Shield with crown below, both reversed.)
Death of Henry I, 1135.

> f. 46a.   *HA* i. 250. Cf. MP I. 19.

ENGLAND, Stephen

11. Coronatur rex Stephanus.
Gules, three lions passant gardant or. (Shield with crown above.)
Coronation of Stephen, 1136.

> f. 46a.   *HA* i. 251. Cf. MP I. 19.
>
> Nephew of Henry I, being s. of William I's dau. Adela, or Alice, by Stephen, Count of Blois. Stephen landed in England a few days after Henry's death on 18 Dec. and was crowned on 22 Dec. 1135. These events took place under the zodiacal sign of the sagittary, and BW 11 (*c.* 1445) gives for Stephen, *Gules, three sagittaries or.* Nicholas Upton, *c.* 1400, gives the same, adding that he bore those arms because he entered England under that sign. (*Uptoni de Studio Militari*, ed. Bysshe, 1654, pp. 129–30.) Ralph Brooke, on the other hand, gives Stephen a single sagittary and, while repeating Upton's explanation, adds that the arms also allude to the victory won by Stephen's archers. (*Catalogue*, 1622, pp. 6–7.) There is no evidence that Stephen bore either the sagittaries or the lions.

JERUSALEM, Fulk

12. Fulco rex Jerosolimitanus moritur.
Or, a cross argent. (Shield uncoloured with crown below, both reversed.)
Death of Fulk, King of Jerusalem, 1143.

> f. 49a.   *HA* i. 271. Cf. MP I. 6.
>
> Fulk, Count of Anjou, m. Melissande, dau. of Baldwin II, King of Jerusalem (d. 1131), and was elected king on the death of his father-in-law. (Runciman, *History of the Crusades*, ii. 233.)
>   Matthew enters his death under the year 1142.

ENGLAND, Stephen

13. Corona et clipeus regis Stephani.
Gules, three lions passant gardant or. (Shield with crown below, both reversed.)
Death of Stephen, 1154.

> f. 53a.   *HA* i. 299. Cf. MP I. 19.

ENGLAND, Henry II

14. Corona et clipeus regis Henrici secundi.
Gules, three lions passant gardant or. (Shield with crown above.)
Coronation of Henry II, 1154.

> f. 53*a*.   *HA* i. 300. Cf. MP I. 19.
>
> S. of Geoffrey of Anjou by Maud, dau. of Henry I and widow of the Emperor Henry V.

FRANCE, Philip II

15. Philippus consecratur in regem Francorum.
Azure, semy de lis or (4, 3, 2, 1). (Shield with crown above.)
Coronation of Philip II, known as Philip Augustus, 1179.

> f. 69*b*.   *HA* i. 417. Cf. MP I. 8.
>
> S. of Louis VII by Adèle de Champagne, d. 1223.

FRANCE, Louis VII

16. Obiit Lodowicus rex Francorum pius.
Azure, semy de lis or (4, 3, 2, 1). (Shield reversed.)
Death of Louis VII, 1180.

> f. 69*b*.   *HA* i. 418. Cf. MP I. 8.
>
> Louis VII 'le jeune', 1137–80, s. of Louis VI by Alice of Savoy, m. Eleanor of Aquitaine who after her divorce m. Henry II of England.

ENGLAND, 'the young king'

17. Corona et clipeus regis Henrici junioris.
Gules, three lions passant gardant or. (Shield with crown below, both reversed.)
Death of Henry, s. of Henry II, 1180.

> f. 70*b*.   *HA* i. 426. Cf. MP I. 19.
>
> Associate king during his father's lifetime, crowned 1170, d.v.p. 1182.

ENGLAND, Henry II

18. Rex Henricus secundus.
Gules, three lions passant gardant or. (Shield reversed with crown below.)
Death of Henry II, 1189.

> f. 77*a*.   *HA* ii. 3. Cf. MP I. 19.

ENGLAND, Richard I

19. Ut dux Ricardus in Angliam coronandus venerit. *Gules, three lions passant gardant or.* (Shield with crown above.)
Accession of Richard I, 1189.

> f. 77*a*.   *HA* ii. 3.
>
> Eldest surviving s. of Henry II. On his first great seal Richard carries a shield of which the dexter half only is visible, this being charged with a lion rampant towards the sinister. Some have inferred that Richard bore two lions combatant, others that he bore a single lion rampant: arguments can be found for both views and failing further evidence the question remains open. In either case the coat was soon discarded and Richard's second seal, cut in 1195, displays the three lions passant gardant which have been the royal arms ever since. (London, *Royal Beasts*, p. 12; Landon, *The Itinerary of King Richard I*, Pipe Roll Society li (1935), Appendix A.)

JERUSALEM, Henry of Champagne

20. De morte Henrici Regis Jerosolimitani.
Or, a cross argent. (Shield uncoloured with crown below, both reversed.)
Death of Henry de Champagne, King of Jerusalem, 1197.

f. 83*b*.   *HA* ii. 61. Cf. MP I. 6.

Henry de Troyes, Count of Champagne, s. of Henry, Count of Champagne by Mary, dau. of Louis VII of France by Eleanor of Aquitaine; m. Isabella, dau. and h. of Amalric I, King of Jerusalem (1174), governed the kingdom of Jerusalem 1192–7 but never became king; d. 1197. (Runciman, *History of the Crusades*, iii. 28–29, 66, 82–83, 93.)

THE EMPIRE, Otto IV

21. Scutum Ottonis imperatoris, cujus medietas de scuto est imperii, alia vero de scuto regis Angliae.
Gules, three lions passant gardant or, dimidiating *Or, a double eagle displayed sable.* (Shield with crown above uncoloured.)
Coronation of Otto IV.

f. 84*a*.   *HA* ii. 65. Cf. C 1.

S. of Henry the Lion, Duke of Saxony, King of Germany 1198–1218, Emperor 1209; d. 1218.

It would seem that after the foundation of the new Roman Empire in the west, Charlemagne adopted the eagle as a symbol of the restored imperium. An eagle was placed on the gable of the palace at Aachen. In the reign of Otto II (973–83) Richerus (*Scriptores Rerum Germanicarum, Richeri Historiarum*, lib. iv (Hanover, 1877), p. 111) writes of a bronze eagle on the palace 'Aeneam aquilam, quae in vertice palatii a Karola Magno acsi volans fixa erat, in vulturnum converterunt. Nam Germani eam in favonium converterant, subtiliter significantes, Gallos suo equitatu quandoque posse devinci.' A tunic of Henry II (1002–24) in the National Museum at Munich is decorated with two-headed eagles. (Dreger, *Künstlerische Entwicklung der Weberei und Stickerei* (Wien, 1904), pp. 77–78 and pl. 55.) It should be remembered that needlework of Byzantine origin or inspiration is frequently adorned with eagles. The great seal of Conrad II (1024–39) shows the emperor with an eagle perched on his right hand. (Posse, *Die Siegel der Deutschen Kaiser und Könige* (Dresden, 1909), pl. 13.) The monk Günther (*Ligurinus*, vii. 504 sq.; Migne, *Patrologia Latina*, vol. ccxii), writing *c.* 1180, speaks of the brilliance of the emperor's eagle, and Otto Morena says that the Milanese promised after the reduction of the city in 1158 to place an eagle on the campanile of the cathedral as a sign of fealty. (*Historia rerum Laudensium;* L. A. Muratorius, *Rerum Italicarum scriptores* (Milan, 1725), tom. vi, col. 1022.)

In MP II. 46 Matthew is uncertain whether the imperial eagle is one-headed or two-headed. In the Chronicles he usually draws the eagle with two heads, and in the dimidiated examples it may be assumed that one head is cut off. C 1 assigns the two-headed eagle to the emperor, and the single-headed to the king of the Romans or the king of Germany (C 1, 8), and that is of some interest as an early instance of a distinction between the two eagles, a distinction which is only established on the imperial seals in 1443. (D. L. Galbreath, *Manuel du Blason* (1942), p. 325, citing Gritzner, '*Symbole und Wappen des alten deutschen Reiches*', Leipziger Studien aus dem Gebiete der Geschichte, viii. 3 (Leipzig, 1902).) About 1314 the two eagles, double and single, were set in the armorial window in the north nave aisle of York Minster. (Harrison, *Painted Glass of York* (1927), p. 42; cf. Purey-Cust, *Heraldry of York Minster*, pp. 371–5.)

ZWR 23 only gives the single-headed eagle, naming it 'Rom', but *Nav.* 1250 gives the double-headed eagle for the emperor. FW 3, 5 distinguishes between the two eagles, and D 2, 4 appears to have made the same distinction, though the roll is too damaged to be read with certainty.

The dimidiated arms here attributed to Otto IV are not a mere invention of the artist but seem to have been used. This dimidiation of the eagle appeared absurd to Thomasin von Zeuklaere. In *Der Wälsche Gast* (*c.* 1216) (ed. H. Rückert, *Bibliothek der gesammten deutschen*

National-Literatur, iii, Quedlinburg und Leipzig, 1852) he says that a man cannot fly with only one wing

> swer mit einem vetich vliegensol
> der mac niht gevliegen fol (lines 12441–2), and

> ich sprach daz niene fol
> in iemens schilt dii lewen gar
> erschînen und ein halber ar (lines 12352–4).

The seal of Mary of Brabant, second wife of Otto IV (1258), shows the arms as here described (Hauptmann, *Die Wappen in der Historia Minor des Matthew Parisiensis*. (Jahrbuch der K. K. Heraldischen Gesellschaft Adler, Neue Folge, 91 Bund, (Wien, 1909), fig. 80.) On the arms of the empire see also *ZWR*, pp. 16–17; Major Oscar Göschen ('Pusikan'), 'Wappen aus den Werken des Matthias von Paris († 1259)' in *Vierteljahrsschrift für Heraldik, Sphragistik und Genealogie*. Herausgegeben vom Verein 'Herold' zu Berlin, IX. Jahrgang, Berlin, 1881.

ENGLAND, Richard I

22. Corona et clipeus regis Ricardi spiculati.
Gules, three lions passant gardant or. (Shield with crown below, both reversed; at the base of the shield is a cross-bow with an arrow in the notch.)
Death of Richard I, 1199.

> f. 85*b*.   *HA* ii. 76. Cf. MP I. 19.

> Richard was shot at the siege of Chaluz in the Limousin. Matthew names the archer Peter Basilius (*CM* ii. 457). Roger of Hoveden names him Bertrand de Gurdun and describes his subsequent execution. (*Chronica*, iv. 82–84.)

ENGLAND, John

23. Corona et clipeus Regis Johannis.
Gules, three lions passant gardant or. (Shield with crown above.)
Accession of John, 1199.

> f. 85*b*.   *HA* ii. 78. Cf. MP I. 19.

> Younger brother of Richard I. In 1177 as Count of Mortain and Lord of Ireland he bore two lions passant one above the other, but on ascending the throne he took the three lions as borne by Richard I. His illegitimate s. Richard de Warenne, de Douvres, or de Chilham, bore two lions passant gardant (B 82).

THE EMPIRE, Otto IV

24. Ut rex Otho Romam veniens ad imperium sit admissus.
Gules, three lions passant gardant or, dimidiating *Or, an eagle displayed sable.* (Shield with three crowns above over which are written respectively Argentea, Aurea, Ferrea. The centre crown encircles a pointed green cap with a gold ball at the top, the other two encircle round green caps.)
Election of Otto IV as emperor, 1209.

> f. 86*b*.   *HA* ii. 83. Cf. MP I. 21.

MANDEVILLE

25. Obiit comes Galfridus de Mandevilla.
Quarterly gules and or. (Shield reversed and on either side the halves of a broken spear point downwards.)

Death of Geoffrey de Mandeville, Earl of Essex, in a tournament, 1216.

f. 97a. *HA* ii. 175. Cf. MP I. 43; II. 22.

Geoffrey FitzPiers, alias Mandeville, Earl of Essex 1213–16, s. of Geoffrey FitzPiers, Earl of Essex 1199–1213, by Beatrice de Say, whose grandmother was Beatrice, sister of the great Geoffrey de Mandeville who was created Earl of Essex by the Empress Maud, and was slain in 1144.

Although shown as *Quarterly gules and or*, with gules in the first and fourth quarters, both here and in MP IV. 10, 24, the arms should really be *Quarterly or and gules*; they are so painted for William FitzPiers in MP I. 43 and II. 22. Matthew is explicit on this point: *quarter devant d'or cum suo pari.*

The quarterly coat belongs to one of the groups of related arms which can be traced back to the infancy of armoury at the beginning of the twelfth century—cf. the Clare chevrons and the Warenne checkers, MP I. 46 and 64—for it must have been borne by Geoffrey de Mandeville, the first earl. Although there is no direct evidence of this, Round pointed out that he was the central figure in a group of families that bore this coat or one derived from it, and further that no hypothesis can explain the adoption of this quarterly coat by these families from any other source or at any other period than from and in the time of Geoffrey (J. H. Round, *Geoffrey de Mandeville*, 388–96; cf. *Genealogists' Magazine*, vii. 223, &c., 469–72.) The leading figures in the group besides FitzPiers are Lacy (MP I. 63), Vere (MP II. 15), Beauchamp of Bedford (MP II. 28, 76), Clavering (MP IV. 39), Say (B 29), and Sackville. Other families whose arms are or may be connected directly or indirectly with the group are Despenser (MP II. 58), Berners (MP II. 78), Fitzwarin (B 184), Eure (B 169), and Rochford (B 208). W. H. B. Bird also suggested that Mascy of Durham may be attached to it. (*Ancestor*, x. 85.)

Both this Geoffrey and his brother William (MP I. 43) were known as Mandeville and bore the quarterly coat undifferenced, but their half-brother John FitzGeoffrey added a bordure vair (B 28). William FitzPiers d.s.p. 1227, and in 1239 the earldom was conferred on his nephew Humphrey de Bohun who set two small quarterly shields on his seal, one on either side of the Bohun achievement (Birch 5720).

VESCY

26. Eustachius de Vescy.

Gules, a cross patonce[1] argent. (Shield reversed.)

Death of Eustace de Vescy of Alnwick and Malton, 1216.

f. 98b. *HA* ii. 187. Cf. MP I. 102; II. 35, 106; IV. 11, 84 : B 76.

S. of William de Vescy, d. 1184/5. This is the usual form of the arms, but for Eustace's s., Sir William de Vescy, Matthew makes the cross moline (MP II. 102), while in MP II. 35 he makes it formy; cf. B 76 where the arms are considered in more detail. (*CP* xii (2) 275–6.)

ENGLAND, John

27. Rex Johannes.

Gules, three lions passant gardant or. (Shield reversed with crown below.)

Burial of King John, 1216.

f. 99b. *HA* ii. 193. Cf. MP I. 19.

ENGLAND, Henry III

28. Rex Henricus tertius.

Gules, three lions passant gardant or. (Shield with crown below.)

First coronation of Henry III, 1216.

f. 100a. *HA* ii. 196. Cf. MP I. 19.

Eldest s. of King John, crowned at Gloucester, when only about nine years old; d. 1272.

[1] In accordance with the recommendation of H. Stanford London *patonce* is used in modern blazon for *paty* (*Coat of Arms*, v, no. 33, pp. 358–65, no. 34, pp. 26–33).

MARSHAL

29. Obiit comes Willelmus Marescallus senior.

Party per pale or and vert, a lion rampant queue fourchée gules. (Shield reversed.)

Death of William Marshal, Earl of Pembroke and sometime Regent of England, 1219.

> f. 104*b*.   *HA* ii. 232.   Cf. MP I. 78, 79; IV. 47.

> These arms were borne by his three elder sons who succeeded in turn to the marshalcy (MP I. 47, 50, 51), but to the fourth and fifth sons who also succeeded to that office Matthew assigns *Per pale gules and vert, a lion rampant queue fourchée argent* (MP I. 78, 79), a variant which is otherwise unknown, and (MP IV. 47) to Gilbert, third son, he also assigns *Party per pale or and vert, a lion rampant argent.* The normal version was later borne by the Bigods, Marshals of England, who acquired the office and arms by the marriage of Hugh Bigod, Earl of Norfolk, with Maud, eldest dau. and coh. of William Marshal I. (*CP* ix. 589–90; x. 358–77.)

MONTFORT

30. Obiit Symon comes Montefortis.

Argent, a lion rampant queue fourchée gules. (Shield reversed, beside it a roundel representing the stone that killed him.)

Death of Simon de Montfort at the siege of Toulouse, 1218.

> f. 105*b*.   *HA* ii. 239. Cf. B 4.

> S. of Simon de Montfort by Amice, sister and coh. of Robert FitzPernel, Earl of Leicester (d. 1204), confirmed as Earl of Leicester 1207, father of Simon de Montfort the leader of the opposition to Henry III. He is depicted in a clerestory window at Chartres holding a shield *Gules, a lion rampant queue fourchée argent,* with a banner *Party indented gules and argent* (Wagner, *Historic Heraldry*, p. 35). Matthew has reversed the tinctures. Both coats belonged to the Montforts in France, for Simon de Montfort had shown the lion on his seal before he acquired the earldom of Leicester (Ddq. 707; Birch 6234), while his brother Amaury, Earl of Gloucester (d. 1216), sealed with the party indented (Ddq. 10138). His younger s., second Earl of Leicester (B 4), also sealed with the lion. (Birch 6235–6; cf. 6686.)

> The banner, which at Chartres is tinctured gules and argent and in B 4 is or and gules, is generally *Party indented argent and gules* as in B II and IV. It was later assigned to the Honour of Hinckley, one of the honours of the Earl of Leicester, and it is so given in the fifteenth century. (DLC 7; PLN 37.)

> In MP IV. 15 the lion's tail is not forked, but that is a mistake. It is clearly forked on the seal of 1195 (*AVD* xi. 481).

MONTFORT

31. Frater . . . ejusdem Symonis.

Argent, a lion rampant queue fourchée gules. (Shield reversed with a roundel as in MP I. 30.)

Death of . . . de Montfort, brother of Simon, at the siege of a castle not far from Toulouse.

> f. 105*b*.   *HA* ii. 239. Cf. MP I. 30.

> Guy de Montfort d. at Albigeois à Vareille, 1220 (*ex. inf.* Dr. P. Adam-Even).

QUINCY, Bohun

32, 33. Obierunt Saerus de Quincy Comes Wintone et Henricus de Boun Comes Herefordie.

32. *Gules, seven voided lozenges conjoined or* (3, 3, 1). (Shield reversed.)
Death of Saher de Quincy, Earl of Winchester, 1219.

f. 106a. *HA* ii. 243. Cf. MP II. 11; IV. 17.

Saher de Quincy was s. of Robert de Quincy (d. 1197), a younger s. of Saher de Quincy (d. *c.* 1158), by Maud, widow of Robert FitzRichard de Clare and dau. of Simon de St. Liz, Earl of Huntingdon. He d. 1219 (*CP* xii (2) 745–51). In the *Book of Seals*, 282, Saher de Quincy (d. 1190) is described as bearing lozengy on his hawberk and on the trappers of his equestrian seal. But it is likely that this was not heraldic but a means of indicating mail. If this is so the earliest known arms of Quincy were a fess and a label as borne by this man on his seal. The label has seven points on the obverse and eight points on the reverse (Birch 6355) while it has eleven points on his seal, *c.* 1212 (Stevenson, *Scottish Heraldic Seals*). These arms, borne before his creation as Earl of Winchester, may be derived from or connected with those of Fitzwalter of Woodham, which were *Or a fess between two chevrons gules*. Robert FitzWalter was s. of Walter FitzRobert s. of Robert FitzRichard de Clare by Maud de St. Liz. (Smith Ellis, *Antiquities of Heraldry*, pp. 196–7). It should be noted that on his equestrian seal (n.d. Birch 6356) the obverse shows a shield of Fitzwalter, while the reverse shows the fess with a label (7), and the legend . . CRETVM COMITIS WINTON . shows that this was after his creation as earl. Similarly, Robert FitzWalter shows voided lozenges in the field on the obverse of his equestrian seal. (Tonnochy, *Catalogue of British Seal-Dies in the British Museum*, no. 332.) Whether the tinctures and the indented shape of the lozenges have any connexion with Clare is a matter of conjecture.

BOHUN

33. Henricus de Boun, comes Herefordie.
Azure, a bend argent between six lions rampant or. (Shield reversed.) This shield is also drawn in the upper margin of the sheet with the legend *scutum de azuro, leones de auro, benda alba*.
Death of Henry de Bohun, Earl of Hereford, 1220.

f. 106a. *HA* ii. 243. Cf. MP IV. 16.

Henry de Bohun, s. of Humphrey de Bohun, was gds. of Margery, sister and h. of Roger, Earl of Hereford, cr. Earl of Hereford 1199, d. 1220, father of Humphrey de Bohun, Earl of Hereford (MP II. 9). (*CP* vi. 457–8.)

There seems to have been some uncertainty about these arms. Matthew gives two versions: (1) as here and in MP II. 9, (2) *Or a bend gules cotised sable* without lions (MP IV. 16). The latter has been found nowhere else and may be a mistake. The former appears on the seal of Humphrey de Bohun in 1238 (Birch 7529), but on another seal used *c.* 1236 (*Book of Seals*, 323) the bend is cotised and the arms *Azure a bend cotised or between six lions rampant*, were regularly used hereafter (B 10; C 123, and many other later rolls and seals).

QUINCY

34. Robertus filius suus primo genitus (i.e. s. of **32**).
Gules, seven voided lozenges conjoined or. (Shield reversed.)
Death of Robert de Quincy, eldest s. of Saher de Quincy, v.p. 1217.

f. 106a. *HA* ii. 243. Cf. MP I. 32.

BOHUN

35. Small shield of Bohun, reversed and uncoloured.

f. 106a. *HA* II 243. Cf. MP I. 33.

D'AUBIGNY

36. Obiit Willelmus de Albineto comes Harundelie.
Gules, a lion rampant queue fourchée or. (Shield reversed.)

Death of William d'Aubigny, Earl of Arundel, 1221.

f. 106b.   *HA* ii. 249. Cf. *MP* I. 72; II. 5; IV. 18, 57 : B 18.

Third Earl of Arundel, s. of William, second earl (d. 1193) and gds. of William de Albini or d'Aubigny, Earl of Arundel (d. 1176), by Adeliza de Louvain, dau. of Godfrey, Duke of Lothier, Count of Brabant and Louvain, and widow of King Henry I. The earldom was variously known as Sussex, Chichester, or Arundel (*CP* i. 233–8).

The lion's tail is usually single as in MP II. 5, &c.

The second earl used a seal engraved with a lion passant looking backwards (Birch 5604).

Hugh d'Aubigny, fifth Earl of Arundel, s. of the above (MP I. 72; II. 5; IV. 57 : B 18), d.s.p. 1243, and his possessions were divided among his sisters and their heirs, the castle and manor of Arundel being awarded to John Fitzalan, s. of the second sister Isabel. He never had the title of earl nor had his s. John (d. 1272), but the latter's s. Richard was summoned to Parliament as Earl of Arundel in various writs. Round, *Geoffrey de Mandeville*, p. 319, &c. (*CP* i. 239–41.)

Both the d'Aubignys of Arundel and the Mowbrays came from St. Martin d'Aubigny (dépt. Manche) in Normandy. They were of the same stock, their respective ancestors William d'Aubigny, Earl of Lincoln (d. 1139) and Nele d'Aubigny (d. 1129) being nephew and uncle. (Loyd, *The Origins of some Anglo-Norman Families*, Harl. Soc. ciii. 7; *CP* ix. 366–7.) Whether the lion was adopted from Brabant or from Henry I, in either case through Adeliza, is an open question, but whichever its source it is probable that the Mowbrays took their arms *Gules, a lion rampant argent* in sympathy with their cousins.

FRANCE

37. Obiit Philippus rex Francorum.
Azure, semy de lis or (3, 3, 2, 1). (Shield reversed.)
Death of Philip Augustus, 1223.

f. 107b.   *HA.* ii. 256. Cf. MP I. 8.

CORNWALL

38. Ut Rex Anglorum Henricus Ricardum fratrem suum cinglo donavit militari.
Argent, a lion rampant crowned or queue fourchée gules, in a bordure sable bezanty. (Shield uncoloured.)
Richard, Earl of Cornwall, knighted 1225.

f. 109b.   *HA* ii. 269. Cf. MP II 3: B 3; C 124.

Younger s. of King John, Earl of Cornwall and Count of Poitou 1225, King of the Romans 1256, d. 1272.

These arms, the lion uncrowned, were borne by the viscounts of Chatellerault, hereditary marshals of Poitou, and by the town of Poitiers. Dr. Adam-Even has argued that it was as Count of Poitou, the title that Richard commonly used, that he bore these arms. (*Études Héraldiques Médiévales; Les Armoiries des Comtes de Poitou*, privately printed c. 1950, p. 5.)

The lion's tail should not be forked. In B 3 and C 124 the lion is crowned as it is on his and on his son's seals (Birch 6328, 6307) and in Westminster Abbey (*RCHM*, pl. 103).

BIGOD

39. Obiit Hugo Bigod, Comes Orientalium Anglorum.
A cross. (Shield reversed and uncoloured.)
Death of Hugh Bigod, Earl of Norfolk, 1225.

f. 110a.   *HA* ii. 274. Cf. MP II. 12 : B 6, 197; C 91.

He m. Maud, sister and coh. of Anselm Marshal, Earl of Pembroke and Earl Marshal. His s. Roger Bigod, Earl of Norfolk and Earl Marshal *jure matris*, bore *Or, a cross gules* (B 6). (*CP* ix. 589–90.)

LONGESPÉE

40. De laudabili morte Willelmi comitis Saresberiensis.

Azure, six lions rampant or. (Shield reversed.)

Death of William Longespée, Earl of Salisbury, 1226.

f. 111*a*. *HA* ii. 281. Cf. B 22.

Natural s. of Henry II, was granted the earldom of Salisbury on his marriage with Ela, dau. and h. of William FitzPatrick, Earl of Salisbury (*CP* xi. 379).

He first sealed with a single lion rampant, but later adopted the six lions shown here and on his tomb in Salisbury Cathedral. This is the shield that appears on the enamel from the tomb of his grandfather, Geoffrey Plantagenet, at Le Mans. It is not known when the change was made. (G. H. White, 'On the Plantagenet Enamel at Le Mans', *CP* xi, Appendix G 141; Birch 6191, 6678, 11375; Wagner, *Historic Heraldry*, p. 40.)

His gtgddau. Margaret, sometimes called Countess of Salisbury, m. Henry de Lacy, Earl of Lincoln. (*CP* xi. 384; cf. B 9.)

FRANCE, Louis VIII

41. Clipeus regis Francorum Ludovici potionati.

Azure, six fleurs-de-lis or. (Shield reversed with crown reversed below.)

Death of Louis VIII, 1226.

f. 112*a*. *HA* ii. 288. Cf. MP I. 8.

S. of Philip Augustus; succ. 1223; d. of poison at Avignon 1226.

FRANCE, Louis IX

42. Clipeus Ludowici filii Ludowici potionati apud Avinionem.

Azure, six fleur-de-lis or (3, 2, 1). (Shield with crown above.)

Coronation of Louis IX, 1226.

f. 112*a*. *HA* ii. 290. Cf. MP I. 8.

St. Louis, s. of Louis VIII by Blanche of Castile; b. 1215; succ. 1226; led the eighth Crusade 1270; d. of the plague at Carthage 1270.

MANDEVILLE

43. Obiit Willelmus de Mandevilla, comes Essexie gloria Anglie.

Quarterly or and gules. (Shield reversed.)

Death of William de Mandeville, Earl of Essex, 1227.

f. 112*b*. *HA* ii. 292. Cf. MP I. 25.

Gtgds. of Beatrice, sister and eventually coh. of Geoffrey de Mandeville, Earl of Essex (d. 1144) and brother of Geoffrey de Mandeville (MP I. 25). (*CP* v. 130–3.)

BREWES

44. Perimitur Willelmus de Brahuse.

Party per pale indented gules and azure. (Shield reversed.)

Murder of William de Brewes, 1230.

f. 116*a*. *HA* ii. 322. Cf. MP IV. 7, 27 : B 55.

S. of Reynold de Brewes, who was third s. of William de Brewes the elder (d. 1211) (MP iv.7). He was hanged by Llwelyn ap Iorwerth, 1230. The descendants of William de Brewes, elder s. of William de Brewes the elder, bore *azure crusuly a lion rampant or.* (*Sussex Arch. Coll.* xxvi. 261; *CP* ii. 302.) Matthew attributes different arms to him in iv. 27.

Henry III sails to Britanny (*see* MP VIII. 2).

BURGH

45. Reimundus de Burgh.

Lozengy — and vair. (Shield reversed and uncoloured.)

Death of Raymond de Burgh, 1230.

> f. 117a. *HA* ii. 326. Cf. MP II. 16.

> Nephew of Hubert de Burgh, Earl of Kent (MP I. 73). (*HA* ii. 326.)

CLARE

46. Obiit comes de Glovernia Gilebertus.

Or, three chevrons gules. (Shield reversed.)

Death of Gilbert de Clare, Earl of Gloucester, 1230.

> f. 116b. *HA* ii. 328.

> Earl of Gloucester and Hertford, s. of Richard de Clare, Earl of Hertford (d. 1217) by Amice, second dau. and coh. of William, Earl of Gloucester (d.s.p.m.s. 1183); d. at Penros in Brittany. (*CP* v. 694–6.)
> The arms of Clare were originally chevronny, as shown on early seals, the change to three chevrons was apparently made by Richard Strongbow, Earl of Pembroke *c.* 1170. (Wagner, *Historic Heraldry*, pp. 36–37.) On the possible derivation of the chevrons from Marguerite de Ramerupe, wife of Hugh II, Count of Clermont-en-Beauvaisis, see MP I. 48.
> Among those whose arms were derived directly or indirectly from Clare are FitzWalter (MP II. 32), Pecche (MP II. 33), Daubeney of Belvoir (MP I. 52), Montfichet (MP II. 24), Sackville of Fawley (B 211), Monmouth (B 92), and Bishop Walter de Merton, founder of Merton College, Oxford. Smith Ellis (*Antiquities of Heraldry*, pp. 199–200) suggested that the single chevron of Stafford and Dabernon may also have a common origin with the Clare chevrons.

MARSHAL

47. Obiit Willelmus comes de Penbroc.

Party per pale or and vert, a lion rampant gules. (Shield reversed.)

Death of William Marshal, Earl of Pembroke, 1231.

> f. 117a. *HA* ii. 331.

> Eldest s. of MP I. 29 (*CP* x. 365–8).

CHESTER

48. Clipeus Cestriae qui jam in dampnum regis prostratus est.

Azure, three garbs or. (Shield reversed.)

Death of Ralph de Blundeville, Earl of Chester, 1232.

> f. 119b. *HA* ii. 349. Cf. MP IV. 6, 7, 34 : B 16 : C 65.

> S. of Hugh 'of Kevelioc', Earl of Chester (d. 1181). (*CP* iii. 167–9.) He is the first earl who is known to have borne the garbs, but Dr. Adam-Even has pointed out what looks like a highly significant coincidence. Count Hugh II of Clermont-en-Beauvaisis (d. 1103) had by his wife Marguerite de Ramerupe, four children. The son Reynold (d. *c.* 1153) and three daughters, Marguerite, wife of Gerard de Gerberoy, Adèle, wife of Gilbert de Clare (d. 1123), and Ermentrude, wife of Hugh d'Avranches, Earl of Chester (d. *c.* 1101), whose nephew Ralph le Meschin, Earl of Chester, (d. *c.* 1129), was great-grandfather of Ralph de Blundeville. The descendants of Reynold, Marguerite, and Ermentrude all bore garbs, while Adèle's descendants the Clares (MP I. 46) bore chevrons like the family of Ramerupe.
> The garbs have been regarded as the arms of the earldom ever since Ralph's time; they were borne by his nephew and successor John le Scot (d.s.p. 1237; MP IV. 34) and by several constables of Chester as Edmund de Lacy (B 9), his grandfather Roger de Lacy, and Roger de Lacy, setting them in a particoloured field (MP IV. 6).

In addition to the garbs Earl Ralph also used a seal with a lion rampant bendways. (Birch 7520, 8530; *Brit. Arch. Assoc.* v. 243, &c.; *Durham Seals*, 584, misblazons this a wolf passant.)

In 1246 the earldom of Chester was annexed to the Crown, but in 1254 it was conferred on King Henry's younger s., Prince Edmund, and that explains the earl's promotion to no. 1 in the 1258 version (III) of B.

In 1264 Simon de Montfort obtained the earldom, but d. the next year, and from then onwards the earldom was in the Crown until 1301 when it was granted to the future king Edward II. (*CP* iii. 170–1.)

BASSET

49. Obiit Warinus Basset.
Blank. (Shield reversed.)
Death of Warin Basset, 1233.

f. 120*b*. *HA* ii. 357. Cf. MP II. 34; IV. 44.

Matthew Paris writes that he was killed at the siege of Cardiff Castle. He was a younger s. of Alan Basset of Wycombe. (Dugd. *Bar.* i. 384.)

MARSHAL

50. De morte Ricardi Marescalli.
Party per pale or and vert, a lion rampant queue fourchée gules. (Shield reversed.)
Death of Richard Marshal, Earl of Pembroke, 1234.

f. 122*a*. *HA* ii. 369. Cf. MP I. 29, &c.

Second s. of MP I. 29 and brother of MP I. 47. (*CP* x. 368–71.)

MARSHAL

51. Gilebertus Marescallus.
Party per pale or and vert, a lion rampant queue fourchée gules.
Henry III restores the marshalcy to Gilbert Marshal, 1234.

f. 122*a*. *HA* ii. 371. d.s.p. legit 1241. Cf. MP V. 29, &c.

Third s. of MP I. 29. (*CP* x. 371–4.)

DAUBENEY of Belvoir

52. De morte Willelmi de Albineto.
Or, two chevrons and a bordure gules. (Shield reversed.)
Death of William Daubeney, 1236.

f. 125*a*. *HA* ii. 390. Cf. MP II. 21 : B 68.

William Daubeney of Belvoir, co. Leics., gtgds. of William Daubeney by Cicely de Belvoir and gds. of William Daubeney (d. 1166) by Maud de St. Liz. His grandmother Maud was dau. of Robert FitzRichard de Clare, from whose arms the chevrons are possibly derived. (Round, *HMC Rutland*, iv. 106–7; Dugd. *Bar.* i. 111–15.) Dugdale makes him s. of William Daubeney who d. 1166.

JERUSALEM and BRIENNE

53. Obiit rex Jerusalem Johannes de Bresne cujus filia nuptui tradita fuit Fretherico imperatori que peperit ei Conradum.

(*a*) *Or, a cross argent, scutum ejus secundum.*
(*b*) *Azure, a fish hauriant or, scutum ejus primum.*

(Two shields reversed between two swords points downwards, with crown reversed below the second, with gloss in Latin beside.)
Death of John de Brienne, King of Jerusalem, 1237.

> f. 125*b*. *HA* ii. 396. Cf. MP I. 6.

> John de Brienne m. in 1210 Maria, dau. of Isabella, Queen of Jerusalem (dau. of Amalric I, King of Jerusalem (d. 1174)) by her first husband Conrad de Montferrat. His dau. Yolanda m. the Emperor Frederick II and d. in 1228 a few days after the birth of her s. Conrad. (Runciman, *History of the Crusades*, ii. 399; iii. 132–3, 173–7.)

CAUNTELO

54. Obiit Willelmus de Cantelupo miles.
Gules, three fleurs-de-lis or. (Shield reversed, uncoloured.)
Death of William de Cauntelo, 1239.

> f. 128*b*. *HA* ii. 419. Cf. MP II. 26 : B 27.

> S. of Walter de Cauntelo (living 1205) seneschal under John. In *HA* ii. 419 he is described as 'natione Neuster', which suggests that the family were new-comers to England. The name is probably from Chanteloup, canton de Bréhal, in La Manche. (*CP* iii. 111; *Beds. Hist. Rec. Soc.* v. 215; *DNB*.)

SAVOY

55. De lugubri morte Willelmi electi Valentini.
Gules, three pales or on a chief sable a lion passant gardant or. (Shield reversed: two mitres attached to the lower sides of the shield and between them the head of a pastoral staff reversed.)
Death of William of Savoy, bishop elect of Valence-sur-Rhône, 1239.

> f. 129*b*. *HA* ii. 427.

> William of Savoy, Bishop of Liège and bishop elect of Valence-sur-Rhône, was one of the eight sons of Thomas, Count and Marquis of Savoy (d. 1253). His sister Beatrice m. Raymond-Berengar IV of Provence (d. 1245), whose dau. Eleanor of Provence m. Henry III. The arms here attributed to him are those of Provence, with a lion passant gardant or on a chief sable which may point to his connexion with the royal family of England. (C. W. Previté-Orton, *Early History of the House of Savoy*, Cambridge, 1912, pp. 417–18.)

TURBERVILLE

56. Obiit Henricus de Trublevilla.
Gules, on a chief sable a demi-lion queue fourchée issuant or. (Shield reversed.)
Death of Henry de Turberville 1239.

> f. 129*b*. *HA.* ii. 427.

> Henry de Turberville, or Trubleville, a prominent soldier, was with Hubert de Burgh in the sea-fight against Eustace the Monk. He distinguished himself at the siege of Milan 1238, where he had been sent to help the emperor. At one time he was seneschal of Gascony. He held the manor of Bradninch Devon, and d.s.p. (*CM* iii. 29, 491; v. 295 : *Cal. Inq.* i, no. 23.) His relationship to John de Turberville (B 185) has not been found. Henry held lands in Dorset in 1206 (Pipe Roll Society lviii. 133). For notice of the family see G. T. Clark, *Limbus Patrum Morganiae et Glamorganiae*, pp. 447–9.

TONY

57. Radulfus de Thoni obiit.
Argent, a maunch gules. (Shield reversed.)

Death of Ralph de Tony, 1239.

f. 129*b*. *HA* ii. 427. Cf. MP II. 25; IV. 25.

Ralph de Tony, s. of Roger de Tony or Toenalius of Conches (d. *c.* Jan. 1208/9) was elder brother of Roger de Tony (MP IV. 25) and was succ. by his son Roger (d. 1264). The family derived its name from Toeni, now Tosni (dép. Eure). He was descended from Ralph de Tony who fought at Hastings and received grants of land in many counties, and whose 'caput baroniae' was at Flamstead, Hertfordshire. In the *Vitae Abbatum* (ed. Wats, p. 998) Matthew says he was descended from those famous knights 'qui a Cigni nomine intitulantur', thus showing that he knew the epics about the Chevalier au Cygne. (For the descent see *Arch.* xcvii. 136.) In MP II. 25 the field is or.

FRENCH NOBLES KILLED BY THE SARACENS AT GAZA, 1240

58–62. Scuta victorum Francorum non procul a Gazre. Capti sunt etiam et occisi multi de Templariis et Hospitalariis (*written above*).
(Three shields reversed and below them the standards of the Hospitallers and of the Templars reversed.)

f. 130*b*. *HA* ii. 433.

DAREINES

58. Dareines.
Gules, two trumpets in pile or.

BARRES

59. De Barres.
Gules, a cross recercly or.
Death of John de Barres.

Cf. MP I. 89.

A John de Barres seals with these arms 1213 (Ddq. 1302) and William des Barres, Lord of Villagenart, Île de France 1299 (Ddq. 1300).

BAR

60. De Bar.
Azure, two barbels addorsed or.
Death of Henry II, Count of Bar, 1240.

S. of Thibaut I (d. 1214). A single barbel appears on a coin of Count Henry I in 1180 and on his equestrian seal in 1189, while the seal of his brother Thibaut I shows a shield with two barbels back to back in 1189. These arms appear on his seal (1230) (Ddq. 796). In C 30 there are crosses on the field of the shield of Henry II. (*AVD* xiii. 434–6.)

THE HOSPITAL

61. Vexillum Hospitalis.
Gules, a cross argent.

Here Matthew draws a plain cross, but in IV. 41 he draws a cross formy. C 22 also has a cross formy. Such evidence as there is suggests that the Hospitallers' cross when used as a badge on the mantle and elsewhere may perhaps have had at first slightly splayed ends, as, for example, on a bulla of 1221 (E. J. King, *The Seals of the Order of St. John of Jerusalem*, pl. III, fig. 2) and on the seal of the Grand Master Garin de Montaigu in 1224 (*Revue Archéologique*, N.S. xxxii (1876), 237; Ddq. 9881). The effigy of John de Dreux at St. Yvod de Braine near Soissons, *c.* 1275, has a mantle with a plain cross.

Mr. J. A. Goodall argues that the cross was originally formy and would derive from the crosses of varying pattern which are seen on the coins of the eleventh and twelfth centuries of the city of Amalfi, whose merchants founded the first hospice. (*Coat of Arms*, v. 372–8.) The available evidence is scanty and it is not unlikely that the two patterns were used indifferently.

THE TEMPLE

62. Vexillum Templi.
Argent, a chief sable.

Cf. MP IV. 42; VIII. 1, 5, 19 : C 21.

This is the well-known banner of the Templars, later known as Beauseant. In C 21 it is surcharged with a red cross.

LACY

63. Obiit comes Cestrie et Lincolnie.
Quarterly or and gules, a bend sable and a label (5) *argent.* (Shield reversed.)
Death of John de Lacy, Earl of Lincoln, 1240.

f. 130b. *HA* ii. 436. Cf. MP II. 20; IV. 37 : B 9.

In the text Matthew refers to the 'comes Lincolnie et Cestrie Johannes cognomento Scotus', thus confusing John the Scot, Earl of Chester (d. 1237), with John de Lacy, Earl of Lincoln (d. 1240). The latter was Constable of Chester and s. of Roger de Lacy, Constable of Chester (MP IV. 6). The arms are derived from those of Mandeville through Alice de Vere, wife of John, constable of Chester, grandfather of this man; Alice being dau. of Alice of Essex, sister of Aubrey de Vere, Earl of Oxford, and of Rohese, wife of Geoffrey de Mandeville, Earl of Essex. (*CP* vii. 676–80; *Genealogists' Magazine*, vii. 469–72.)

WARENNE

64. Obiit comes Warannie Willelmus.
Checky azure and or. (Shield reversed.)
Death of William, Earl Warenne, 1240.

f. 130b. *HA* ii. 437. Cf. MP II. 36; IV. 7 : B 7.

William de Warenne, Earl of Surrey, s. of Hamelin Plantagenet (d. 1202, illegitimate s. of Geoffrey of Anjou) by Isabel, dau. and h. of William de Warenne, third Earl of Surrey (d. 1148). (*CP* xii (1) 500–3.)

This gold and blue checkered shield is of peculiar interest as to quote G. H. White: 'it belongs to one of the three groups of allied shields which can be traced back to the dawn of heraldry, originating before the middle of the 12th century'. (*CP* xii (1), Appendix J.) The other groups are the Mandeville group of quartered shields (MP I. 25) and the Clare group of chevrons (MP I. 46).

The families bearing the checkered shields all descended from Isabel de Vermandois, dau. of Hugh de Crepi the Great, Count of Vermandois. She married twice, firstly Robert de Beaumont, Count of Meulan and Earl of Leicester, and secondly William de Warenne, second Earl of Surrey (d. 1138). By her first marriage she had two sons, Waleran, Count of Meulan and Earl of Worcester (d. 1166), and Robert Bossu, Earl of Leicester (d. 1168). Some of Waleran's descendants bore checky or and gules, while others tilted the checkers and bore lozengy or and gules. Robert's descendants also bore checky, but the tinctures are not recorded. Isabel also had two children by her second husband, a s. William, third Earl of Surrey (d. 1148), whose descendants bore the familiar checkers or and azure, and a dau. Gundred, wife of Roger, second Earl of Warwick (d. 1153), whose descendants bore *Checky or and azure, a chevron ermine* (*a bend ermine* in MP I. 70; II. 13; IV. 49). According to Smith Ellis a family of Clinton, descended from Gundred's dau. Agnes, wife of Geoffrey de Clinton, also bore checky or and azure, but differenced it by an ermine chief. (G. H. White, op. cit., and *Trans. Royal Historical Society*, 4th s. xiii. 62;

Wagner, *Historic Heraldry*, p. 46; *Genealogists' Magazine*, vii. 221–2; Smith Ellis, *Antiquities of Heraldry*, p. 179.)

Smith Ellis also includes in this group the Dreux family who bore *Checky or and azure in a bordure gules* (the earls of Richmond added a canton ermine). This family descended from Robert, Count of Dreux, s. of Philip I of France, who was brother of Hugh the Great, the father of Isabella.

The Courtenay coat in B 109 must also belong to this group, and it seems possible that Clifford (B 30, 31), Vaux (B 33), and Tateshal (B 50) do also, but the links have not been found.

MARSHAL

65. De miserabili morte comitis Gileberti Marescalli apud Hertford.
Party per pale or and vert, a lion rampant gules. (Shield reversed.)
Death of Gilbert, Earl Marshal, 1241.

> f. 132a. *HA* ii. 451. Cf. MP I. 29, 51, &c.

> Killed accidentally in a tournament at Hertford (*HA* ii. 451): same person as MP I. 51.

SEGRAVE

66. Obiit Stephanus de Segrave.
Gules, three garbs or. (Shield reversed.)
Death of Stephen de Segrave, 1241.

> f. 133a. *HA* ii. 457. Cf. MP IV. 48 : B 176 : C 98.

> S. of Gilbert de Segrave (d. 1201). The garbs are derived from the earls of Chester. Stephen de Segrave held lands in Segrave, Leics., from the earls of Chester and was enfeoffed in Mountsorrel and other lands by Ranulph, Earl of Chester (1217–31). (*CP* xi. 596 n.) He was father of Gilbert de Segrave (B 176).

> B 176, C 98, and several later rolls make the garbs argent on sable. D 114 calls them 'gerbes de aveyne'.

MAREYS

67. Arma Willelmi de Marisco de proditione convicti et Londoniis suspensi.
Or, a lion rampant sable. (Shield, banner, and sword broken.)
Execution of William de Mareys, 1242.

> f. 133b. *HA* ii. 462. Cf. MP I. 68; IV. 64.

> William de Mareys or de Marisco was s. of Geoffrey de Mareys (MP I. 68). In May 1235 a certain Henry Clement was murdered and suspicion falling on William de Mareys he fled to Lundy Island. Although he professed his innocence, it would appear likely that he had murdered Clement because he suspected him of connivance in the incident at the Curragh in April 1234 where Richard, Earl Marshal, was wounded and captured. The Earl d. a fortnight later. At Lundy William maintained himself for seven years as a pirate. In 1238 a man who attempted to assassinate Henry III confessed that he had been sent by William, who was eventually captured and hanged in 1242. The breaking of the shield and weapons was presumably a part of the ceremony of degradation. (Powicke, *Henry III and the Lord Edward*, ii, Appendix B, 740–59.)

MAREYS

68. Patris Willelmi scilicet Galfridi.
Gules, a lion rampant argent. (Shield reversed.)
Death of Geoffrey de Mareys, 1245.

> f. 133b. *HA* ii. 462. Cf. MP I. 67; IV. 64.

> Geoffrey de Mareys, justiciar of Ireland 1215–21, 1226–8, 1230–2, was younger brother of William de Mareys of Huntspill, Som. Although not concerned in the murder of Henry Clement

by his s. William (MP I. 67) he fled to sanctuary. After the attempt on the life of the king, of which his s. was accused, he went to Scotland, probably to seek the protection of the Comyns with whom he was connected. He was driven thence 1244 and d. 1245.

His arms are the same as those of his s. save for the tinctures. His great-great-great-nephew, Herbert de Mareys, bore *Argent, a lion rampant sable* (L 190). In MP IV. 64 Matthew attributes to him *Per fess gules and vert, a fess argent between in chief two roundels argent and in base a crescent argent.* It has been suggested (*Royal Society of Antiquaries of Ireland*, lxii. 60 n.) that these may have been borne by him as justiciar, but the fanciful character of the coat suggests that it was an invention of Matthew who at the time of writing the *CM* did not know the true arms. (Powicke, *King Henry III and the Lord Edward*, ii, Appendix B, 740–59; *DNB*; E. St. J. Brooks, *Royal Society of Antiquaries of Ireland*, lxii. 50–74.)

HENRY, King of the Romans

69. Scutum Henrici filii imperatoris.
Or, a double eagle displayed sable, dimidiating *Gules a cross recercly argent.* (Shield reversed.) Death of Henry, King of the Romans, 1242.

> f. 134*b.*   *HA* ii. 468. Cf. MP I. 21; IV. 51.

> S. of the Emperor Frederick II by his first wife Constance of Aragon, m. Margaret of Austria, d. 1242. (*Cambridge Medieval History*, vi. 88, 98.) The Babenberg Dukes of Austria bore *gules, a fess argent* (*ZWR* 28) and the recercly cross has not been found elsewhere for this family.

WARWICK

70. Scutum comitis de Warewic.
Checky azure and or, a bend ermine. (Shield reversed.)
Death of Thomas, Earl of Warwick, 1242.

> f. 134*b.*   *HA* ii. 468. Cf. MP II. 13, 104; IV. 49 : B 20.

> S. of Henry, Earl of Warwick (d. 1229), d.s.p. 1242. Margaret, his sister and h., m. in 1243 as her second husband John de Plescy (B 24) who was invested with the earldom by 1247 and d. 1263. (*CP* xii (2) 364–6.)
> Matthew paints a bend in all three places, but B, C, and all later authorities give a chevron ermine. It is uncertain whether the bend is a mistake or an earlier form of the arms. It is possible that Matthew took them from an equestrian seal in which the shield borne across the rider's chest showed only half the chevron which therefore looked like a bend. The coat is one of those derived from Vermandois. It has often been called Newburgh, but although that name was used by a younger branch of the family, there is no evidence that the earls of Warwick who derived from Beaumont-le-Roger (dept. Eure) were ever called Newburgh.
> Newburgh, i.e. Neubourg (dépt. Eure), was part of the honour of Beaumont-le-Roger, and was granted before 1116 to Robert, seneschal of Normandy, a younger s. of Henry, first Earl of Warwick (d. 1123). (Loyd, *Anglo-Norman Families*, Harl. Soc. ciii. 13, 72.)
> The attribution of the name to the earls of Warwick and to the above arms is probably due to John Rous, the fifteenth-century chronicler of the earls, for he called the first earl 'sir herre Newburgh' and said that he was Earl of Newburgh in Normandy and Earl of Warwick in England. (*The Rous Roll*, ed. Courthope, nos. 13, 19, 31.)

BURGH

71. Scutum Ricardi de Burgh.
Lozengy vair and gules. (Shield reversed.)
Death of Richard de Burgh, justiciar of Ireland, 1242. [n.s. 1243]

> f. 134*b.*   *HA* ii. 468. Cf. MP I. 45; II. 16.

> S. of William de Burgh, brother (probably elder) of Hubert de Burgh, Earl of Kent (MP I. 73), who had received from John a large grant in Connaught. He m. Egidia, a dau. of William de Lacy, feudal lord of Ulster, and was the ancestor of the earls of Ulster; d. Feb. 1243 (*CP* xii (2) 172–2.)

D'AUBIGNY

72. Scutum comitis Harundelie Hugonis.

Gules, a lion rampant or. (Shield reversed.)

Death of Hugh d'Aubigny, Earl of Arundel, 1243.

    f. 135*b*. *HA* ii. 477. Cf. MP I. 36.

    Brother of William d'Aubigny, Earl of Arundel (d.s.p. 1224), and younger s. of MP I. 36. (*CP* i. 238–9.)

BURGH

73. Scutum comitis Cancie.

Lozengy vair and gules. (Shield reversed.)

Death of Hubert de Burgh, Earl of Kent, 1243.

    f. 135*b*. *HA* ii. 477. Cf. MP I. 45; II. 16.

    Justiciar and Regent of England 1216–27, created Earl of Kent 1227, d. 1243. His s. and h., John de Burgh (C 104), is occasionally referred to as 'sometime earl of Kent', although in fact none of Hubert's issue had the title. (*CP* vii. 133–42; Birch 5769.)

FITZMATHEW or HERBERT

74. Obiit Herbertus filius Mathei in Wallia miles strenuus lapide obrutus.

Party per pale gules and azure, three lions rampant or. (Shield reversed.)

Death of Herbert Fitz Mathew, 1245.

    f. 138*a*. *HA* ii. 500. Cf. MP II. 71; IV. 61 : B 78.

    Herbert FitzMathew, s. of Mathew FitzHerbert; he was seneschal of Gascony 1242–3. His cousin Reynold FitzPiers, s. of Piers FitzHerbert, brother of Mathew FitzHerbert, bore *Gules, three lions rampant or* (B 77). (*CP* v. 442; cf. Birch 9738.)

REVIERS

75. Die Sancti Valentini obiit Baldwinus comes Devonie miles juvenis et elegans.

Or, a lion rampant queue fourchée azure. (Shield reversed.)

Death of Baldwin de Reviers, Earl of Devon, 1245.

    f. 138*a*. *HA* ii. 509. Cf. MP II. 17; IV. 35, 60 : B 12 : C 146.

    Invested with the earldom of Devon and the lordship of the Isle of Wight 1239; succeeded by his s. Baldwin (B 12). (*CP* iv. 318–19.) The shield is wrongly placed and should have been on f. 134*a*.

CLARE

76. Milicia Ricardi comitis de Clare, *above the last word is written* Glovernia.

Or, three chevrons gules. The shield is on a small square of parchment pasted on to the margin.

Richard de Clare, Earl of Gloucester, knighted 1245.

    f. 138*b*. *HA* ii. 502. Cf. MP I. 46 : B 5.

    S. of Gilbert de Clare, Earl of Gloucester (MP I. 46); d. 1262.

PROVENCE

77. Obiit Reimundus comes Provincie pater reginae.

Or, four pales gules. (Shield reversed, on small square of parchment pasted on to the margin.)

Death of Raymond Count of Provence, father of Queen Eleanor, 1245.

f. 139a.   HA ii. 509. Cf. MP II. 44, 84; IV. 65; V. 1.

S. of Alphonso, Count of Provence, who was a younger s. of Alphonso II, King of Aragon. (Powicke, *The Thirteenth Century*, p. 101.)

MARSHAL

78. Marescallus Walterus obiit.
Party per pale gules and vert, a lion rampant queue fourchée argent. (Shield reversed.)
Death of Walter, Earl Marshal, 1245.

f. 139a.   HA ii. 509. Cf. MP I. 29; IV. 66.

Fourth s. of MP I. 29 and younger brother of MP I. 47. (*CP* x. 374–6.) The tinctures are different from those borne by his father and his elder brothers. His younger brother Anselm Marshal (MP I. 79) differences in the same manner. In MP IV. 66, however, Walter Marshal is given the same arms as his father and elder brothers, *Per pale or and vert, a lion rampant gules*.

MARSHAL

79. Obiit Anselmus frater dicti Comitis Marescalli.
Party per pale gules and vert, a lion rampant queue fourchée argent. (Shield reversed.)
Death of Anselm Marshal, brother of Walter, Earl Marshal, 1245.

f. 139a.   HA ii. 509. Cf. MP I. 29; IV. 67.

Fifth and youngest s. of MP I. 29 and younger brother of MP I. 47, 50, 51, 78. (*CP* x. 376–7.) The tinctures are the same as those given for 78 above.
   On Anselm's death the marshalcy passed to his nephew Roger Bigod. (B 6, 17; cf. MP I. 39.)

CHATEAUNEUF

80. Obiit Fulco de Novo Castro in Purificatione beate Marie, Londoniis domini regis consobrinus et sepultus in ecclesia Westmonasterii.
Gules, a chief vair. (Shield reversed.)
Death of Fulk de Chateauneuf or Castro Novo, 1247.

f. 141a.   HA iii. 19.

Fulk de Chateauneuf, described by Matthew as 'Domini regis consobrinus' and as 'quondam consanguineus noster' in the Close Rolls (1242–7, p. 498), was granted the manor of Glatton, Hunts. (*Cal. Pat. Rolls*, 1242, p. 269), which he surrendered on being granted the wardship and marriage of Christiane, dau. and h. of Robert de Marieys (ibid., 1243, p. 412; *V.C.H. Hunts.* iii. 178). He d. 1247. Segur de Chateauneuf also described as 'consanguineus', may have been his brother and received in 1253 'compensation for his land lost in the king's service in Angoulême until he have recovered that land' (*Cal. Pat. Rolls*, 1253, p. 257). This seems definitely to connect the persons called Chateauneuf with Angoulême. They were probably relatives of the king on the side of his mother Isabel of Angoulême. As she was an heiress they may have been of bastard stock and may have come from Castillon-sur-Dordogne.

RASPE

81. Obiit Andegravius Duringie ad cujus promotionem ut imperaret dominus papa infinitam effudit pecuniam. Hic Henricus Raspe dicebatur.
(*a*) *Gyronny of six or and azure, a roundel between six smaller roundels gules all with white rims.*
(*b*) *Azure, an eagle displayed or.* (Two shields reversed.)

Death of Henry Raspe, Landgrave of Thuringia and King of Germany, 1247.

f. 141a. *HA* iii. 19. Cf. C 45.

S. of Herman, Landgrave of Thuringia (d. 1217), succ. his nephew Herman II in 1241, d.s.p. 1247. The first shield is presumably that of the landgraves of Thuringia and the second that of the empire of which the field should be sable. (*AVD* xv. 492–3; *Cambridge Medieval History*, vi. 81, 107.)

HOLLAND and ZEALAND

82. Scutum Willelmi comitis, Primum scutum ejusdem de Holandia, aspirantis ad imperium.

(*a*) *Or, a lion rampant gules armed azure.*

(*b*) *Azure, on a chief gules a demi-lion rampant issuant or.* (Two shields.)

William, Count of Holland and Zealand, elected king of Germany, 1247.

f. 141b. *HA* iii. 23. Cf. MP VII. 8.

S. of Florence IV, Count of Holland and Zealand, d. 1256. (*AVD* xiv. 434–7.)

LUSIGNAN-VALENCE

83. Scutum Willelmi de Valentia.

Buruly (13) *azure and argent, a label* (5) *gules, each point charged with three lions passant gardant or.*

William de Lusignan, Seigneur de Valence, knighted by his half-brother Henry III, 1247.

f. 142a. *HA* iii. 29. Cf. MP I. 86; II. 63 : B 23 : C 71, 72.

William de Lusignan, half-brother of Henry III, was s. of Queen Isabel, widow of King John by her second husband Hugh X de Lusignan 'le Brun', Count de la Marche (MP I. 86 : C 71). He was called de Valence from the name of his birthplace in Saintonge. (Powicke, *The Thirteenth Century*, p. 139 n.) He came to England in 1247, m. Joan de Munchensy, dau. of Warin de Munchensy by Joan, fifth dau. of William the Marshal, and in her right became Lord of Pembroke, though he was never invested with the earldom. (*CP* x. 377–81.) He d. 1296.

Matthew gives William this same coat in all three places, but on his only known seal he differences the Lusignan buruly with an orle of martlets gules (Birch 14088–92; Eygun, *Sceaux de Poitou*, 432), and that coat is assigned to him in B 23 and C 72 and was borne by his descendants. It also appears quartered by the three leopards of England on an enamel shield in the Museum at Reggio Emilia, Italy. (*Coat of Arms*, iii. 5, 45, 87.)

ENZIO, King of Sardinia

84. Capitur Ensius, filius Fretherici a Bonaniensibus.

Party per pale vert and or, a double eagle displayed sable.

Capture of Enzio, King of Sardinia, natural s. of Frederick II, by the Bolognese, 1249.

f. 145b. *HA* iii. 56.

SCOTLAND

85. Scutum regis Scocie.

Or, a lion rampant gules and a bordure flory counter flory gules. (Shield reversed.)

Death of Alexander II, King of Scots, 1249.

f. 146*b*.   *HA* iii. 65. Cf. MP II. 48; IV. 80 : C 15.

S. of William the Lion, King of Scots 1165–1214. Although there is no evidence, it is very likely that William the Lion may have used a lion in some way or other, unless he derived his name from his ferocity in battle, and that would be a reason for adopting the lion as his cognizance. Alexander II shows a lion on his great seal. (Stevenson, *Scottish Heraldic Seals*, p. 4.)

Matthew is uncertain how to draw these arms. Here he sets the lion within a red bordure charged with demi-fleurs-de-lis projecting inwards from the inner and outer edges respectively. In MP II. 48 the lion is enclosed by a very narrow single tressure which is straddled by ten demi-fleurs-de-lis projecting from the outer edge of the shield, while in MP IV. 80 there is a single tressure whence demi-fleurs-de-lis project towards the lion. The charge ought to be a double tressure flory and counter flory. It is so represented on the great seal of Alexander III 1249–86 (Stevenson, *Scottish Heraldic Seals*, p. 5), and it is so drawn in *Wijn.* 777 and 1272 and in FW 12. *Nav.* 1259 blazons it 'un tresehour de gueueles double et floure'. The examples in MP are the earliest known of the tressure in the arms of Scotland.

LUSIGNAN

86. Scutum Comitis de Marchia et filii ejusdem.

Buruly (13) *argent and azure.* (Shield reversed.)

Death of Hugh le Brun, seigneur de Lusignan, Count de la Marche, 1249.

f. 146*b*.   *HA* iii. 66. Cf. MP I. 83; II. 63.

Hugh X de Lusignan, m. Isabel of Angoulême, widow of King John. He was father of Hugh XI (d. 1250) of Guy, Sire de Cognac (d.s.p. 1288), and of William, Sire de Valence (MP I. 83). His gtgds. Hugh XIII, d.s.p. 1303, having pledged La Marche to King Philip the Fair. Guy differenced the buruly with an orle of six red lions, William with an orle of red martlets, and another branch, the kings of Jerusalem, with a single red lion. The number of stripes on seals, &c., varied to twenty and over. (*AVD* x. 232; *CP* x. 377; *ChP* 5; Ddq. 844; *Genealogist*, N.S. xxi (1905) 78, &c.)

GENEVA

87. Scutum Petri de Genevre.

(*a*) *Sable, a lion rampant argent.* (Shield reversed.)

(*b*) *Argent, a lion rampant sable.* (Smaller shield below as if in correction.)

f. 146*b*.   *HA* iii. 66.

According to Matthew, Peter de Geneva was a Provençal of humble birth to whom the king m. Maud, dau. of William de Lacy, by which marriage Peter obtained lands in Ireland. (*HA* iii. 66; *CM* v. 90–91.) He also held the manor of Dilwyn, co. Hereford (*Book of Fees*, 1271, 1481). The allegation of humble birth is inaccurate. Peter was in fact s. of Humbert de Genève by Agnes of Savoy, aunt of Count Peter of Savoy (B 101). He d.s.p. 1249. His widow m. Geoffrey de Geneville (B 103) (see *Genealogist*, N.S. xxi. 6, &c.).

B 104 assigns the first of the above coats to Peter's younger brother Ebal, but the counts of Geneva bore *Checky or and azure* (reduced to nine pieces, *c.* 1250) from 1224, and this appears on seals of Peter's uncle, Count William II, though William's s. and h. Radolphe in 1252 relegated the checky to his secretum and sealed with *A bend between two lions*. The lion probably came from Peter's mother, as several members of the house of Savoy sealed with a lion. (*Genealogist*, loc. cit.; Galbreath, *Armorial Vaudois*, i. 272; ii. 624.)

BALLIOL

88. Scutum Rogeri de Bailloil.

Gules, an escutcheon voided argent. (Shield reversed.)

Death of Roger de Balliol, 1249.

f. 146*b*.   *HA* iii. 67. Cf. MP II. 53 : B 169.

Matthew names him s. of John de Balliol (*HA* iii. 67), but he is really Roger FitzJohn of Eure or Iver, Bucks., Warkworth, Northumb., and Clavering, Essex. He was s. of John FitzRobert by Ada dau. of Hugh de Balliol and sister of John de Balliol (*MP* ii. 53). Matthew was in error about his parentage. His arms are given correctly in B 169 (*Cal. Pat. Rolls* 1247–58, p. 47).

BARRES

89. Per unum istud scutum accipe scuta Barrensium scilicet nobilium Francorum. *Azure, a lion rampant gules* dimidiating *Or, a cross recercly sable.* (Shield reversed.) Death on the Crusade of many French nobles in Cyprus and on the sea, 1249.

f. 146*b*.   *HA* iii. 66. Cf. MP I. 59.

This is evidently a composite shield. Jean des Barres, Seigneur of Oissorey, bore on his seal (1253) *Lozengy, impaling a lion rampant* (Ddq. 1305).

90–95 THE ARMS OF NOBLES SLAIN IN THE HOLY LAND, 1250

LONGESPÉE

90. Comitis Willelmi Longaespate. *Azure, six lions rampant or.* (Shield reversed, and above two hands issuing from a cloud holding a dove.) Death of Sir William Longespée.

f. 148*b*.   *HA* iii. 84. Cf. MP I. 40.

Sir William Longespée II, s. of William, Earl of Salisbury (MP I. 40), killed at the battle of Mansourah. (*CP* xi. 382–3.) Though referred to as Earl by Matthew Paris, his claim to the earldom was unsuccessful.

ST. OMER

91. Castellani de S. Aedemaro. *Azure, a fess or.* (Shield reversed.) Death of William, Castellan of St. Omer.

f. 148*b*.   *HA* iii. 84.

William, Castellan of St. Omer, succ. his brother William *c.* 1245. His father and his brother both show a fess on their seals, but his seal bore *billetty a fess.* He used this seal in 1247 after he had succ. his brother. He appears to have left for Palestine in 1248 when his sister was acting in his office. The billets are probably a fraternal difference, which he did not trouble to remove on succeeding his brother. (A. Hermand and L. Deschamps de Pas, *Histoire sigillaire de la ville de Saint-Omer* (Paris, 1860), pp. 20–22 and pls. v, vi.)

GHENT

92. Castellani de Gant. *Sable, a chief ermine.* (Shield reversed.) Death of the Castellan of Ghent.

f. 148*b*.   *HA* iii. 84.

Possibly Hugh, Castellan of Ghent, Lord of Heusden, whose seal 1229 shows a chief. (J. Th. de Raadte, *Sceaux armoiriés des Pays-Bas* (Bruxelles, 1897), tome i. 474.)

BOULOGNE

93. Comitis Bolonie.

Gules, a lion rampant argent. (Shield reversed.)

f. 148*b*. *HA* iii. 84.

Philip Hurpel, s. of Philip Augustus by Agnes de Méranie, m. Mahaut, dau. and h. of Renaud, Count of Dammartin, by Ide, dau. and h. of Matthew, Count of Boulogne. (*AVD* xii. 358–66.)

ARTOIS

94. Comitis Atrabatensis Roberti.

Azure, six fleurs-de-lis or, a label (7) gules. (Shield reversed; beside the shield is a black bird emblem of evil, Robert of Artois being held to be the cause of the disaster at Mansourah.)

f. 148*b*. *HA* iii. 84. Cf. C 31.

Robert, Count of Artois, second s. of King Louis VIII of France, by Blanche of Castile, killed at Mansourah 1250. The label should be charged with golden castles (for Castile); it is painted as a strip at the very top of the shield. (Pinoteau, *Héraldique Capétienne*, I.)

COUCY

95. Engelramus de Coucy.

Barry of eight pieces argent and vairy of gules and argent. (Shield reversed.)

f. 148*b*. *HA* iii. 84.

It was Raoul de Coucy, s. of Enguerrand de Coucy, who was killed at Mansourah. (Du Plessis, *Histoire de la Ville et des seigneurs de Coucy* (Paris, 1728), p. 68.)

THE EMPIRE

96. Scutum imperatoris F[retherici].

Or, a double eagle displayea sable. (Shield reversed; on either side of the shield is a crown inverted, the dexter inscribed 'Corona Jerusalem', the sinister 'Corona Sicilie', with the addition 'Hic sunt adepte'.) Lower down are three other crowns also inverted with the following rubric: 'Triplici corona coronatur imperator Romanorum: Aurea ratione imperii Romani quod quasi aurum toti mundo. Argentea, ratione Alemannie, quae nummismata argentea ditatur, et habundat commerciis. Necnon est famosa, unde vulgariter dicitur imperator Alemannie. Argenteum enim sonorum est. Ferrea ratione Italie, quae armis et cominu urbibus roboratur ferrum namque pro armis accipitur, scilicet materia pro materiato.'

Beneath this again: 'Rex autem Anglie tres in scuto suo gerit leopardos, quia rex, dux et comes est.'

Death of Frederick II, 1250.

f. 149*a*. *HA* iii. 88. Cf. MP I. 21.

S. of the Emperor Henry IV by Constance, Queen of Sicily, succ. his father as king of Sicily 1197, elected emperor 1212, crowned emperor 1220.

ARMS OF FIVE KINGS WHO HAD TAKEN THE CROSS

Multi quoque reges crucesignantur in diversis mundi partibus.

Five shields with crowns beside them and with red crosses on the top of each shield.

CASTILE

97. Scutum regis Castelle crucesignati.

Gules, a triple-towered castle argent with windows gules. (Shield with crown beside.)
St. Ferdinand III, King of Castile, 1217–52, and of Leon, 1230–52.

f. 150a. *HA* iii. 95.

S. of Alphonso VIII of Leon by Berengaria of Castile. The castle of Castile appeared in 1178 under Alphonso VIII. Ferdinand III sealed in 1225 with the lion-shield of Leon with Castile as counterseal (*ex. inf.* P. Adam-Even), but from 1230 when he became king of Leon he quartered the lion of Leon as on his seal 1237. (Ddq. 11245.)

FRANCE

98. Scutum regis Francorum, sed vexillum prostratum in bello.

Azure, six fleurs-de-lis or. (Shield with crown at side). Beside the shield is a banner reversed, *Azure, three fleurs-de-lis or.*
St. Louis IX, 1226–70.

f. 150a. *HA* iii. 95. Cf. MP I. 8.

The prostrate banner refers to the defeat and capture of Louis IX at Mansourah 1250.

ENGLAND

99. Scutum regis Anglorum crucesignati.

Gules, three lions passant gardant or. (Shield with crown beside.)
Henry III, 1216–72.

f. 150a. *HA* iii. 95.

NORWAY

100. Scutum regis Norwagie crucesignati.

Gules, three galleys or, above the first a cross formy argent. (Shield with crown beside.)
Haakon IV, d. 1263.

f. 150a. *HA* iii. 95. Cf. MP IV. 73.

Although this coat with the cross in chief has not been found elsewhere it cannot be dismissed as a mere fruit of Matthew's imagination, for apart from the fact that Matthew had visited Norway in 1248, probably before either the *Historia* or the *Chronica* was compiled, similar coats are to be found in several rolls. PCL, *c.* 1450 (i. 59), attributes *Gules, three dragon-headed barges or* to the Lord of the Isles, long a Norwegian dependency, and RH (25) sets the three gold galleys in a blue field for the king of Norway, while still earlier WNR (16) and the LMRO (i. 27) attribute *Azure, a single masted golden galley* to the king of Norway. Reinfried von Braunschweig also assigns that last coat 'meister lieher Schif von finem gold' to 'Kunic Palaveize Norwaege'. It would therefore seem clear that one or more galleys, the long ships of the Vikings, were used as a Norwegian device, perhaps for the Scottish isles (ships of divers fashions are still borne for Lorn, Orkney, and Caithness) side by side with the modern lion-coat. The cross alludes to Haakon's resolve to go on a Crusade which was taken in 1250.

The lion is first known on seals of Haakon IV (1217–63) and Magnus VI (1263–80). On these it has neither axe (the emblem of St. Olaf) nor crown (cf. *ZWR* 17). These two features were added by Magnus's son Erik Magnusson (1280–99), before 1283, and it is noteworthy that this new version *Gules, a lion rampant or holding an axe argent* (alias *azure*) appears in FW 20, D 14, G 21, and *Wijn* 1275 (cf. 1306), all of which date from Erik's accession or soon after (see P. Warming, L'Apparition de la Hache dans les armes de Norvège, *Archivum Heraldicum*, 1954, pp. 38–40). PCL (i. 5) names this coat 'Sanctus Olavus rex'.

In this connexion it is worth noting that in Matthew's drawing of the battle of Stamford Bridge, Harold Hardrada bears three axes on his shield (MP VIII. 27 (g)), and in another drawing Sweyn of Denmark bears axes (MP VIII. 21, 24). In RH 835, however, *Or, three axes sable* is attributed to the King of Norway, and in PCL *Azure, three axes or*, quarters the galleys in the shield of the Lord of the Isles. On the other hand, the three axes in varying tinctures are assigned to Denmark in several other rolls: D 16, G 14, FW 17, LMRO 121, and in WNR 5.

JERUSALEM

101. Scutum Regis Jerusalem cognomento Bresne.
Or crusuly argent, a cross argent. (Shield with crown beside.)
John de Brienne, King of Jerusalem, 1210–37.

> f. 150*a*.   *HA* iii. 95. Cf. MP. I. 6.

VESCY

102. Scutum Willelmi de Wescy.
Gules, a cross moline argent. (Shield reversed.)
Death of William de Vescy, 1253.

> f. 156*b*.   *HA* iii. 147. Cf. MP I. 26.
>
> S. of Eustace de Vescy (MP I. 26), he was of Alnwick and Malton, W. Northumberland, and father of John (d.s.p. 1288/9) and of William (d.s.p. s. legit. 1297). (*CP* xii (2) 276–8.)

MP II

British Museum MS. Cotton Nero D I
Liber Additamentorum, ff. 170, 170*b*, 185, 198, 198*b*

Nero D I, f. 170*b*. Forty-two painted shields with names and 'blazons' arranged in seven rows of six, with three more shields added in the margins; no. 1, in outline to the left of the top row; nos. 44 and 45 painted but mostly torn away, to the right of the last two rows, next to nos. 37 and 43 respectively. There are legends at the extreme top of the page now badly rubbed and partly cut away. All that is now legible is: — over 3: Corn . . .; 4 Clare; 6 . . . sc bla'c . leo gul'; 7: Come' Wa. . . .

JERUSALEM

1. I'r'l'm.
Scutum aureum crux alba cum multis parvis crucibus albis.
Or crusuly argent, a cross argent.

> Cf. MP I. 6, 101 : C 14.
>
> John de Brienne, King of Jerusalem, d. 1237. A small outlined shield near the foot of MP II. 2. The crosslets are not shown. (Runciman, *History of the Crusades*, iii. 177.)

ENGLAND

2. Domini Regis.
Scutum de gules, leones aurei.
Gules, three lions passant gardant or.

> Cf. MP I. 19.
>
> Henry III 1216–72.

RICHARD, Earl of Cornwall

3. Comitis Ricardi, comitis scilicet Pictavie.
Scutum album, leo gules, bordura nigra besantie de or.
Argent, a lion rampant gules crowned or in a bordure sable bezanty.

> Cf. MP I. 38 : B 3 : C 124.

> Richard, Earl of Cornwall and Poitou, d. 1272: same person as MP I. 38. (*CP* iii. 431.)

CLARE

4. Comitis de Clare.
Scutum aureum, tres cheveruns gules.
Or, three chevrons gules.

> Cf. MP I. 46, 76 : B 5.

> Richard de Clare, Earl of Gloucester, d. 1262: same person as MP I. 76. (*CP* v. 700.)

D'AUBIGNY

5. Comitis de Harundel.
Scutum gules, leo aureus.
Gules, a lion rampant or.

> Cf. MP I. 36, 72.

> Hugh d'Aubigny, Earl of Arundel, d.s.p. 1243: same person as MP I. 72.

MONTFORT

6. Comitis de Legrecestria.
Scutum album, leo gules.
Argent, a lion rampant queue fourchée gules.

> Cf. MP I. 30 : B 4.

> Simon de Montfort, Earl of Leicester, second s. of MP I. 30; confirmed in the earldom 1239 with the consent of his elder brother Amaury; slain at Evesham 1265. (*CP* vii. 543–7.)

WARENNE

7. Comitis Warenne.
Chekere de auro et azuro.
Checky or and azure.

> Cf. MP I. 64. B 7.

> Probably same person as MP i. 64.

LONGESPÉE

8. Willelmi Longaspata.
Scutum azureum vj leones aurei.
Azure, six lions rampant or.

> Cf. MP I. 40 : B 22.

> Sir William Longespee: same person as MP I. 90.

BOHUN

9. Comitis de Hereford.

Scutum azureum leones aurei benda album [sic].

Azure, a bend argent between six lions rampant or.

> Cf. MP I. 33; IV. 16 : B 10.

> Humphrey de Bohun, Earl of Hereford, s. of Henry, Earl of Hereford (MP I. 33); d. 1275. These arms appear on his seal in 1238 (Birch 7529), but more usually the bend is cotised or, as in B 10, and on his seal in 1236 (*Book of Seals*, 323) and in 1259 (Birch 5720). The version in MP IV. 16 is otherwise unknown.

FERRERS

10. Comitis de Ferrers.

Scutum varium aur' et gules.

Vairy or and gules.

> Cf. MP II. 62; VII. 1 : B 15.

> William de Ferrers, Earl of Derby, s. of William de Ferrers, Earl of Derby; d. 1247. (*CP* iv. 194–6; Birch 5917.) In MP II. 93 the vairy is gules and or, in MP II. 108 gules and argent, but these rough sketches are not of the authority of the finished paintings.

QUINCY

11. Comitis Wintonie.

Scutum gules losenges de or.

Gules, seven voided lozenges conjoined or (3, 3, 1).

> Cf. MP I. 32.

> Roger de Quincy, Earl of Winchester, d.s.p.m. 1264, s. of Saher de Quincy, Earl of Winchester (MP I. 32), d.s.p.m. 1264. (*CP* xii (2) 751–4.)

BIGOD

12. Comitis Bigod.

Scutum aureum crux gules.

Or, a cross gules.

> Cf. MP I. 39 : B 6, 89, 197.

> Roger Bigod, Earl of Norfolk, s. of MP I. 39, Marshal of England *jure matris* (see MP I. 79); d.s.p. 1270. (*CP* ix. 590–3.)

WARWICK

13. Comitis de Warewic.

Scutum eschekeratum de or et de azure, bende . . .

Checky or and azure, a bend [ermine].

> Cf. MP I. 70; IV. 49 : B 20.

> Thomas, Earl of Warwick, d.s.p. 1242: same person as MP I. 70. (*CP* xii (2), 365.) It is possible that Matthew did not know the word for ermine and therefore left a blank.

CHESTER

14. Comitis Cestrie.

Scutum de azuro garbe de or.

Azure, three garbs or.

> Ranulph de Blundeville, Earl of Chester, d.s.p. 1232: same person as MP I. 48. (*CP* iii. 167–9.)

VERE

15. Comitis Oxonie.

Quarterium ubi stella alba de gules aliud cum suo [pari] aureum.

Quarterly gules and or, a mullet argent in the first quarter.

Cf. MP II. 88 : B 11.

Hugh de Vere, Earl of Oxford, d. 1263. (*CP* x. 213–16.) The arms are derived from Geoffrey de Mandeville whose wife Rohese was sister of Aubrey de Vere, Earl of Oxford, Hugh's grandfather.

BURGH

16. Comitis Cancie.

Losenga media maskele de albo et azuro alia quarteria de gules.

Lozengy vair and gules.

Cf. MP I. 45, 71, 73; IV. 28, 58.

Hubert de Burgh, Earl of Kent, d. 1243: same person as MP i. 73. The arms are usually *Lozengy of gules and vair*, and are so painted by Matthew in several other places (I. 45, 71, 73; IV. 28, 58). Here the blue panes of the vair are omitted, but it is impossible to say whether this is a mere oversight or whether when he came to paint the shield Matthew had forgotten the arms and misinterpreted his own unintelligible blazon.

REVIERS

17. Comitis Devonie.

Scutum aureum leo de azuro.

Or, a lion rampant azure.

Cf. MP I. 75.

Baldwin de Reviers, Earl of Devon, d. 1245 (*CP* iv. 318–19): same person as MP I. 75.

MARSHAL

18. Comitis Marescalli.

Medieta viridis alia aurei leo gules an[te] leonem gules. (*Ante* may be *autem*; neither makes sense.)

Per pale or and vert, a lion rampant gules.

Cf. MP I. 29, 51, &c.

This coat is probably for Gilbert, Earl Marshal, d. 1241. His younger brothers, Walter and Anselm, are given a lion rampant argent (MP I. 78, 79), though it should be noted that in MP IV. 66 Walter is given a lion rampant gules. (*CP* x. 371–4.)

HUNTINGDON

19. Comitis Huntundune.

Scutum aureum tres pali aurei.

Or, three piles meeting in base gules.

Cf. B 14.

John le Scot, Earl of Huntingdon and Chester, s. of David, Earl of Huntingdon, brother of William the Lion, King of Scotland, by Maud, sister and coh. of Ralph de Blundeville, Earl of Chester; d.s.p. 1237. (*CP* iii. 169–70.)

In MP IV. 34 he is given the arms of Chester. The equation of *pali* and *piles* should be noted.

LACY

20. Comitis Lincolnie.

Cantel anterior de or et correspondens alia cantella de gules, benda nigra que Gallice sable dicitur.

Quarterly or and gules, a bend sable and a label (5) argent.

> Cf. MP I. 63.

> John de Lacy, Earl of Lincoln, d. 1240: same person as MP I. 63. (*CP* vii. 676–80.) The 'blazon' omits the label.

DAUBENEY of Belvoir

21. Daubeni.

Scutum de dor cheveruns cum bordura de gules.

Or, two chevrons and a bordure gules.

> Cf. MP I. 52 : B 68.

> William Daubeney, d. 1236: same person as MP I. 52. (Round, *HMC Rutland*, iv. 106–7; Dugd. *Bar.* i. 112–15.)

MANDEVILLE

22. Willelmi de Mandevilla.

Ad quatre quarters, quarter devant d'or cum suo pari.

Quarterly or and gules.

> Cf. MP I. 25.

> William de Mandeville, Earl of Essex, d.s.p. 1227: same person as MP I. 43. (*CP* v. 130–3.)

HUNTINGFIELD

23. Rogeri de Huntingfield.

Scutum de or bende de gules a iiij gasteus de blanc.

Or, on a fess gules three roundels argent.

> Cf. B 131.

> Roger de Huntingfield of Huntingfield and Mendham, Suffolk; d. 1257. (*Cal. Inq.* i. 394; *CP* vi. 664.) An example of *bende* used for a horizontal band.

MONTFICHET

24. Ricardi de Munfichet.

Scutum de or iij cheveruns de gules vel rastel de azuro vel lambel.

Or, three chevrons gules a label (5) azure.

> Cf. B 80.

> Great-gds. of William de Montfichet, the founder of Stratford Langthorne Abbey, Essex; succ. his father Richard, 1203 and d. 1267. (Farrer, *Feudal Cambridgeshire*, 234; *Book of Seals*, 97; Birch 11866.)
>
> Family and arms derived from the marriage of William de Montfichet to Margaret, aunt of Richard de Clare 'Strongbow', Earl of Pembroke (cf. MP I. 46), and the variation of the tinctures in B 80 suggests that the arms were originally chevronny or and gules, though this was afterwards reduced to three chevrons as in the case of Clare.(Wagner, *Historic Heraldry*, p. 37.)

TONY

25. De Tony.

Scutum de or, manche de gules.
Or, a maunch gules.

> Cf. MP I. 57; IV. 25.
>
> Ralph de Tony, d. 1239: same person as MP I. 57. (*CP* xii (1) 769–71.)

CAUNTELO

26. Willelmi de Cantelupo.

Scutum de gules flores aurei.
Gules, three fleurs-de-lis or.

> Cf. MP I. 54 : B 27.
>
> William de Cauntelo, s. of William de Cauntelo (MP I. 54), d. 1251. (Dugd. *Bar.* i. 732.)

BEAUCHAMP

27. Johannis de Bellocampo.

Scutum album aquila nigra secundum dictum, sed a contrario secundum alium.
Argent, an eagle displayed sable, beak and legs or.

> Cf. B 96, 204.
>
> Possibly s. of William de Beauchamp of Eaton Socon, Beds.; nephew and h. of Hugh (d. 1187) and of Roger (d. 1218); d. 1241. If this identification is correct, he is father of B 96 who bears different arms, and this makes this identification very doubtful. (Dugd. *Bar.* i. 224–5.)

BEAUCHAMP of Bedford

28. Willelmi de Bellocampo.

Quarter de or ante cum suo pari, alia de gules, la fesse de gules.
Quarterly or and gules, a bend gules.

> Cf. MP II. 76 : B 54, 196.
>
> Here *fesse* is used for *bend*.
>
> William de Beauchamp, Baron of Bedford, s. of Simon de Beauchamp, succ. 1216 and d. 1260. The arms are derived from Geoffrey de Mandeville whose widow Rohese de Vere m. secondly Payn de Beauchamp of Bedford, grandfather of this man. (Dugd. *Bar.* i. 223–4; *VCH Beds.* ii. 29–30, iii. 10–12; *Genealogists' Magazine*, vii. 224.)

BASSINGBOURNE

29. Johannis de Bassingbourne.

Scutum superius de gules leo aureus, inferius scutum de albo fesse de gules aves de gules.
Argent, a bend between five martlets gules, on a chief gules a lion passant gardant or.

> Cf. B 35; C 136.
>
> John de Bassingbourne, d. 1237; s. of Warin; an evil counsellor of King John according to Matthew. (*CM* ii. 533.) He held castle of Beningfield, Northants., and lands in several counties; last mentioned in *Close Roll* 1236 p. 234 when he was given four pollard trees for his hearth.
>
> In B 35 and C 136 Warin de Bassingbourne, who was probably John's gds., bears *Gyronny or and azure*. The arms attributed to John by Matthew are those of Furnival with a chief of England. No explanation of these has been found, but it is possible that the lion was attributed to him by Matthew because of his connexion with King John. (Dugd. *Bar.* i. 680.) Matthew terms the lion passant gardant 'lion' and not 'leopard'.

CRESSY

30. Rogeri de Cressi.

Scutum aureum lune de gules.

Or, three crescents gules.

> Roger de Cressy of Hodsock, Notts., and Melton, Yorks., m. Sibyl, dau. and h. of John de Braytoft, Lincs.; d. *c.* 1245. (*CP* iii. 528.) His seal, thirteenth-century, bears seven crescents (*Book of Seals*, 383), a canting coat, but his s. William bore *Argent, a lion rampant queue fourchée sable* (E 594).

NEVILLE of Essex

31. Hugonis de Novilli (*the last letter is torn*).

Anterior quarter cum suo pari . . . (remainder torn away).

Quarterly indented both ways gules and vert, a bend or.

> Cf. MP IV. 19, 69; V. 4.
>
> Hugh de Neville of Great Hallingbury, Essex; gds. of Alan de Neville who was brother of Gilbert, the grandfather of Isabel who m. Robert FitzMeldred, ancestor of Neville of Raby. Hugh was appointed Chief Justice and Keeper of the Forest 1224; d. 1234. (*CP* ix. 479–80.) This version of the arms is otherwise unknown; they are usually *Per chief* (or *Per fess*) *indented gules and vert, a bend or*, so in MP IV. 19, 69, and on Hugh's counter seal on BM Harl. ch. 54 B 14. In N 684 Sir Thomas de Nevile (Lincs.) also parts his field per chief though the tinctures are different, *De or od le chef endente de vert e une bende de goules.*

FITZWALTER

32. Roberti filii Walteri.

Scutum de or cheveruns de gules.

Or, a fess between two chevrons gules.

> Cf. B 186.
>
> Robert FitzWalter of Woodham Walter, Suffolk, gtgds. of Richard FitzGilbert de Clare and s. of Walter FitzRobert (d. 1198); father of B 186; d.1235. (*CP* v. 472.) The arms are a variant of Clare (MP I. 46). (Wagner, *Historic Heraldry*, p. 37.)

PECCHE

33. Hamonis Peche.

Scutum album cheveruns de gules scilicet pars superior et inferior.

Argent, a fess between two chevrons gules.

> Cf. B 60.
>
> Of Bourn, Cambs.; d. 1241; s. of Gilbert Pecche by Alice, dau. of Walter FitzRobert of Dunmow, Essex, and sister of MP II. 32. The arms are derived from Clare through FitzRobert (later FitzWalter). For his s. Gilbert see B 60. (Dugd. *Bar.* i. 677; *CP* x. 334–5.)
>
> This is one of the items which suggests that the 'blazons' are mere memoranda for the guidance of Matthew when he came to paint and that he relied on his memory to complete the picture.

BASSET

34. Basseth.

Scutum album unde de gules.

Barry wavy of six pieces or and gules.

> Cf. MP IV. 44 : B 93.
>
> Gilbert Basset of Wycombe, Leics., s. of Alan Basset and elder brother of Warin Basset (MP I. 49) and of Philip Basset (B 93); d. 1240/1. (Dugd. *Bar.* i. 384.) *Album* is a mistake for *aureum*; the painting is correct.

VESCY

35. Willelmi de Vesci.

Scutum de gules crux alba debet esse pes alba.
Gules, a cross formy fitchy at the foot argent.

Cf. MP I. 26, &c. : B 76.

William de Vescy, s. of Eustace de Vesci (MP I. 26) of Malton and Alnwick, d. 1253. (Clay, *Extinct and Dormant Peerages*, p. 227; *CP* xii (2) 276.) Same person as MP I. 102.

On the dexter side of the shield is written 'Cr[edo] scutum comitis de Albermarla' (cf. MP II. 38).

Matthew was quite uncertain as to the pattern of the Vescy cross. Here he painted it as a cross formy, then added in ink a small point at the foot, but he did not paint that white. In I and IV he draws a cross patonce for Eustace de Vesci, d. 1216 (MP I. 26; IV. 11), but a moline cross for William (MP I. 102; IV. 84). See also B 76 where the Vescy arms are further considered.

ARGENTINE

36. Ricardi de Argenton.

Scutum de gules cuppe argentee.
Gules, three covered cups argent.

Richard de Argentine was s. of Reynold de Argentine of Melbourn, Cambs. He was one of Matthew's informants. (*CM* iii. 164.) The arms, and possibly the name, allude to the serjeanty of bearing a silver cup at the coronation, by which the manor of Great Wymondley, Herts., was held. (*Camb. Ant. Soc.* xxviii. 16–79.)

FLANDERS

37. Comitis Flandorum.

Scutum nigrum leo aureus.
Sable, a lion rampant or.

Cf. MP II. 43; VII. 11.

Thomas of Savoy, uncle of Queen Eleanor of Provence, m. Johanna, dau. and coh. of Baldwin IX, Count of Flanders; d. 1259. At his wife's death s.p. 1233 he resigned Flanders and Hainault to her sister Margaret who m. William de Dampierre and was mother of Guy de Dampierre (C. 29). He stayed at St. Albans in 1244. (*CM* iv. 378.)

The colours should be reversed, *Or a lion sable*; this is the coat of Brabant (cf. MP II. 43).

FORZ

38. Comitis de Aubemarle.

Scutum de gules crux variata de albo et azuro.
Gules, a cross vair having the vertical arms formy and the horizontals patonce.

Cf. B 13; C 60.

William II de Forz, titular Count of Aumale; succ. 1214; d. 1241; s. of William de Forz of Holderness, Yorks. (d. 1195), by Hawise, Countess of Aumale. He was gdfather of Thomas, Earl of Aumale (C 60). Aumale is in Normandy. On the blazoning of the cross see B 13 and *Coat of Arms*, v. 359. The evidence of seals, &c., proves that it was really patonce, but the ends of the arms were often drawn with barely distinguishable indentations, and that fact may explain why Matthew made the perpendiculars formy.

FITZNICHOL

39. Radulfi filii Nicholai.

Scutum de gules pentafolium de or bordura escal' de argent.

Gules, a pierced cinquefoil or in an orle of escallops argent.

> The orle of silver scallops is omitted in the painting. Ralph FitzNichol 'senescallus hospitii regis' 1236, 'domini regis senescallus' 1250; d. 1257. (*CM* iii. 363; v. 101, 616.)

HERRING

40. Roberti Harenc.

Scutum de gules iij har[engs] de argent.

Gules, three herrings hauriant two and one, argent.

> A tenant of the Bishop of Rochester in Snodland, Kent, 1242–3. (*Book of Fees*, 667, 682.)

MUSCHET

41. Roberti Muschet.

Scutum de azuro et tres muschet de or.

Azure, three sparrow hawks or.

> A muschet is a kind of sparrow-hawk. No mention of Robert Muschet has been found. Luard, in the index to *Chronica* (vii. 422), identifies him with Robert de Muschamp, who d. 1249/50, but that must be a mistake, for the latter sealed with *Three bars and a chief*. (*Durham Seals*, 1848, pl. 21.) The heirs of Ralph Muschet held lands in Edlesborough, Beds., 1242–3, and in the same year Adam Muschet paid scutage for land in Peatling Magna, Leics. Early in the thirteenth century William Muschet was a tenant of the Bishop of Ely in Hackbleach, Norfolk, and in the fourteenth century members of the family held lands in Thriplow, Ditton, and Stow-cum-Quy, co. Camb. (*Book of Fees*, 630, 876, 949; *Feudal Aids*, i. 144, 155, 161, 180.)

TOULOUSE, Count of

42. Comitis Tholosie.

Comes Tholose qui dicitur comes Sancti Aegidii.

Scutum de gules crux aurea.

Gules, a Toulouse cross or.

> Raymond VII, Count of Toulouse, d. 1249, leaving a dau. and h. Jeanne who m. Alphonse of Poitou (cf. C 42). (*AVD* ix. 393–6.) Modern French heralds blazon the Toulouse cross clechée, vidée et pommettée, and that is exactly how Matthew has drawn it (cf. *Coat of Arms*, v. 360, fig. 3a).

BRABANT

43. Dux Braibante.

Scutum nigrum leo aureus.

Or, a lion rampant sable 'vacat'.

> Cf. MP II. 80 : C 46.

> The blazon is correct. The painting is the coat of Flanders (MP II. 37) as Matthew evidently realized, for 'vacat' is written below the shield. Duke Henry II d. 1248; father of Henry III. (Bigot 43; *AVD* xiv. 95–96.)

ARAGON or PROVENCE

44. *Paly of eight pieces gules and or.*

> Cf. MP I. 77; IV. 65; V. 1 : C 9.

> This is one of the two shields added in the outer margin and only the two dexter pales are left.

The tiny fragment of legend is now illegible, but at the left foot of the shield is written 'Quod debet esse octo linee'. Either James I, King of Aragon, 1213–76, may be meant, or Raymond of Provence, his cousin (MP I. 77). (See C 90 for note on Aragon.)

FURNIVAL

45. *Argent, a bend between [six] martlets gules.*

Cf. MP II. 77 : B 147, 148, 149.

Only a small portion of the dexter side of the shield is left with a part of a bend and two birds, enough, however, to show that the arms were those of Furnival as in MP II. 77 below. The superscription is lost except for 'Gu'.

f. 170a. Twenty-five shields in five rows of five with three more below and five in the lower part of the right-hand margin. Names and 'blazons' as on the recto. Of the thirty-three shields sixteen are painted, fourteen in trick, and three blank.

EMPEROR

46. Scutum Imperatoris Rome.
Scutum aureum aquila biceps vel moniceps nigra.
Or, a double eagle sable. (Painted.)

Cf. MP I. 21, 96.

Frederick II, d. 1250.

FRANCE

47. Scutum Regis Francorum.
Scutum azureum vj gladioli flores aurei [sic].
Azure, six fleurs-de-lis or. (Painted.)

Cf. MP I. 8, 42.

St. Louis (IX), 1226–70.

SCOTLAND

48. Scutum regis Scocie.
Scutum de auro leo reptans [de gules] et flores in bordura similiter.
Or, a lion rampant in a single tressure flory gules. (Painted.)

Cf. MP I. 85; IV. 80 : C 15.

Alexander II, 1214–49. The tressure is drawn as a thin red line parallel to the edge of the shield and straddled by ten demi-fleurs-de-lis projecting from the edge of the shield. The shield of the king of Scotland in the roof of the monks' choir in St. Albans, painted in the reign of Edward III, shows a similar single tressure. It suggests that this manuscript may have been used by the artists who painted the shields on the roof. (*Arch.* li. 441.)

BAUCEY

49. Scutum Nichol de Moles [sic].
Hug' de Baucei pictavensis.
Scutum aureum ferrum molendinum de gules.
Or, a cross moline gules. (Painted.)

The second name is correct. The arms are those of Baucey or Baussay. In Bigot 249–9 (1254) Pierre and Guillaume de Bausai (Baussay-le-Noble, dépt. Vienne), sons of Hugues VII, both bear *D'or a j fer de molin de gueules* the latter differencing *au lalbel d'azur*. Both are described as 'Banneret et Angevins'. (See also *ChP* 26 and sources there cited.)

Nicholas de Moles or Moels bore *Argent, two bars in chief three roundels gules* (B 83).

KENNET

50. Scutum N. de Kenetz.

Scutum de gules caniculi de argento.

Gules, three dogs (kennets) passant argent. (Uncoloured.)

Nicholas, s. of Peter de Kennet of Kennet, Cambs., sealed with these arms 1252–3. (*Book of Seals*, 381.) The arms are canting, a kennet being a small hunting dog. In F 101 the dogs are drawn with noses down as though following a scent. (Farrer, *Feudal Cambridgeshire*, pp. 148–9.)

UMFRAVILLE

51. Scutum Gileberti de Humf'mvile.

Scutum de gules pentafolium aureum bordura de azuro.

Gules, a cinquefoil pierced [or] in a bordure azure. (Shield uncoloured.)

Cf. MP IV. 62 : B 122.

Gilbert de Umfraville of Prudhoe and Redesdale, Northumberland, m. 1243 Maud, Countess of Angus, dau. and h. of Malcolm, Earl of Angus, and may have become Earl of Angus *jure uxoris*; d. 1245. (*SP* i. 167–8; but cf. *CP* i. 146–7.) In MP IV. 62 and B 122 the border is charged with horseshoes argent.

Gilbert's father, Richard de Umfraville (d. 1223) sealed with a cinquefoil (not on a shield) in early thirteenth century. (*Durham Seals*, 2507.)

Gilbert's s. and h. Gilbert, second Earl of Angus, and his descendants, bore *Gules crusuly or, a cinquefoil or*. (H 24; D 117; E 33; Lawrance, p. 45.)

PERCY

52. Ricardi de Percy.

Scutum d'azuro vque fesse d'argent endentes clausi superius ferri argentei.

Azure, a fess of five fusils argent, the tips of the fusils touch the top edge of the shield. (Uncoloured.)

Cf. B 41, 119.

Younger s. of Jocelin de Louvain by Agnes de Percy, dau. and coh. of William de Percy, whose name he took. His elder brother, Henry de Percy (d. 1198), probably bore *Azure, a fess of five fusils or*, for his (Henry's) s. William bore the fusils on his seal (c. 1240; see *Arch. Aeliana* (1941), p. 87) and William's s. Henry de Percy (d. 1272) bore them of gold (B 41).

Richard m. (1) Alice, (2) Agnes, dau. of Geoffrey de Neville of Raby, and d. 1244, leaving a s. Henry. (*CP* x. 449–52.) The use of a fess engrailed by Piers Percy (B 119), who was probably descended from Picot de Percy of Wharram and Sutton-upon-Derwent, puts the origin of this coat back to a date before the Louvain marriage. The exact relationship of Picot de Percy to William de Percy of Topcliffe, great-grandfather of Agnes de Percy, is not known, but he was probably closely related. (*CP* x. 435 note (*b*); *Whitby Cartulary*, ii. 707–8; Clay, *Extinct and Dormant Peerages*, p. 159.)

BALLIOL

53. Johannes de Bailloil.

Scutum de gules aliud de argent.

Gules, a voided escutcheon argent. (Tricked.)

Cf. MP; II. 67 : B 36.

John de Balliol, d. 1268 (s. of Hugh, d. 1228), Regent of Scotland, Lord of Barnard Castle, m. Devorguilla, dau. and coh. of Alan, lord of Galloway. His third s. John became King of Scots 1292; d. 1315. (*NCH* vi. 73; *DNB*.)

Devorguilla's mother was Margaret, dau. and coh. of David, Earl of Huntingdon and of Chester, younger s. of King Malcolm III, and thus she transmitted a claim to the Crown of Scotland. On her seal she gave precedence to her own arms and bore Galloway (*azure, a lion rampant crowned or*) impaling Balliol (seal 1252, *Oxford Deeds of Balliol College*, Oxford Hist. Soc. lxiv. 227, and pl. facing. p. 363). This coat is now used by Balliol College of which John was one of the founders.

BALLIOL

54. Eustachii fratris ejusdem Johannis.

Scutum d'azuro aliud d'or multe cruces in campo.

Azure crusuly, a voided escutcheon or. (There are no crosslets in the drawing; the shield is painted blue but the outline of the escutcheon is uncoloured.)

Cf. MP I. 88; II. 53 : B 36, 40.

Eustace, younger brother of John (MP II. 53), d. 1272. (*NCH* vi. 73.)

ROS of Helmsley

55. Roberti de Ros.

Scutum de gules tres utres d'argent.

Gules, three bougets argent. (Uncoloured.)

Cf. B 66, 173.

These are the arms of Ros of Helmsley. Robert de Ros, known as Furfan or Furson, s. of Everard de Ros by Rohese, dau. of William Trussebut, Lord of Warter, Yorks., and in her issue h. of her brother Robert, m. Isabel, widow of Robert de Brus and illegitimate dau. of William the Lion of Scotland; d. as a Templar, 1226. This is sometime before 1244, which is probably the date of the compilation. It is possible, but unlikely, that Matthew was referring to Robert de Ros of Wark, second s. of Robert de Ros of Helmsley. His arms were, however, *Or, three bougets sable* (see B 173), and Matthew may have made a mistake. (*CP* xi. 92–93.)

The arms are canting derived from Trussebut, *trois bouces*. Agatha Trussebut, sister of Rohese, bears a bouget on her seal (late twelfth or early thirteenth century), though not on a shield (Birch 13991), and Richard de Trussebut, whose relationship has not been established, bore *Argent three bougets gules* (E 817) .Smith Ellis suggested (*Antiquities of Heraldry*, p. 201) that the earliest arms of Ros were roses, because Cossington of Kent, who, he said, descended from Ros, bore *roses*. But Ros of Kent, from whom the manor of Acrise passed to the Cossingtons, appears to have had no connexion with Ros of Helmsley. The Kentish family take their name from Ros in Calvados; the Yorkshire family doubtless took theirs from Ros in Holderness, and Ellis's argument does not apply to them. (*CP* xi. 90; Loyd, *Anglo-Norman Families*, p. 86.)

Robert de Ros of Helmsley was father of William de Ros (B 66) and of Robert de Ros of Wark (B 173).

GIFFARD and HUSSEY

56. G[iffard] eis et Heusey.

Scutum de ermine iij benda de gules.

Ermine, three bars gules. (Uncoloured.)

These are later the arms of Giffard of Yester, but it is more probable that they are intended for one of the Osbern Giffards, of whom there were three. (1) Sir Osbern Giffard of Winterbourne Houghton, Dorset, d. 1237. (2) His s. Sir Osbern Giffard living 1301/2. (3) Sir Osbern Giffard, natural s. of King John, d. 1248. The arms of the second were *Ermine two bars gules, on a chief gules a lion passant gardant or* (sl. 1285/6 PRO; A 220; E 521; Q 578; G 206). It has been considered with some reason that these were the arms of no. 3 and that the leopard proclaimed his royal parentage (*Ancestor*, iii. 227). However, this would seem to be precluded by the fact that similar arms were undoubtedly borne by no. 2. It is probable that it was no. 1 to whom Matthew was referring; the leopard may have been omitted by error, or more probably it was added by the son. (*CP* v. 649–53; *Genealogist*, n.s., xxxviii. 128–34.)

The same arms attributed to Hussey probably refer to Sir Matthew Hussey (Husee, Hose, or Huse), s. of Henry Hussey of Harting, Sussex (d. 1235); he m. Agnes, dau. and coh. of Hugh de Saundford, d. 1253. (*HKF* iii. 85–86; *CP* vii. 1.)

ODINGSELES, DODDINGSELES

57. Gerardi et Willelmi Dodingseles.

Scutum album j fesse de gules ij stelle de gules in capite.

Argent, a fess gules in chief two mullets gules. (Uncoloured.)

> Cf. B 142; C 157.

> Gerard de Odingseles, s. of Hugh de Odingseles of Maxstoke, Warw., had succ. by 1239 and d. 1266. William, brother of Gerard, held the manor of Solihull, Warw., and was dead 1271 (*VCH Warw.* iv. 138, 218; Dugd. *Warw.*, p. 228.)

> Birch 12287 describes the seal of William as having estoiles in chief, but seals in the PRO (A 3259, 3261) and at Maxstoke Castle (*Arch.* xxxviii. 272), and all rolls except B 142 support mullets.

DESPENSER

58. Hugonis Dispensatoris.

Album ubi benda nigra aliud gules a or frette.

Quarterly of argent with gules fretty or, over all a bend sable. (Uncoloured except for the bend.)

> Cf. MP IV. 79 : B 114.

> Hugh le Despenser of Loughborough, Leics., s. of Hugh le Despenser (d. 1238); slain at Evesham 1265. His s. Hugh was created Earl of Winchester 1322. Geoffrey le Despenser (MP IV. 79) was younger brother of Hugh, the father of this man.

> The coat is derived from Mandeville (MP I. 25) either through Beauchamp of Bedford (MP II. 28, 76) of whom the Despensers were tenants, or through Lacy (MP I. 63), constables of Chester, to whom the Despensers were 'dispensatores'. (Wagner, *Historic Heraldry*, p. 50; *CP* iv. 259.)

LEXINGTON

59. Johannis de Lexington.

Scutum de argento crux de azuro.

Argent, a cross patonce azure. (Uncoloured.)

> Cf. B 155.

> John de Lexington of Laxton, Notts., d.s.p. 1257, s. of Richard de Lexington and brother and h. of Robert. He was a councillor of Henry III, became a judge, and from 1238 had custody of the Great Seal for several short periods. He was one of Matthew's informants. (*CM* v. 384.) His younger brother and h. Henry was Bishop of Lincoln 1254–8. (*DNB*; Dugd. *Bar.* i. 743.)

> Although we have blazoned the cross patonce, it is actually drawn as a moline cross with a small point or tooth projecting between the flukes of each arm, and that is probably what was meant by the blazon *furchée au kanee* in B 155 q.v. (See also 'Patee, Patonce and Formy' in *Coat of Arms*, v. 358.)

NAVARRE

60. Regis Navarie.

Scutum de azuro benda alba utrobique lineata auro.

Azure, a bend argent cotised or. (Shield blank.)

> Cf. C 6, 42.

> Blanche, h. of Navarre, m. Theobald, Count of Champagne, and their s. Theobald reigned as king of Navarre 1234–53 (C 6).

The arms are those of Champagne (see C 42), and the blank shield may indicate that Matthew was uncertain how they ought to be drawn, which would hardly be surprising in view of the variations. (See Appendix II).

TATESHAL or TATTERSHALL

61. Roberti de Tateshale.

Scutum scaccaratum auro et gules. (Blank shield.)

Checky or and gules.

Cf. B 50.

Robert de Tateshal of Lincs., d. 1249. His s. Robert (d. 1273) bore *Checky or and gules, a chief ermine* (B 50). (*CP* xii (1), 649–50.)

The fact that the shield has been left blank suggests that a certain time had elapsed from the writing of the blazons before the shields were drawn. Probably Matthew had notes of the blazons, but when he sat down to draw the shield he was aware of an omission in this instance and therefore left the shield blank.

FERRERS

62. Comitis de Ferrariis.

Scutum variatum auro et gules.

Vairy. (Uncoloured.)

Cf. MP II. 10.

William de Ferrers, Earl of Derby 1190–1247: same person as MP II. 10. (*CP* iv. 194–6.)

LUSIGNAN

63. Comitis de Marchia.

Scutum burele de azuro et argento, quot lineas vis primam tamen de argento.

Buruly argent and azure (15 bars). (Uncoloured.)

Cf. MP I. 83, 86; II. 64; IV. 72 : B 23 : C 71, 72.

Hugh le Brun, Seigneur de Lusignan, Count de la Marche: same person as MP I. 86.

LUSIGNAN-VALENCE

64. Willelmi de Valentia filii ejus.

Similiter ut patris cum hiis quinque lambelli de gules pendentes a superiori linea argenti ita tamen quod prima linea argentea sit libera, in quolibet lambello iij leopardi transeuntes.

Barry (15) *argent and* [*azure, a label* (5) *gules on each point three lions of England*]. (Uncoloured.)

Cf. MP I. 83, 86; II. 63; IV. 72 : B 23 : C 72.

William de Valence, s. of MP II. 63, came to England 1247, d. 1296: same person as MP I. 83. The 'blazon' of Matthew shows that his notes were made from a coloured representation of the arms.

LUSIGNAN

65. Guidonis de Lichetum fratris ejusdem Willelmi. (Shield blank, no 'blazon'.)

Cf. C 71.

Guy de Lusignan, Sire de Cognac, second s. of Hugh, Count de la Marche (MP I. 86). He was knighted by Henry III in 1242; d.s.p. 1288. (*Genealogist*, N.S. xxi. 78, &c.)

CREVEQUER

66. Hamonis de Crevequer.

Scutum de or crux de gules perforata,

[*Or*], *a cross gules voided throughout.* (The cross is painted.)

Cf. B 61.

A canting coat, croix crévé au cœur. Hamo de Crevequer of Chatham and Leeds Castle, Kent, d. 1263; s. of Robert de Crevequer; m. Maud, sister and coh. of William de Avranches. His father's seal, *c.* 1200, bears fleurs-de-lis, probably three though only two are visible. (Streatfield, *Excerpta Cantiana*, p. 8; *Arch.* lxv. 262, pl. 32; Dugd. *Bar.* i. 592.)

BALLIOL

67. Johannis de Bailloil.

Gules, a voided escutcheon argent. (Painted: no blazon.)

Cf. MP II. 53.

Same man as MP II. 53.

GREY of Codnor

68. Richard de Grai.

Scutum album tres fesse auree (sic for *azuree*). (Uncoloured.)

Argent, three bars azure.

Cf. B 42, 43.

Richard de Grey of Codnor, d. 1271. The coat is canting, the bars being read as 'grés' steps. The arms are usually *Barry of six argent and azure* as on Richard's seal (Birch 6078) and in nearly all rolls from B 42 (q.v.) onwards. (*CP* vi. 134–5.)

SIWARD

69. Ricardi Suard.

Scutum nigrum cum cruce alba et vastellis albis.

Sable, a cross recercly between four roundels argent. (Uncoloured, the second roundel is omitted.)

Cf. MP IV. 75.

Member of the royal council, 1234; m. Philippa, Countess of Warwick, dau. and coh. of Thomas Basset and widow of Henry, Earl of Warwick; d. 1248. (*CM* iii. 292, 363; *Book of Fees*, 451, 455; *CP* xii (2) 365.)

THWENG

70. Roberti de Tuengue.

Scutum album cum fesse rubea et papaginibus viridibus.

Argent, a fess gules between three popinjays vert. (Uncoloured.)

Cf. B 133.

S. of Marmaduke of Thweng; m. Maud, widow of Richard de Autrey and possibly dau. of Roger de Kilton. She brought Kilton, Yorks., to the Thwengs. He was father of Marmaduke (B 133); last mentioned 1246. (*CP* xii (1) 737–8.)

FITZMATHEW or HERBERT

71. *Tres leones rampanz unus in quartero rubeo alius in quartero azurino tertius in pede et totum scutum scintillatum auro.*

Party per pale; the dexter half painted gules, the sinister tricked azure. The dexter half was tricked 'aureum', but that was carefully and almost completely erased and 'gules' superscribed.

Cf. MP I. 74; IV. 61 : B 78.

The arms should be: *Party per pale gules and azure étincelé (semy of sparks) or, three lions rampant or.* They are the arms of Herbert FitzMathew (MP I. 74). In MP I. 74 and B 78 there are no sparks, but in MP IV. 61 they are clearly drawn. It might be thought that they are a mere fancy of the artist, but the above 'blazon' shows that they must have appeared in some representation of the arms; they were perhaps a kind of diaper. Cf. the arms attributed to Hungary in C 11 and 'Scintillatum auro', *Coat of Arms*, ii. 111–13. Same person as MP I. 74.

CASTILE and LEON

72. Scutum regis Castelle et Leonum, videlicet moderni sed non patris, pater enim portavit scutum tale quale comes Provincie Reimundus.

An uncoloured shield with 'blazons' written against the four quarters thus:

[1] *Campus hujus quarteri rubeus castrum de auro.*
[2] *Campus hujus quarteri albus leo de purpura.*
[3] *Campus iste albus leo de purpura.*
[4] *Campus rubeus castrum de auro.*

Viz. *Quarterly; 1* and *4 Gules, a triple towered castle or; 2* and *3 Argent, a lion rampant purpure.*

Cf. MP I. 97.

Ferdinand III, King of Castile 1217 and Leon 1230–52. The lion of Leon first appears crowned and with a human head on the coins of Alphonso VII, King of Leon and Castile and Emperor of Spain (d. 1157). His brother Ferdinand II of Leon (d. 1188) used a lion as *signum* (mark serving in lieu of signature), and this lion, tinctured purpure in a silver field and with a gold crown, was soon after adopted as the arms of Leon.

The castle of Castile appeared in 1178 under King Alphonso VIII (d. 1214) gds. of Alphonso VII.

St. Ferdinand III, s. of Alphonso VIII by Berengaria of Castile, sealed in 1225 with the lion-shield of Leon with Castile as a counterseal (*ex. inf.* Dr. Adam-Even), but from 1230, when he became King of Castile and Leon, he quartered the two coats (Pinoteau).

On Ferdinand's seal in 1237 and on that of Alphonso X in 1255 (Ddq. 11245, 11247), on the monument in Westminster Abbey to Ferdinand's dau. Eleanor, consort of Edward I (d. 1290), in MP IV. 83, and in *Wijn.* 1258 the arms are depicted as here, but elsewhere Leon has the precedence, as, for example, *Nav.* 1251; *ZWR* 2; FW 10; D 3 and *Clipearius* 3:

> Rex Hispanie duos gilvo tibi nigro leones
> In niveoque duas urbes rubeas ibi pones.

PROVENCE

73. 'Rubeum', three pales 'aurum'.

Gules, three pales or. (Uncoloured.)

Cf. MP I. 77; II. 44; IV. 65.

Raymond, Count of Provence, d. 1245. A stroke points from this shield to the name Reimundus in MP II. 72 showing that these are his arms, although in MP I. 77 he bears *Or, four pales gules.*

74–78. These five shields are drawn in the lower part of the right-hand margin and are smaller than the others on this page.

LANCASTER: BOYS

74. Scutum de Lancastre quod iam cecidit.

Argent, two bars gules and a canton gules. Leopardus aureus in quartero (above the shield).

Hernoldi de Bois sine leopardo (beside the shield).
Hernoldi de Bosco (within the chief).

Cf. B 49.

William de Lancaster was s. of Gilbert FitzRoger FitzReinfrid by Hawise de Lancaster, the h.
of Kendal. (*CP* vii. 371.) He d.s.p. 1246 when the issue of his sisters, Hawise, wife of Piers de
Brus (B 48), and Alice, wife of William de Lindsay (B 205), were found to be his heirs. (*CP*
vii. 371; *VCH Lancs.* i. 361–4; cf. Birch 6171.)

Ernald de Boys, Chief Forester, d. 1255 (*Cal. Pat. Rolls*, 1249–58, p. 394). Cf. MP VII. 6.

As it is painted the shield is that of Boys. Lancaster bore the same with a lion passant gardant or in the canton.

MAUDUIT: MOSLE

75. Willelmus Mauduit (above the shield).
Nicholaus de Moles, sed quaere iij turtelli superius (beside the shield). (Painted.)
Argent, two bars gules.

Cf. B 65, 83.

William Mauduit of Hanslope, Bucks., d. 1256. (Dugd. *Bar.* i. 399.) See B 65, where he bears
these arms, and equestrian seal. (Cast at Soc. Ant. F 27.)

Nicholas de Moels bore *Argent, two bars gules with three roundels gules in chief* (B 83). He was Lord
of Cadbury, Som., probably d.c. 1264 (*CP* ix. 1–4); see also B 83.

BEAUCHAMP

76. Galfredi de Bellocampo.
Quarterly argent and sable. (Painted.)

Cf. MP II. 28 : B 54, 196 : C 150.

S. of Simon de Beauchamp of Bedford. Younger brother of William (MP II. 28 : B 54). (*Beds.
Hist. Rec. Soc.* i. 1–25.) He m. Joan dau. and coh. of Robert Daubeny of Cainho: he was
living 1256/7.

FURNIVAL

77. de Furnival.
Argent, a bend between six martlets gules. (Painted.)

Cf. MP II. 45 : B 147, 148, 149.

It is difficult to suggest which member of the family is referred to. (See B 147–9.)

BERNERS

78. de Berners.
Quartere de or et viridi auro ante.
Quarterly [or and vert] a label (9). (Uncoloured.)

Cf. B. 146 : C 149.

The arms are derived from Mandeville from whom the Berners held Roding Berners, Essex
(*Book of Fees*, 480, 920; Morant, *Hist. of Essex*, ii. 474), but this branch bore the arms without
a label. The entry probably refers to John de Berners who had a tenement at Nosterfield,
Cambs., 1231, and is described as John the elder in 1254. (*HKF* iii. 215.)

f. 185 (BM 186). Two shields in the lower left-hand corner of the page, the
upper blank, and the lower charged with a five-pointed label. The names and
blazons are written in Matthew's own hand, above, between, and below, the shields.

PLATE II

British Museum MS., Cotton Nero D I f. 198 (B.M. 200)

FLANDERS

79. Comitis Fland'.

Scut' dor leo niger.

Or, a lion rampant sable.

Cf. MP II. 37.

BRABANT

80. Com' de Braib'.

Scut' dor leo gul' rastel daz'.

Or, a lion rampant gules, a label azure.

Cf. MP II. 43.

These are not the arms of Brabant which were *Or a lion rampant sable*, nor has anyone been identified who was styled Count of Brabant. The label may be a cadency mark for Henry, elder s. of Henry II, Duke of Brabant 1235–48. (*AVD* xiv. 96.)

SAVOY

81. Pet' de Sabaudia.

Scut' dor leo rubeus rastel dazur.

Or, a lion rampant gules, a label azure. (No shield: blazon in margin.)

Cf. MP IV. 40 : B 101.

Peter, sixth s. of Thomas I, Count of Savoy, succ. his nephew Boniface as Count of Savoy 1263 and d. 1268. He was uncle of Eleanor of Provence, wife of Henry III. He came to England and was given the Honour of Richmond, being popularly known as Earl of Richmond. (*CP* x. 805; *Coat of Arms*, iii. 241.) He is usually considered to have borne *Or, a lion rampant gules* (Galbreath, *Armorial Vaudois*, ii. 624; *Genealogist*, N.S. xxi. 10, n.) and bears a lion rampant on his seal. In MP IV. 40 and B 101 he is attributed *Gules, a cross argent*, i.e. the cross of Savoy.

f. 198 (BM 200). On this sheet are twenty-seven shields roughly drawn in seven rows of 3, 3, 5, 5, 4, 4, and 3 respectively. There are legends over the shields in Matthew's hand. The first shield of row 2, MP II. 85, is larger than the others and is set horizontally. The shields are neither coloured nor tricked, and most of them are unnamed. Plate II.

GENEVA

82. Petrus de Genef.

Scutum nigrum leo argenteus.

Sable, a lion rampant queue fourchée argent.

Peter de Geneva, d. 1249.

Cf. MP I. 87. Same person as MP I. 87.

[BURGH]

83. *Rubea et varia.*

Lozengy (7) gules and vair.

Cf. MP I. 73.

Probably Hubert de Burgh, Earl of Kent.

[ARAGON or PROVENCE]

84. *Auro et rubea.*

Paly (10) *or and gules*—on the sixth pale the word *aurum* is written.

Cf. MP I. 77, &c.

Probably Raymond Count of Provence

PERCY

85. Ricardus de Perci.

Scutum dazur' fesse endente argent.

Azure, a fess indented argent.

Cf. MP II. 52.

Richard de Percy, d. 1244: same person as MP II. 52. Here the charge is clearly drawn as an indented fess of five points with an appreciable gap between the inner points. In MP II. 52, on the other hand, the charge is drawn as a fess of five fusils. In both cases the upper points touch the edge of the shield.

[FITZWALTER]

86. *Scutum aurum ch . . . cum benda rubea.*

Or, a fess between two chevrons gules.

(Part of the field is painted or.)

Cf. MP II. 32 : B 186.

[CAUNTELO]

87. *Scutum rubeum flores aurei.*

Gules, three fleurs-de-lis or.

Cf. MP I. 54.

[VERE]

88. *Quarterly, a mullet* (8) *in the first quarter.*

Cf. MP II. 15 : B 11.

[HOLLAND]

89. *Scutum aureum leo rubeus.*

Or, a lion rampant gules.

Cf. MP I. 82.

Possibly William, Count of Holland, d. 1256: same person as MP I. 82.

[LACY]

90. *Quarterly, a bend and a label* (5).

Cf. MP I. 63.

[MONTFORT]

91. *Leo rubeum* [sic] *scutum album.*

Argent, a lion rampant gules.

Cf. MP I. 30; II. 6.

Probably Simon de Montfort, Earl of Leicester, d. 1265.

[WARENNE]
92. *d'auro et azuro.*
Checky or and azure.
  Cf. MP I. 64.

[FERRERS]
93. *Rub' et auro.*
Vairy gules and or.
  Cf. MP II. 10.

[BIGOD]
94. *Scutum aurum crux rubeus.*
Or, a cross gules.
  Cf. MP I. 39.

[BOHUN]
95. *Benda alba scutum azureum leones aurei.*
Azure, a bend argent between six lions rampant or.
  Cf. MP I. 33, 35; II. 9.

[CLARE]
96. *Scutum album ch. gules.*
Argent, three chevrons gules.
  Cf. MP I. 46.
  Probably meant for Clare, in which case the field should be or.

[CORNWALL]
97. *Scutum album bordura nigra bezanti aurei leo rubeus coronatus auro.*
Argent, a lion rampant gules crowned or and a bordure sable bezanty.
  Cf. MP I. 38.

[ENGLAND]
98. *Scutum rubeum leones aurei.*
Gules, three lions passant gardant or.
  Cf. MP I. 19.

[LONGESPÉE]
99. *Scutum de azuro leones aurei.*
Azure, six lions rampant or.
  Cf. MP I. 40.

[CHESTER]
100. *Scutum de azuro garb' aurea.*
Azure, three garbs or.
  Cf. MP I. 48.

[MANDEVILLE]?

101. *Quarterly azure and gules.*
(*az* and *gul* written in the respective quarters.)

Cf. MP I. 25.

Perhaps a mistake for Mandeville, *quarterly or and gules.*

[D'AUBIGNY]

102. *Scutum rubeum leo argenteus.*
Gules, a lion rampant argent.

Cf. MP I. 36.

[FORZ]

103. *Scutum rubeum crux variata.*
Gules, a cross patonce vair. The upper arm extends to the edge of the shield and the spreading end is not shown. The vair is not shown in the drawing.

Cf. MP II. 38, where another variant of this cross is drawn.

[WARWICK or CLIFFORD]

104. *De azura et auro benda alba.*
Checky azure and or, a bend argent.

Cf. MP. I. 70 : B 20.

Probably meant for the Earl of Warwick though in that case the bend should be ermine. It might be meant for Walter Clifford of Clifford, although in B 30 the bend is gules. As there is no other example of Clifford in MP, the latter attribution is unlikely.

[MONTFICHET]

105. *Scutum de gules chev. de azur.*
Gules, three chevrons azure, a label (5).

Cf. MP II. 24. Above the shield is written faintly *scutum aur* (?).

[VESCY]

106. *Scutum rubeum crux alba.*
Gules, a cross patonce argent.

Cf. MP I. 26; IV. 11.

[DAUBENEY]

107. *Scutum aureum bordura cum cheverones rubeis besanta aurea.*
Or, two chevrons gules and a bordure gules bezanty.

Cf. MP I. 52; II. 21, in neither of which is the bordure bezanty.

[FERRERS]

108. *Scutum variatum rubeum et album.*
Vairy gules and argent.

Cf. MP II. 10.

f. 198 (BM 200) dorse. Here are five items with names or blazons or notes of tincture. There are no visible shields, but the way the tinctures are arranged in

MP II. 110 and 111 suggests that in those cases the shields may have been sketched in with a plummet, and there are indeed faint marks consistent with that suggestion. The leaf has been turned sideways for these items.

ODINGSELES
109. Odingseles.
Scutum album une fess de gules, et iii stelle similiter de gules.
Argent, a fess and three mullets gules.

Cf. MP II. 57.

There are only two mullets for Gerard de Odingseles in MP II. 57 and for William his brother and heir in B 142. Close by is written 'xxxvj milia marcas cepit rex de episcopatu Wintoniense vacante'.

DESPENSER
110. *Gules et or frette blanc nigra blanc.* The last three words are written below the first three.

Cf. MP II. 58.

From the way in which the tinctures are placed it is probable that they were on a shield which must have been very lightly sketched. Only a few meaningless traces remain.

BALLIOL
111. J. de Bailliol.
Gules argent gules. The words are written one above the other.

Cf. MP I. 88.

Here, as in MP II. 110, the arrangement of the tinctures suggests that they were tricking a shield, of which no trace remains.

BALLIOL
112. Eustachi fater (*sic*) Johannis de Bailloil.
Scutum d'azuro falsum scutum dor cruces dor.
Azure crusuly or, a voided escutcheon or.

Cf. MP II. 54.

GIFFARD and HUSSEY
113. Giffard et Heuse.
Scutum d'ermine tres benda de gules.
Ermine, three bars gules.

Cf. MP II. 56.

Below are sketched six mullets in red ink.

MP III

Corpus Christi College, Cambridge MS. 26
Chronica Majora, ed. H. R. Luard, vols. i and ii, to p. 336; Rolls Series 57

p. 160. Edmund Ironside and Canute (*see* MP VIII. 4).

HAROLD, King of England
1. Scutum et corona Regis Haroldi sibi Regnum usurpantis.

Azure, a lion rampant or. (Shield and crown.)

> p. 172.   *CM* i. 537. Cf. MP I. 1; III. 2; VIII 29 (*p*).
>
> This precedes the account of Harold's coronation, 1066.

HAROLD, King of England

2. Scutum Haroldi Regis.

Azure, a cross moline sable and over all a lion rampant or. (Shield reversed with crown above.)

Death of Harold, 1066.

> p. 174.   *CM* i. 542. Cf. MP I. 1; III. 1; VIII. 29 (*p*).
>
> The sable cross is probably a sign of mourning.

ENGLAND, William I

3. Scutum Willelmi Bastardi Conquestoris. In hoc *scuto tres leopardi vel leones figurantur.* Quia rex est, est et comes et Anglie gubernator.

Gules, three lions passant gardant or. (Shield and crown.)

Coronation of William I.

> p. 174.   *CM* ii. 1. Cf. MP I. 2.

ENGLAND, William I

4. Moritur Willelmus Conquestor Anglie.

Gules, three lions passant gardant or. (Shield and crown reversed.)

Death of William I.

> p. 180.   *CM* ii. 23. Cf. MP I. 2.

ENGLAND, William II

5. Creatur Willelmus Rufus in regem.

Gules, three lions passant gardant or. (Shield and crown.)

Accession of William Rufus, 1087.

> p. 181.   *CM* ii. 25. Cf. MP I. 4.

ENGLAND, William II

6. Corona et clipeus Willelmis secundi videlicet Rufi sagittati.

Gules, three lions passant gardant or. (Shield and crown reversed, bow and arrow pointing at the shield.)

Death of William Rufus, slain by an arrow while hunting in the New Forest, 1099.

> p. 212.   *CM* ii. 111. Cf. MP I. 4.

ENGLAND, Henry I

7. Clipeus et corona regis Henrici I.

Gules, three lions passant gardant or. (Shield and crown.)

Coronation of Henry I.

> p. 212.   *CM* ii. 115. Cf. MP I. 5.

> p. 220. Two Templars (*see* MP VIII. 5).

ENGLAND, Henry I

8. De morte Henrici regis.
Gules, three lions passant gardant or. (Shield, crown, and sword reversed.)
Death of Henry I, 1135.

> p. 225. *CM* ii. 161. Cf. MP I. 5.

ENGLAND, Stephen

9. Scutum et corona regis Stephani.
Gules, three lions passant gardant or.
Accession of Stephen, 1135.

> p. 225. *CM* ii. 162. Cf. MP I. 11.

ENGLAND, Stephen and Henry II

10. De morte regis Stephani et coronatione regis Henrici secundi.
Gules, three lions passant gardant or. (Shield, two crowns: one reversed, the other upright, sword reversed.)
Death of Stephen and coronation of Henry II, 1154.

> p. 238. *CM* ii. 204. Cf. MP I. 14.

ENGLAND, Henry, son of Henry II

11. Pomposum principium (*in red*), vitae brevis (*in black*). In medietate rubea vitale, in nigra vero accipe Mortale auspicium (*in red*).
Party per pale gules and sable, three lions passant gardant or. (Shield and crown at an angle.)
Coronation of the associate king Henry, 1170.

> p. 261. *CM* ii. 274. Cf. MP I. 17.
>
> Matthew's remark about the sable half of the shield shows that it was a sign of mourning and not a difference.

FRANCE, Philip II

12. Philippus consecratur in regem Francorum.
Azure, six fleurs-de-lis or. (Shield and crown.)
Coronation of Philip II during his father's lifetime.

> p. 274. *CM* ii. 314. Cf. MP I. 8, 15.

ENGLAND, Henry, son of Henry II

13. Corona et scutum Henrici Regis junioris qui vivente patre obiit.
Gules, three lions passant gardant or, dimidiating Sable. (Shield and crown reversed.)
Below is written *mors* in black, *vita* in red.
Death of Henry, son of Henry II, 1183.

> p. 276. *CM* ii. 319. Cf. MP I. 17.

p. 279. Capture of the Cross by Saladin (*see* MP VIII. 6).

MP IV

Corpus Christi College, Cambridge, MS. 16

Chronica Maiora, ed. H. R. Luard, vols. ii from p. 336, iii, iv, v, vi, vii, Rolls Series 57

ENGLAND, Henry II

1. Obiit magnanimus Rex Henricus secundus sed in amaritudine cordis.
Gules, three lions passant gardant or. (Shield and crown reversed.)
Death of Henry II, 1189.

f. 1*b.* *CM* ii. 344. Cf. MP I. 14.

ENGLAND, Richard I

2. Corona et scutum bellipotentis Regis Ricardi.
Gules, three lions passant gardant or. (Shield and crown.)
Coronation of Richard I, 1189.

f. 2. *CM* ii. 348. Cf. MP I. 19.

ENGLAND, Richard I

3. De morte regis Ricardi.
Gules, three lions passant gardant or. (Shield reversed, cross-bow above, below a crown reversed between two swords downwards.)
Death of Richard I, 1199.

f. 17*b.* *CM* ii. 451. Cf. MP I. 22.

ENGLAND, John

4. Johannes coronatur in regem Anglorum.
Gules, three lions passant gardant or. (Shield with crown above.)
Coronation of John, 1199.

f. 18. *CM* ii. 456. Cf. MP I. 23.

THE EMPIRE, Otto IV

5. (*a*) Otto creatur in imperatorem Romanorum.
Or, a double eagle sable.
(*b*) Scutum mutatum pro amore regis Anglie.
Gules, three lions passant gardant or, dimidiating *Or, a double eagle sable.* (Two shields one above the other, and above them three crowns side by side, superscribed respectively 'Corona argentea', 'Corona aurea' and 'Corona ferrea': the middle one has a pointed green cap with a gold ball on top, the others have round green caps.)
Election of Otto IV as emperor, 1199.

f. 18. *CM* ii. 457. Cf. MP I. 21, 24, 96. Plate I.

LACY

6. Rogerus Cestrie Constabularius.
Party per pale gules and azure, three garbs or. (Shield reversed.)

Death of Roger de Lacy, Constable of Chester, 1211.

> f. 29. *CM* ii. 532. Cf. MP I. 48, 63.
>
> S. of John de Lacy, Constable of Chester, and gds. of Robert FitzEustace and of Aubrey de Lisours. His grandmother was dau. of Robert de Lisours by Aubrey, dau. and in her issue coh. of Robert de Lacy, s. of Ilbert de Lacy who d. 1093. (Clay, *Extinct and Dormant Peerages*, pp. 115–16.) He was father of John de Lacy, Earl of Lincoln (MP I. 63).
>
> The arms are those of the Earl of Chester differenced.

BREWES

7. Willelmus de Braose.

Per fess gules and azure, three garbs or. (Shield reversed.)

Death of William de Brewes, 1211.

> f. 29*b*. *CM* ii. 532. Cf. MP I. 44; IV. 27 : B 55.
>
> William de Brewes, Lord of Bramber, was s. of William, Lord of Braiose (now Briouze) in Normandy. He rebelled against King John; d. 1211. From him descended William de Brewes (B. 55), and William de Brewes (MP I. 44; IV 27). The elder line bore *Azure, crusuly a lion rampant or* (B 55) the younger *Party per pale indented gules and azure* (MP I. 44). No reason can be given why he should be attributed with a variation of the arms of Chester.

Oppression of the common people by King John (*see* MP VIII. 8).

ARMS OF THE FAITH

8. Scutum Fidei.

Drawing of a shield-shaped device comprising four roundels, one in the centre and one at each corner, joined by lines in orle and in pale. The central roundel is labelled 'deus' the others respectively dexter, sinister, and base 'pat' (*pater*), 'spts' (*spiritus*), and 'fili'(*filius*). Between the central and the lowest roundel (*filius*) is a cross labelled 'v'bu' caro f'm est' (*Verbum caro factum est*). The lines joining the outer roundels are each inscribed 'non est', those joining the central roundel to the other three are each inscribed 'est'.

> f. 45*b*. *CM* ii. 647.
>
> This is probably one of the earliest examples of this device. There is a similar shield in the De Quincey Apocalypse where a young penitent woman uses it to ward off the attacks of the devil (late thirteenth century). (Saunders, *English Illumination*, i. 69 and ii, pl. 73.) In WB iv. 8 and PLN 8 this device is called the Arms of the Faith, but RH 115 assigns it to St. Michael, and elsewhere it is called the Arms of the Trinity.

THE SOUL

9. Scutum anime.

A device similar to MP IV. 8 but with the roundels differently named, viz. centre 'anima', dexter 'memoria', sinister 'voluntas', and lowest 'racio' : lines labelled 'non' join the three corner roundels, those joining the central roundel to the others are labelled 'est'.

> f. 45*b*. *CM* ii. 647.

MANDEVILLE

10. Obiit Galfridus de Mandeville.

Quarterly gules and or. (Shield and sword reversed.)

Death of Geoffrey de Mandeville, Earl of Essex, 1216.

> f. 46. *CM* ii. 650. Cf. MP I. 25.
>
> Same person as MP I. 25.

VESCY

11. *Gules, a cross patonce argent.* (Shield reversed.)
Death of Eustace de Vescy, 1216.

> f. 48*b*.   *CM* ii. 666. Cf. MP I. 26, 102; II. 35, 103; IV. 84 : B 76.
> Same person as MP I. 26.

ENGLAND, John

12. Vae labenti coronae Anglie. Obiit rex Anglie Johannis primus tributarius.
Gules, three lions passant gardant or. (Shield and sword reversed, crown at an angle.)
Death of King John, 1216.

> f. 48*b*.   *CM* ii. 669. Cf. MP I. 23.

ENGLAND, Henry III

13. Coronatur Henricus tertius rex, qui iccirco tertius quia Henricus junior licet successione tertius obiit patre vivente, nec unquam regnavit.
Gules, three lions passant gardant or. (Shield and crown above.)
Coronation of Henry III, 1216.

> f. 49.   *CM* iii. 1. Cf. MP I. 28.

Siege of Lincoln by King Louis and the Barons (*see* MP VIII. 9).
Sea-fight on St. Bartholomew's Day, 1217 (*see* MP VIII. 10).

MARSHAL

14. Obiit Willelmus Marescallus miles incomparabilis.
Party per pale or and vert, a lion rampant gules. (Shield reversed.)
Death of William, Earl Marshal, 1219.

> f. 54.   *CM* iii. 43. Cf. MP I. 29, &c.
> Same person as MP I. 29.

MONTFORT

15. Obruitur lapide petrarino comes de Monteforte S'.
Argent, a lion rampant gules. (Shield reversed.)
Death of Simon de Montfort, Earl of Leicester, 1218.

> f. 56.   *CM* iii. 57. Cf. MP I. 30.
> Same person as MP I. 30.

BOHUN and QUINCY

16. Obierunt hoc anno Henricus de
17. Boun comes Hertfordie [*sic*] Saherus de Quincy, comes Wintoniensis.
16. *Or, a bend gules cotised sable.* (Shield reversed.)
17. *Gules, seven voided lozenges conjoined or.* (Shield reversed.)

> f. 56.   *CM* iii. 60. Cf. MP I. 33, 32.
> Same persons as MP I. 33, 32.

D'AUBIGNY

18. Obiit comes Harundel.
Gules, a lion rampant or. (Shield reversed.)
Death of William d'Aubigny, Earl of Arundel, 1221.

> f. 57. *CM* iii. 66. Cf. MP I. 36.
>
> Same person as MP I. 36.

NEVILLE

19. Obiit Hugo de Neville.
Per fess indented gules and vert, a bend or. (Shield reversed.)
Death of Hugh de Neville, 1222.

> f. 58. *CM* iii. 71. Cf. MP II. 31; IV. 69; V. 4.
>
> Same person as MP II. 31: Matthew is in error in entering his death under this year. (*CP* ix. 479.)

FRANCE, Philip Augustus

20. Philippus rex Francorum.
Azure semy of nine fleurs-de-lis or. (Shield and crown reversed.)
Death of Philip Augustus, 1223.

> f. 58b. *CM* iii. 77. Cf. MP I. 37.

Capture of Bedford Castle (*see* MP VIII. 12).

FRANCE, Louis VIII

21. De morte Lodovici regis Francorum apud Avinionem.
Azure semy of nine fleurs-de-lis or. (Shield and crown reversed.)
Death of Louis VIII at Avignon, 1226.

> f. 64. *CM* iii. 116. Cf. MP I. 41.

FRANCE, Louis IX

22. De coronatione Lodovici regis Francorum filii Lodovici ejus defuncti.
. . . *three fleurs-de-lis.* . . . (Small shield and crown.)
Coronation of Louis IX, 1226.

> f. 64b. *CM* iii. 118. Cf. MP I. 42.

BREAUTÉ

23. De morte Falcasii et de presagio mortis ejus.
Gules, a cinquefoil argent. (Shield reversed.)
Death of Fawkes de Breauté, 1226.

> f. 64b. *CM* iii. 120.
>
> Fawkes de Breauté, a military adventurer in the service of King John, was banished in 1225 and d. 1226. (*DNB*.)

MANDEVILLE

24 Willelmus comes Essexie.
Quarterly gules and or. (Shield reversed.)
Death of William de Mandeville, Earl of Essex, 1227.

> f. 64b. *CM* iii. 121. Cf. MP I. 43.
>
> Same person as MP I. 43.

TONY

25. De morte Rogeri de Thony militis.
Argent, a maunch gules. (Shield reversed.)
Death of Roger de Tony, 1227.

> f. 67b.   *CM* iii. 143. Cf. MP II. 25.
>
> Younger brother of Ralph de Tony (MP I. 57). (*CP* xii (1) 770, note *k*.)

THE EMPIRE, Frederick II

26. Epistola imperatoris Fretherici ad regem Anglorum.
Scutum imperatoris scuti campus aurea, aquila nigra.
Or, a double eagle sable.
Letter from Frederick II to Henry III, 1229.

> f. 72b.   *CM* iii. 175. Cf. MP I. 96.

BREWES

27. Willelmus de Braose.
Gules, four piles meeting in base or. (Shield reversed.)
William de Braose hanged by Llewellyn ap Iorwerth, 1230.

> f. 75b.   *CM* iii. 194. Cf. MP I. 44.
>
> S. of Reynold de Brewes, who was younger s. of William de Brewes (d. 1211; MP IV. 7), who had obtained extensive possessions in Radnor and Builth. (*Arch. Camb.* 6th s. x. 337–54; *Sussex Arch. Coll.* v. 1–5; viii. 97–103; xxvi. 261.)

Henry III sails for Britanny, 1230 (*see* **MP VIII. 13**).

BURGH

28. Reimundus de Burgo.
Lozengy gules and vair. (Shield reversed.)
Raymond de Burgh, nephew of Hubert de Burgh, drowned in the river Lea, 1230.

> f. 76b.   *CM* iii. 199. Cf. MP I. 45.
>
> Same person as MP I. 45.

CLARE

29. Obiit Gilebertus comes Glovernie.
Or, three chevrons gules. (Shield reversed.)
Death of Gilbert de Clare, Earl of Gloucester, 1230.

> f. 76b.   *CM* iii. 200. Cf. MP I. 46.
>
> Same person as MP I. 46.

MARSHAL

30. Obiit comes Willelmus Marescallus.
Party per pale or and vert, a lion rampant gules. (Shield reversed.)
Death of William, Earl Marshal, 1231.

> f. 76b.   *CM* iii. 201. Cf. MP I. 29, 47.
>
> Same person as MP I. 47.

A knight (*see* **MP VIII. 14**).

CHESTER

31. De morte Ranulphi comitis Cestrensis.

Azure, three garbs or. (Shield reversed.)

Death of Ralph Blundeville, Earl of Chester, 1232.

f. 81*b*. *CM* iii. 229. Cf. MP I. 48; IV. 6.

Same person as MP I. 48.

Fight between Richard Marshal and Baldwin de Guisnes (*see* MP VIII. 15).

MARSHAL

32. Scutum Marescalli.

Per pale or and vert, a lion rampant queue fourchée gules. (Shield; field tricked 'ex auro viridique', lion 'gules'.)

Deeds of Richard, Earl Marshal, in Ireland, 1234.

f. 88*b*. *CM* iii. 277. Cf. MP I. 50. Plate I.

Same person as MP I. 50.

The Marshal on horseback (*see* MP VIII. 16).

FITZWALTER

33. De morte Roberti filii Walteri.

Or, a fess between two chevrons gules. (Shield reversed.)

Death of Robert FitzWalter, 1235.

f. 95*b*. *CM* iii. 334. Cf. MP II. 32 : B 186.

Same person as MP II. 32.

CHESTER

34. De morte J. Comitis Cestrie.

Azure, three garbs or. (Shield reversed.)

Death of John le Scot, Earl of Chester and of Huntingdon, 1237.

f. 103*b*. *CM* iii. 394. Cf. MP II. 19.

Same person as MP II. 19.

REVIERS

35. Devene. Quomodo rex Baldwinum baltheo cinxit militari.

Or, a lion rampant azure.

Baldwin de Reviers, knighted and invested with the earldom of Devon, 1239.

f. 131*b*. *CM* iv. 1. Cf. MP I. 75.

Same person as MP I. 75.

WARENNE

36. De morte comitis de Warenne.

Checky azure and or. (Shield reversed.)

Death of William, Earl Warenne, 1240.

f. 132*b*. *CM* iv. 12. Cf. MP I. 64.

Same person as MP I. 64.

Defeat of the French at Damascus (*see* MP VIII. 17).

LACY

37. De morte J. comitis Lincolnie.
Quarterly or and gules, a bend sable and a label argent.
Death of John de Lacy, Earl of Lincoln, 1240.

> f. 134*b*.   *CM* iv. 34. Cf. MP I. 63.
>
> Same person as MP I. 63.

MULTON

38. De morte Thomae de Muletuna.
Argent, three bars gules. (Shield reversed.)
Death of Thomas de Multon, 1240.

> f. 136*b*.   *CM* iv. 49. Cf. B 158.
>
> S. of Thomas de Multon of Egremont, Cumberland, father of B 158. (*CP* ix. 339–400.)

FITZROBERT

39. Hoc etiam anno obiit Johannes filius Roberti, vir nobilis et unus de praecipiis baronibus in plaga Anglie borealis.
Quarterly or and gules a bend sable. (Shield reversed.)
Death of John FitzRobert of Clavering, 1240.

> f. 140.   *CM* iv. 80. Cf. B 169.
>
> S. of Robert FitzRoger (d. 1214). The arms are derived from the quarterly coat of Mandeville (MP I. 25) through Vere. Alice de Vere, sister of Geoffrey de Mandeville's wife Rohese and widow of Robert de Essex, m. as her third husband Roger FitzRichard of Warkworth and Clavering. From that marriage descended in direct line Robert FitzRoger (d. 1214), John FitzRobert above named (d. 1240), Roger FitzJohn (B 169). The last named was Lord of Iver (Eure), Bucks., Clavering, Essex, &c.; he succ. his father 1240; d. 1249. His s. and h. Robert FitzRoger d. 1310, and his s. and h. John FitzRobert assumed the name of Clavering. (*NCH* v. 25; Clay, *Extinct and Dormant Peerages*, pp. 20–21.)

SAVOY

40. Quam pomposo fastu rex Petrum de Sabaudia fecerit militum.
Gules, a cross argent.
Peter of Savoy, knighted 1241.

> f. 141.   *CM* iv. 85. Cf. MP II. 81 : B 101.
>
> The cross of Savoy is one of the earliest coats for which there is evidence, as it appears on the seals of counts Amadeus and Humbert in 1143 and 1151. (*AHS*, 1925, p. 8; Galbreath, *Armorial Vaudois*, ii. 623.) For the connexion between the houses of Savoy, Joinville, and Geneva see *Genealogist*, N.S. xxi. 1, &c.
>
> Same person as MP II. 81.

41–43. Ecce tria signa omnia magis in fidelibus formidabilia.

HOSPITAL

41. Vexillum Hospitalis.
Gules, a cross formy argent. (Banner with five streamers.)

> f. 141.   *CM* iv. 85. Cf. MP I. 61. Plate I.

TEMPLE

42. Vexillum Templi.
Argent, a chief sable. (Banner.)

f. 141. *CM* iv. 85. Cf. MP I. 62; VIII. 1, 5, 16 : C 21. Plate I.

FRANCE

43. Oloflamma Francie.
Gules. (Banner with eight streamers.)

f. 141. *CM* iv. 85. Plate I.

BASSET

44. Obiit Gilbertus Basset.
Barry wavy of six or and gules. (Shield reversed.)
Death of Gilbert Basset, 1240/1.

f. 141*b*. *CM* iv. 89. Cf. MP II. 34 : B 93.

Brother of MP I. 49 and B 93: same person as MP II. 34.

BISSET

45. Obiit Johannes Biset summus Anglie forestarius.
Azure, ten bezants. (Shield reversed.)
Death of John Bisset, chief forester of England, 1241.

f. 141*b*. *CM* iv. 89.

LACY

46. Obiit Walterus de Lacy.
Or, a fess gules. (Shield reversed.)
Death of Walter de Lacy, 1241.

f. 141*b*. *CM* iv. 93. Cf. MP I. 63.

S. of Hugh de Lacy, Lord of Meath, who was s. of Gilbert de Lacy, s. of Emma, dau. of Walter de Lacy (d. *c.* 1085). This last may have been brother of Ilbert de Lacy (d. *c.* 1093) from whom descended the Lacys, earls of Lincoln (see MP I. 63). Walter de Lacy sealed with these arms temp. John (Birch 11203). (Eyton, *Antiquities of Shropshire*, v. 240; *DNB*; Orpen, *Ireland under the Normans*, iii. 286–7.

Sea-fight between Pisans and Genoese (*see* MP VIII. 18).

MARSHAL

47. De miserabili morte comitis Gileberti Marescalli.
Party per pale or and vert, a lion rampant argent. (Shield, sword, and spear reversed.)
Death of Gilbert, Earl Marshal, at the tournament at Hertford, 1241.

f. 147*b*. *CM* iv. 136. Cf. MP I. 51.

Same person as MP I. 51.

SEGRAVE

48. De morte Stephani de Segrave.
Sable, three garbs or, bands and ears gules.

Death of Stephen de Segrave, 1241.

> f. 152. *CM* iv. 169. Cf. MP I. 66.
>
> Same person as MP I. 66.

49–54. De obitu quorundem militum.
Death of several nobles in 1242.

GAUNT

49. Gileberti de Gant.
Or, three bars azure and a bend gules. (Shield and sword reversed.)
Gilbert de Gaunt, d. 1242.

> f. 155*b*. *CM* iv. 194. Cf. B 72. Plate I.
>
> Gilbert de Gaunt, Earl of Lincoln (d. 1156), descended from the Domesday tenant, showed on his seal a shield *Barry* without a bend (*Book of Seals*, no. 297). This was his nephew. (*CP* v. 625, vii. 672–5; *Ancestor*, ix. 143.)

French troops in Poitou die of the plague (*see* drawings).

WAKE

50. Hugonis Wake.
Or, two bars gules and in chief three roundels argent. (Shield and sword reversed.)
Hugh Wake, d. 1241.

> f. 155*b*. *CM* iv. 194. Cf. MP IV. 50 : B 51. Plate I.
>
> S. of Baldwin Wake of Bourne and Haconby by Isabel Briwere; m. Joan, dau. and h. of Nicholas de Stuteville; d. 1241. (*CP* xii (2) 298–9; Dugd. *Bar.* i. 539–40.)

KYME

51. Philippi de Kyme.
Or, a chevron gules and a bordure sable bezanty. (Shield and sword reversed.)
Philip de Kyme, d. 1242.

> f. 155*b*. *CM* iv. 194. Cf. B 127. Plate I.
>
> S. of Simon de Kyme of Kime in Kesteven, Lincs. A Philip de Kyme seals in the thirteenth century with a *Chevron and in base an estoile* (Birch 11140), and this is probably the same man. (*CP* vii. 356; Dugd. *Bar.* i. 620–1; *HKF* ii. 117–27.)

THE EMPIRE

52. Henrici filii Imperatoris.
Party per pale or and vert, a double eagle sable. (Shield reversed.)
Death of Henry, s. of Frederick II by Constance of Aragon, 1242.

> f. 155*b*. *CM* iv. 194. Cf. MP I. 69; VII. 2. Plate I.
>
> Same person as MP I. 69.

WAKE

53. B. Wake.
Barry of six argent and gules, in chief three roundels azure. (Shield and sword reversed.)
B. Wake, d. 1242.

> f. 155*b*. *CM* iv. 194. Cf. MP IV. 53. Plate I.

Luard suggests that this is an error for Hugh Wake, although the arms for Hugh are given above (MP IV. 50). Baldwin, father of Hugh, d. 1213, and no other Baldwin has been found who d. at this time. (*CP* xii (2) 297–9.)

WARWICK

54. Comitis de Warewic.
Checky azure and or, a bend ermine. (Shield and sword reversed.)
Thomas, Earl of Warwick, d. 1242.

f. 155*b*. *CM* iv. 194. Cf. MP I. 70. Plate I.

Same person as MP I. 70.

BURGH

55. Obiit Ricardus de Burgh.
Party per pale gules and or, a bordure vert. (Shield and sword reversed.)
Death of Richard de Burgh, 1242.

f. 160*b*. *CM* iv. 232. Cf. MP I. 71.

Younger s. of William de Burgh, elder brother of Hubert de Burgh, Earl of Kent.

LACY

56. Obiit Hugo de Lacy.
Vert, a bordure or. (Shield and sword reversed.)
Death of Hugh de Lacy, 1242.

. 160*b*. *CM* iv. 232. Cf. MP I. 63; IV. 46.

Brother of Walter de Lacy (MP IV. 46) and was Lord of Ulster. A drawing of his seal, early thirteenth century (Bowditch MS., p. 73), shows a fess and a bend. (Eyton, *Antiquities of Shropshire*, v. 240; Orpen, *Ireland under the Normans*, iii. 286–7.)

D'AUBIGNY

57. Obiit comes Harundelle, Hugo de Albineto.
Gules, a lion rampant or. (Shield and sword reversed.)
Death of Hugh d'Aubigny, Earl of Arundel, 1243.

f. 162. *CM* iv. 243. Cf. MP I. 72.

Same person as MP I. 72.

BURGH

58. Obiit comes Cantie, Hubertus de Burgh.
Lozengy gules and vair. (Shield and sword reversed.)
Death of Hubert de Burgh, Earl of Kent, 1243.

f. 162. *CM* iv. 243. Cf. MP I. 73.

Same person as MP I. 73.

WALES

59. Quomodo Griffinus Leolini filius de Turri Londoniarum corruens expiravit.
Quarterly or and gules, four lions passant counterchanged. (Shield reversed.)

Death of Gruffydd ab Llywelyn, Prince of Wales, in an attempt to escape from the Tower of London, 1244.

f. 169.   *CM* iv. 296. Cf. C 13.

Younger s. of Llewlyn ap Iorwerth (d. 1242) and brother of MP IV. 68. For a note on the arms, see C 13.

Loss of Jerusalem, 1244 (*see* MP VIII. 19).

REVIERS

60. Obiit Baldewinus comes Devonie vel Insule.
Or, a lion rampant azure. (Shield reversed.)
Death of Baldwin de Reviers, Earl of Devon and Lord of the Isle of Wight, 1245.

f. 183*b*.   *CM* iv. 406. Cf. MP I. 75 : B 12 : C 146.

Same person as MP I. 75.

FITZMATTHEW

61. Herbertus filius Matthaei jactu lapidis obrutus obiit in crastino Purificationis Sancte Marie.
Party per pale gules and azure étincelé or, three lions rampant or. (Shield reversed.)
Death of Herbert FitzMatthew, killed by a stone in the campaign against the Welsh, 1245.

f. 183*b*.   *CM* iv. 408. Cf. MP I. 74, II. 71.

Same person as MP I. 74.

UMFRAVILLE

62. Gilebertus de Humframvilla.
. . . a cinquefoil and a bordure semy of horseshoes. (Shield reversed, uncoloured.)
Death of Gilbert de Umfraville, 1245.

f. 184*b*.   *CM* iv. 415. Cf. MP II. 51 : B 122.

Same person as MP II. 51.

CLARE

63. Die Pentecostes rex apud Londonias Ricardum de Clare balteo cinxit militaris.
Or, three chevrons gules. (Shield and sword.)
Richard de Clare, knighted 1245.

f. 185.   *CM* iv. 419. Cf. MP I. 46, 76.

Same person as MP I. 76.

MAREYS

64. Obiit Galfridus de Marisco exul, pauper et profugus.
Party per fess gules and vert, a fess between two roundels in chief and a crescent in base all argent. (Shield reversed.)
Death of Geoffrey de Mareys, 1245.

f. 185*b*.   *CM* iv. 422. Cf. MP I. 68.

Same person as MP I. 68.

PROVENCE

65. Obiit Reimundus comes Provinciae, pater reginarum Anglorum et Francorum.
Gules, three pales or. (Shield, sword, and spear reversed.)
Death of Raymond, Count of Provence, 1245.

f. 194. *CM* iv. 485. Cf. MP I. 77; II. 84; V. 1.

Same person as MP I. 77.

Gannoc [Deganwy] Castle (*see* MP VIII. 20).

MARSHAL

66. Comes Marescallus Walterus obiit.
Party per pale or and vert, a lion rampant gules. (Shield reversed.)
Death of Walter, Earl Marshal, 1245.

f. 195. *CM* iv. 491. Cf. MP I. 29, 78.

Same person as MP I. 78.

MARSHAL

67. Anselmus frater ejus obiit.
Party per pale or and vert, a lion rampant gules. (Shield reversed.)
Death of Anselm Marshal, 1245.

f. 195. *CM* iv. 491. Cf. MP I. 29, 79.

Same person as MP I. 79.

WALES

68. De morte David principis Norhwallie.
Quarterly or and gules, four lions passant counterchanged. (Shield reversed, bow and two arrows beside.)
Death of David, Prince of Wales, 1246.

f. 198. *CM* iv. 517. Cf. MP V. 3.

S. of Llewllyn ap Iorwerth (d. 1240), brother of MP IV. 59. (Lloyd, *History of Wales* ii. 692, &c.)

NEVILLE

69. Moritur Johannes de Novilla Anglie prothoforestarius.
Per fess indented gules and vert, a bend sable. (Shield reversed; above it a hunting horn hanging from a hook.)
Death of John de Neville, Chief Forester, 1246.

f. 204*b*. *CM* iv. 563. Cf. MP II. 31; V. 4 : B 178.

S. of Hugh de Neville (MP II. 31). The horn and the marshal's hammer (MP VIII. 8) seem to be the earliest recorded examples of official badges, anticipating the broad arrow of the royal butlery by a century or so. ('Official Badges', *Coat of Arms*, iv. 92, &c.)

CHATEAUNEUF

70. Obiit Fulco miles domini regis consanguineus.
Gules, a chief vair. (Shield and spear reversed.)
Death of Fulk de Chateauneuf, 1247.

f. 210*b*. *CM* iv. 604. Cf. MP I. 80.

Same person as MP I. 80.

THURINGIA

71. De morte Andegravii Duringie.

Gyronny of eight or and azure, a roundel in an orle of smaller roundels gules edged argent.
(Shield and spear reversed.)
Death of Henry Raspe, Landgrave of Thuringia, 1247.

> f. 211.   *CM* iv. 610. Cf. MP I. 81.
>
> Same person as MP I. 81.

LUSIGNAN—VALENCE

72. De tirocino Willelmi de Walentia fratris domini regis uterini.

Buruly argent and azure, a label (5) gules, on each point three lions passant gardant or.
William de Valence, knighted.

> f. 215*b*.   *CM* iv. 644. Cf. MP I. 83; II. 63, 64 : B 23 : C 71.
>
> Same person as MP I. 83.

NORWAY

73. Scutum regis Norwagie nuper coronati qui dicitur rex Insularum.

Gules, three galleys with dragon heads at each end or, one above the other. (Shield and crown.)
Coronation of Haakon IV, 1247.

> f. 216*b*.   *CM* iv. 650. Cf. MP I. 100.

FERRERS

74. De obitu comitis de Ferrariis.

Vairy or and gules. (Shield reversed.)
Death of William, Earl Ferrers, 1247.

> f. 216*b*.   *CM* iv. 654. Cf. MP II. 10.
>
> Earl of Derby 1191–1247: same person as MP II. 10.

SIWARD

75. Ricardus Suard infirmatus est ad mortem.

Sable, a cross patonce between four roundels argent. (Shield reversed.)
Death of Richard Siward, 1248.

> f. 217.   *CM* v. 2. Cf. MP II. 69.
>
> Same person as MP II. 69.

THE EMPIRE.

76. Obiit autem circa eadem tempora principum mundi maximus Frethericus stupor quoque mundi et immutator mirabilis.

Or, a double eagle sable. (Shield reversed.)
Death of the Emperor Frederick II, 1250.

> f. 242.   *CM* v. 190. Cf. MP I. 96.

CAUNTELO

77. Obiit Willelmus de Cantelupo.

Gules, three fleurs-de-lis or. (Shield reversed.)

Death of William de Cauntelo, 1251.

> f. 247. *CM* v. 224. Cf. MP I. 54; II. 26; VII. 5.

> S. of William de Cauntelo (MP I. 54), father of VII. 5: same person as MP II. 26.

PEYVRE

78. Paulinus nomine, cognomento Piper. Scutum album flores de auro, reliqua rubra.

Argent, on a chevron gules three fleurs-de-lis or. (Shield reversed.)
Paulyn Peyvre, d. 1251.

> f. 250. *CM* v. 243. Cf. B 152.

> Paulyn Peyvre, king's esquire of Toddington, Beds., was s. of Roger Peyvre (dead 1228) (*Beds. Hist. Rec. Soc.* x. 316–19 and 356, pedigree 11). He left a s. John then a minor, who d. 1257, and a younger s. William of Thorpe Market, Norfolk, who d. 1278. (*CP* x. 513–14; *Book of Seals*, 112, 166.)

DESPENSER

79. Obiit Galfridus Dispensator miles.

Quarterly or fretty sable and argent, a bend sinister sable. (Shield reversed.)
Death of Geoffrey le Despenser, 1251.

> f. 250b. *CM* v. 245. Cf. MP II. 58 : B 114.

> Younger brother of Hugh le Despenser who was father of Hugh le Despenser (MP II. 58). (*CP* iv. 260.)

SCOTLAND

80. Rex Scotie balteo donatur militari.

Or, a lion rampant in a tressure flory inwards only gules. (Shield, between lance and sword.)

> f. 254. *CM* v. 267. Cf. MP I. 85; II. 48.

> Alexander II, King of Scots; knighted 1252.

SANDFORD

81. Obiit Nicholaus de Sanford.

Barry wavy of six argent and gules. (Shield reversed.)
Death of Nicholas de Sandford, 1252.

> f. 255. *CM* v. 273. Cf. B 115, 116.

> Of Aston Sandford, Bucks., probably brother of Gilbert de Sandford (d. 1248), s. of John de Sandford, who held the manor of Great Hormead, Herts., and other lands by the serjeanty of the Queen's Chamberlain. Gilbert de Sandford bore *Barry wary six argent and azure* (F 111). Nicholas is described (B 116 q.v.) as brother of William de Sandford, but in B II. 116 he is called s. of William de Sandford and a label azure is added to his arms. That it was the same family which held the serjeanty and Aston Sandford is established by the succession of earls of Oxford descended from Alice, dau. and h. of Gilbert de Sandford, to both the serjeanty and the lands in Buckinghamshire. (*VCH Bucks.* iv. 8; *Coll. Top. and Gen.* v. 199; Round, *The King's Serjeants and Officers of State*, pp. 132–5.)

MOUNTENEY

82. Hernaldi de Munteinni.

Scutum de azuro, cetera de auro.

Azure, a bend between six martlets or. (Shield reversed with broken spear.)

Arnold de Mounteney, killed in a tournament, 1252.

f. 262*b*.　*CM* v. 318. Cf. B 145.

Probably the Arnold de Mounteney (brother of Sir Robert) who m. a dau. of Gerard de Furnival (d. 1219) by Maud de Lovetot (Hunter's *Hallamshire*, ed. 1869, p. 390; Clay, *Extinct and Dormant Peerages*, p. 81) and that marriage may explain his use of a variant of the arms of Furnival.

SPAIN

83. Scutum regis Hyspanie.

Scutum regis Hyspanie Campus de gules castrum de auro, campus de argento leo de auro [*sic*].

Quarterly, 1 and 4 gules, a triple towered castle or, 2 and 3 argent, a lion rampant or.

Alphonso X the Wise, King of Castile and Leon, 1252–84.

f. 277.　*CM* v. 399. Cf. MP II. 72.

S. of Ferdinand III of Castile and Leon (MP II. 72).

VESCY

84. Moritur Willelmus de Wescy.

Gules, a cross moline argent. (Shield reversed.)

Death of William de Vescy, 1253.

f. 279.　*CM* v. 410. Cf. MP I. 26, 102; II. 35, 103; IV. 11 : B 76

Same person as MP I. 102.

MP V

Chetham Library, Manchester, MS. 6712

Flores Historiarum, ed. H. R. Luard, Rolls Series 95

PROVENCE

1. Reimundus comes Provincie.

Gules, three pales or. (Shield reversed.)

Raymond, Count of Provence, d. 1245.

f. 184*v*.　*FH* ii. 304. Cf. MP I. 77; II. 44, 84; IV. 65.

Same person as MP I. 77.

MARSHAL

2. Obiit comes Marescallus Walterus . . . obiit Anselmus frater ipsius.

Party per pale or and vert, a lion rampant gules. (Shield reversed.)

Death of Walter, Earl Marshal, and of his brother Anselm, Earl Marshal, 1245.

f. 184*v*.　*FH* ii. 305. Cf. MP I. 29, 78; IV. 66.

Same person as MP I. 78.

WALES

3. Et cito post memoratus David de medio sublatus in morte sua paucos pro pro-ditione sua meruit habere lamentatores.

Or, three roundels vert, on a chief dancetty vert a lion passant sable (Shield reversed.)
Death of David, Prince of Wales, 1246.

> f. 185*v*. *FH* ii. 308. Cf. MP IV. 68.
>
> Same person as MP IV. 68.

NEVILLE

4. Obiit Johannes de Novilla, prothoforestarius Anglie.
Azure, a cinquefoil or and a bordure or. (Shield reversed.)
Death of John de Neville, 1246.

> f. 186*v*. *FH* ii. 312. Cf. MP II. 31; IV. 69.
>
> Same person as MP IV. 69.

MP VI

British Museum Claudius D VI

Abbreviatio Chronicorum Angliae, ed. Sir Frederic Madden, in vol. iii of *Historia Anglorum*

ENGLAND, William II

1. De morte regis Willelmi II scilicet Rufi.
Gules, three lions passant gardant or. (Shield reversed, in trick, crown above.)
Death of William II, 1100.

> f. 16*b*. *HA* iii. 177. Cf. MP I. 4.

ENGLAND, Henry I

2. Henricus.
Gules, three lions passant gardant or. (Shield, in trick, with crown above.)
Accession of Henry I, 1100.

> f. 16*b*. *HA* 177. Cf. MP I. 5.

NORMANDY

3. Obiit . . . Robertus dux quondam Normannorum.
(Blank shield reversed with crown.)
Death of Robert, Duke of Normandy, 1134.

> f. 20*b*. *HA* iii. 186.
>
> Eldest s. of William I. It should be noted that Matthew knew of no arms for Normandy.

ENGLAND, Richard I

4. Ricardus.
Gules, three lions passant gardant or. (Shield in trick, and cross-bow, both reversed; there is a faint yellow wash on the lions.)
Death of Richard I, 1199.

> f. 36*b*. *HA* iii. 218. Cf. MP I. 19.

ENGLAND, John

5. Johannes.

Gules, three lions passant gardant or. (Shield in trick; faint yellow wash on the lions.)
Accession of King John, 1199.

>   f. 36*b*.   *HA* iii. 219. Cf. MP I. 23.

FERRERS

6. Scutum comitis de Ferrariis.

Vairy or and gules. (Shield reversed.)
Obiit comes de Ferrariis Willelmus, filius Willelmi, vir discretus et legum terrae
peritus.

>   f. 90*b*.   *HA* iii. 333. Cf. MP II. 10; VII. 1.

>   William de Ferrers, Earl of Derby, s. of MP II. 10, d. 1254.

THE EMPIRE, Henry s. of Frederick II

7. Scutum Henrici filii imperatoris.

Gules, three lions passant gardant or, dimidiating, *Or, a double eagle sable*.

>   f. 91*b*.   *HA* iii. 336. Cf. MP I. 69; VII. 2.

>   Henry s. of Frederick II by Isabel dau. of King John, d. 1254.

THE EMPIRE, Conrad of Sicily

8. Scutum Conradi regis Siculorum.

Or, a double eagle sable and in chief a crescent gules enclosing a small roundel gules.

>   f. 92*a*.   *HA* iii. 338. Cf. MP VII. 3.

>   S. of the Emperor Frederick II by Yolanda, Queen of Jerusalem, dau. of John de Brienne.

THE EMPIRE, Manfred of Apulia

9. Manfredus creatus est.

Or, a double eagle sable and over all a fess argent.
The nobles of Apulia do homage to Manfred as their king, 1254.

>   f. 92*a*.   *HA* iii. 338. Cf. MP VII. 4.

>   Base s. of Frederick II, d. 1266.

CAUNTELO

10. Obiit Willelmus de Cantelupe.

Gules, three fleurs-de-lis or. (Shield reversed.)
Death of William de Cauntelo, 1254.

>   f. 92*a*.   *HA* iii. 339. Cf. MP II. 26; VII. 5.

>   S. of William de Cauntelo (MP II. 26). (Dugd. *Bar* I 732.)

MUNCHENSY

11. Scutum Warini de Munchensil.

Or, three escutcheons vair. (Shield reversed.)
Death of Warin de Munchensy, 1255.

>   f. 94*a*.   *HA* iii. 346. Cf. MP VII. 7 : B 25 : C 87.

>   Brother and h. of William de Munchensy (dead April 1208) of Norfolk. (*CP* ix. 421.) On
>   variations in the arms see B 25.

MP VII

British Museum Royal MS. 14 C VII

Chronica Majora, ed. H. R. Luard, v. 421–748; Rolls Series 57

FERRERS

1. Obiit Willelmus, comes de Ferrariis.

Vairy or and gules. (Shield reversed.)

Death of William, Earl Ferrers, 1254.

> f. 159.   *CM* v. 43. Cf. MP II. 10.
>
> Same person as MP VI. 6.

THE EMPIRE, Henry, son of Frederick II

2. Obiit Henricus filius Fretherici imperatoris, nepos regis Anglie.

Gules, three lions passant gardant or, dimidiating *Or, a double eagle sable.* (Shield reversed.)

Death of Henry, s. of Emperor Frederick II by Isabel, dau. of King John, 1254.

> f. 162*b*.   *CM* v. 448. Cf. MP VI. 7.
>
> Same person as MP VI. 7.

THE EMPIRE, Conrad of Sicily

3. De morte regis Siculorum Conradi.

Or, a double eagle sable and in chief a crescent enclosing a roundel gules.
(Shield reversed, crown below.)

Death of Conrad, King of Sicily, 1254.

> f. 164*b*.   *CM* v. 459. Cf. MP VI. 8.
>
> Same person as MP VI. 8.

THE EMPIRE

4. Scutum principis M.

Mortuo Conrado filio Fretherici imperatoris suscitatur Memfredus filius ejusdem Fretherici naturalis in ecclesie Romane persecutionem.

Or, a double eagle sable and over all a fess argent.

> f. 165*a*.   *CM* v. 460. Cf. MP VI. 9.
>
> Same person as MP VI. 9.

CAUNTELO

5. Obiit Willelmus de Cantelupo.

Gules, three fleurs-de-lis or. (Shield reversed.)

Death of William de Cauntelo, 1254.

> f. 165*b*.   *CM* v. 463. Cf. MP II. 26; VI. 10.
>
> Same person as MP VI. 10.

BOYS

6. Obiit Hernaldus de Bosco.
Argent, two bars and a canton gules. (Shield reversed, with uncoloured banner.)
Death of Ernald de Boys, one of the chief foresters, 1255.

> f. 170*b*. *CM* v. 487. Cf. MP II. 74.
>
> Same person as MP II. 74.

MUNCHENSY

7. De morte nobilis baronis Warini de Muntcheinsil.
Or, three escutcheons vair. (Shield reversed.)
Death of Warin de Munchensy, 1255.

> f. 174. *CM* v. 504. Cf. MP VI. 11 : B 25.
>
> Same person as MP VI. 11.

HOLLAND

8. Willelmus de Holandia jam promotus in regem Alemannie interimitur.
Or, a lion rampant queue fourchée gules. (Shield, sword, and inverted crown.)
Death of William of Holland, King of Germany, 1256.

> f. 182*b*. *CM* v. 549. Cf. MP I. 82.

FITZNICHOL, MAUDUIT

9, 10. Obierunt Radulphus filius Nicholas et Willelmus Mauduit.
Two blank shields.

> f. 195*b*. *CM* v. 616.

FLANDERS

11. Obiit comes Flandrie Thomas.
Sable, a lion rampant or. (Shield and spear reversed.)

> f. 217*b*. *CM* v. 741. Cf. MP II. 37, 43.
>
> The tinctures are reversed, these being really the arms of Brabant. Cf. MP II. 43.

MP VIII

Heraldic details from the drawings of scenes

BM Royal MS. 14 C VII

THE TEMPLE

1. Two Templars on one horse with helmets, hauberks, surcoats: shields slung behind their backs. The banner *Argent, a chief sable,* is planted to the right. There is an unfinished sketch of the same picture on the right.

> f. 42*b*. *HA* i. 223; WS xiv. 19 and pl. xix. Cf. MP I 62; IV. 42; VIII. 5, 19 : C 21.
>
> Matthew tells the story of how the first two Templars, Hugh de Payens and Godfrey de St. Omer, were so poor that they had only one horse. 'Qui primo adeo pauperes licet strenui fuerunt,

quod unum solum dextrarium illi duo habuerunt; unde propter primitivae paupertatis memoriam, et ad humilitatis observantiam, in sigillo eorum insculpti sunt duo unum equum equitantes'. (*HA* i. 223.) This device is not shown on any of the seals of the Order in England described by Birch (*Catalogue of British Museum Seals*, 4485–4493), nor on any of those recorded by Miss Lees (*Records of the Templars in England in the Twelfth Century*, OUP, 1935). In France seals of *c*. 1202 (Ddq. 9859), 1259 (Ddq. 9863), 1298 (Ddq. 9865) show this device.

The name Beauseant applied to the banner means party of two colours. The term 'baucent', of which it is a corruption, was originally applied to piebald and skewbald horses. (Godefroy *Dictionnaire de l'Ancienne Langue Française*, i. 602.)

It was suggested by Inderwick (*Calendar of Inner Temple Records*, i, p. lxix), that the Pegasus of the arms of the Inner Temple was taken from a blurred impression of the seal, the two knights being interpreted as wings. The Pegasus was adopted in the reign of Elizabeth I. It is leaping and not walking as the Templars horse and was probably adopted as a fabulous animal. Gray's Inn at this date also took a griffin for their arms.

Matthew also states that the Templars put red crosses on their mantles in the time of Pope Eugenius III, 1145–1153. (*HA* i. 223.) (Lees, *Records of the Templars in England in the Twelfth Century*, 169 n. 3. *Brit. Arch. Assoc. Journ.* xxxviii. 122–6. Curzon, *La Règle du Temple*, Paris, 1886, p. 87 n. 3. Redslob, 'Versuch einer Feststellung und Deutung des ursprünglichen Siegels des Templerordens', *Zeitschrift der Deutschen Morgenländischen Gesellschaft*, xvi. 245–57, Leipzig, 1862.)

ENGLAND, Henry III

2. Rex Henricus navigat in Brittanniam.
A ship, the sail charged *Gules, three lions passant gardant or*.
Henry III sails to Brittany, 1230.

> f. 116*b*.   *HA* ii. 323; WS xiv. 19 and pl. xix.

BM. Nero D I

OFFA

3. A cavalry engagement between Offa, King of Mercia, and the sons of Rigan. Offa bears a shield charged with a saltire. Two of his followers have surcoats and shields respectively charged with a *Saltire between four roundels*, and *Semy of hammers*. The latter was apparently painted by Matthew, but the saltire and roundels are additions by a later hand, as is the saltire on the shield of Offa in f. 3*a*. Offa's two opponents, Brut and Sweyn, sons of Rigan, one of the chief men of the kingdom, bear respectively *Gyronny* and *A lion rampant*, tinted at a later date pale yellow. The saltires on banner and shield borne by Offa's squire on f. 10*a* are probably in Matthew's own hand.

> f. 3*b*.   WS xiv. 22 and pl. xxiii; *Ancestor*, v. 108–9.

Corpus Christi College, Cambridge, MS. 26

EDMUND IRONSIDE and CANUTE

4. Edmund Ironside and Canute in single combat at Deerhurst, 1016.
(*a*) Aedmundus ferreum latus.
Surcoat: *Argent, semy of crosses pommy gules*.
(*b*) Cnuto rex Dacie.
Shield: *Gules, a bordure or and over all two ships argent with sails azure*.

> p. 160.   *CM* i. 498; WS xiv. 5 and pl. ii.

> There is, of course, no evidence that these or any other arms were borne by these persons. It is also unlikely that Edmund's surcoat was meant to be heraldic, for such surcoats powdered

with crosses sometimes mingled with roundels or annulets appear in several other drawings. In another drawing Edmund wears quite different arms. (MP VIII. 19).

On the other hand, Canute's ships may have been meant for his arms since Matthew records these galleys for the King of Norway in MP I. 100 and MP IV. 73.

THE TEMPLE

5. Two Templars on one horse.
Shields and banner: *Argent, a chief sable.*

p. 220.   *CM* ii. 144; WS xiv. 5 and pl. iii. Cf. MP I. 62; IV. 42; VIII. 1, 19: C 21.

6. Capture of the Cross by Saladin, 1187. The unnamed Christian knight who holds the Cross has a shield: *Brown* (? *gules*)*, a lion rampant or.*

p. 279.   *CM* ii. 328; WS xiv. 6 and pl. iii.

Corpus Christi College, Cambridge, MS. 16

7. Battle of Bouvines, 1214. King Philip II of France unhorsed while Hugh de Boves flees.

FRANCE, Philip II

(*a*) Rex Francorum Philippus.
Shield: *Vert, three fleurs-de-lis or.*

Elsewhere (MP I. 15, &c.) Philip II is assigned *Azure semy of fleur-de-lis or.*

BOVES

(*b*) Hugh de Boves.
Surcoat and trappers: *Semy of quatrefoils (some barbed vert) and small rings gules.*
Shield: *Argent, a quatrefoil in an orle of rings gules.*

Hugh de Boves, one of the leaders of King John's army in Flanders, was drowned near Yarmouth 1215. (*CM* ii. 578, 622.)

BOULOGNE

(*c*) Reynold de Boulogne.
Shield: *Argent, semy of annulets gules.*
(*d*) A mounted knight.
Shield: *Argent, a cross recercly gules between four roundels azure*; trappers are semy of the same design.

f. 37.   *CM* ii. 580; WS xiv. 13 and pl. xiv.

Reynold de Dammartin, Count of Boulogne, m. Ida, dau. and h. of Matthieu d'Alsace.

8. Oppression of the common people by King John 1215. One of John's minions wears a surcoat: *Argent, semy of hammers gules.*

f. 44*b*.   *CM* ii. 640; WS xiv. 8 and pl. viii.

The king's attendant is probably meant for the marshal or perhaps one of his staff; cf. MP VIII. 15 and 16 below where Richard Marshal are both shown wearing hammers, although elsewhere (MP I. 29, 50; IV. 30, 32) Matthew gives the usual arms, *Per pale or and vert, a lion rampant gules.* The hammers are probably a canting device associated with the marshalcy.

ENGLAND

9. Siege of Lincoln by King Louis and the barons 1217.
Banner on Lincoln Castle: *Or, three lions passant gardant argent, alternately with two gemel bars.* A man on the tower wears a surcoat: *Argent, (?) two crosses pommy or.*

f. 51*b*. *CM* iii. 23; WS xiv. 9 and pl. ix.

The banner is presumably meant for the royal arms, although the gemel bars have not been found elsewhere. These tinctures are also found in MP VIII. 12.

10. Sea-fight on St. Bartholomew's Day 1217, at which Eustace the Monk was defeated. In the French ship are five banners with the legend VEXILLUM ROBERTI DE CURTENAI ET ALIORUM MAGNATUM FRANCIE.
(*a*) *Or, a chief gules.*
(*b*) *Or, three crescents gules.*
(*c*) *Gules, two wide bars vert.*
(*d*) *Vert, a fess or fimbriated gules.*

COURTENAY

(*e*) *Or, three roundels in pale gules* (the upper part of the shield is tinted vert).
(*f*) *Argent, semy of roundels gules,* borne by one of the soldiers in the English ship on his surcoat.

f. 52*b*. *CM* iii. 28; WS xiv. 9 and pl. ix.

Robert de Courtenay, s. of Peter of France, s. of Louis VI, was taken prisoner at this fight. (Powicke, *The Thirteenth Century*, p. 13).

11. Fight at Damietta, 1218, between Christians and Saracens. Three shields:
(*a*) *Or, a cross flory gules,* a thin line marks *a bordure,* borne by a Saracen.
(*b*) *Five voided lozenges gules, a bordure vert,* borne by a Christian on the ground.
(*c*) *A bordure engrailed gules, in another bordure gules,* borne by a Christian.

f. 54*b*. *CM* iii. 48; WS xiv. 9 and pl. x.

ENGLAND and BREAUTÉ

12. Capture of Bedford Castle by the king and surrender of Fawkes de Breauté, 1224.
Banner on castle: *Or, three lions passant gardant argent.* Banner over gallows: *Vert, with narrow edge of white at top and bottom, two bars between two cinquefoils argent.*

f. 60. *CM* iii. 87; WS xiv. 10 and pl. ix.

On the false tincturing of the royal banner cf. MP VIII. 9. The second banner is probably meant for Breauté, some of whose men were hanged. (Cf. MP IV. 23.)

ENGLAND, Henry III

13. Henry III sails for Brittany 1230.
Sail of ship: *Gules, three lions passant gardant or.*

f. 75*b*. *CM* iii. 194; WS xiv. 12 and pl. xii. Cf. MP VIII. 2.

14. A knight bears a shield, *a cross recercly gules, a bordure vert.*

f. 79*b*. *CM* iii. 214.

MARSHAL and GUISNES

15. Fight at Monmouth between Richard Marshal and Baldwin de Guisnes, 1233.
(*a*) Richard Marshal.
Shield: *Argent* (? *or*), *a hammer sable* (perhaps one of three).
(*b*) Baldwin de Guisnes.
Back of saddle: *Brown, two annulets argent.*

> f. 85.   *CM* iii. 254; WS xiv. 12 and pl. xii.

> On the hammer as a badge of the Marshal see MP VIII. 8 and 16. The Guisnes annulets are of doubtful heraldry.
>   Baldwin de Guisnes was a Fleming in the royal service and governor of Monmouth Castle. (*CM* iii. 234.)

MARSHAL

16. Richard, Earl Marshal.
Shield: *Argent* (? *or*) [*three*] *hammers gules* (only one is shown). Surcoat: *Or, powdered with hammers gules.* Crest: *A hammer gules.* There is a hammer on the back of the saddle.

> f. 88*b*.   *CM* iii. 277; WS pl. xiv, pp. 12–13, pl. xii. Cf. MP VIII. 8, 15. Plate I.

17. Defeat of the French at Damascus, 1240. Two broken banners:
(*a*) *Quarterly vert and or.*
(*b*) Brownish: this is probably intended for the Oriflamme.

> f. 133*b*.   *CM* iv. 26; WS xiv. 13 and pl. xiv.

PISANS and GENOESE

18. Sea-fight between the Pisans and the Genoese. Four banners:
   (*a*) and (*b*) Pisan: *Per fess or and vert, two annulets gules, with a bordure or and a small band of or between the or and the vert.*
   (*c*) and (*d*) Genoese: *Per fess or and azure, two annulets argent in pale.*

> f. 146.   *CM* iv. 125; WS xiv. 14 and pl. xiv.

THE TEMPLE

19. Loss of Jerusalem 1244.
Banner: *Argent, a chief sable.*

> f. 170*b*.   *CM* iv. 306; WS xiv. 16 and pl. xvii. Cf. MP I. 62; IV. 42; VIII. 1, 5 : C 21.

> Here the banner of the Temple is drawn as *Per fess sable and argent.*

ENGLAND, Henry III

20. Gannoc [Deganwy] Castle, 1245.
The English banner flies over the castle: *Gules, three lions passant gardant or.*

> f. 194*b*.   *CM* iv. 486. Cf. MP I. 28, &c.

La Estoire de Seint Aedward le Rei, edited M. R. James, Roxburghe Club, 1920.

Cambridge University Library MS. Ee iii 59 (Edward).

DENMARK, Sweyn

21. Oppression of the men of St. Edmund's lands by Sweyn.

Suanus rex. Sweyn has a surcoat white with two battleaxes of which the blades are partly coloured blue. One of Sweyn's men carries a banner, *Or, a battle axe proper.*

f. 4. James, pl. 3.

On the axe as, the alleged arms of Denmark and Norway. cf. C 17, 18.

EDMUND IRONSIDE and CANUTE

22. Edmund Ironside and Canute in combat.

Edmund has shield, surcoat, and his horse trappers, *Field of pale wash, semy of martlets sable, two bars vert cotised gules.* Beside is a picture of Edmund embracing Canute in which his surcoat is, as above, with the field in a pale orange tint.

f. 5. Cf. MP VIII. 4; James, pl. 5.

A KNIGHT

23. Meeting between Alured and Godwin at which one of the four knights present bears a shield edged with pale red bearing *a cross azure.*

f. 5*b*. James, pl. 6.

DENMARK, Sweyn and his followers

24. Death of Sweyn by drowning.

His shield, *Azure, three battleaxes argent,* has fallen into the sea. In the ship are his men and four shields are shown:

(*a*) *Gules, a chevron between two sixfoils in chief and a septfoil in base argent.*

(*b*) *Pale blue, a lion rampant uncoloured.*

(*c*) *Uncoloured, a chevron between three roundels azure.*

(*d*) *Uncoloured, a battleaxe azure.*

f. 12. James, pl. 19.

DANES

25. St. Edward announces the death of Sweyn, which he has seen in a vision. From the side of the ship hang eight shields:

(*a*) *Pale green wash, a chevron azure between three birds gules* (the chevron has a bulbous point).

(*b*) *Pale wash, three bars gemel sable.*

(*c*) *Pale wash, a lion rampant azure.*

(*d*) *Bendy of a pale wash and azure.*

(*e*) *Pale wash, three bars gemel gules.*

(*f*) *Pale brown wash, a lion rampant or.*

(*g*) *Pale wash, a lion rampant sable.*

(*h*) *Pale wash, fretty azure.*

f. 12*b*. James, pl. 20.

NORWAY

26. Landing of Harold Hardrada, King of Norway, and defeat of the Earl of Northumbria. From the ships hang three shields:

(*a*) *Barry of six argent and sable.*

(*b*) *Bendy argent and sable.*

(c) *Azure, a beast uncoloured.*
(d) A Norseman bears a shield, *Gules, a lion rampant argent.*
Englishmen bear shields:
(e) *Pale wash, probably three bars sable, with very small cotises sable.*
(f) *Brown, a boar passant uncoloured between three roundels argent.*
(g) *Gules fretty argent.*
(h) *Barry of six gules and pale wash.*

  f. 31. James, pl. 57.

NORWAY and others

27. Battle of Stamford Bridge 1066. The English bear shields:
(a) *Gules,* borne by a fallen knight.
(b) *Azure, [three] cinqfoils argent.*
(c) *Pale brown wash, two piles charged with annulets.*
(d) *Gules, a fess between [three] roundels argent.*
(e) *Azure, a mermaid argent:* the knight's surcoat bears mermaids and stars.
(f) A knight killing the King of Norway wears a surcoat *Gules with five flowers of a varying number of petals argent.*

The Norwegians bear shields:
(g) *Gules, three axes argent,* borne by Harold Hardrada.
(h) *Gules, a fess and in chief a chevron argent,* the triangle formed by the fess and the chevron is vert with a white dot in the middle, in sinister chief is a white dot and another below the fess.
(i) *Gules, a pair of wings argent:* only the sinister half is shown.
(j) *Azure, a demi-lion rampant and below in pale two lions heads couped argent.*
(k) *Azure, a lion rampant argent.*

  f. 32b. James, pl. 60.

NORMANS

28. William, Duke of Normandy, sails for England.
(a) Banner: *Three roundels uncoloured.*
(b) Shield: *Brown, a fess vert between three roundels uncoloured.*
(c) Shield: *Green wash, a chevron brown, in base a roundel brown.*
(d) Shield: *Chevrons outlined.*
(e) Blank shield.
(f) Shield: *Gules, marked with lines bendy sinister.*
(g) Banner: *Brown, a lion rampant uncoloured.*
(h) Banner: *Gules.*

  f. 34. James, pl. 63.

NORMANS and ENGLISH

29. The battle of Hastings.
This vigorous and confused scene shows many banners and shields, and it is difficult to distinguish Normans from English.
(a) Banner: *Orange wash, on a chief azure two chevrons one sable, one gules, and in base a sixfoil azure pierced gules.*

(*b*) Banner: *Vert, a broad fess sable semy of white dots between two dots gules.*

(*c*) Shield: *Pale wash, a label* (5) *gules.*

(*d*) Banner: *Gules, an elongated indeterminate device coloured dark.*

(*e*) Banner: *Per fess argent and azure, in chief a fess between two dots gules and in base a chevron between two dots sable.*

(*f*) Shield and surcoat: *Pale wash, three lions rampant gules* trapper: *semy of lions.*

(*g*) Shield: *Pale wash, a fess gules and in base a crescent gules.*

(*h*) Banner: *Azure, on a bend gules a bend sable.*

(*i*) Banner: *Pale wash, two annulets between two pairs of thin lines gules.*

(*j*) Shield: *On a fess gules billets* (?) *sable, on a chief vert two roundels uncoloured each charged with a fess gules and in base a similar roundel.*

(*k*) Shield: *Reddish wash, an elaborate rosace, outer line sable, inner part white with azure centre with an eight-pointed device sable with black dots between each point.*

(*l*) Trapper: *Pale wash, semy of crescents with dots between the horns gules.*

(*m*) Shield: *Vert, on a broad fess checky argent and sable a fess gules.*

(*n*) Trapper: *Pale wash, semy of lions rampant gules.*

(*o*) Banner: *Pale wash, two lions rampant in pale gules.*

HAROLD (?)

(*p*) Shield: *Gules, an eagle displayed sable,* borne by an Englishman pierced in the eye by an arrow and presumably Harold. Cf. MP I. 1; III. 1, 2.

(*q*) Shield: *Gules, two pales argent and over all two bars sable.*

(*r*) Shield: *Faint touches of azure, a cross outlined gules between three [or four] roundels gules.*

(*s*) Banner: *Azure, a cross argent between four roundels gules.*

f. 34*b*.   James, pl. 64.

Trinity College, Dublin, MS. E i. 40. Reproduced by W. R. L. Lowe and E. F. Jacob, with description by M. R. James, Oxford, 1924

30. Soldiers find Amphibalus baptizing converts.

(*a*) Surcoat and back of saddle: *Brown with uncoloured voided lozenges.*

(*b*) Back of saddle: *Brown, a fess between two chevrons uncoloured.*

f. 41*a*.   Life of St. Alban; Lowe and Jacob, pl. 23.

31. Massacre of the converts by soldiers of the rulers of Verulam.

(*a*) Shield: *Vert, two [three] hammers uncoloured and a bordure uncoloured.*

(*b*) Back of saddle: *White, two hammers gules.*

(*c*) Shield and back of saddle: *A lion passant, field and charge painted with greenish wash.*

f. 41*b*.   Life of St. Alban; Lowe and Jacob, pl. 24.

32. Fight between pagans and Christians over the body of Amphibalus.

(*a*) Christian with shield: *Uncoloured, three hammers outlined in red and small red crosses in the field*; back of saddle has two red hammers on uncoloured field.

(*b*) A pagan bears a circular shield uncoloured, *a cross with elaborate floriated ends in gules and lozenge boss in vert, a bordure gules.*

(*c*) A pagan bears a circular shield uncoloured, *with red crescents and small red dots between the horns, and little red circles in the field.*

(*d*) A pagan bears a heater-shaped shield: *Azure, a lion rampant white, a bordure vert.*

48*a*.   Life of St. Alban; Lowe and Jacob, pl. 28.

33. Offa, King of Mercia sets out on an expedition.

(*a*) A horseman sounding horn wears a surcoat, *Vert, a lion passant gardant gules.*

(*b*) A knight with shield and surcoat: *Vert, three lions passant gules*; the shield has *a bordure or.*

(*c*) King Offa. Shield: *Vert, two lions passant gardant tinted with pink wash*; the upper lion is crowned. Back of saddle vert, the tails and hind legs of two lions are just visible.

f. 55*b*.   Life of St. Alban; Lowe and Jacob, pl. 39.

34. Offa's victory.

(*a*) Banner, surcoats of two horsemen, and shield of one all bear *Vert, three lions passant gules.*

(*b*) A pagan has a shield of *brown wash and a bordure vert.*

f. 56*a*.   Life of St. Alban; Lowe and Jacob, pl. 40.

GLOVER'S AND WALFORD'S
ROLLS

I. GLOVER'S ROLL

INTRODUCTION

As was recorded in *A Catalogue of English Mediaeval Rolls of Arms*; four versions of this roll can be distinguished, but of these III and IV are mere selections comprising only about one-quarter of the items in I and II.

VERSION I. COOKE'S

Version I is known from two late sixteenth-century copies.

Copy (*a*), now belonging to Sir Anthony Wagner, is on ff. 10–16*b* of the whilom Wrest Park MS. 16. It is in the handwriting of Robert Glover, Somerset Herald 1570–88, and was copied in February 1585/6 from a manuscript then in the custody of Robert Cooke, Clarenceux 1567–93. It is headed:

> The copie of an old rolle of parchemin wherein these Armes followenge were blazoned verbatim as followeth.

It contains 214 items, of which the great majority comprise name and blazon together with an outline drawing of the arms. For convenience these drawings are hereinafter referred to as tricks, although the tinctures are rarely marked.

Copy (*b*), College of Arms MS. 2 G 3, ff. 60–66*b*, is in the handwriting of the above-named Robert Cooke, and is thus headed:

> Armes of the nobilitye in Kyng Henry the 3 tyme taken out of a very Auncient Rolle in parchment written in the same tyme as appereth by the hand. The Rolle was lent unto me Robart Cooke alias Clarencieulx by one Mr. Harvy of Lecestershyer[1] in A⁰ 1586. Thes armes of the nobilitye in H. 3. tyme conteyneth vij leaves.[2]

This copy has names and tricked shields but not blazons except in three cases, no. 6 where the blazon is part of Cooke's note on the name, and nos. 160 and 164 where Cooke did not understand the blazon and gave it in lieu of a trick. This copy comprises 215 items, including one, 176, Gilbert Segrave, which is lacking from (*a*). The rest are the same and in the same order as in (*a*) and most but by no means all of the tricks match (*a*)'s blazons. Cooke has often modernized the names and some of the less obvious are amplified and explained. Save in a few cases these modernizations are ignored in the following text.

The fact that both this and Glover's copy of version II are said in the headings to have been taken from a roll belonging to one Harvy of Leicestershire, led to the assumption that this is a copy of version II and it is listed in *CEMRA* as II *b*. Since then, collation of the different versions and copies has, however, proved

---

[1] According to J. G. Nichols, Harvy also owned a copy of the Caerlaverock poem, the original of Glover's transcript which was published by Sir Harris Nicolas in 1864. He may perhaps be identified as Francis Harvey, a bencher of the Middle Temple, Recorder of Leicester 1612, serjeant at law 1614, Judge of the Common Pleas 1624. (*Herald and Genealogist*, ii. 378, iv. 475.)

[2] i.e. of Cooke's manuscript.

conclusively that this is really a copy of version I and that it and II *a* were copied from two different rolls, both, as it happened, belonging to Harvy.[1]

VERSION II. HARVY'S

Of version II only one copy has been found, College of Arms MS. L 14 (Miscellanea Curiosa), vol. i, ff. 38–42. This, like I *a,* is in Glover's hand and was copied in 1586. It is headed:

The Copy of an ould rolle of Armes in parchemin and in blazon: made and written in the reigne or tyme of King H: 3 and is in the hands of one Harvy of Leicestershire. 1586.

The entries, 218 in number, are in blazon, but thirteen, needlessly as it seems, are accompanied by marginal tricks, viz. 14, 19, 68, 82, 96, 101, 120, 128, 170, 173, 188, 190, and 208.

Of the 218 entries nos. 1–211 correspond to version I and are in the same order, but the last seven items are found in no other version. They were evidently added about 1310, and that, we may take it, is when Harvy's roll was written. (Glover's statement that the roll was 'written' as well as 'made' in the time of Henry III need not be considered sacrosanct.)

Although this version was certainly copied from I, it underwent some editing in the process. The blazons were modernized, some of I's shortcomings were supplied, a number of the Christian names were changed, and four items, 106, 108, 110, and 111, which are either incomplete or obscure in I (*a*) and blank in I (*b*), were omitted.

VERSION III. ST. GEORGE'S

The third version of Glover's Roll is known from three copies:

a. MS. Add. 29796 in the British Museum;
b. MS. Harl. 6589, f. 11*b*;
c. Antiquaries MS. 664, roll 8, vol. i, ff. 23–24.

Of these (*b*) and (*c*) were certainly, and (*a*) was probably, copied from a roll which belonged to Richard St. George, Norroy, in 1607, and about 1640 to his son Sir Henry, also Norroy. That roll is now lost. It comprised 54 painted shields with names and Anglo-French blazons below, all but one of these, James Audley's, being found also in versions I and II. The roll may be dated soon after 1258.

VERSION IV. GRIMALDI'S

What Sir Anthony Wagner called version IV of this roll is really extracts from Grimaldi's Roll (*CEMRA*, p. 62), an apparently mid fourteenth-century compilation with painted shields and superscribed blazons which survives in an early fifteenth-century copy written and limned by the same hand or hands which executed Queen Margaret's copy of Thomas Jenyns's Book.[2] This copy, which is now

---

[1] This collation was greatly facilitated by the late B. R. K. Moilliet, who undertook the tedious task of recopying all the different versions, texts, and tricks on to index cards item by item so that their identity or otherwise was instantly visible.

[2] Add. MS. 40851; *CEMRA*, p. 73 and pl. vi.

in the John Rylands Library, Manchester[1], was printed by its then owner Stacey Grimaldi in 1835.[2] About half the items date from *c.* 1350, but Oswald Barron observed that many of the names and coats in the latter part, no. 43 onwards, are identical with names and coats in Glover's Roll, though the order is different and the blazon has been assimilated to fourteenth-century forms. Actually, these items seem to derive from an earlier collection than Glover's Roll, for instead of Rauf FitzRandolf (I. 140) Grimaldi's Roll gives his father Randolf FitzRobert of Middleham (105) and he died in 1252.

The four versions having been thus shortly described we must next examine certain points at more length, beginning with

VERSION I

Contents

The roll opens with the king and his eldest son. Then follow 20 English earls, while the remainder, nos. 23–215, comprises lords and knights. These are drawn from almost every English county from Devon to Kent in the south to Northumberland and Cumberland in the north, but it is impossible to detect any logical principle either in the choice of the men or in the order in which they are presented. The roll, indeed, seems to be the personal collection of someone who set down names and arms as they occurred to him. Again and again one can see how the compiler's mind was led from one item to the next, nearly half the entries being linked in one way or another. Most of these links appear in the succeeding notes, and it would be tedious to list them here. Sometimes we find a family group like Balliol, 36–40, Furnival, 147–9, and Bohun, 188–90. Sometimes a group of neighbours, it may be from the western marches like 30–32 and 181–5, or from the uorth as 119–22, or a group of foreigners like 101–4. Sometimes similarity in the arms is the explanation as with Lancaster, Wake, and Welle, all bearing two bars, 49–53, or Percy whose engrailed fess suggests Montagu, 44, in one place and Newmarch, 121, in another. More often still kinship or alliance affords the clue as, to give but a few examples, 48–49, 66–68, 77–78, 124–5, 171–2, and 210–11.

Date

Nicolas, in the preface to his edition of II, argued that the original was probably compiled between 1240 and 1245, since the Earl of Warwick's arms, 20, are those of 'Newburgh', extinct in 1242, while Sir John de Plescy, 24, Earl of Warwick from 1247, has not that title. Moreover, the Earl Marshal, 17, and Earl of Norfolk, 6, are separate persons as they were not after the extinction of the Marshal family in 1245; and Baldwin de Reviers, 12, was not Count de l'Isle before 1240. But Nicolas's date is certainly too early since, as pointed out in *CEMRA*, Hugh de Balliol, 37, was only born *c.* 1240, and Geoffrey de Geneville, 103, had not settled in England before 1251. Furthermore, Randolf FitzRobert, who is named in IV. 105, died in 1252, and he is replaced in the other versions by his son Ralph Fitz-Randolf (I. 140). In the light of these facts we shall not be far out if we date the

---

[1] Western (French and Italian) MS. 88. See *Illustrated Catalogue of the Heraldic Exhibition at Burlington House*, 1894, no. 157, p. 46.

[2] *Col. Top. and Gen.* ii. 320 seq.

compilation soon after 1252, say in 1253, when John Neville, 'cowe de rat', 177, died.

At the same time, although the roll as it now exists cannot have been compiled before 1252, it does embody a proportion, perhaps even a considerable proportion, of earlier material. Hugh Wake, 51, for instance, died in 1241, John Vipont, 99, in 1242, Herbert FitzMatthew, 78, in 1245, William de Lancaster, 49, in 1246, Roald of Richmond, 213, in or before 1248, and Roger FitzJohn of Eure, 169, in 1249. Moreover, there are other entries which would apply just as well to a man who died in the 1240's as to his namesake of a later generation. So, for example, no. 50 may mean either the Robert de Tateshal who died in 1249 or his son. No. 72 may be meant either for the Gilbert de Gaunt who died in 1242 or for his son and successor, and no. 27 would fit either William II de Cauntelo who died in 1251 or William III who died 1254. This being so it is more than probable that the 1253 compiler used an earlier collection which he incorporated wholly or in part in his own roll, and that it was this earlier collection rather than the 1253 roll which was used by the Grimaldi compiler. Such evidence as there is suggests that the earlier collection may be dated between 1240 when Baldwin de Reviers became Count de l'Isle and 1242 when John Vipont died. It may conveniently be referred to as the 1240 collection.

Original form

That the original of version I as compiled in 1253 was in blazon only is incontrovertible. Both Glover and Cooke refer to the manuscript which they copied as 'in blazon' or 'written', and neither says anything of illustrative shields whether painted or tricked.

It is equally clear that copies I (a) and I (b) were made from one and the same roll, borrowed by Cooke from Harvy and lent by him to Glover. This is shown by the fact that both copies omit the surname Geneville in no. 102 and that both err in making the field azure instead of argent in 132, 152, and 156.

Nor is there any reason to doubt that that roll was the 1253 original. Although the ideas of sixteenth- and seventeenth-century heralds on dating manuscripts must be taken with more than a grain of salt, the facts that Glover described the manuscript as an old roll and Cooke thought that it was written in the time of Henry III do show that it must have been of considerable age, and so far nothing has been found to suggest that it was not the original.

Tricks

The tricks, on the other hand, both those which accompany the text in I (a) and those which replace it in I (b), must date from 1586 when these copies were made. They are, in fact, no more than Glover's and Cooke's attempts to interpret the old and unfamiliar language of the original. In I (a), as was to be expected from a herald of Glover's calibre, the great majority of the drawings correctly translate the blazon, and such discrepancies and blanks as there are mostly arise from the obscurity or inaccuracy of the original. There are, nevertheless, a few cases in which Glover seems, whether of purpose or through inattention, to have substituted a later and more familiar coat for that blazoned. So for Cauntelo, 27, he draws leopard faces jessant de lis instead of fleurs-de-lis, and for Hugh Balliol,

37, he sets the Galloway lion in the centre instead of in the canton. The Gorges whirlpool, 192, may be another instance, for the text's *roele* suggests a coat of concentric rings as tricked in II rather than the spiral whirlpool which was drawn by both Glover and Cooke. In the case of Richmond, 213, the literal interpretation of the text gives a coat which is otherwise unknown, and Glover draws that cut on Roald's seal which is usually attributed to the family.

Robert Cooke, though energetic in the more remunerative duties of a herald, was neither as learned nor as accurate as Glover, and his tricks in I (*b*) are often at variance with the blazons in I (*a*). These vagaries are mentioned in the succeeding footnotes and it would be pointless to detail them here. It may, however, be observed that a number of the mistakes can be accounted for by changes in the meanings of the terms used. So, for example, Cooke draws Welle's *bastons*, 53, as bendlets instead of bars; the estoiles of Hansard and Beneteby, 75, 126, are drawn as wavy-rayed estoiles instead of straight-rayed molets; the Hay sun, 87, is given the human features which were only introduced at the end of the fifteenth or beginning of the sixteenth century, and *frette* (90, 114, &c.), which in the thirteenth and fourteenth centuries meant what is now called fretty, is drawn as a fret, a pattern which only dates from Tudor days.

Defects

Although I (*a*) gives the oldest version of the 1253 text and is unquestionably the best extant authority, it is not accurate enough to be reproduced word for word. One item, 176, Gilbert Segrave, is omitted, and more than a score of others are defective in one way or another. Whenever possible these defects have been remedied in the ensuing text, the emendations being placed in brackets. They are also noticed and when necessary discussed in the footnotes (see 13, 32, 42–43, 44, 46, 86, 102–3, 106, 108, 110, 111, 113, 114, 127, 132, 152, 156, 160, 164, 176, 179, 185, 197, 210). Most of these defects are repeated in either I (*b*) or II if not in both, or else the item is omitted or incomplete. This shows that the mistakes were not due to careless copying by Glover but were repeated by him from the original. This is strikingly confirmed by no. 86 where the field is blazoned *argent* but tricked by Glover (*b*) (azure), and by the blank shield which Glover left against no. 197. The fact that both I (*b*) and II have corrected the mistakes in these two cases and in 32, 114, 127, and 179, in no way invalidates the above conclusion, for Cooke's tricks are not to be trusted and the author of version II edited the 1253 text as and when he thought fit.

VERSION II

Version II was evidently copied from version I. The names are the same and in the same order, and many of the blazons are word for word the same, while those which have been modernized generally follow the older wording closely, the change in most cases being limited to the omission of *od* or *ove* or its replacement by *a*, and similar trivialities.[1] Moreover, in five cases (113, 160, 164, 185, 210) I's errors or omissions are repeated in II, and this is the more significant as in other cases the copyist did not scruple to remedy I's shortcomings. On the other hand, it may be objected that several Christian names have been changed twice,

[1] Further reference to the changes is made below in considering the language of the roll.

William for Baldwin Dakeny (I. 46), William for Gilbert de Gaunt (I. 72), William for Paulin Peyvre (I. 152), and Robert for William Morteyn (I. 215). These men have not been identified, but it seems possible that they were the most prominent members of the families when the roll was copied.

It can also be accepted that this version was made by a Northcountryman, for three of the seven whose arms were added at the end were Northumbrians and the others hailed from Durham, Cumberland, and Westmorland. However, until Robert Shafto's dates, 212, shall have been found, the version can only be dated or in soon after 1310, since Richard FitzMarmaduke's arms, 214, are differenced by a bend, and his father only died in 1310, while no. 215, Odinel Heron, died in or before 1312.

As for the tricks, although the original manuscript of version I had no illustrative shields, it would seem that the tricks which accompany II. 14, 19, 68, 82, 96, 101, 120, 128, 170, 173, 188, 190, and 208, were copied from the 1310 manuscript and that they are not referred to in the heading to Glover's copy because he deemed them too few or too trivial to mention. Indeed, it is hard to imagine why anyone should have thought it worth while to illustrate those coats, for twelve of the thirteen blazons are perfectly simple and straightforward. The only one which might possibly be misunderstood is 188, *Rauf de Gorges roele d'argent et d'azur*. This is identically the same blazon as in I. 192, but whereas in that case Glover and Cooke both drew a spiral whirlpool, here the draughtsman took *roele* literally and drew *Azure, four concentric annulets argent*. This goes far to confirm the above assumption that Glover copied the tricks from the 1310 manuscript and that the 1253 roll had no illustrations.

VERSION III

Version III comprises 54 items, or 55 if the conflated no. 20 be broken into its components. In one case, 14, William de Munchensy is substituted for his father Warin (I. 25) who died in 1255, and in another, 16, John FitzJohn replaces his father John FitzGeffrey who died in 1258. Of the rest all but one, 34, James Audley, occur in I. They are, moreover, in the same order except that the Earl of Chester, i.e. Prince Edmund (I. 16), has been promoted to the first place (the King and Prince Edward are omitted) and Sir John de Plescy (III. 12; I. 24) precedes instead of following William de Valence. Item 20 also breaks the order. From the sequence of coats in I we should expect to find here *Roger de Leyburne d'azur od six leonceulx d'argent* (I. 34) and that is probably what the compiler meant to insert, but actually all three copies give *Roger de . . . meri* (*Someri* in I a) *esquartele de or e de gules*. That can only be explained as a conflation of *Roger de Someri d'or deus leopartz d'azur* (I. 97) and *Le Comte de Maundevill esquartele d'or et de gules* (I. 19),[1] though if this version was taken from I, it is hard to see how those two items came to be thus telescoped, seeing how widely they are separated there.

The blazons also generally agree with I, the omission of *pate* in blazoning the Aumale cross (7) and the use of *fauses roeles* for the Plescy annulets (12) and *bastons* for the Welle bars (32) being particularly striking. The only material differences are the addition of an orle of martlets on the Chaworth buruly (see the note to I. 56)

[1] William de Say also bears *Quarterly or and gules*, but his blazon is quite different, *au tiel sanz le bordure* (I. 29).

and perhaps the change of Robert de Ros's label from azure to or (45). Most of the other variations are merely verbal. The following may, however, be mentioned:

5. Vere is blazoned quarterly gules and or instead of I's somewhat misleading or and gules.
14. The Munchensy scocheons are blazoned with the older bendy instead of barry.
23. Hugh de Balliol. *En la cornere* is omitted and the Galloway scocheon is painted in the centre of the shield.
24. Eustace de Tours. I's *au tiel*, which ignores Hugh and refers back to John de Balliol, is translated into *Gules au faus escuchon de argent*.
29. The Tateshal checky is argent, instead of or, and gules.
35. Breuse. *Poudre al le eschu* has been added.
39. The Crevequer cross is *perce* instead of *faux*.
49. Gaunt's barry is or, instead of argent, and azure.
50. *En beliff* is omitted in blazoning the Grelley bends.
53. The arms of Vescy are blazoned *de gules a une croix de argent* and are painted with a plain cross, an apparent confusion of the family's two coats.

These variations are referred to again in the notes on I. 11, 25, 37, 38, 50, 55, 56, 61, 72, 73, and 76. It may also be remarked that all the coats in III are in the first third of I.

In view of these discrepancies it would be rash to assert that this version was extracted from I, and yet the two collections have so much in common that it would be equally rash to exclude that possibility. The inclusion of Sir John de Plescy, 12, under that name and not as Earl of Warwick, might seem to point to the 1240 collection as the source of this roll, but that is ruled out by the presence, amongst others, of Hugh de Balliol who was only born *c.* 1240, and William de Valence who only came to England in 1247. The source of the collection must therefore remain an open question. Nor, if III does consist of extracts from I, is there anything to show why these particular items were picked out and the other three-quarters left. A possible explanation is that the roll was intended as a textbook on heraldry, whence the provision of both blazons and painted shields, and that the 54 coats were chosen to that end. This idea is referred to again in the section on instructional rolls.

In contrast to the uncertainty as to its source the date of this version is clear. It must have been compiled in 1258, for Reynold de Mohun, 40, died in that year, and John FitzGeffrey (I. 28), the father of no. 16, John FitzJohn, also died in 1258. That may also be the date of execution, for the style as reproduced in (*c*) points to the thirteenth century.

Of the three copies (*c*) is evidently nearest the original. It is one of the Hatton–Dugdale facsimiles made *c.* 1640 (*CEMRA*, p. xxi), and is headed 'Sr H. St George his roule—old Roll—S'. It shows that the lost original was a roll, presumably of vellum, $4\frac{5}{8}$ in. wide by 6 ft. 4 in. long, with painted shields, two by two, with names and Anglo-French blazons below. The shields measure $1\frac{7}{8}$ by $2\frac{1}{8}$ in. To judge from other Hatton–Dugdale facsimiles which have been compared with the originals, the paintings can be taken as reliable copies, but the transcription of the legends is not always word-perfect, and several emendations have had to be made in the text hereunder.

(*a*) is a late sixteenth-century copy which imitates the original in its arrangement but not in the style of the paintings. The blazon is given twice below each shield, first in thirteenth-century and then in sixteenth-century language. The roll is headed with the Tudor royal arms, but it is not said whence or by whom it was copied.

(*b*) is the work of Nicholas Charles, Lancaster Herald 1608–13. It is headed:

The Coppy of an ould role in the Custody of Richard St. George, Norroy: taken out of the originall by me N.C. 1607, both in Coulors and in Blazon.

The phrase 'both in Coulors and in Blazon' refers to the original, for Charles's copy gives the blazons only and they are modernized with a free use of symbols instead of words. This is the only copy which includes William Martin, 43.

There are many small discrepancies between (*a*) and (*c*). These might conceivably be due to the copyists having used different originals, but it is more likely that they merely indicate that the copyist of (*a*) did not reproduce his original letter for letter, perchance because of unfamiliarity with the old script, or perhaps the original was already difficult to decipher.

VERSION IV

The so-called version IV (*CEMRA*, p. 7) is not and may never have existed as a separate document. It is, as stated above, merely selected items from Grimaldi's Roll (*CEMRA*, p. 62—short reference P), a compilation which cannot have been made before 1337 when William de Montagu was made Earl of Salisbury (P 65) and Robert de Ufford, Earl of Suffolk (P 64), and which may be appreciably later as it is only known from a fifteenth-century manuscript written and limned by the same hands which executed Queen Margaret's copy of Thomas Jenyns's Book (TJ), a comprehensive collection which *CEMRA*, p. 73, dates *c*. 1410, but which may really have been compiled for Queen Margaret's marriage in 1445.[1] It may also be mentioned that not only were P and TJ executed by the same hands but that both show a marked north-country influence. Intrinsically, these extracts from P have no better claim to be rated as a separate roll or version than similar extracts from TJ and other comprehensive rolls, and the only reason for treating them here as a version of Glover's Roll is that they are so described in *CEMRA*.

Although Grimaldi's Roll cannot have been compiled before 1337 and may be appreciably later, many names and coats, apart from the assimilation of the language to fifteenth-century usage, are identical with Glover I. In one case, however, instead of Rauf FitzRandolf (I. 140), P 105 gives his father Randolf FitzRobert of Middleham who died in 1252. This shows that the compiler of P drew on a source anterior to Glover I. The 1240 collection at once comes to mind and many of the names are those of persons living at that time. The exact relationship of Grimaldi's Roll to Glover's Roll it will be impossible determine until the former shall have been edited.

The order of the items in the two versions, IV and I, differs widely, and IV includes two men, 80 and 81, James Audley and William Beauchamp of Elmley, who might well have been in the 1240 collection but who are neither in I nor II, although Audley is in III.

---

[1] No definite opinion can be expressed as to the date of P and TJ until these rolls shall have been examined item by item and all, or at least the great majority, of the individuals identified.

II. WALFORD'S ROLL

INTRODUCTION

THIS Roll was named after the late Weston Styleman Walford, F.S.A., 1802–79, who edited one manuscript of it in 1864. Two versions are distinguished in *CEMRA,* pp. 7–9, both being in blazon.

VERSION I. CHARLES'S

What Sir Anthony Wagner called Version I is only known from British Museum MS. Harl. 6589, f. 12, 12*b*. This is a copy made, like Glover III (*b*), by Nicholas Charles, Lancaster. It is headed 'The coppy of a very antient Rolle made as may be supposed in the tyme of K. H. 3'. Charles does not say who owned the roll when he copied it. It was from this manuscript that Walford printed the roll in *Archaeologia* (xxxix. 373–87), entitling it 'A Roll of Arms of the Thirteenth Century'. It was reprinted privately later in 1864, together with Charles's and St. George's Rolls, in *Three Rolls of Arms of the Latter Part of the Thirteenth Century*, edited by W. S. Walford and C. S. Perceval. It is to that reprint that reference is made when necessary in the following pages.

This manuscript includes marginal sketches of three coats, nos. 89 Robert Mortimer, 172 Richard Talbot, and 184 Henry de Bautersem. Walford ignores these, but Sir Anthony Wagner suggested that they may have represented paintings in the original. That is possible, but there is no evidence either for or against the suggestion.

VERSION II. LELAND'S

Of version II two copies are known, one at Oxford and the other in Dublin. Copy (*a*) is in Bodleian MS. Top. Gen. c. 1 (3117), Lelandi Collectanea, vol. i, pp. 897–905, where it is headed 'The Copy of an ould roule of Armes'. This was made by the antiquary John Leland (*c.* 1506–52), but there is nothing to indicate where or when he copied it, or to whom the original belonged. This copy was printed by Thomas Hearne in *Johannis Lelandi Antiquarii de Rebus Brittannicis Collectanea cum Thomae Hearnii Praefatione, Notis et Indice*, 1st edn., 1715, i. 897–905; 2nd edn., London, 1770, vol. ii, part i, pp. 610–16. Walford (p. 1) thought that Hearne's edition is 'so inaccurately printed, as is evident on the face of it, that no reliance can be placed on any passage that is not supported by other authority'. It is true that Hearne's text is not letter-perfect, but very few of his misrenderings are material, and in fact many of the apparent inaccuracies are in Leland's manuscript, from which the following copy is printed.

Copy (*b*) is in Dublin, in the National Library of Ireland, Trinity College MS. E 1–17, ff. 9–10*b*. This appears in *CEMRA* as III (*a*), unplaced, but on examination it proved to be a somewhat disordered and modernized copy of version II, and it has therefore been renumbered II (*b*). There is no heading to this copy and nothing as to the original from which it was copied. From the handwriting it appears to have been written in the time of Henry VIII or somewhat later by someone who was certainly not a skilled scrivener. It is often difficult to read; contractions are used freely; erasures and corrections are numerous, and the vagaries of spelling are remarkable even for that age. A detailed comparison of the text with copy (*a*) suggests that it was written at dictation by someone unused to that exercise. It would also seem that the reader modernized the text as he went along, though unfamiliarity with the language and armory of the period forced him to repeat many items almost word for word, as, for example, in the somewhat cryptic Rapperswil entry 141, in 94 where he repeats (*a*)'s mistakes *FitzMarmion* and *ebartile* for *FitzWarin* and *écartelé*, and in 172, Estoteville, where he repeats (*a*)'s *cos* which I, rightly or wrongly, altered to *lions*. Nevertheless, in a few cases he seems to have tried to emend the text. So in 29 he translated *roundeles d'or* (rings or annulets) by bezants and then had to make the crosslets within them gules, and in 148 he gave the Dunbar coat the silver rose-strewn border which was normal in Tudor days, but which had not been added when this roll was compiled. The substitution of *rormy* (sic) for *d'azur* in the Hungary entry, no. 11, may be another attempt to emend an incomplete text; this is referred to in the notes hereunder. Most of the variations are of no importance, and indeed, the whole copy might have been ignored were it not that in nos. 120–1, Henry and Anseau de Chevreuse, it has expanded two items which both I (150–1) and II (*a*) (110–11) have, or appear to have, telescoped. At first sight one is tempted to assume that II (*b*) has here preserved the original version of the roll, but on second thoughts the fact that the corresponding items in I and II (*a*) are virtually identical seems to show that the expansion must be credited to the II (*b*) copyist. The conflation of the entries for Walter Mauduit and Enald de Boys in II (*b*) 85 is obviously accidental and of no significance.

It has been suggested that the copyist of II (*b*) may have been Bartholomew Butler, who, after serving successively as Hampnes, Rouge Croix, and York, was Ulster King of Arms from 1522 to 1566. He was the first to hold that post, which then ranked as a king of arms extraordinary in England.

Apart from the variations mentioned above, the text of II (*b*) is substantially the same as that of II *a*, from which it may well have been copied; if not, then both must have been made from the same original. Nevertheless, although the text is the same the order of the items differs considerably, the derangement being in large blocks, thus:

		(*b*)	(*a*)
f. 63		1–11	1–11
,,		12–28	34–50
,,	col. 2	29–50	12–33
f. 63*b*		51–65	127–41
,,		66–74	169–78*
,,	col. 2	75–100	142–68
f. 64	cols. 1, 2	101–37	91–126
f. 64*b*		138–77	51–90

(*a*) 179–86 are missing from (*b*)

The most likely reason for a derangement of that nature is that II (*b*) was copied from a manuscript of which the leaves were loose and out of order, but the coincidence of the blocks with the pages and even the columns of this copy is difficult to reconcile with such a supposition.

COPY III (b)

A fourth copy of this roll is listed in *CEMRA* as III (*b*). This was in the former Wrest Park MS. 16, 'Ancient Rolls', ff. 22–25*b*. After the Wrest Park sale in 1922 that particular volume was broken up and sold piecemeal, and so far all attempts to learn the whereabouts of those leaves have been fruitless. Copies of Glover I and Falkirk II from the same volume are now in Sir Anthony Wagner's library (see p. 89 above), and as these are in the handwriting of Robert Glover it is probable that this roll was also copied by him. It is not known which version it gives.

Differences between I and II

There can be no doubt that versions I and II both come, though perhaps not directly, from a single original. Clerical errors apart the contents are practically identical, and though there are variations in the order it will be seen from the tables on pages 100–102 that there are many blocks in which the order is exactly the same.

For reasons which will appear below it is probable that the original roll was in blazon and II (*a*) may be taken as a pretty accurate copy. In any case the language is contemporary or nearly contemporary with the compilation, and for that reason it has been taken as the master copy in this edition. In version I the language has been modernized and seems to date from the fourteenth century (cf. Glover II) rather than from *c.* 1275.

Another reason for preferring II (*a*) as the master copy is that it includes four coats, nos. 7, Castile, 14, Jerusalem, 66, Lasser, and 166, Creyke, which are omitted from I, no doubt inadvertently. It also gives correctly two coats, 30–31, Bar and Artois, which version I has conflated.

Whether the order of I or II (*a*) is nearer the original is a more difficult question. Sir Anthony Wagner thought that the order of I is 'more rational' and therefore perhaps original, but it may also be argued that it is more likely that the copyist of I rationalized the order of a somewhat haphazard original, than that the copyist of II (*a*) muddled his original. However, little weight can be attached to either argument, for it is difficult to see any system in the arrangement of either version.

Contents

The roll opens with a score of emperors and kings, among whom II, oddly enough, includes the Welsh prince Llewelyn ap Griffith. Then follow:

21–22, the Crusading Orders of the Temple and the Hospital;

23–45, foreign counts, all but the last, Thuringia, from France or Flanders;

46–51, foreign dukes ranging from the French frontiers to Poland;

52–57, foreign counts;

58–60, three Englishmen;

61–64, four Scotsmen;

65–107, mostly English but with a few foreigners intermingled;

108–30, foreigners, mostly counts, but with some of lesser rank and also the

King of Portugal, the Duke of Burgundy, and three English earldoms—
Hereford, Cornwall, and Winchester;

131–73, Englishmen, born or domiciled;

174–85, foreigners.

In I an attempt was perhaps made to rationalize the order of the opening group
of sovereigns if only by putting the Emperor of Constantinople in the second place.
But in the rest of the roll the variations of the order appear to have neither rhyme
nor reason. Nor is it possible to detect any logical scheme or occasion which would
account for the somewhat motley collection which the roll contains. Probably we
shall not be far out if we suggest that this is another personal collection, but whereas Glover's Roll contains the recollections of a stay-at-home Englishman, Walford's
seems to be the work of someone who had spent much of his active life abroad,
clerk, merchant, or perhaps a herald, and who had jotted down from time to time
the arms he met in his travels. Some such explanation would account for the high
proportion of foreign coats. It would also account for the inclusion of a dozen or
more persons who had died before the roll was finished. And lastly it would go
some way to explain the omission of the earls of Gloucester, Surrey, Lincoln, and
Oxford, and other prominent Englishmen whose arms are duly noted in the earlier
collection. The presence of such sequences as 61–64, four Scots, 71–72, Lusignan-
Marche and Lusignan-Valence, 127–9, Dammartin and Trie, 144–5, Warwick
and Plescy, and the Longespée and Bardolf brothers, 75–76 and 137–8, tends to
confirm that hypothesis, although such sequences are neither as numerous nor as
conspicuous as they are in Glover's Roll.

Yet, even if that theory be sound, it still remains to explain the discrepancies
in the language of the two versions and in the order of the items. The variation of
the language may be and probably is due to no more than the fancy of the copyist,
but that could hardly explain the variations in the order, nor can one detect any
principle underlying those changes. The variations seem, indeed, to be quite
erratic. Sometimes, especially in the opening section of sovereigns, the items
seem to have been changed about one by one. Elsewhere one finds more or less
considerable blocks in which the order is identical. Thus the following tables
show one group of 29 and another of 23 items, as well as many smaller blocks of
14, 13, 12 down to 3, 2, and even 1.

Tables comparing the order of items in the two versions of Walford's Roll

In Version I items 7, 14, 31, 66, 166 are omitted

TABLE I

Version II	Version I	
1–22	1–21	Sovereigns and Orders: order different and numbers 7, 14 omitted in Version I and no. 18 later in the roll
23–45	22–43	Foreign: no 31 omitted in Version I
46–51	73–78	,,
52–57	44–49	,,
58–59	79–80	English
60–63	50–53	Aumale and the Scots
64	81	Scot

Version II	Version I	
65	54	Chester
66	—	Lasser
67–68	82–83	English
69	55	Châlon
70	84	Comyn
71–72	56–57	Lusignan
73–85	85–97	Mixed
86–99	125–38	English
100–11	140–51	Mixed
112	72	Burgundy
113–22	58–67	Foreign
123–5	98–100	English earldoms
126	18	Portugal
127	71	Dammartin
128–9	69–70	Trie
130	68	Vienne
131–42	104–15	English
143–4	101–2	English earldoms
145	116	Plescy
146	103	Reviers
147–9	117–19	English
150	139	Beauchamp
151–5	120–4	English
156–9	152–5	English
160–1	157–8	English
162	156	FitzWarin
163–5	159–61	English
166	—	Creke
167–85	162–80	English and foreign

TABLE II

Version I	Version II	
1–21	1–22	Sovereigns and Orders: order different
22–43	23–45	Foreign
44–49	52–57	,,
50–53	60–63	Aumale and the Scots
54	65	Chester
55	69	Châlons
56–57	71–72	Lusignan
58–67	113–22	Foreign
68	130	Vienne
69–70	128–9	Trie
71	127	Dammartin
72	112	Burgundy
73–78	46–51	Foreign
79–80	58–59	English
81	64	Scot
82–83	67–68	English
84	70	Comyn
85–97	73–85	Mixed

Version I	Version II	
98–100	123–5	English earldoms
101–2	143–4	,,
103	146	Reviers
104–15	131–42	English
116	145	Plescy
117–19	147–9	English
120–4	151–5	English
125–38	86–99	English
139	150	Beauchamp
140–51	100–11	Mixed
152–5	156–9	English
156	162	FitzWarin
157–8	160–1	English
159–61	163–5	English
162–80	167–85	English and Foreign

There is no evidence to explain these variations in the order, but the virtual identity of the blazons in such cases as 11, *Le Roy de Hongerye de or estenzele a deux passans d'azur*, and 42, *Le counte Chaumpaine d'azur a une bende d'argent a custeres d'or diaspres*, and their close resemblance in many other cases, shows that the originals of I and II were both copied from a single text, and proves conclusively that they cannot be independent translations of a painted roll. The differences in the language of I would then be due to nothing more than the copyist's preference for the vocabulary and grammar with which he was familiar. Having made those points we may now hazard a guess that the original notes were written on loose sheets, on such scraps of vellum as came to hand at the time. Such bits and pieces would easily get out of order, and we may take it that there was a great deal of derangement between the making of the transcripts from which the present manuscripts I (*a*) and II (*a*) were copied. At the same time it is impossible to say which of those transcripts was made first. It is even possible that neither version preserves the original order, for the pieces might have been disarranged before either transcript was made. An objection to this suggestion is that it does not cover the opening section of the roll, where, apart from Sicily and Navarre and the two Orders, 5–6 and 21–22, no two items are in the same order and position in I and II respectively. Here Sir Anthony Wagner is clearly right in considering the order of I 'more rational', and we can only suggest that possibly I's copyist tried to re-arrange the sovereigns in order of precedence.

Date

The key to the dating of the roll is afforded by the fact that the arms of Bardolf of Wormegay are borne by a William Bardolf both in B 70 and in C 138, but whereas Thomas Bardolf, who wears the cinquefoils on a crusuly field, is described in B 71 as William's son, in C 138 William is called Thomas's brother.[1] It follows that B 70 is the William who died in 1275 and that C 138 is his son and successor of the same name. It also follows that the roll cannot have been compiled before

[1] Actually, as shown in the note to B 70, it is probable that there were two brothers named Thomas, but this point has no relevance for the dating.

1275. Both Walford, p. 5, and Sir Anthony Wagner, p. 8, notice the above facts, but whereas Walford thought that the roll was compiled 'about 1280', Sir Anthony Wagner says '*c.* 1275'. The difference is small, but the earlier date, *c.* 1275, is certainly to be preferred, since no. 59, John FitzJohn, died in that year, and no.148, Guy de Rochford, died in 1274, while several others, e.g. 94, 133, 136, and 176, died only a few years before that. This last fact is not, however, conclusive, for the roll includes several others who died in the 1250's, e.g. 75, 87, 93, 164, and 169, and for the earls (or earldoms) of Winchester, Pembroke, and Warwick (125, 143–4) it gives the arms of Quincy, Marshall, and 'Newburgh', extinct in 1264, 1245, and 1242 respectively.

III. GENERAL CONSIDERATIONS

Language

THE language of both Glover and Walford is French and resembles that of the northern French (Picard) roll known as the *Armorial Bigot*,[1] which is almost exactly contemporary with Glover. A comparison of the three rolls proves that armory had already acquired a technical vocabulary of some extent and that certain broad principles were already accepted in blazoning. At the same time neither the vocabulary nor the grammar was rigidly established. The principal variations and changes will be noticed in succeeding pages.

Blazon

Perhaps the first points to strike the reader are that in all these manuscripts the field is blazoned first and that the charges are commonly introduced by *with*.

The fifteenth-century 'doctors', or teachers of heraldry, laid down that the little words *of*, *and*, and *with* must be used as sparingly as possible, or, still better, eschewed completely, and modern textbooks tend to a similar attitude. The thirteenth-century herald had no such inhibition, and B I bristles with 'withs' and 'ands'. The principal charge is nearly always introduced by *ove* (*ov*, *od*), e.g. *de gules ove trois lupards d'or*. Only in 13 cases out of 177 is this replaced by *a* (*al*, *au*) and in one case by *et*, and only in 3 cases is there no link between field and charge, e.g. *d'azur vj leonceux d'or*. Nor did the compiler hesitate to repeat the preposition before secondary charges. In 49 cases *ove* is either repeated or is followed by *a* or *et*. In 7 more cases these links occur three times and in one blazon (B 188) 4 times.

In the short 1258 version, B III *a* has almost ousted *ove*, introducing the principal charge 43 times to *ove*'s 4. In no case is the link omitted, nor did the compiler scruple to repeat *a* or *ove* whenever there was more than one charge.

In B II, which dates from 1310 but in which many entries follow the earlier

---

[1] Edited by Dr. Paul Adam-Even in *Archives Héraldiques Suisses*, lxiiie année, 1949. Dr. Adam-Even dates it between Nov. 1253 and Sept. 1254.

phraseology, there is a strong tendency to omit the link. The figures are: no link 87, *a* 72, *ove* 24, *et* 1.

In C, on the other hand, *c.* 1275, *a* is used almost invariably, *o* and *et* occurring but once each and *e* twice, if indeed *o* and *e* are not clerical errors for *a*. The link is never omitted.

To a great extent these variations were probably due to the whim of the different scribes, but we may deduce that between 1240 and 1310 the older *ove* was being gradually superseded by *a*,[1] and that there was a growing inclination to dispense with any link between field and charge.

In more elaborate coats the blazon is simple and straightforward, with such formulae as *D'or a deus cheverons de gules et la bordure de gules* (B 68), *D'or od deux barres de gules ov trois turteux de gules en chief* (B 51), *D'argent ove un cheveron de gules od florettes d'or en la cheveron* (B 152). The following points may, however, be noticed.

In such coats as Furnival, Baskerville, and the like, modern usage insists that the ordinary must be named first, but B I puts the secondary charges first in 9 cases out of 13 (60, 133, 145, 147, 149, 183, 186, 188, 189), and of the 4 cases where the ordinary is given the precedence (46, 107, 178, 179) 3 should probably be counted rather as examples of an ordinary in a powdered field than as an ordinary between small charges. C puts the ordinary first in 7 cases out of 9, and B II in 9 cases out of 14. It is also worth noting that in 5 of those 9 cases (141, 143, 145, 182, 184) B II blazons the ordinary (bend or fess) between, *entre*, the minor charges. This is the earliest example which has been observed of this use of 'between'. Another innovation in this version is in the coat of Shafto (212), which is blazoned *Goule sur ung bende d'argent trois moletes dazure*. At first sight one suspects that Glover had inadvertently translated the old blazon into the language of his own day, but a search of the fourteenth-century rolls shows that both formulae are used in Cotgrave's Ordinary, *c.* 1340.[2] Nevertheless, it was long before the older fashion of blazon was completely ousted. B II affords another foretaste of later practice in *mascle voyde du champ* (8).

In the great majority of cases the blazon is silent as to the position of the charge or charges, thus showing that the conventional arrangements were already well recognized. So one is left to infer that the Baskerville fess is between the three roundels (183) and that the bends of Bohun and Furnival are between the lions and martlets (10, 147). The fact that one charge is on another is, however, expressed, as in the case of St. John 110, where the molets are *en le chief*, and Hunting-field 131, where the roundels are *en la fesse*. Otherwise it is only when the position of a charge is unusual or when there is room for doubt that the position is stated. The Vere molet for instance is *en le quartier devant* (11); Hugh Balliol bears the Galloway scocheon either *en la cornere* (I. and II. 37) or *dedenz* (IV. 127); and the roundels of Devereux are *en le chief* (45). In this last case *en le chief* means in modern parlance 'in chief', and it is similarly used in several other coats. Elsewhere, as in the above-mentioned coat of St. John, it would be rendered on the chief.

Charges in orle are variously blazoned. William de Valence, 23, bears *la*

---

[1] *Ove* and its variants are, however, still found in TJ and other fifteenth-century rolls.

[2] Both formulas are also found at the end of the Ashmolean Roll, e.g. 505, *Argent in un fees geuls deins trois mertletes sable iij mascles d'or voides*. The bulk of that roll dates from *c.* 1335, but the last 30 or so entries, including the above, may be late additions.

bordure des merloz, but FitzNichol has *les scalops entour*, 154, and Frank Bohun bears *merlots en le urle*, 190. In C such charges are commonly described as *bordeans*.[1]

The fact that the Monmouth fess is over all, 92, is not expressed, and the use of exactly the same phrasing to blazon Pecche, 60, and FitzWalter, 186, suggests that the fess in those coats was originally over rather than between the two chevrons, an idea which is supported by the drawing of the Pecche shield in III, 38. On the other hand, the blazoner was careful to specify that John de Courtenay's silver bars are *sur le tout* and not merely on the green half of the shield (109).

The above examples are all taken from B I, but the remarks apply equally to C and even to B II, although, as already mentioned, the latter does sometimes use 'between', *entre*.

Patterned fields

It may be noticed that in blazoning parti-coloured fields and charges, whatever the pattern, both these rolls name the metal or fur before the colour. In most cases that is how the arms were borne, but there are three exceptions. In Glover's Roll the arms of Vere, 11, are blazoned *Esquartele d'or et de gules ove une estoille d'argent en le quartier devant*. If that blazon were to be interpreted literally, it would place the silver molet on a field of gold, but in fact the arms were always represented as *Quarterly gules and or*, and Matthew Paris is careful to specify that the first quarter is of gules.[2] Again, in Walford's Roll, 4, the King of Spain is said to bear *Esquartele de argent e de goules* although the fact that the blazon goes on to mention the castles before the lions shows that the red quarters of Castile came before the silver quarters of Leon. Lastly, the Earl of Pembroke (C 143) is said to bear *Party d'or e de vert a un leon rampant party de or et de gules en lunge*, whereas if the earl ever did bear such a parti-coloured lion it must have been per pale gules and or; otherwise the gold half of the lion would have been invisible against the gold field.

It is evident that in these three examples the metal was named first deliberately, and this must be because it was deemed more honourable than the colour. Indeed, Dr. Adam-Even has found this enjoined in at least one French tractate. No such rule is, however, to be found in any of the English treatises. On the contrary, Johannes de Bado Aureo states explicitly that in quarterly coats the tincture of the dexter chief quarter must be named first.[3] On the other hand, he says on another page, on the authority of his mentor Franciscus de Foveis, that whenever the base of the shield is of a single tincture that tincture must be named first,[4] so that in the case of a barry or buruly field the tinctures must be named from the base upwards. That rule was certainly not observed by the compilers of these rolls, but it may have been known to Matthew Paris,[5] and it was followed in some later rolls.[6]

[1] In this connexion it is to be noticed that II replaces the FitzNichol *scalops entour* by *le champ pleyn des escallopes*, which at least to a modern armorist is not the same thing.

[2] II. 48. The blazon in Cotgrave's Ordinary, *c.* 1340, is almost word for word the same as in Glover's Roll except that *gules* is inserted before *devant*.

[3] Ed. Bysshe, p. 27.

[4] Ibid., p. 23.

[5] II. 63. *Comes de Marchia, scutum burele de azuro et argento, quot lineas vis primam tamen de argento.*

[6] See 'Some Medieval Treatises on English Heraldry', *Ant. Journ.* xxxiii (1953) 179–80.

Powdered fields

Neither powdered nor semy is used in B I or II, though it is inserted once in III. 35, *Willame de Breuse de azur a lion de or a croisile de or pudre al le eschu*. Two formulas are used. Sometimes the adjective is preferred, as bezanty and billetty (3, 52, 53, 85–86, 120, 209), but more frequently we find the noun either alone (55, 181) or preceded by 'and' or 'with' (40, 71, 107, 123, 152, 178–9, 197). In all these cases it would seem that the number of the charges was indifferent, and in most cases that it was more than 6, for the presence of 6 charges is expressed in 12 cases (10, 22, &c.)

In C, on the other hand, *poudre a* is used 12 times as against the adjective 9. It is used with a variety of charges including crosses and fleurs-de-lis. The adjectives are *besantee, billette, estenzele,* and *flurete.*

The addition of *pudre al le eschu* in B III's blazon of de Breuse is probably due to a misunderstanding. Both I and II. 55 blazon *d'azur od un leon d'or croiselez* (*croisele* in II) *d'or*, where *croiselez* or *croisele* is almost certainly the adjective crusuly. The compiler of III seems, however, to have read it as the noun crosslets and therefore added powdered in the field.

In B whichever way the powdering is blazoned it is named last of all except in two cases (120, 209) where billetty precedes the charge. In C the powdering is always blazoned first.

Tinctures[1]

Six tinctures are found in these two rolls, and in C they are invariably blazoned by the modern names. In B *or, azure, gules,* and *vert* are also so blazoned, but in all three versions *noir* is used more often than *sable*,[2] while *blanc* occasionally replaces *argent*.[3]

Gules is the most popular of the six tinctures, and is followed by *or, argent, azure, sable,* and *vert* in that order. *Vert* only occurs thrice in B I, but 8 times in C. *Purpure* is not found in B, and in C it only occurs once, for the lion of Leon, and then only in two copies, copy II (*a*) making that beast *azure*.

Of the furs *ermine* occurs rather more often than *vair* in B (15 to 11), but less often in C (8 to 11). No variant of ermine is found in either roll, but vairy or and gules occurs once in B and twice in C; vairy or and azure also occurs in C. Both ermine and vair are usually combined with gules. The exceptions in B are: 20, ermine with checky or and azure; 50, ermine with checky or and gules; 174, ermine and vert; and 57, vair and paille. Vair plain occurs twice and vairy or and gules, also plain, once. In C ermine is combined twice with checky or and azure, once with checky or and gules, and once with azure.

More interesting than the furs is the appearance in these two rolls of two *pannes*, a class of tincture which is of extreme rarity in English armory. In B 57 Philip Marmion wears *vair, a fess paille,* and in C *diapré* occurs twice, once in the arms of Champagne, 42, *d'azur a une bende d'argent a custeres d'or diasprez,* and once in those

---

[1] In this section only the field and the principal charge have been counted, secondary charges being ignored.

[2] 21 times out of 24 in I; 18 out of 26 in II.

[3] 4 times out of 75 in I; only once in II; never in III.

of the Count de l'Ile, 146, *de goules a treis barres d'or diaspres*. These terms *paille* and *diapré* are considered at some length in Appendix 2.

The proportion of plain to patterned fields is a little over 2 to 1 in B and rather more than $2\frac{1}{2}$ to 1 in C.[1] In both rolls barry (including buruly) and quarterly fields are roughly twice as frequent as any other pattern. In B the figures are: quarterly 12 examples, barry (and buruly) 11, vair (and vairy), checky, fretty, and lozengy 6 each, ermine, undy (barry wavy), and party per pale 4 each, paly 2, bendy, gyronny, paly wavy, and roele 1 each. In C there is no example of fretty or roele, but there is one chevronny field. The figures are: barry 13, quarterly 10, paly 7, vair and checky 6 each, lozengy and per pale 2 each, ermine, bendy, chevronny, gyronny, and undy 1 each.

Colour on colour

Only two examples of colour on colour and one of metal on metal occur in the two rolls. In Glover's Roll Henry de Bohun (B 189) changes his paternal bend and cotices from argent to *gules* although the field is *azure*. In Walford's Roll the King of Cyprus is said to bear *vert* semy of roundels *gules*, a cross throughout or (C 16), and the King of Jerusalem bears *argent* crusuly *or*, a cross potent *or* (C 14).[2]

Charges

In both rolls nearly half the patterned fields bear no charge or only a label. There is, however, no example in either roll of an uncharged plain field like the plain red shield carried by Sir Eumenious de la Brette at Caerlaverock and the plain black shield used by Sir Thomas Holand in the 1350's.

The so-called ordinaries and sub-ordinaries are much the commonest charges. Rather more than half the coats in the two rolls contain one or more ordinaries. These are sometimes accompanied by some common charges as St.John *d'argent od chief de gules et deux estoiles d'or en le chief*, but more often the shield only contains one or more ordinaries, as, for example, Foliot, *de gules od une bende d'argent*, Daubeney, *d'or a deus cheverons de gules et la bordure de gules*. Commonest of all these charges is the fess with its diminutive the bar. Then come the bend, chief, cross, chevron, and border. The scocheon, whole or voided, canton, roundel, saltire, lozenge, whole or voided, and pile also occur.

Of the other charges the lion figures in about one coat in five in the two rolls, usually as the sole or principal charge, but sometimes in company with an ordinary. No other beasts are found in B, but C provides a horse, an ox, and a hind, though it must be added that the two former are only in coats of somewhat doubtful authenticity (17, 18). Birds are more varied. The eagle, martlet, and popinjay occur in both rolls: cocks, corbies, and herons appear in B which also provides the

---

[1] Fretty and the furs are counted as patterns. Powdered fields, crusuly, billetty, &c., are, however, counted as plain, partly because in several cases the powdering is a mere difference, and partly because the blazons do not distinguish between, e.g. a fess on a billetty field and one between, say, 10 billets.

[2] The reluctance to set metal on metal and colour on colour seems never to have extended to labels and other difference marks added over all, nor to those cases where either the field or the charge is parti-coloured. Examples of both are numerous in both rolls.

indeterminate *avoz* (I. 201). Both B II and C change these into martlets, but they must originally have been falcons. The only fish in B is the luce or pike, but the barbel and dolphin also appear in C. The common charges are too numerous to mention here. Many are obviously canting.

Canting arms

Roughly 1 in 16 of the coats in these two rolls are canting. Many of these are familiar, as Ferrers's vairy, Lucy's luces, Gorges' *gurges* or whirlpool, the *trois bouz* of Trussebuts borne by Ros, the castle and lion of Castile and Leon, the *bars* or barbel of Bar, and the dolphin of Dauphiné borne by the Count of Forez. Others, though less familiar, are scarcely less obvious, as the *merlettes* of Merlay, the oak of Oksted, the *fers* or horseshoes borne by Montgomery as tenant of Ferrers, the rakes or *râteaux* of Réthel, Tierstein's *Tier* or hind on a mount of *Stein*, the hammers or *martels* of Martell, and the cummin-sheaves of Comyn. Less obvious, but still undoubtedly canting, are the *grés* or steps figured by Grey's barry, the cross *crévé au cœur*, i.e. voided, of Crevequer, Moels' *meules* or millstones, Vipont's *vi* points (drawn as annulets), the birds (falcons) of Fauconberg, the Maltravers fretty and the brays which the Genevilles borrowed from their cousins of Broye. So, too, the paly wavy of B 214 may have been intended to suggest the whiskers whence Gernons got his name. The sharp-pointed fusils of Montagu (Mont-aigu, de Monte Acuto) and Percy are also canting. In the latter case there seems to be a double allusion. As piercing they point to the name Percy, whilst as mill-picks they recall the twelfth-century Picot de Percy.

Terminology

Reference has already been made to changes in the meaning of certain terms and to the use of *blank* and *noir* as alternatives for silver and sable. Another important point is the use of *baston, bende,* and *bendé*. In B *baston* is used thrice in I for the horizontal bar (49, &c.), and once each in II and III, but it is also used once in II. 214 for a narrow bend, the diagonal. So, too, although *bende* is generally used in its modern sense for the diagonal charge (B 9, &c.), it is also used once (IV. 93) for the horizontal fess, and the adjective *bende* is used once each for barry (I. 32) and bendy (117). In other words, to B's compiler *baston* and *bende* merely meant a band or stripe, and neither word had any fixed directional significance. This is brought out clearly by the blazon of the Grelley bends as *bendes en beliff*, that is diagonal or slantwise stripes. III. 50 omits *en beliff*, but whether the compiler did not understand the term or thought it superfluous it is impossible to say.

Annulets are blazoned as voided roundels, *fauses roeles* (I. 24, 99) or *faux rondelettes* (II. 24, 99), but C 12 omits *fauses* and merely blazons *roundeles*, and in B IV. 88 Vipont bears *anelettes*.

The martlet is still a little *merle, merlotte,* and the fact that the eagle is displayed is taken for granted in B but stated in C.

The term canton does not appear in B I or III where its place is taken by *quartier* (49, &c.) and *cornere* (32, &c.). *Cantelle* is, however, used in C and *canton* in B II. 105.

Of the crosses the plain cross is naturally the commonest. It occurs alone (B 6, &c.), charged (B 197), and between other charges (B 46). In B it is merely a *croix* but in C it is more often blazoned *croix passant*, though *passant* is apt to be omitted when there are other charges. The diminutive *croisele*, *croiselette* is always used when there is more than one, usually as a powdering on the field. It is to be noticed that the pattern of these crosslets is never stated. Presumably, their exact shape was of no importance in those days.

Next to the plain cross comes the cross paty (see plate III, no. 3), which is borne by the Earl of Aumale in both B and C, by Vescy and Lexington in B, and by Rauf Basset in C. For the Earl of Aumale both rolls blazon *croix* with no distinguishing adjective; for Vescy B writes *croix furchee* and for Lexington *croix furchee au kanee* (*kauee* ?), all of which shows that there was still no accepted description for this cross in the mid-thirteenth century. The term *pate* does, however, appear in C's blazon of Rauf Basset, and that is the earliest known appearance of the term. C also applies this term to the Toulouse cross, which on seals is always *clechee*. C's use of *pate* for the Toulouse cross is important, for it points to the word's derivation from the Latin *patens*, 'spreading', rather than from *patte*, 'a paw', and that is borne out by the blazon of the Swilton and Trussel crosses as *pate e florette* and *pate flurette* in 2nd Dunstable 5 and Boroughbridge 41, both those crosses being really formy, flory at the ends. B II's use of *patonce* to blazon the Vescy cross is probably Glover's mistake for *furchee* or some other, perhaps illegible, word, for *patonce* is not found again before the fifteenth or sixteenth century.[1]

The only other cross in B is the canting cross *crévé au cœur* of Crevequer, which is blazoned *faux croix* in I. 61 and *croyz perce* in III. 76.[2]

In C, besides Basset's *croix patee* and the Toulouse *croix pate et perse*, we find the cross *byllette*, i.e. potent, of Jerusalem (14), the cross *engrele* of Gournay (82), and the cross *rescersele* or moline of Paveley and Baucey (160, 177). None of these call for any comment, but the use of *fourme* to blazon the Hospitallers' cross (22) is surprising, for the term does not appear again in any roll of arms for more than half a century; it is next found in the Carlisle Roll of 1334 (no. 106) and in Cotgrave's Ordinary, *c.* 1340, in both of which it blazons the Berkeley crosslets.

The lion, plural *leonceux*, is usually rampant, this pose being assumed in B I and III, but blazoned in II and IV, and generally though not invariably in C. A lion *passant* is so blazoned except in C 95, Somery, where it is apparently assumed that as there are only two lions they must perforce be passant one above the other. A lion passant gardant is a *leopard* or *lupard* in all the manuscripts, but B II sometimes writes *leopard passant* and a *leopard rampant* occurs in C 115. Other postures of the lion are not to be found in these rolls unless we are to interpret B IV. 50's blazon of the Bohun lions, *leonceaux rampantz embelif*, as meaning lions saliant. It is also possible that Hugh Bigod's lion was saliant—see the note to B 89. A demi-lion, *leon recope*, was borne by Geneville. Crowned lions and lions with forked tails also occur.

Other terms to which attention may be invited are *de l'un et l'autre*, *embelif*, *endente*, *engrele*, *estoile*, *fess*, *furchee*, *lozenge*, *peus*, *rey de soleil*, *roele*, and *roundel*, all of which occur in B, and *estenzele* and *ruell* which are only found in C.

---

[1] The earliest example which I have noticed is in a sixteenth-century addition to Collingborne's Book.

[2] B II. 217 also includes Lamplugh's *crois florettee*, flory at the ends, but that is one of the fourteenth-century additions.

Differencing

Neither Nicolas nor Walford considered differencing in their introductions to these two rolls, but in 1939 Sir Anthony Wagner remarked how few are the instances in Glover's Roll where one coat is borne by two individuals.[1] The six instances are:

19, 29. Mandeville and Say, two cousins, *Quarterly or and gules.*

26, 39. Herbert and Martin Chamberlain, *Gules, three escallops or* (these two men have not been identified but it may be presumed that they were near relatives).

95, 143. William de Beauchamp and Hugh de Ferrers, *Vair plain.*

115–16. William and Nicholas Sandford, brothers, *Undy argent and gules.*

141, 191. FitzBrian and Savage, *Barry or and gules.*

194–5. Le Fort de Vivonne and Columbers, *Argent, a chief gules.*[2] (This is also attributed to Alein Lasser in C 66.)

As a seventh instance we should perhaps count 65 and 202, William Mauduit, *Argent, two bars gules,* and Nicholas FitzMartin, the same with a label azure, for it is at least possible that the label was a mere brisure and that the FitzMartin arms were already the same as Mauduit's, as they certainly were by 1301 (see no. 65).

In Walford's Roll, although there are several cases in which, unless the name is mistaken, a cadet is given the undifferenced arms of the head of the family, there are only two instances of identical arms being attributed to different persons, viz:

58, 171. Nevile of Hornby and FitzGerald, *Argent, a saltire gules*; and

61, 131, 154. Dunbar, Mowbray, and Merck, *Gules, a lion argent*;

and in this case it is perhaps significant that Dunbar soon enclosed his lion in a rose-strewn border, whilst it is a question whether the Merck lion ought not to have a forked tail.

It may also be mentioned that this roll attributes to one Baldwin Pecche the vairy or and gules of Ferrers (C 165); this coat appears for Ferrers in Glover's Roll though not in Walford's.

It is thus apparent that the need to differentiate the arms worn by different persons was already recognized in the first half of the thirteenth century, and this is amply confirmed by the evidence of the Bigot Roll of 1254, in which Dr. Adam-Even found that no less than 27 per cent of the 295 coats display a major *brisure* (bend, border, or label), while twenty years or so later, 1265–70, more than 40 per cent of the 256 coats in the first and slightly earlier portion of the Wijnbergen Roll are differenced in one way or another. Moreover, in one case the Bigot Roll is at pains to mention that a brother bore the undifferenced arms, *les porte entires.*[3] It may also be recalled that in 1300 the author of the Caerlaverock Poem could

[1] *Heralds and Heraldry*, p. 18.

[2] The two St.John entries, 110–11, are ignored as both are incomplete. Nor have we included 18 and 88, the Earl of Arundel and John Fitzalan, as these are probably successive generations. 89, Hugh Bigod, is said to bear that same coat, but his lion seems to have been saliant or even passant. Rokely and Fitzwilliam are mentioned by Sir Anthony Wagner as both are assigned lozengy ermine and gules in version II, but I. 136–7, a version which was not known when Sir Anthony Wagner wrote, rightly makes the Fitzwilliam coat argent and gules.

[3] The family in question, von Schinnen, 77–78, were Germans, and differencing for cadency seems always to have been exceptional in Germany.

write that many marvelled to see Hugh Poyntz and Brian Fitzalan both wearing the same barry coat (line 346).

In the following paragraphs it will be convenient to distinguish two categories of differences. On the one hand are cadency brisures, that is the bearing of a differenced version of the pronominal coat by junior members of that family, sons, brothers, cousins, and so forth. On the other hand, there are derivative arms, that is the adoption or adaptation of the arms of another person by reason of alliance, dependence, affection, or what not.

Cadency

In MP, as Mr. Tremlett has pointed out, cadency brisures are rare and are almost confined to the sons of the Emperor Frederick II. In these two rolls they are relatively numerous, though less numerous than in the two French rolls mentioned above.

In Glover's Roll we found thirty-two indubitable examples of cadency brisures. In eleven of these the difference mark is a label (2, 38, 43, 67, 81, 146, 158, 166, 187–8), and to these should perhaps be added the FitzMartin coat, 202, mentioned above. Ten coats are differenced by the change of one or more tinctures (47, 78, 86, 102–3, 119, 143, 149, 173, 189); six add a bend (14, 72) or some other charge or charges (23, 171, 197, 200); two powder the field with crosslets (40, 71); one changes the charge from a bend to a fess (31), and another adds a small scocheon of his mother's arms (37), a type of difference which is commoner in the Low Countries than in Great Britain. Lastly, one, Geoffrey Beauchamp of Bedford, makes a double change, both altering the tinctures and removing the bend from his paternal coat.

Walford's Roll, as already suggested, is or appears to be less scrupulous than Glover's in recording cadency brisures, for there are some eight entries of apparent cadets who are given the undifferenced coat of the head of the family,[1] whilst only thirty-seven coats are definitely recognizable as differenced for cadency. Among these eleven are marked with a label (5, 27, 31, 73, 126, 129, 149, 177, 178, 182, 183); two are differenced by the addition of an ermine canton (24, 76); two by a border (24, 26); and seven by the addition of other charges (72, 96, 109, 174, 180, 181, 185). In nine cases the tinctures are changed (49, 53, 58, 68, 79, 106, 114, 117, 128). In two cases the charge is multiplied, both Alfonso of Portugal, 126, and the Count of Poitiers, 23, bearing a semy of towers instead of the single castle of Castile. In one case, Chevreuse, 110, a charge is changed. Only in two cases, 134, 137, is the field made crusuly, and in one case, 109, billetty.

It need hardly be remarked that there is no sign of the petty charges or stigmata which English heralds introduced in the fifteenth century. In that system the label was taken as the difference of the eldest son v.p., but in the thirteenth century there was no such restriction on its use and it was rightly rated by Dr. Adam-Even as a major difference. It would, indeed, appear from these two rolls that there were no rules or principles whatsoever to govern the selection of brisures, and that the particular method of differencing any particular coat was at the choice of the wearer.

[1] 74, 81, 86, 107, 111, 142, 162, 164.

Derived arms

A few lines after his allusion to the absence of overlapping in Glover's and later rolls, Sir Anthony Wagner observed that 'the frequency of significant similarity' is no less striking. He then went on:

That the members of one family would normally distinguish their several coats by making small alterations and additions has always been well known. Camden observed further that 'About this time did many Gentlemen begin to bear Arms by borrowing from their Lords Arms of whom they held in Fee, or to whom they were devoted . . .' (*Remains*, ed. 1674, p. 277). Less obvious, but not less certain, is the collateral adoption of like arms by families linked by intermarriage.[1]

In that paragraph Sir Anthony Wagner has indicated two main sources of derivative arms, feudal dependence (or sometimes perhaps mere local proximity) and collateral adoption. Both sources are illustrated in this volume, particularly in Glover's Roll.

Most of the groups of derivative arms are more conveniently considered in the notes to the respective texts,[2] but attention may be drawn here to the Genevilles' use of the horse-brays of Broye (B 102), an extreme case of collateral adoption which is perhaps paralleled in England by the Aldham use of the de la Hay sun (B 87).

Marshalling and composed arms

The practice of uniting two distinct coats of arms in a single shield by dimidiation or impalement goes back to the twelfth century as is shown by the seals of Robert of Pinkney, c. 1195 (*Arch.* lxxxix, pl. vi. f.) and Isabel Mauduit, *nee* Basset, c. 1220. Quartering came in somewhat later since the earliest known example dates from 1230 when St. Ferdinand of Spain quartered the arms of his two kingdoms of Castile and Leon. This last coat occurs both in MP (II. 72) and in Walford (C 4), but that is the only example of quartering in the three rolls. Walford also affords an example of dimidiation (or impalement) in the arms of the Count of Poitiers, the dexter semy of France, the sinister semy of Castile (C 7).

Glover's Roll has no example of either quartering or impalement, but two items seem to foreshadow the later custom of bearing the arms of an heiress wife 'in pretence'. Hugh Balliol (B 37) bears Balliol with a scocheon of Galloway, his mother's arms, over all, while the Merlay coat (B 139) is even nearer to the modern usage, for that might be read as semy of Merlay with Stuteville in pretence.

Other cases of the union of two coats in a single shield may be seen in the arms of Geneville, in effect Broye with a chief of Brienne (B 102–3; C 106), and of Bautersem (C 184), in which a chief of Berthout is added to the voided lozenges of Bautersem. Another possible instance of such combination is the coat worn by John FitzGeoffrey (B 28) and his son John FitzJohn (C 59); this should perhaps

---

[1] *Heralds and Heraldry*, p. 19. Smith Ellis worked out many examples of the collateral adoption of arms and came to interesting and original conclusions, but unhappily, as Sir Anthony Wagner pointed out ibidem, many of his genealogical and other assumptions were incorrect, and his work needs verification and revision.

[2] See, for example, Mandeville, Warenne, Clare, Chester, Stuteville, Balliol, Furnival, and Tony.

be read as Mandeville in a border of Ludgarshall. It is also possible that the rather odd coat assigned to John Courtenay in B 109 may be a combination of Warenne and the Isle of Wight (C 146).

Comparative value of the two rolls

Neither Glover's nor Walford's Roll lists more than a fraction of those bearing arms in England in the middle and latter half of the thirteenth century, for the two together comprise less than 270 English armigers (including successive generations of the same family) whereas c. 1312 the Parliamentary Roll names over a thousand.[1] In fact, as was said on earlier pages, neither roll is anything more than the personal collections of someone interested in heraldry, who set down names and arms as they occurred to him or came to his notice. Moreover, as we studied the rolls we felt more and more strongly that of the two men the compiler of Glover's Roll was both more knowledgeable and more reliable. The sequences referred to on page 91 show that he was well acquainted with the intermarriages of those families whose arms he noted; differences are scrupulously recorded and such defects as have been detected are mere clerical errors. In Walford's Roll, on the other hand, there are many names whose bearers cannot be traced, so many that one cannot avoid a suspicion that either the names or the arms (if not both, e.g. 166–7) are mistaken;[2] in other cases cadency brisures are omitted, while clerical errors are hardly less numerous and in some cases are certainly more serious than those in Glover's.

Arrangement

Broadly, the presentation of these two rolls is the same as for the Matthew Paris Shields, with the text in italics printed in the upper part of the page, the normalized or key name above, and the notes, whether biographical, armorial, or other, in smaller type below.

For Glover's Roll the Wagner–Wrest Park manuscript, I (a), has been taken as the master text as being nearer to the original version. It is printed first and is annotated as fully as space would permit. Although the drawings which accompany the text in that manuscript and which replace it in I (b) only date from 1586, they are an integral part of the existing manuscripts and it was therefore deemed preferable to mention them in the text. Where there is no such note it is to be understood that the sketches correctly interpret the blazon.

In the notes the first line in each case gives the numbers of the corresponding items in versions II, III, and IV, a dash showing that the item is missing from that version (these references are not preceded by 'B'). References to the Matthew Paris shields (MP) and to Walford's Roll (C) are also given there when appropriate.

Variations and related items in versions II, III, and IV and in Walford's Roll are dealt with as far as possible in the notes to Glover I. The notes to those manu-

---

[1] It has been estimated that in the later thirteenth century there were about 1,500 knights in England and about as many more who held lands whose value put their holders in the social class of knights. (Sir M. Powicke, *The Thirteenth Century*, 1953, p. 541.)

[2] In no. 11, for instance, the arms of Denmark are mutilated and are wrongly attributed to Hungary.

scripts are therefore limited to items which do not appear in the earlier text, together with a few points which could not conveniently be handled there.

For Walford's Roll, version II, the Leland manuscript has been taken as the master text as giving the older and fuller text, and it alone has been annotated. References to the corresponding items in version I and in copy II (*b*) (these are not preceded by 'C'), together with those to the MP Shields and to Glover's Roll (B), are given in the first line of the notes.

In all versions of both rolls editorial emendations of the text are bracketed and are explained in the notes.

GLOVER'S ROLL

VERSION I

ENGLAND

1. *Le Roy d'Angleterre port l'escu de gules ove trois lupards d'or.*

(*a*) No shield.

(*b*) 'Kyng Henry the 3.' *Gules, three lions passant gardant or.*

Cf. 1, —, —: MP I. 19.

Henry III succ. 1216, d. 1272.

ENGLAND

2. *Son filz au tiel ove label d'asure.*

(*a*) No shield.

(*b*) 'Edward prince of Walles the Kynges son.' As 1 with a label azure.

Cf. 2, —, —.

Edward, eldest s. of Henry III, afterwards King Edward I. He was never Prince of Wales, that title being only created by him for his s. Edward of Carnarvon in 1301.

On an equestrian seal of 1267 the label appears to have only three points, but on the counterseal it has five. This suggests that the number was unimportant at that time, and that is confirmed by the fact that his brother Edmund Crouchback's label has three and sometimes five points. (Sandford 103.)

CORNWALL

3. *Le Comte de Cornewaill d'argent ou un leon de gules coronne d'or ove le bordure noir besante d'or.*

(*b*) 'Richard Erle of Cornwall.'

Cf. 3, —, 46: MP I. 38; II. 3: C 124.

Same person as MP I. 38.

MONTFORT

4. *Le Comte de Leycestr' de gules ove un leon blank la cowe furchee. Et la baner party endente d'or et de gules.*

(*a*) Trick only.

(*b*) 'Simon Erle of Lecester' (*Gules, a lion with a forked tail argent*). This banner was also over the armes of 'Simon Mountforth, erle of Lecester' (banner in the margin). *Per pale indented argent and gules.* Amaury de Montfort, Earl of Gloucester sealed with shield party indented (DD q. 10138). This banner was later assigned to the honour of Hinckley (DCL f. 2 b).

Cf. 4, 2, 56: MP I. 30, 31; II. 6; IV. 15.

Same person as MP I I. 6.

CLARE

5. *Le Comte de Gloucestre d'or ove trois cheverons de gules.*

Cf. 5, —, 45: MP I. 46, 76: B 81.

Richard de Clare, Earl of Gloucester, s. of Gilbert de Clare (MP I. 46), succ. 1230, d. 1262: same person as MP I. 76.

BIGOD

6. *Le Comte de Northfolk d'or ove une croix de gules.*

(*b*) 'The erle of Norff. This erle of Norff. or a crosse gules.'

> Cf. 6, —, —; MP I. 39; II 12: B 89, 197: C 91.
>
> Roger Bigod, Earl of Norfolk, succ. 1225, d.s.p. 1270: same person as MP II. 12.
>
> His nephew and successor Roger, Earl of Norfolk and Marshal of England 1270–1306, s. of Hugh le Bigod (B 89), **took** what seems to have been the arms of the marshalcy, *Party per pale or and vert a lion rampant gules* (see B 17 and cf. C 91). It may be noted that the equestrian seal of Roger, his uncle, has a lion passant at the foot. (*CP* ix. 590–4; Birch 5708.)

WARENNE

7. *Le Comte de Garenne eschekere d'or et d'azure.*

> Cf. 7, —, 48: MP I. 64; II. 7; IV. 36.
>
> John de Warenne, Earl of Surrey, d. 1304, s. of William (MP I. 64). (*CP* xii (1) 503.)

QUINCY

8. *Le Comte de Wyncestr' de gules ove sept faulses losenges d'or.*

(*a*) and (*b*) *Seven voided lozenges joined* (3, 3, 1).

> Cf. 8, 3, 59: MP I. 32, 34; II. 11; IV. 17: B 153.
>
> Roger de Quincy, Earl of Winchester, s. of Saher de Quincy, Earl of Winchester (MP I. 32), d.s.p.m. 1264: same person as MP II. 11. (*CP* xii (2) 751–4.)

LACY

9. *Le Comte de Nichole esquartele d'or et de gules ove une bende noir et un label d'argent.*

(*b*) 'The erle of Lyncolne.'

> Cf. 9, —, —: MP I. 63; II. 20; IV. 6, 37, 46, 56.
>
> Edmund de Lacy, Earl of Lincoln, s. of John de Lacy, Earl of Lincoln and Constable of Chester (MP I. 63), succ. 1240, d. 1258. As Constables of Chester he and his father used seals with three garbs. (Birch 11188; cf. MP I. 48; IV. 6: B 16.) His son Henry de Lacy abandoned the quarterly coat and bore *Or, a lion rampant purpure* (K, line 40), a coat which may allude to his wife Margaret Longespée (see MP I. 40). (*CP* vii. 680–7.)

BOHUN of Hereford

10. *Le Comte de Herford d'asur ove sys lyonceaux d'or ove une bende blanche a deux cutices d'or.*

> Cf. 10, 4, 50: MP I. 33, 35; II. 9; IV. 16: C 123.
>
> Humphrey de Bohun, Earl of Hereford, s. of Henry de Bohun, Earl of Hereford (MP I. 33), succ. 1220, d. 1275. (*CP* vi. 459, &c.): same person as MP II. 9.

VERE

11. *Le Comte d'Oxenford esquartele d'or et de gules ove une estoille d'argent en le quartier devant.*

(*a*) and (*b*) *Quarterly or and gules with a mullet of five points argent in dexter chief.*

> Cf. 11, 5, 33: MP II. 15.
>
> Hugh de Vere, Earl of Oxford, succ. 1221, d. 1263: same person as MP II. 15. (*CP* x. 213, &c.)
>
> B I (*a*), B II, and B IV all blazon *quarterly or and gules*, and B I (*b*) tricks the same. But MP II 15 and B III paint and blazon *quarterly gules and or* and that is how the arms have always been borne. B IV also paints *quarterly gules and or* in spite of its blazon.

REVIERS

12. *Le Comte del Yle d'or ove un leon d'asur.*

Cf. 12, 6, —: MP I. 75; II. 17; IV. 35, 60: C 146.

Baldwin de Reviers, Earl of Devon, s. of Baldwin de Reviers, Earl of Devon (MP I. 75), Lord of the Isle of Wight, succ. 1245, d.s.p.s. 1262. (*CP* iv. 318, &c.) The coat here assigned is the familiar Reviers lion, but C 146 gives *Gules trois barres d'or diasprez.* That coat has not been found elsewhere: it has been suggested by Sir Anthony Wagner that it is related somehow to the silver bars in the coat (B 109) attributed to Baldwin's cousin, John de Courtenay. In this connexion it may be noted that Pembroke and Warwick, the earldoms that precede this earldom in C, are given arms of families extinct in 1245 and 1242 respectively. This suggests that the three diapered bars of C 146 may have been arms of an earlier Lord of the Isle.

FORZ

13. *Le Comte d'Aubemarle de gules ove un croix de veer.*
(*a*) and (*b*) *A cross patonce.*

Cf. 13, 7, 63: MP II. 38: C 60.

William de Forz, Count of Aumale, succ. 1214, d. 1241. (*CP* i. 355.) Same person as MP II. 38, or his s. William de Forz, Count of Aumale, who m. Isabel sister and h. of Baldwin de Reviers (B 12) and d. 1260.

Though B I and B II both blazon a cross without specifying the pattern, both draw the cross patonce, and it is blazoned paty in B II and B IV and thus painted by Matthew Paris and so cut on the seals of this and other earls (*Book of Seals*, 66, 445; Birch 6044) and so depicted with the blue lion of Reviers on an embroidered surcoat (*Vetusta Monumenta*, vi, pl. XVIII.)

HUNTINGDON

14. *Le Comte de Huntingdon pale d'or et de gules ove une bend noir.*
(*b*) 'John Scot erle of Hountingdon in the lyffe of Davyd his father and Randolff erle of Chester his uncule.'

Cf. 14, —, 62: MP II. 19.

Same person as MP II. 19.

FERRERS

15. *Le Comte de Ferrers verre d'or et de gules.*

Cf. 15, 8, 52: MP II. 10, 62.

Either William de Ferrers, Earl of Derby 1190–1247 (MP II. 10), or his s. William, Earl of Derby 1247–54. (*CP* iv. 194–8.) The latter on his seal bore *Vairy, a bordure charged with horseshoes.* (Birch 5920.) This variant was also used by his younger s. William de Ferrers of Groby (E 70).

CHESTER

16. *Le Comte de Cestre d'asur ove trois garbes d'or.*

Cf. 16, 1, 55: MP I. 48; II. 14; IV. 6, 31, 34: C 65.

B IV. names him Le Comte Randolf de Chestre, i.e. Ralph de Blundeville, succ. 1181, d.s.p. 1232 (MP I. 48), and who was succ. by his nephew John, Earl of Huntingdon (MP II. 19: B 14), s. of his sister Maud. (*CP* iii. 167–9.) In 1253 the earldom of Chester was conferred on King Henry's younger s. Prince Edmund, and that explains the earl's promotion to no. 1 in the 1258 version, B III.

118 GLOVER'S ROLL

MARSHAL

17. *Le Comte Marschall party d'or et de vert ove un leon gules.*

Cf. 17, —, 47: MP I. 29, &c.

On the death of Anselm Marshal, Earl of Pembroke in 1245, the office passed to his nephew Roger Bigod (MP II. 12: B 6) and thereafter these arms were assumed by the Bigods as pertaining to the marshalcy. In C 143 the coat is attributed to the earldom of Pembroke, but the Bigods were not earls of Pembroke, and William de Valence, who had that title from about 1259 to 1296, is not known to have used these arms.

D'AUBIGNY

18. *Le Comte d'Arundell de gules au un lion d'or.*

Cf. 18, —, 54: MP I. 36, 72; II. 5; IV. 18, 57.

Hugh d'Aubigny, Earl of Arundel, brother of William d'Aubigny, Earl of Arundel (d.s.p. 1224), and younger s. of William d'Aubigny, Earl of Arundel (MP I. 36); d.s.p. 1243. (*CP* i. 238–9.) Same person as MP I. 72.

MANDEVILLE

19. *Le Comte de Maundevill esquartele d'or et de gules.*

Cf. 19, —, 67: MP I. 25, 43.

William de Mandeville, Earl of Essex, brother of Geoffrey de Mandeville, Earl of Essex (MP I. 25) and s. of Geoffrey FitzPiers, Earl of Essex, d.s.p. 1227: same person as MP I. 43. (*CP* v. 130–3.)

WARWICK

20. *Le Comte de Warwik escheker d'or et d'azur ove un cheveron d'ermyn.*

Cf. 20, 9, 51: MP I. 70: C 144.

Thomas, Earl of Warwick, d.s.p. 1242: same person as MP I. 70. (*CP* xii (2) 365.)

BURGH

21. *Le Comte de Kent masclee de veer et de gules.*
(*a*) *Lozengy gules and vair.*

Cf. 21, 10, 57: MP I. 73.

Hubert de Burgh, Justiciar and Regent of England 1216–27, Earl of Kent 1227, d. 1243: same person as MP I. 73. (*CP* vii. 133–42.)

LONGESPÉE

22. *Le Conte de Salesbury d'azur vi leonceux d'or.*

Cf. 22, 11, 66: MP I. 40; II. 8.

B IV adds the surname 'Longespée'.

William de Longespée, Earl of Salisbury, d. 1226 (MP I. 40). This entry might refer to his s. William who d. 1250 (MP I. 90), although the latter was unsuccessful in his claim to the earldom. It might even apply to the latter's s. William who d.s.p.m. 1257, and whose dau. Margaret commonly called Countess of Salisbury, m. Henry de Lacy, Earl of Lincoln. (*CP* xi. 379–84.)

LUSIGNAN VALENCE

23. *Will'm de Valence burle d'argent et d'asur ove la bordure des merloz de gules.*
(*a*) tricks the buruly of 14 stripes, (*b*) of 10.

Cf. 23, 13, 44: MP I. 83; II. 63, 64; IV. 72: C 71.

William de Valence, half-brother of Henry III, came to England in 1247 and d. 1296: same person as MP I. 83. (*CP* x. 377–81.)

PLESCY

24. *Sire Johan de Pleysys d'argent ove six fauses roueles de gules.*
(*a*) and (*b*) Six annulets.

Cf. 24, 12, —.

This entry probably refers to John de Plescy (Plessis or Plassetis), who m. Margaret, sister and h. of Thomas, Earl of Warwick (B 20), and was invested with the earldom in 1247. (*CP* xii (2) 366–7.) The inclusion of Sir John among the barons shows that the compiler included earlier material without bringing it up to date. John de Plescy was a Poitevin, perhaps a younger brother of Pierre, seigneur de Plessis, and d. 1263, leaving a s. Hugh by his first wife Christian, dau. and h. of Hugh de Sandford of Hooknorton. His second wife predeceased him without issue and the earldom passed to her cousin William Mauduit. (*CP* x. 548.)

MUNCHENSY

25. *Warin de Mounchansy d'or ove trois escucheons barres de veer et de gules.*
(*a*) *Escutcheons barry of six vair and gules.*
(*b*) *Escutcheons gules each with two bars vair.*

Cf. 25, 14, 76: MP VI. 11; VII. 7: C 87.

Warin de Munchensy of Winfarthing, Norfolk, was brother of William de Munchensy (dead 1208) and d. 1255: same person as MP VI. 11. (*CP* ix. 421; Manning and Bray, *History of Surrey*, ii. 269.) His s. William was summoned to Parliament 1264, d. 1289; he must have been the William of B III. 14.

B I and B II blazon the escutcheons barry, while B III and B IV say bendy, but all four versions draw barry. This is an instance of the early use of bend and cognate terms in the sense of stripe irrespective of direction. The drawings have five, six, and eight respectively, showing that little importance was attached to the number of stripes in such coats. More striking are the facts that MP makes the escutcheons wholly vair (VI. 11), that Warin's widow, Denise, dau. and h. of Nicholas de Anesty, sealed with three escutcheons of vair (Birch 6685), and that this version is also given for William in D 131, although E 149 and F 30 make his escutcheons barry as here.

CHAMBERLAIN

26. *Herberd Chamberleyn de gules ove trois skalops d'or.*
(*b*) 'Harbart the Chamberlen'.

Cf. 26, —, —: B 39.

Herbert Chamberlain may possibly be identified with Herbert FitzPiers of Blaen Llyfni, s. of Piers FitzHerbert, who d.s.p. shortly before 27 May 1248. (*CP* v. 465 n. (*d*).) Piers Fitz-Herbert was the second s. of Herbert FitzHerbert who was gds. of Herbert the Chamberlain of Henry I, and whose elder s. and one gds. were also Chamberlains. (Tout, *Chapters in the Administrative History of Medieval England*, i. 76–77; Eyton, *Antiquities of Shropshire*, vii. 146–56; *EYC* ii. 167–8.) However, later members of the family of FitzHerbert bore three lions rampant, and the arms here suggest a relationship to Martin Chamberlain (B 39), whose family is centred in East Anglia and who appears to have no connexion with the Chamberlain/FitzHerbert family whose property was in Yorkshire, Shropshire, and Hereford.

CAUNTELO

27. *Will'm de Cantelowe de gules ove trois floretts d'or.*
(*a*) and (*b*) *Three leopards' faces jessant de lis.*

Cf. 27, 15, 74: MP I. 54; II. 26; IV. 77; VI. 10; VII. 5.

William de Cauntelo, s. of William de Cauntelo (MP I. 54), d. 1251 (MP II. 26), or former's s. William de Cauntelo who d. 1254. (*CP* i. 22–23; iii. 111.)

Although all four versions blazon the arms with fleurs-de-lis and B III and B IV paint fleurs-de-lis, both B I and B I (*b*) trick leopard faces jessant de lis, thus proving that the tricks are not contemporary with the compilation.

This odd charge, which modern heralds blazon as a leopard's head jessant de lis, that is sprouting a fleur-de-lis (the head, or rather mask, may be inverted or not), has never been adequately studied. In the case of the Cauntelo family the available evidence is far from clear, but it may be suggested with some diffidence that it is a cadency brisure for the sake of the cant, *tête de lupar* (leopard) or *de loup* (wolf). In any case *Gules, three fleurs-de-lis or* is the early form of the arms, and that seems to have been retained in the senior line as long as there was a male surviving. Three fleurs-de-lis are on seals of William, s. of William de Cauntelo (MP I. 54), which Birch dates *c.* 1228–9, and on the seal of the same, or of another, William early in Henry III's reign (Birch 8312, 8310). They are also on the seals of William de Cauntelo (MP II. 26) in 1248 and on that of Millicent, dau. of William (d. 1234) in 1287 (*Book of Seals*, 346, 137), while *Gules, three fleurs-de-lis or* is attributed to Sir George Cauntelo, her brother (D 107; E 246; F 60). It is true that HE 143 paints Sir George's arms as *Gules, three leopards faces inverted jessant de lis or* (*Heralds' Commemoration Exhibition Catalogue* (1934), pl. XX), but that seems to be the only place where the charge is attributed to the senior line, and it is belied by the Fitzwilliam version of that roll (FW 116) which gives Sir George the three fleurs-de-lis without any leopards' heads. The Everard Green version also belies Heralds' Roll. In this Sir George's arms appear as *Gules, three fleurs-de-lis argent,* each with an inverted leopard-face of gold superimposed (no. 90), but a scrutiny of the Roll shows that the shield was originally painted with three white fleurs-de-lis and that the leopard-faces were added afterwards.

For the cadets the evidence is too confused to be examined here. It must suffice to say that the earliest known appearance of the heads is on the seal of Sir Nicholas de Cauntelo, a younger brother of William de Cauntelo (d. 1254), who bore *Three leopard faces jessant de lis between three crosses crosslet* (seal, 13th cent.; Birch 8308); and his s. William, Lord Cauntelo 1299 (d. 1301), is assigned *Gules, a fess vair between three leopard faces jessant de lis or* (H 73; K line 381). His seal on the Barons' Letter 1301 shows a fess between three fleurs-de-lis without heads. Most of the later entries of the coat in the rolls give leopard-faces jessant de lis, and it would seem that the heads were first added by Sir Nicholas de Cauntelo near the end of the thirteenth century.

It may be mentioned that the Everard Green version of the Heralds' Roll gives for John de Cauntelo *Azure, three inverted leopard faces jessant de lis or* (142). In this case there is nothing to suggest that the roll has been tampered with. The John in question is presumably the younger brother of the Nicholas mentioned above.

FITZGEOFFREY

28. *Johan le fitz Geffrey esquartele d'or et de gules ove la bordure de veer.*

Cf. 28, 16, 75: C. 59.

John FitzGeoffrey, Justiciar of Ireland 1245–56, d. 1258, s. of Geoffrey FitzPiers, Earl of Essex (see B 19), by his second wife Aveline de Clare. His half-brothers Geoffrey and William de Mandeville, earls of Essex (d. 1216 and 1227), discarded the bordure. B II assigns this coat to his s. John FitzJohn, Lord FitzJohn 1264, d. 1276 (C 59), thus showing that that version was not compiled before 1258. (*CP* v. 122, 433.)

Geoffrey FitzPiers was the second s., but eventually h., of Piers de Ludgarshall, who is said in The Rows Roll to have borne *Vair plain.* (*The Rows or Warwick Roll*, ed. Courthope, 1859, no. 45.) This may explain the bordure, and it seems a more likely explanation than the escutcheons of vair in the arms of Aveline's first husband William de Munchensy (see B 25). On the other hand, it is conceivable that Rows inferred the Ludgarshall vair from John's bordure.

SAY

29. *Will'm de Say au tiel sanz le bordure.*
(*a*) and (*b*) *Quarterly or and gules.*

Cf. 29, 20, —.

William de Say, gtgds. of William de Say by Beatrice, sister of Geoffrey, aunt and eventually h. of Geoffrey de Mandeville, Earl of Essex; he d. 1272. (*CP* xi. 470; Birch 13318.) The arms were also borne by Mandeville (see B 19).

CLIFFORD

30. *Walter de Clifford eschekere d'or et d'asur ove une bende de gules.*

Cf. 30, 17, 94: MP II. 104: B 31.

Walter, s. of Walter de Clifford of Clifford, Hereford, succ. 1222, d.s.p.m. 1263, and was succ. by his nephew Roger de Clifford (B 31). (Dugd. *Bar.* i. 336–7.) His nephew changed the bend to a fess, which he retained even after succeeding to the family estates.

CLIFFORD

31. *Roger de Clifford au tiel ove une fesse de gules.*
(*a*) and (*b*) *Checky or and azure a fess gules.*

Cf. 31, 18, 93: B 30.

B IV blazons Roger's arms with a bend but paints with a fess. The other versions both blazon and paint a fess.
    Roger de Clifford, nephew and h. of Walter de Clifford (B 30), was s. of Roger de Clifford (d.v.p. 1231/2). He d. 1285 and was succ. by his gds. Robert, s. of Roger (d.v.p. 1282) by Isabel, dau. and h. of Robert de Vipont. (*CP* iii. 290; Dugd. *Bar.* i. 336–7.)

MORTIMER of Wigmore

32. *Roger de Mortymer bende a chief pale a corneres geronne [d'or et d'azur] ove un escucheon [d'argent].*
(*a*) *Barry of six, on a chief a pale, the corners gyronny, over all an escutcheon.*
(*b*) As (*a*) but with two pales on the chief.

Cf. 32, —, 73: C 102.

Version (*a*) omits the tinctures, but they are given in B I (*b*) and B II. The simple blazon of B I and B II (the latter substitutes 'barre' for I's 'bende'), may be compared with the more complicated version on B IV where the shield is painted like (*a*) trick. On the origin of this coat see Wagner, *Historic Heraldry*, p. 51.
    Roger de Mortimer of Wigmore, s. of Ralph de Mortimer (d. 1246), d. 1282. (*CP* ix. 276–81.)

VAUX of Gilsland

33. *Johan de Vaulx eschekere d'argent et de gules.*

Cf. 33, 19, 98: C 164.

John de Vaux, s. of Robert, succ. his brother William before 1253, and d. 1287 leaving two daughters and coheiresses. (Dugd. *Bar.* i. 526; *Cal. Inq.* ii, no. 653.)

LEYBURN

34. *Roger de Leyburn' d'azur od six leonceulx d'argent.*

Cf. 34, —, —: C 74.

Roger de Leyburn, s. of Roger de Leyburn (d. *c.* 1251), d. 1271. (*CP* vii. 631–4.)

BASSINGBOURNE

35. *Warin de Bassingburn' geronne d'or et d'asur.*
(*a*) *Gyronny of twelve pieces.*
(*b*) and B IV. *Gyronny of eight pieces.*
    B III. *Gyronny of six per pale and per saltire.*

Cf. 35, 21, 135: MP II. 29: C 136.

Warin de Bassingbourne was probably gds. of John de Bassingbourne (MP II. 29), and was dead 1269. (*Cal. Inq.* i, no. 708.)

BALLIOL

36. *Johan de Baillol de gules od un faus escuchon d'argent.*

Cf. 36, 22, 95: MP II. 53: B 37, 38, 40.

John de Balliol, Regent of Scotland, m. Devorguilla of Galloway, d. 1268: same person as MP II. 53. (Clay, *Extinct and Dormant Peerages*, p. 6; *NCH* vi. 73.)

BALLIOL

37. *Hugh son filz au tiel od un escuchon d'asur ove un leon d'argent coronne d'or en la cornere.*

(*a*) and (*b*) The blue escutcheon fills the voiding of the Balliol charge.

Cf. 37, 23, 127: B 36, 38, 40.

Hugh de Balliol was the eldest s. of John (MP II. 53: B 36), whose arms he differences by adding an escutcheon of his mother's arms. B IV calls him Hugh Balliol of Bywell; he d.s.p.c. 1271. (Clay, *Extinct and Dormant Peerages*, p. 6; *NCH* vi. 74.)

The blazon in B I and B II can only mean that the shield of Galloway was borne in one or other canton, and his seal of *c.* 1269 shows the voided escutcheon of Balliol with the shield of Galloway over all in the sinister canton. Nevertheless, all four versions of this roll draw the coat with the shield of Galloway filling the void of the Balliol charge. B III. 23 omits the words *en la cornere* and the blazons both of B IV and TJ 100 expressly describe the blue escutcheon as 'dedenz'.

BALLIOL of Red Castle and Tours

38. *Eustas de Tours au tiel od un label d'or.*

(*a*) and (*b*) *Gules, a voided escutcheon argent and a label or.*

Cf. 38, 24, —: B 36, 37, 40: C 142.

'Au tiel' refers back to no. 36. The description 'de Tours' identifies this as Eustace de Balliol of Red Castle, co. Forfar, and of Tours. He was living 1284. Surtees, *Durham*, iv. 60 makes his father Ingelram (living 1228) to be a younger s. of Bernard de Balliol of Bywell, great-grand-father of John de Balliol (MP II. 53), but J. R. Walbran (*History of Gainford*, facing p. 147) makes Bernard and Ingelram cousins. Tours has not been identified.

CHAMBERLAIN

39. *Martin Chaumberleyn de gules ove trois skalops d'or.*

Cf. 39, —, —: B 26.

Martin the Chamberlain held of the Earl of Oxford in Cambridgeshire and Essex *c.* 1236–48. (*Book of Fees*, 580, 608, 900, 921, 925, 1162; Farrer, *Feudal Cambs.*, p. 122.) He also held of the honour of Richmond in 1236. (Farrer, *Feudal Cambs.*, p. 24.) He was perhaps chamberlain to the Earl of Oxford or to the Earl of Richmond.

BALLIOL

40. *Eustace de Baillol dazur al faus escuchon d'or al croisel d'or.*

(*a*) *A voided escutcheon in an orle of eight crosses crosslet, with three more in the voiding.*

(*b*) *Azure, a cross crosslet within a voided escutcheon or.*

Cf. 40, —, —: MP II. 54.

He was a younger brother of John de Balliol, Regent of Scotland (MP II. 53; *NCH* vi. 73): same person as MP II. 54.

PERCY

41. *Henry de Percy d'azur od le fesse engrele d'or.*

(*a*) and (*b*) *A fess of five fusils.*

> Cf. 41, —, 83: MP II. 52.

> Henry de Percy, succ. 1245 and d. 1272. He was s. of William de Percy who was s. of Henry, elder brother of Richard de Percy (MP II. 52). (*CP* x. 455–6.)
>
> B IV blazons the fess indented but paints a fess of five fusils as in B I and that has always been the normal form. The fusils have been sometimes called mill-picks, which may be a pun on the idea of piercing. (*Arch. Aeliana*, N.S. iv. 164, cf. Montagu (B 44).)

GREY of Codnor

42. *Richard de Grey barre d'argent et d'asur.*

(*a*) and (*b*) *Barry of six.*

> Cf. 42, —, —: MP II. 68.

43. *Johan de Grey au tiel od un label de gules.*

(*a*) *A fess of five fusils and a label.*

(*b*) *Or, a dance azure and a label gules.*

These two entries have been considered together because they have been interchanged.

> Cf. 43, —, —.

> Richard de Grey of Codnor, d. 1271: same person as MP II. 68. He was succ. by his s. John de Grey who d. 1271/2 (B 43). (*CP* vi. 133–5.) Both sealed with a barry of six pieces, John differencing with a label of five points. (Birch 6078, 10260.)
>
> In B I the items are interchanged making John's 'au tiel' refer to the Percy fess. B II gives them in the correct order.
>
> The trick in B I (*b*) of a dance for a fess is a mistake which is paralleled in the Parliamentary Roll in two instances. Sir Philip de Neville's arms (N 659) are blazoned with a dance although he actually bore the fusilly fess of Daubeney, and the fusilly fess of Montagu (N 149) is called a dance.

MONTAGU

44. *Will'm Mountagu blank od un fesse engrelle de trois peices de gules.*

(*a*) *A fess of three fusils not reaching the sides of the shield.*

(*b*) *Argent a fess of five fusils gules.*

> Cf. 44, —, —.

> The words *de trois peices* have been supplied from B II. They must have been lacking in the original text for B I (*a*) omits them and B I (*b*) draws the fess of five fusils. The sharp-pointed fusils may allude to the name Mont-aigu. William de Montagu of Shepton Montacute, Somerset, d. 1270. (*CP* ix. 77.)

DEVEREUX

45. *Will'm de Everus gules od un fesse d'argent ove trois turteaus d'argent en le chief.*

(*b*) *Argent, fess and three roundels in chief gules* (i.e. the tinctures transposed).

> Cf. 45, 25, —.

> Sir William Devereux of Lyonshall, Herefords., s. of Stephen Devereux, d. 1265. (Dugd. *Bar.* ii. 175.) B II and B III both tincture the arms as in A and that coat is given in F 80 and E 57 and later rolls. The version (B I (*b*) with the tinctures reversed is the coat of Devereux of Bodenham, Lords Ferrers of Chartley, Viscounts Hereford, and Earls of Essex, whose kinship to this line has not been ascertained.

DAKENY

46. *Baudewin de Abygny d'azur od la crois d'or et quartier leunces d'or.*

(*a*) Trick blank.

(*b*) 'Bauldewen Albignye', *Azure a cross and a canton or.*

Cf. 46, 26, —.

B III gives the name as 'Baudewin Dakeni', B II as 'William Dakigny'; the latter has not been identified. Baldwin (possibly s. of Roger) de Akinny or d'Acquigny, of Whittlesford, Cambs., and of Holkham, Norfolk, fl. 1241–69. (*Feudal Cambs.* 260; *Cal. Charter Rolls*, ii. 73; *Cal. Pat. Rolls*, 1266–72, p. 332).

The name appears later as Dakeny (E 120; N 611; TJ 72) and in Tudor manuscripts (e.g. Walls Book of Arms, Glover's Ordinary) it becomes Dabeny or Dawbeny, a perversion which may perhaps be traced to the marriage of Roger Dakeny (d. 1286) to Joan, dau. of William d'Aubigny. (*Beds. Hist. Rec. Soc.* xix. 149, 170; *Cal. Inq.* ii, no. 616.)

The arms are given correctly in B III (*b*) *A cross between four lions or.* In B I (*a*) Glover wrote *quartier lentes* and in B II *quartires leonceus. Lentes* must be a misreading of *leuces*, i.e. leunces or leonceux, while *quartier* and *quartires* are obviously meant for *quatre.* B I (*b*)'s cross and canton can only be explained on the assumption that Cooke took *quartier* for *quarter* and ignored *lentes* or *leuces*, failing to recognize it as a contraction for leonceux.

MARMION

47. *Will'm Marmyon de veer od un fesse de gules.*

Cf. 47, 27, —: B 57: C 159.

William Marmion, s. of Robert Marmion of Tamworth, Staffs. (d. 1241/2), was dead 1276. (*CP* viii. 514–18.) For a discussion on the arms see Appendix I.

BRUCE of Skelton

48. *Piers de Brus d'argent od un leon d'azur.*

Cf. 48, 28, 96.

Piers de Brus, or Bruce, Lord of Skelton and Annandale, succ. 1242, and d. 1272, leaving as coh. his four sisters, Agnes, wife of Walter de Fauconberg (B 201), Lucy, wife of Marmaduke de Thweng (B 133), Margaret, wife of Robert de Ros (B 173), and Laderana, wife of John Bellew. His mother was Hawise, sister and coh. of William de Lancaster, Lord of Kendal (MP II. 74: B 49). (*CP* v. 267–8; *Yorks. Arch. Journ.* xiii. 246–7).

LANCASTER

49. *Will'm de Lancastre d'argent od deus bastons de gules od un quartier de gules od un leopard d'or en le quartier.*

(*a*) and (*b*) *Two bars on a canton a lion passant gardant.*

Cf. 49, —, —: MP II. 74.

B II blazons 'deux barre'. William de Lancaster d.s.p. 1246 (*CP* vii. 371): same person as MP II. 74.

TATESHAL or TATTERSHALL

50. *Robert de Tatreshale eschekere d'or et de gules od un chief enermyne.*

(*a*) and (*b*) *Checky, a chief ermine.*

Cf. 50, 29, 99: MP II. 61.

Robert de Tateshal of Lincs., s. of Robert (MP II. 61), d. 1273. (*CP* xii (1) 649–50.) *Enermyne* is probably a participle meaning ermined.

WAKE

51. *Hugh' Wake d'or deux barres de gules od trois turteux de gules en chief.*

Cf. 51, 30, 77: MP IV. 50, 53.

Hugh Wake of Bourne, d. 1241 (*CP* xii (2) 298–9): same person as MP IV. 53.

STAFFORD

52. *Robert de Estafford d'argent od un cheveron de gules besande d'or.*

(*a*) *Three bezants on the chevron.*

(*b*) *Argent, on a chevron gules three martlets.*

Cf. 52, 31, 78.

Robert de Stafford succ. his brother Hervey in 1241, both being sons of another Hervey: d. 1261. (*CP* xii (1) 171–2.)

B I, B II, and B III all make the field silver, but some of the later rolls (e.g. E 656, F 420, TJ 1583) make it gold and the roundels silver.

Robert's gds. Edmund was summ. to Parliament in 1298 as Baron Stafford, and it is probably to him that B IV refers: he removed the bezants and bore, *a chevron* (seal, Barons' Letter 1301).

WELLE

53. *Robert de Welle d'argent od deux bastons de geules bezante d'or.*

(*a*) *Two bars with three bezants on each.*

(*b*) *Argent, on two bars gules six bezants.*

Cf. 53, 32, —.

All three versions blazon this with bastons but only B I (*b*) draws bends. B I (*a*) and B III both draw bars. His seal shows two bars. (Birch 14344.) Robert de Welle, s. of William de Welle of Well, Withern, Lincs., d. 1265. (*CP* xii (2) 438; *Misc. Gen. et Her.* 5th s. ix. 44.)

BEAUCHAMP of Bedford

54. *Will'm Beauchamp esquartele d'or et de gules od un bend de gules.*

Cf. 54, 33, 79: MP II. 28, 76: B 196.

William de Beauchamp, d. 1260: same person as MP II. 28. (Dugd. *Bar.* i. 224.)

BREWES

55. *Will'm de Breuse d'azur od un leon d'or croiselez d'or.*

(*a*) *Crusuly of ten crosses crosslet dispersed irregularly.*

(*b*) Gives the lion a gold crown.

Cf. 55, 35 —: MP IV. 7, 27.

William de Brewes, Lord of Bramber and Gower, succ. 1232, d. 1290. He was s. of John, who was s. of William de Brewes (MP IV. 7). (*CP* ii. 302.)

B III (*a*) and (*c*) paint the crusuly of plain crosses couped, but B I and B III (*b*) trick the crosses crosslet and they are so engraved on the seal of William's s., William de Brewes, in 1324, the lion being uncrowned. (Birch 7797.)

CHAWORTH, CHAURCES

56. *Patrick de Chaursey burle d'argent et de gules.*

(*a*) *Buruly of twelve pieces.*

(*b*) *Barry of six pieces argent and gules, an orle of martlets sable.*

Cf. 56, 36, —.

B II, like B I (*a*), blazons the arms as *Barry argent and gules*, but B III, like B I (*b*), adds *an orle of sable martlets.*

Patrick, s. of Pain de Chaworth (d. 1237), d. 1258, was succ. by his sons Pain (d.s.p. 1279) and Patrick. The latter d. 1283 s.p.m. holding Stoke Bruerne, Shittlehanger, and Alderton, Northants. (*HKF* iii. 414; Dugd. *Bar.* i. 517.)

About 1235 the elder Pain sealed with a barry shield (*Book of Seals*, 470; Birch 5802), but by 1270 the younger Pain and by 1280 his brother Patrick had added *an orle of martlets*. (Birch 5803, 8512.) The omission of the martlets in B I and B II and their inclusion in B III confirms that B I used the 1240 collection and suggests that the martlets were added by Patrick who d. 1258. Nevertheless, the barry coat without martlets is given in FW 129. The orle of martlets appears in E 87 and later rolls.

MARMION

57. *Philip Marmyon de veer od la fesse de paile.*
(*a*) Vair, a fess gules fretty or.

Cf. 57, —, —: B 47: C 159.

For discussion of these arms see Appendix I.

Sir Philip Marmion, s. of Robert Marmion, who was elder half-brother of Robert Marmion, father of William Marmion (B 47); Sir Philip d.s.p.m. legit. 1291. (*CP* viii. 510–12.)

DUNSTANVILLE

58. *Walter de Dunstanvill d'argent frette de gules od un quartier de gules od un leopard d'or en le quartier.*
(*a*) Fretty of six bastons.

Cf. 58, —, —.

Walter de Dunstanville of Castlecombe, Wilts., succ. 1240, d. 1270, leaving a daughter Petronilla, wife of Robert de Montfort. (Dugd. *Bar.* i. 591.)

NEVILLE of Raby

59. *Robert de Nevill de gules od un saut' d'argent.*

Cf. 59, 37, 84: C 135.

The Nevilles of Raby, co. Durham, were descended from Robert FitzMeldred, whose seal displays a saltire. (Durham Seals 1742.)

B IV describes Robert as of Raby. He had succ. his father Geoffrey by 1242 and d. 1282. (*CP* ix. 495–6.)

PECCHE of Bourne

60. *Gilbert Pecche d'argent od deus cheverons de gules od la fesse de gules.*

Cf. 60, 38, —: MP II. 33.

Gilbert Pecche of Bourn, Cambs., s. of Hamo Pecche (MP II. 33), succ. 1241, d. 1291. (*CP* x. 334–5.)

CREVEQUER

61. *Hamon Crevecœur d'or ove une faux crois de gules.*

Cf. 61, 39 —: MP II. 66.

Hamo de Crevequer, d. 1263: same person as MP II. 66.

MOHUN

62. *Reynaud de Moun gules ove le maunche d'ermyne.*

Cf. 62, 40, 125.

B II blazons the maunch argent, but other versions ermine, which is correct.

Reynold de Mohun of Dunster, Som., succ. his father Reynold in 1213 and d. 1258. (*CP* ix. 19–20.) His gtgds. John de Mohun (d. 1330) changed the arms to *Or, a cross engrailed sable*, probably derived from the saltire engrailed of his wife Ada, dau. of Robert de Tibetot. (Seal 1301, Barons' Letter; *CP* ix. 19–20.)

AGUILLON

63. *Robert Agulon de gules ove une flour d'argent.*

(*a*) *A fleur-de-lis.*

(*b*) Tricks the field azure.

Cf. 63, 41 —: C 158.

Robert Aguillon of Perching, Sussex, s. of William Aguillon (d. 1244), Sheriff of Surrey and Sussex 1267; d. 1286. (*Suss. Arch. Coll.* lxxix. 56 sqq.) C 158 makes the fleur-de-lis or.

CAMOYS

64. *Rauf de Camoys d'or a chief de gules od trois turteux d'argent el chief.*

Cf. 64, 42, 97.

Ralph de Camoys d. 1259. His s. Ralph (C 151) d. 1277. (*CP* ii. 506.)

MAUDUIT

65. *Will'm Maudeut d'argent od deus barres de gules.*

Cf. 65, 43, 126: MP II. 75: B 83.

William Mauduit of Hanslope, Bucks., d. 1256: same person as MP II. 75. B III makes the bars much narrower than in other cases. In B III the entry in copies (*a*) and (*b*) is virtually identical with B I and B II, viz. *Willame Maudit de argent a deus barres de gul'*. Copy (*b*), on the other hand, has this: *Will'm Martyn de argent two barres gules. W'm Maudet port le mesme.* This must be an emendation by the copyist of (*b*), since the William Martin to whom the entry presumably refers was only born *c.* 1257. He succ. his grandfather Nicholas as Lord of Kemeys in 1282, was summoned to Parliament in 1295, and died in 1324.

ROS of Helmsley

66. *Will'm de Ros de gules a trois bouz d'argent.*

(*a*) and (*b*) *Three bougets.*

Cf. 66, 44, 82: MP II. 55: B 67, 173.

William de Ros of Helmsley, s. of Robert de Ros (MP II. 55), d. 1264. He was father of Robert (B 67), and elder brother of Robert de Ros of Wark (B 173). (*CP* xi. 93.)

ROS of Belvoir

67. *Robert son filz au tiel od label d'asur.*

Cf. 67, 45, —: MP II. 55: B 66, 173: C 132.

Robert de Ros, s. of William (B 66), d. 1285. He acquired Belvoir by his marriage to Isabel, dau. and h. of William Daubeney of Belvoir (B 68). (*CP* xi. 95.)

DAUBENEY of Belvoir

68. *Will'm Daubeney de Beauvoir d'or a deus cheverons de gules et la bordure de gules.*

Cf. 68, 46, 100: MP I. 52; II. 21.

William Daubeney, s. of William Daubeney (MP I. 52), d.s.p.m. 1247. His dau. and h. m. Robert de Ros (B 67). (*HMC Rutland Papers*, iv. 106, &c.; Nichols, *Leics.* ii. pt. 1, p. 27.)

HARCOURT

69. *Richard de Harecourt d'or od deus barres de gules.*

Cf. 69, 47, 124.

Sir Richard Harcourt held lands in Market Bosworth, Leics., of the Earl of Winchester, and also lands at Staunton, Oxon.; d. 1258. (*Cal. Inq.* i, no. 411.)

BARDOLF of Wormegay

70. *Will'm Bardolf d'azur od trois quintefoilles d'or.*
(*a*) and (*b*) The cinquefoils pierced.

71. *Thomas son filz au tiel a croisseles d'or.*
(*a*) *Semy of nine crosses crosslet, three pierced cinquefoils.*
(*b*) *Azure, three pierced cinquefoils or and a label gules.*

Cf. 70, 48, 101: C 137, 138.

Cf. 71, —, —.

William Bardolf succ. his father Doun or Dodo in 1209 and d. 1275. He inherited the barony of Wormegay, Norfolk, from his mother Beatrix de Warenne. He was succ. by his s. William (C 138). (Dugd. *Bar.* i. 681; *CP* i. 417.) Neither Dugdale nor *CP* mention any Thomas, but Thomas Bardolf and his father are named as overlords at Hallington, Lincs., in 1267. Whether this Thomas is identical with C 137 is doubtful.

GAUNT

72. *Gilbert de Gaunt barre d'argent et d'asur od un bende de gules.*
(*a*) and (*b*) *Barry of six pieces argent and azure, a bend gules.*

Cf. 72, 49, 102: MP IV. 54: C 86.

Both B I and B II make the field argent and azure, but B III and B IV say or and azure. This probably intended for Gilbert de Gaunt of Hunmanby and Swaledale, Yorks., second but eldest surviving s. of Gilbert de Gaunt (MP IV. 54). He d. 1274. Version II substitutes an unidentified William for Gilbert. (*CP* v. 625, vii. 672–5; *Ancestor*, ix. 143.)

GRELLEY

73. *Thomas Greley de gules od trois bendes d'or en beliff.*
(*a*) *Three bends not enhanced.*
(*b*) *Gules, three bends enhanced or.*

Cf. 73, 50, —.

Thomas de Grelle, Grelley, or Gresley, succ. 1230, d. 1262. (*CP* vi. 107 n. (*d*); *VCH Lancs.* i. 326, &c.) B I (*a*) and B II blazon the 'bendes' as *en beliff* to show that they are slantwise and not bars as in some other cases. B III 50 omits *en beliff*.

E 53 and other early rolls give the arms as drawn in B I and B III, but later rollsfrom CVL onwards enhance the bends as in B I (*b*)'s trick.

MOWBRAY

74. *Roger de Mowbray de gules od un leon d'argent.*

Cf. 74, 51, 85: C 131.

Roger, younger s. of William de Mowbray of Lincs. (d. *c.* 1224), succ. his elder brother Nele in 1230 and d. *c.* November 1266. His s. Roger de Mowbray (C 131) was summ. as Lord Mowbray in 1295 and d. 1297. (*CP* ix. 375; Birch 12005.)

The family descended from Nele d'Aubigny, younger brother of William (d. 1139) (MP I. 36), and Smith Ellis deduced that the Mowbray lion is that of d'Aubigny differenced. (Smith Ellis, *Antiquities of Heraldry*, p. 207.)

PLATE III

93

151

76

184

95

136

103

GLOVERS ROLL. NOS. 93, 151, 76, 184, 95, 136, 103

HANSARD

75. *Gilbert Haunsard de gules od trois estoilles d'argent.*
(*a*) *Three six-pointed mullets.*
(*b*) *Gules, three estoiles with eight wavy rays argent.*

Cf. 75, 52, —.

Sir Gilbert Hansard, s. of Sir John, occurs from 1252 (*Cal. Charter Rolls*, 9 Nov. 1252, p. 409) and was dead by May 1301. (*Cal. Close Rolls*, Edw. I, iv. 491.)

B III draws the 'estoiles' as mullets and that is the usual form of the arms—see, for example, E, F, and later rolls. Estoile is also used for mullet in K both for Hansard and for Vere.

VESCY

76. *Will'm de Vescy de gules od une crois d'argent furchee.*
(*a*) *A cross patonce,* see plate III.
(*b*) *Gules, a cross patonce argent*: and below that a small shield, *Sable, a plain cross or.*

Cf. 76, 53 —: MP I. 26, 102; II. 35; IV. 11, 84.

Sir William de Vescy of Alnwick and Malton, Northumb., d. 1253. He was s. of Eustace de Vescy (d. 1216; MP I. 26; IV. 11) and father of John (d.s.p. 1288/9) and of William (d.s.p. legit 1297). (*CP* xii (1 (ii)) 276–83.): same person as MP I. 102.

Cross fourchy is now generally taken to mean either a cross moline, or one similarly forked but with the eight points cut off straight. In MP (I. 102; IV. 84; cf. II. 35) the cross is moline, but for Eustace it is patonce (I. 26; IV. 11) as is tricked here, and such a cross is on the seals of William de Vescy who d. 1297, and on that of his mother Agnes de Ferrers. (Birch 14111, 6726; *Durham Seals*, 2537, 2540; *Book of Seals*, 525.) The tomb of his illegitimate s. William of Kildare (Lawrance, p. 47) shows a cross patonce with a bend over all, although N 1030 gives him *Or, a cross sable.*

B II describes the cross as *patonce* but that term is otherwise unknown before the sixteenth century and it may be Glover's translation of patee. B I (*b*)'s second trick is an inversion, possibly accidental, of the coat *Or, a cross sable,* which was used side by side with the cross patonce and which was taken by Sir Gilbert de Aton on his succeeding William of Kildare in the Vescy estate (see *The Pedigrees and Early Heraldry of the Lords of Alnwick,* by George Tate and W. H. D. Longstaffe, Alnwick, 1866). B III has confused the two coats, for it omits *furchee* from the blazon and paints *Gules, a plain cross argent.*

FITZPIERS

77. *Reynaud le fitz Piers de gules od trois leonceux d'or.*

Cf. 77, 54, —: MP I. 74; II. 71; IV. 61: B 78.

Sir Reynold FitzPiers, s. of Piers FitzHerbert, who was brother of Matthew FitzHerbert, father of Herbert FitzMatthew (MP I. 74: B 78), m. as second wife Joan, dau. and h. of William le Fort de Vivonne (B 194); d. 1286. He was cousin of Herbert FitzMatthew (MP I. 74). (*CP* v. 465.)

FITZMATTHEW or HERBERT

78. *Herberd le fiz Maheu party d'azur et de gules od trois leonceux d'or.*
(*b*) *Per pale argent and gules, three lions rampant or.*

Cf. 78, —, —: MP I. 74; II. 71; IV. 61: B 77.

Herbert FitzMatthew of Stokenham, Devon, d.s.p. 1245. (*CP* v. 442.): same person as MP I 74.

KERDESTON

79. *Fuke de Escherdestone de gules od un salter d'argent engrelle.*
(*a*) and (*b*) *A saltire engrailed.*

> Cf. 79, —, —: C 139.

> In 1242/3 Fulk de Kerdeston held of Walter FitzRobert in East Ryston, Norfolk. He also held in Newton, Norfolk. (*Book of Fees*, 903, 909.)

MONTFICHET

80. *Richard de Mounfychet d'or od trois cheverons de gules od label d'azur.*

> Cf. 80, —, —: MP II. 24.

> B II reverses the tinctures and blazons *Gules, three chevrons or and a label azure* though Matthew tinctures as here. Richard de Montfichet, d. 1267: same person as MP II. 24. (Farrer, *Feudal Cambs.*, p. 234.)

CLARE

81. *Will'm de Clare au tiel.*
(*a*) and (*b*) *Or, three chevrons gules and a label azure.*

> Cf. 81, —, —: MP I. 46, 76: B 5: C 73.

> William, brother of Richard de Clare (MP I. 76), was born 1228 and d. of poison at breakfast with Prince Edward at Winchester in 1258. (*CP* v. 695, n. (*m*).) Thomas de Clare, who bore the same arms (C 73), was his nephew.

DOUVRES

82. *Richard de Douvre de gules a deux leopardz d'or.*

> Cf. 82, —, —.

> Richard, bastard s. of King John, variously known as FitzRoy, de Warenne, de Chilham, or de Dover, d. late 1245 or early 1246, leaving by his wife Rohese, dau. and h. of Fulbert de Douvres, Lord of Chilham, Kent, a s. Richard who m. as second husband Maud, Countess of Angus (*New England Historical and Genealogical Register*, cv. 39–40; *Genealogist*, N.S. xxii. 105–10; Sandford, p. 57.) The name comes from Douvres, about 10 km. north of Caen. (Round, *Family Origins*, p. 213.)

MOELS

83. *Nichol de Moeles d'argent od deux barres de gules ove trois moeles de gules en le chief.*
(*a*) *Two bars with three roundels in chief.*
(*b*) *Argent, two bars with three pierced mullets in chief gules.*

> Cf. 83, —, —: MP II. 75.

> Nicholas de Moels, Moles, Moules, or Mules, Lord of Cadbury, Som., probably d. c. 1264. (*CP* ix 1–4.)
> The name comes from Meulles in Calvados, and the three 'moeles' are canting *meules* or millstones. Originally they may have been shown as millstones, but all known representations of the arms show roundels. In B II the charges are called *moletes*. Nicolas transcribed that as 'molets' and interpreted it as mullets, straight-rayed stars, but the manuscript has moletes, that is meulettes or little millstones. The word is used again for roundels in the arms of Baskerville (B 183) and there too B I (*b*) tricks mullets. It occurs again in Walford's Roll where John de Plescy bears *molettes de goules perces* (C 116).

BARANTINE

84. *Dru de Barantyn noir ove trois egles d'or.*

Cf. 84, —, —.

Dru de Barantin occurs from 1228 (*Cal. Pat. Rolls,* 1225–1232, p. 227) and was dead by January 1267 (ibid., 1266–1272, p. 26.)

ZOUCHE

85. *Alain la Zouche de gules besante d'or.*
(*a*) and (*b*) *Ten bezants* (4, 3, 2, 1).

Cf. 85, —, 103: B 86: C 94.

Alan la Zouche of Ashby, s. of Roger la Zouche, d. 1270. His s. and h. Roger d. 1285. (*CP* xii (2) 932–5). His appearance in C 94 shows that that roll is not in every entry as late as 1275.

ZOUCHE

86. *Will'm la Zouche d'argent besante d'or.*
(*a*) *Azure, ten roundels or.*
(*b*) *Azure, bezanty or a canton ermine.*

Cf. 86, —, 104: B 85.

B I (*a*) blazons the field argent and that, no doubt, is what was in the 1253 manuscript. Glover, however, has tricked it '*b*' (i.e. azure), and it is azure B I (*b*), B II, and B IV. B I (*b*)'s canton seems to be an interpolation.

William la Zouche of Marston, Beds., and of Cambs. and Essex, occurs from 1243; he was dead by 1272. He m. Maud, widow of John de Trailly. He was brother of B 85. (*CP* xii (2) 957; *VCH Beds.* iii. 243; Farrer, *Feudal Cambs.*, pp. 14, 86, 103, 125–6; *Cal. Inq.* i, p. 106 and no. 795.)

HAY

87. *Rauf de la Haye blank od une rey de soleil de gules.*
(*a*) No shield.
(*b*) *Argent, a sun in splendour (with human features) gules.*

Cf. 87, —, —: C 93.

Rey de soleil, rais or *raie,* is an old term for a sun, or rather for a star-like charge, which was commonly represented as a many-rayed mullet as, for example, on the seal of Jeanne de la Hay, *c.* 1300. (Birch 10599.) The human features are an anachronism due to Cooke, for they were not introduced until Tudor days.

Sir Ralph de la Hay, of Lindsey, Lincs., d. 1254, leaving by his first wife Eustachia a s. John, who d. *c.* 1274. (A. R. Wagner, 'The Origin of the Hays of Erroll', *Genealogists' Magazine,* xi. 535–40; xii. 1–6.)

As his second wife Ralph m. Isabel, dau. and coh. of William de Montagu of Shepton Montacute, Som. She survived him and took as her second husband Thomas de Aldham (d. 1275), and it is to be remarked that the Aldhams bore *Azure, a sun or* (A 16 for Sir Thomas, N 263 for Isabel's gds. Sir Francis). The similarity between this and the Hay coat suggests that both were derived from Montagu, but there is no evidence that Montagu ever bore a sun. In that case it must be assumed that the Aldhams borrowed the sun from Hay, just as the Geneville descendants of Felicity de Brienne (fl. *c.* 1140) took horse-brays from the family of her first husband Simon de Broye (see 102–3 below). From Aldham the sun passed to St. Clere whose heiress carried it in the fifteenth century to Gage.

The meaning of the old blazon had been forgotten in the course of time and the Aldham *raie* was changed into a pile wavy issuing from the dexter chief bendways, or even into a bend wavy, while the Hay arms as quartered by Grenville in the 1620 visitation of Cornwall had become *Or, a pile wavy gules.*

Sir Ralph's inclusion in C 93 is another proof that that roll is partly retrospective.

FITZALAN

88. *Johan le fitz Alein de gules ove un leon d'or.*

Cf. 88, —, —.

This is the coat of d'Aubigny, Earl of Arundel, and was assumed by John Fitzalan, Lord of Clun and Oswestry (succ. 1240, d. 1267), s. of Isabel, sister and in her issue coh. of Hugh d'Aubigny, Earl of Arundel (B 18). (*CP* v. 391; i. 239; Round, *Peerage and Family History*, p. 120, &c.)

BIGOD

89. *Hugh' le Bygot au tiel.*

(*b*) *Gules, a lion rampant 'in bend' or.*

Cf. 89, —, —: MP I. 39; II. 12: B 6, 197: C 91.

Hugh le Bigod, Justiciar of England, d. 1266, second s. of Hugh, Earl of Norfolk 1221–5 (MP I. 39) and brother of Roger, Earl of Norfolk (MP II. 12). He m. Joan, dau. and h. of Nicholas de Stuteville and widow of Hugh Wake (MP IV. 53: B 51) and their s. Roger (d. 1306) succ. his uncle as Earl of Norfolk and Earl Marshal in 1270, assuming the coat *Party or and vert a lion rampant gules* which his uncle had inherited from the Marshals. (*CP* ix. 590 n. (*c*), 593; Birch 7471.)

The text of B I (*a*) appears to mean that Hugh bore *Gules, a lion rampant or*, but B II adds the words *mais le lion passant*, and C 130 gives Hugh's arms as *Gules un leon passant d'or*. Both the seal and counterseal of Hugh's grandfather Roger, Earl of Norfolk 1189–1220, display a shield charged with a lion passant (*Book of Seals*, 337), and a lion prowls at the foot of the equestrian seal used by Hugh's father. (Birch 5708; cf. B 6.)

The trick in B I (*a*) might be meant for a lion passant or for one rampant embelif, but B I (*b*) clearly tricks *a lion rampant embelif* and adds the marginal note *in bend* so that there shall be no mistake. In that connexion it is worth noting that Sir Simon le Bigod, who m. Maud, dau. and coh. of Richard de Felbrigg, is supposed to have been a younger brother of Hugh the Justiciar; his gds., another Sir Simon, temp. Edward II, took the name Felbrigg, and his s. Sir Roger de Felbrigg alias Bigod sealed in 1351/2 with *Or, a lion salient gules.* (*Yorks. Arch. Journ.*, xxxii. 73, 208–9.)

B 197 is presumably another brother of this Hugh.

VERDUN

90. *John de Verdon d'or frette de gules.*

(*b*) *Or, a fret* (modern style) *gules.*

Cf. 90, —, 86.

John de Verdun alias le Boteler of Alton, Staffs., s. and h. of Theobald le Boteler by Rohese, dau. and h. of Nicholas de Verdun, d. c. 1274, leaving a s. and h. Theobald. (*CP* xii (2) 246–8.)

TONY

91. *Rauf de Tonny d'argent ove le maunche de gules.*

Cf. 91, —, —: MP I. 57; II. 25; IV. 25.

Ralph de Tony, d. 1239: same person as MP I. 57.

MONMOUTH

92. *Johan de Monemewe d'or od trois cheverons de gules ove une fesse d'azur.*

(*a*) and (*b*) *Three chevrons, over all a fess.*

Cf. 92, —, —.

John, Lord of Monmouth, succ. 1248, d. 1257. Having no son he gave the castle and honour of Monmouth to Prince Edward. The arms are derived from the chevrons of Clare, John's ancestor

Baderon, Lord of Monmouth, having m. Rose, sister to Strongbow, Earl of Pembroke. (Bradney, *Monmouthshire*, i. 4, 5; Dugd. *Bar.* i. 442–3.) It does not appear how this John was related to John de Monmouth (C 88).

BASSET

93. *Philip Basset ounde d'or et de gules.*

(*a*) See plate III.

(*b*) The lines are drawn nearer to the modern nebuly.

Cf. 93, —, 106: MP II. 34.

Philip Basset of Wycombe, s. of Alan Basset (d. 1241) and younger brother of Gilbert Basset (MP II. 34), appointed Justiciar 1261, d.s.p.m. 1271. (Dugd. *Bar.* i. 383–4; Birch 6579, 7192.)

BLOUNT

94. *Will'm le Blount masclee d'or et de noir.*

(*a*) *Lozengy or and sable.*

(*b*) *Undy* (as B 93) *of six pieces sable and or.*

Cf. 94, —, 123.

William le Blount, or Blund, of Ixworth, Suffolk, s. of William le Blount, was slain at Lewes 1265, and left no issue. His sisters Agnes, wife of William de Criketoft, and Rohese, wife of Robert de Valoynes, shared his lands. (Dugd. *Bar.* i. 518; *Cal. Inq.*, vol. i, no. 585; Croke, *The Croke Family*, i. 105–7.)

B II and B IV agree with B I (*a*) in making the arms *Lozengy or and sable*, and the same coat is given for William le Blount, probably the same person as William of Ixworth in FW 620; P 123; TJ 1042. B I (*b*)'s trick, *Barry wavy sable and or*, is probably a draughtsman's variation of the lozengy coat engendered by the knowledge that *Barry wavy or and sable* was a Blount coat. It was borne by the Blounts of Elmley Lovett and Sodington, Worcs., who were descended from Stephen le Blount, uncle of William le Blount of Ixworth. (Croke, *The Croke Family*, i. 102–12, ii. 120–8.)

BEAUCHAMP of Hatch

95. *Robert de Beauchamp de veer.*

(*a*) See plate III.

Cf. 95, —, —.

Robert de Beauchamp of Hatch, Som., succ. his father Robert before 1251 and was dead 1266. (*CP* ii. 48; *Som. Arch. Soc. Proc.* xxxvi. 20–59.)

BEAUCHAMP of Eaton Socon

96. *Will'm de Beauchamp de Eton de gules frette d'argent.*

(*a*) *Fretty of six batons.*

(*b*) *Gules, fretty argent* 'but a fret' in the margin. The trick is something between six batons and a modern fret.

Cf. 96, —, — 107: MP II. 27.

William de Beauchamp of Eaton Socon, Beds., d. 1258/9 leaving sons William and Ralph. His father John (d. 1241) was s. of William fitz Geoffrey (a gds. of William de Mandeville, third Earl of Essex) by Olive de Beauchamp, and took the name Beauchamp on succ. his uncle Roger at Eaton 1220–1. (*Beds. Hist. Rec. Soc.* ii. 80–83, 91, and frontispiece; *Genealogist*, N.S. xxix. 79 seq.; *Book of Seals*, 309; Dugd. *Bar.* i. 224.)

The fretty coat appears on the seal of William's ancestor Hugh de Beauchamp (d. 1187).

SOMERY

97. *Roger de Somery d'or deus leopartz d'azur.*

(*a*) and (*b*) *lions passant gardant.*

> Cf. 97, 20, —.
>
> Roger de Somery, of Dudley, Staffs., succ. 1229 and d. 1273; his s. Roger d. 1291. Roger's seal displays lions passant. (*Book of Seals*, 13.) B II blazons *lions passant* and C 95 blazons *deux leons*. The *leopartz* of B I may be a mistake, but it suggests that the pose of the head was still unimportant and that no clear distinction was drawn between a lion passant and a lion passant gardant. The arms are derived from Paynel, John de Somery, grandfather of Roger, having m. Hawise, sister and h. of Gervase Paynel. (Dugd. *Bar.* I. 612–13; *CP* xii (1) 109–13.)
>
> B III. 20 is a conflation of this entry with B 19 (see p. 94 above).

MOHAUT

98. *Roger le Monhaut d'azur od un leon d'argent.*

> Cf. 98, —, —.
>
> Roger de Mohaut, or Montalt (now Mold, Flints.), s. of Roger, succ. 1232 and d. 1260. (*CP* ix. 12.)

VIPONT

99. *John de Veupont de gules od six fauses roueles d'or.*

(*a*) and (*b*) *Six annulets.*

> Cf. 99, —, 88.
>
> John de Vipont, of Westmorland, s. and h. of Robert (d. 1227), d. 1242 leaving Robert his s. (d.s.p.m. *c.* 1265) in ward to the king. (Dugd. *Bar.* i. 349; *Beds. Hist. Rec. Soc.* xix. 170.)

BRUCE

100. *Robert de Bruys d'or od un sautor de gules au chief de gules.*

> Cf. 100, —, 72.
>
> Robert de Brus, or Bruce, of Annandale, succ. 1245, d. 1295. He was a competitor for the crown of Scotland in right of his mother, Isabel, dau. of David, brother of William, King of Scotland. (*CP* ii. 358.)

SAVOY

101. *Piers de Saveye de gules ove une croix d'argent.*

(*b*) 'Peter of Savoy after erle of Richemond'.

> Cf. 101, —, —: MP II. 81; IV. 40.
>
> Peter of Savoy, d. 1268: same person as MP II. 81.

GENEVILLE

102. *Simon de Genville noir od trois breys d'or al chief d'argent od un demi leon de gules.*

(*a*) Similar to 103.

(*b*) Blank shield.

103. *Geffrey de Genville d'azur od trois breys d'or od un chief d'ermyne et un demi lion de gules.*

(*a*) See plate III.

(*b*) Similar.

> **102–3.** Cf. 102–3, —, —: C 106.
>
> Both B I (*a*) and B I (*b*) omit the surname in 102, which must therefore have been lacking in the original.

The brays of Geneville were taken from the canting arms of Simon de Broye, first husband of Felicity de Brienne (fl. *c.* 1140), though the Genevilles were descended from Felicity's second husband and had no connexion with Broyes.

Geoffrey and Simon, who differenced their paternal coat by changing the tincture of chief and field respectively, were younger brothers of John, Lord of Joinville, the historian of the Seventh Crusade. Geoffrey (B 103), Lord of Vaucouleurs, was b. *c.* 1226, settled in England *c.* 1251, and was summoned to Parliament 1299 and 1314. His wife Maud de Lacy was widow of Peter de Geneva, elder brother of B 104. Simon, youngest of the three brothers (B 102), was Lord of Marnay and d. 1277. ('The Geneville Brays', *Coat of Arms*, iii. 84; *CP* v. 628, &c. *Genealogist*, N.s. xxi. 1, &c. Birch 6059.)

GENEVA

104. *Eble de Genevre noir a un leon d'argent.*

Cf. 104, —, —: MP I. 87.

Ebles or Ebal de Geneva, younger brother of Peter de Geneva (MP I. 87), d.s.p. 1259. (*Genealogist*, N.s. xxi. 6 sqq.; Galbreath, *Armorial Vaudois*, I. 272.)

BOYS

105. *Ernaud de Boys d'argent od deux bastons de gules od quartier de gules.*
(*a*) and (*b*) *Two bars and a canton.*

Cf. 105, —, 110: MP II. 74; VII. 6: C 153.

For more than 200 years the head of the family of Boys was called Ernald. This probably refers to Ernald who d. 1255 (MP II. 74; VII. 6). His s. (C 153), last of the name, d. 1277, sealed with these arms and a label (5). (*CP* ii. 202; *Book of Seals*, 500.)

106. . . . *croix noir.*
(*a*) and (*b*) Blank.

B II omits this. It may refer to Upsale. Arnold de Upsale sealed with a cross *c.* 1190 (*EYC* ix. 156) and *Argent a cross sable* is borne by John de Upsale in G 142 (*c.* 1282).

DEINCOURT

107. *Johan Deyncourt d'azur od le daunce d'or et billettes d'or.*
(*a*) and (*b*) *A dance between ten billets* (4, 3, 2, 1).

Cf. 106, —, 91.

John Deincourt, s. of Oliver, succ. 1246 and d. 1257. (*CP* iv. 118, n. (*c*)).

108. . . . *Gaddesden d'argent a deux barres noir od trois estoilles noir en le chief.*
(*a*) *Two bars and in chief three mullets of six points.*
(*b*) *A blank.*

There is no corresponding entry in B II, B III, or B IV. The name Gaddesden is cancelled in B I (*a*), and B I (*b*)'s blank shows that it must have been so in the original.

The arms are assigned to le Moigne, or Moyne in the PE (II. 16), AN (224), and later rolls.

A similar coat with pales instead of bars is given for Gaddesden or Gatesden of Herts. and Warws. in Glover's Ordinary and later dictionaries, but according to a note by the late Sir W. St. John Hope a seal (not identified) of John de Gatesden, temp. Henry III, in the PRO displays a shield which appears to be charged with two bars. John de Gatesden, of Gatesden, Herts., d. 25 November 1258 leaving a dau. and h. Margaret. (*Cal. Inq.* i, no. 454.)

COURTENAY

109. *Johan de Courtenay party les armes le Comte de Garenne et de vert deux barres d'argent sur le tout.*
(*a*) *Per pale, the dexter checky or and azure, the sinister vert and over all two bars argent.*
(*b*) Shield blank.

Cf. 107, —, —: MP VIII. 10 (*e*).

B II gives the name 'John de Courteny' but no arms. The blazon of B I (*a*) seems to be correctly represented by the trick.

John de Courtenay of Okehampton, d. 1274, grandfather of the first Courtenay, Earl of Devon, was s. of Robert de Courtenay (d. 1242) by Mary de Reviers whose mother Mabel was dau. and h. of Robert de Beaumont, Count of Meulan by Maud, dau. and coh. of Reynold de Dunstanville, Earl of Cornwall. (*CP* iii. 465, &c.; iv. 315–17.) This explains the dexter half of the shield, William de Warenne having m. Robert de Beaumont's widow. (*CP* xii (1), appendix J.) The silver bars remain unexplained, though it seems possible that they may be in some way related to the three diapered bars which C 146 assigns to John's cousin Baldwin de Reviers, Earl of the Isle (of Wight) or of Devon—see B 12.

ST. JOHN

110. . . . *d'argent od chief de gules et deux estoiles d'or en le chief.*
(*a*) *On a chief two mullets of six points.*
(*b*) *A blank space.*

B II. ignores the entry. The arms are those of St. John (see B III).

ST. JOHN

111. . . . *St. Johan au tiel.*
(*a*) As B 110.
(*b*) '. . . St. John': shield blank.

Cf. —, —, 112.

B II ignores the entry, B IV names 'Robert de Seint John' with arms as B 110. Sir Robert de St. John of Basing, d. 1267. His s. John (C 163) d. 1302. (*CP* xi. 322–5; Birch 6401.)

LUCY

112. *Geoffrey de Lucy de gules od trois luces d'or.*
(*a*) and (*b*) *Three luces hauriant.*

Cf. 108, —, 111.

Geoffrey de Lucy, of Newington, Kent, d. 1252. His father Geoffrey d. 1234, and his s. Geoffrey was dead before 5 June 1284. (*CP* viii. 257.)

B IV assigns the same arms to Richard de Lucy, probably brother of Geoffrey who d. 1234. (*CP* viii. 257 n. (*c*).) Moreover, as B IV draws on an earlier source than B I and B II it is conceivable that Richard was the elder s. and died before 1253, Geoffrey then taking the undifferenced arms.

C 134 seems to refer to a different branch.

TREGOZ of Ewyas

113. *Robert de Tregoz de gules od deux gemelles d'or et un leon [d'or] en le chief passant.*
(*a*) *Three gemel bars in chief a lion passant.*
(*b*) *Gules, three gemel bars in chief a lion passant or.*

Cf. 109, —, —: C 97.

Both B I *a* and B II make the lion gules which is impossible on a red field. It was no doubt misblazoned in the 1253 original. B I (*b*) is probably correct in making the lion gold in which case the reference is to Robert de Tregoz of Ewyas, Hereford, d. 1268, s. of Robert de Tregoz (who was a younger brother of Geoffrey de Tregoz of Blunts Hall, Essex, whose gds. appears in C 97) by Sibyl, dau. and h. of Robert d'Ewyas. (*CP* xii (2) 16; *Sussex Arch. Coll.* xciii. 34–58.)

DESPENSER

114. *Hugh' le Despenser esquartele d'argent et de gules od un bend* [*de sable*] *lescu* [*le gu*] *frette d'or.*

(*a*) The 2nd and 3rd quarters only are fretty.

(*b*) *Quarterly argent and gules with a fret in second and third quarters and a bend sable over all.*

Cf. 110, —, 90: MP II. 58; IV. 79.

B I (*a*) no doubt followed the 1253 original in omitting *de sable* and writing *lescu* for *le gu*. Both faults are corrected in B II. B I (*b*)'s trick is correct save that the 2nd and 3rd quarters should be fretty: the fret was a Tudor invention. The arms are given correctly in B II and B IV.

Hugh le Despenser was killed at Evesham 1265: same person as MP II. 58.

SANDFORD

115. *Will'm de Samford ounde d'argent et de gules.*

(*a*) and (*b*) *Barry of six pieces.*

116. *Nichol son frere ounde d'argent et de gules.*

(*a*) *Bendy of six pieces.*

(*b*) *Bendy of six argent and gules, a label azure.*

Cf. 111–12, —, —: MP IV 81: C 140.

Both B I (*a*) and B I (*b*) call Nicholas William's brother. B II makes Nicholas William's s. and differences with a label gules. Nicholas de Sandford d. 1252: same person as MP IV. 81.

MONTFORT

117. *Piers de Mounfort bende d'or et d'azur.*

(*a*) *Bendy of ten pieces.*

(*b*) *Or, six bends azure.*

Cf. 113, —, —.

Piers de Montfort of Beaudesert, Warws., succ. his father Thurstan 1216, still under age 1231, slain at Evesham 1265, and was succ. by his s. Piers who d. 1287. His seal displays *Bendy of six*. (*CP* ix. 123, &c.; Birch 11873.)

DARCY

118. *Philip Darsy d'argent od trois roses de gules.*

(*a*) *Three sexfoils unpierced.*

(*b*) *Argent, three pierced cinquefoils gules.*

Cf. 114, —, —.

Both B I (*a*) and B I (*b*) draw the roses exactly like the Vere sexfoils of B 134.

Sir Philip Darcy of Nocton, Lincs., s. of Norman, succ. *c.* 1253 and died 1264. (*CP* iv. 50.)

PERCY

119. *Piers Percy d'or a la fesse engrelle d'azur.*
(*a*) and (*b*) *A fess of five fusils.*

> Cf. 115, —, —: MP II. 52: B 41.

> Piers Percy, who d. 1266/7, held Wharram Percy in chief and lands in Sutton-upon-Derwent, Carnaby, and Bolton Percy of the Percy fee. Picot de Percy, from whom Piers is probably descended, was tenant in 1086 of William de Percy of Topcliffe at Sutton-upon-Derwent and elsewhere, and was probably closely related to his overlord. Piers was sheriff of Yorkshire 1263/4. (*CP* x. 435, n. (*b*); *The Whitby Chartulary*, ii. 707-8; *Cal. Inq.* i, no. 653; *VCH* Yorks. ii. 262.)

LOUVAIN

120. *Matheu de Lowayn de gules billette d'or od la fesse d'argent.*

> Cf. 116, —, —.

> Matthew, s. of Godfrey de Louvain (brother of the Count of Louvain), succ. *c.* 1226 and d. 1258. (*CP* viii. 178.) The collocation of this and B 119 was no doubt suggested by the connexion of Percy with Louvain (MP II. 52).

NEWMARCH

121. *Adam de Neufmarche de gules od le fesse engrelle d'or.*
(*a*) *A fess of five fusils.*
(*b*) *Gules a fess engrailed* (modern) *or*, and in the margin: *Gules, a fess of five fusils argent* 'this is the truer'.

> Cf. 117, —, —.

> Adam de Novomercato of Yorks. (s. of John living in 1242/3), succ. his grandfather Adam, 1247; summ. to Parliament 1264, d. 1283. (*EYC* viii. 141; *CP* ix. 546, &c.) His seal 1274 (Westminster Abbey Muniments 9014) bears *A fess of five fusils*.

> The origin of this family is unknown (Loyd, *Anglo-Norman Families*, p. 72), but it may be assumed to come from a French Neufmarché, in which case it could be anglicized as Newmarket. But Newmarch is the accepted version.

UMFRAVILLE

122. *Gilbert Umframville d'or od la quintefoill de gules od un bordure d'asur od fers d'argent.*
(*a*) *A pierced cinquefoil in a bordure charged with eight horseshoes.*
(*b*) *Or, a pierced cinquefoil gules in a bordure azure* (no horseshoes).

> Cf. 118, —, —: MP II. 51; IV. 62.

> B II misblazons the horseshoes gules.
> Sir Gilbert de Umfraville, d. 1245. (*CP* i. 146.): same person as MP II. 51.

DEIVILLE

123. *Johan de Eyville d'or od une fesse de gules od florettes de l'un et l'autre.*
(*a*) *A fess between five fleurs-de-lis* (2, 2, 1) *and charged with two fleurs-de-lis.*
(*b*) *Gules, a fess flory on both sides or*, i.e. with three demi-fleurs-de-lis projecting above and two below the fess.

> Cf. 119, —, —.

> B I (*b*)'s trick misinterprets the blazon.
> Sir John d'Eiville of Egmanton, Notts., s. of Sir Robert d'Eiville by Denise, dau. of Sir Thomas Fitzwilliam of Spotborough, occurs from 1257 onwards; d. 1291. (*CP* iv. 130–3.)

MAULEY

124. *Piers de Mauley de veer od la manche de gules.*

Cf. 120, —, 113.

This is one of the coats to which B II adds a marginal trick for no apparent reason. Piers de Mauley of Mulgrave, Doncaster, succ. his father Piers, a Poitevin, while still a minor in 1242, and d. 1279. (*CP* viii. 558.) His s. Piers (d. 1308) sealed the Barons Letter in 1301 with *Or, a bend sable* (cf. N 61), a coat inherited from the first Piers's mother-in-law Joan, dau. and h. of William Fossard of Mulgrave and Doncaster. The maunch appears to have been the original Mauley coat. (Clay, *Extinct and Dormant Peerages*, pp. 132–3; *EYC* ii. 327–33; *CP* viii. 58–59; cf. P 114; TJ 1132.)

MEINILL

125. *Esteven de Menyl d'asur od trois gemels d'or au chief d'or.*
(*b*) 'Stiven Menill'; *azure, three gemel bars or, and a chief argent.*

Cf. 125, 121, —.

B I *a* is correct in making the chief or. B II gives the Christian name as Freinon, but it is emended (by Glover?) in the margin to 'Steven'.

Stephen de Meinill, s. of Robert de Meinill of Whorlton, Yorks., was under age in 1219, and d. 1269. (*CP* viii. 623.) He was descended from Robert de Meinill and Gertrude de Fossard. (*EYC* ii. 327; *Guisborough Cartulary* ii. 78–80; Clay, *Extinct and Dormant Peerages*, p. 135.) The collocation of this and B 124 shows that the compiler was aware of the two men's common descent from Fossard.

BENETEBY

126. *Nichol de Beneteby d'azur od trois estoilles d'argent.*
(*a*) *Three mullets of six points.*
(*b*) *Azure, three estoiles of eight wavy rays argent.*

Cf. 122, —, —.

No person of this name has been identified. It might be a misreading of Boltby. Nicholas de Boltby held lands at Boltby, Yorks., and at Langley, Haydon, Northumb., d. 1272. (*Book of Fees*, 597, 1111, 1129, 1130; *Cal. Inq.* i., no. 824.) There is no heraldic evidence to support this conjecture.

KYME

127. *Will'm de Kymbe d'or od cheveron de gules od la bordure noir.*
(*a*) *Three chevrons in a bordure.*
(*b*) *Or, a chevron gules in a bordure sable.*

Cf. 123, —, —: MP IV. 52.

William de Kyme, younger s. of Philip (d. 1242; MP IV. 52), succ. his brother Simon in 1248 and d. 1259, holding Kyme in Kesteven and other lands in Lincs. and Yorks. His s. Philip d. 1323. (*CP* vii. 352; *HKF* ii. 124; Dugd. *Bar.* i. 620.)

B I (*a*) writes 'cheverons' by mistake for the singular. B I (*b*) tricks and B II blazons one chevron and that is correct (cf. WJ 1213).

BASSET of Drayton

128. *Rauf Basset d'or od trois peus de gules a un quartier d'ermine.*
(*a*) and (*b*) *Three piles meeting in base with a canton ermine.*

Cf. 124, —, 115.

Ralph Basset of Drayton, s. of Ralph Basset (d. between 1254–61), who was gtgds. of Richard Basset, the Justiciar (d. 1144), d. 1265. (*CP* ii. 1–2.)

The progenitor of the family was Ralph Basset, the Justiciar, Lord of Montreuil-au-Houlme, dép. Orne (Loyd, *Origins of some Anglo-Norman Families*, p. 12). He d. *c.* 1127 (*DNB*) and was succ. by his s. Richard, the Justiciar, who d. 1144. Richard m. Maud, dau. of Geoffrey Ridel, and had four sons—Geoffrey, who adopted his mother's name of Ridel and was ancestor of the Bassets of Weldon; Ralph Basset of Drayton, grandfather of the Ralph whose arms are here blazoned; William Basset of Sapcote from whom were also descended the Bassets of Cheadle and Blore and the Bassets of Fledborough; and Gilbert Basset from whom descended the Bassets of Wycombe (MP I. 49; II. 34: B 93) and probably the Bassets of Tehidy. William Wyrley in *The True Use of Armorie* (1592) (ed. 1853, pp. 15–18) expounds the relationship of the various Basset coats on the basis of this pedigree, for which the evidence is not complete, but which is probable. The Basset heraldry presents a problem to which no satisfactory explanation has been found, namely the use of two distinct coats: (1) *Barry wavy* borne by Wycombe, Tehidy, and Sapcote lines with varying tinctures, (2) *Three piles* borne by Drayton, Weldon, Fledborough, and Cheadle lines, while both Sapcote and Cheadle lines at times used both coats.

COLEVILE

129. *Walter de Colleville d'or od une fesse de gules.*

Cf. 125, —, —.

Walter de Colevile, s. of Roger, of Bytham Castle, Lincs., d. 1277. (*CP* iii. 374.)

AMUNDEVILLE

130. *Richard de Mundeville d'azur frette d'argent od la fesse de gules.*

Cf. 126, —, 121.

Richard de Amundeville of Berkswell, Warws., joined the baronial party in the war and in 1297, when he must have been old, he surrendered the manor of Berkswell to the Earl of Warwick in return for a pension of £100 a year. (*VCH Warws.*, iv. 29; Dugd. *Warws.*, 717).

HUNTINGFIELD

131. *Roger de Huntingfield d'or od la fesse de gules a trois torteus d'argent en la fesse.*
(*a*) Or, on a fess gules three roundels argent.
(*b*) Or, a fess and in chief three roundels argent.

Cf. 127, —, —: MP II. 23.

B II's blazon agrees with (*a*) which is correct.
Roger de Huntingfield of Mendham, Suffolk, d. 1257: same person as MP II. 23. (*CP* vi. 664, 671; *Cal. Inq.* i, 671, no. 394.)

VERE

132. *Robert de Veer d'azur [argent] od la crois de gules.*
(*a*) Argent, a cross gules.
(*b*) Azure, a cross gules.

Cf. 128, —, —.

This is one of the cases where the 1253 roll confused azure and argent. The manuscript of B I (*a*) makes the field 'azure' and B I (*b*) tricks it likewise, but B I (*a*) tricks it 'ar' and B II both blazons and tricks argent. Moreover TJ 848 gives the arms of Mons. Nichol de Veer as *D'argent et une croice passant de goules a labelle dazure.*
Robert de Vere of Twywell and Slipton, Northants., was descended from Robert de Vere, a s. of Aubrey de Vere, chamberlain of Henry I (*Northants. Rec. Soc.* iv. 86–87); he was living in 1246. (*Book of Fees*, 937; *Feudal Aids*, iv. 12.)

THWENG

133. *Marmaduk de Thwenge d'argent ove trois papelays vert et une fesse de gules.*
(*a*) *A fess between three popinjays.*
(*b*) *Argent a fess between three popinjays gules.*

Cf. 129, —, —: MP II. 70: C 103.

Marmaduke de Thweng, s. of Robert de Thweng (MP II. 70), d. *c.* 1282/3. (*CP* xii (1) 738–9.)

VERE

134. *Simon de Veer gules od trois sixtefoilles d'ermyne.*
(*a*) *Three sixfoils.*
(*b*) *Gules, three pierced cinquefoils ermine.*

Cf. 130, —, —.

The charges both in B I (*a*) and (*b*) are drawn exactly like the Darcy roses of B 118. There was no certainty as to the number of petals: TJ 1018 blazons and paints cinquefoils, whereas F 45 and WLN 698 paint pierced sixfoils.

Simon de Vere of Sproatley, Yorks., was s. of Walter de Vere who was s. of Adam of Goxhill, Lincs., by Gundreda, dau. and h. of Guy de Vere. In 1267 he was described as the King's enemy and his lands were granted to John Comyn. (*Cal. Pat. Rolls*, 1266–72, p. 67.)

DAUBENEY

135. *Rauf Daubenay de gules od la fesse engrelle d'argent.*
(*a*) *A fess of five fusils.*
(*b*) *Gules, a fess of five fusils argent.* The fess does not reach the edges of the shield.

Cf. 131, —, —.

Ralph Daubeney of South Petherton, Barrington, and Chillington, Som., d. 1292. He was s. of Ralph Daubeney of Ingleby, Lincs., and younger brother and h. of Philip Daubeney of Ingleby, who d. 1224. (*CP* iv. 94–95.)

ROKELY

136. *Richard de la Rokele mascle d'ermyne et de gules.*
(*a*) *Lozengy* as B. 21, plate III.

Cf. 132, —, —.

Sir Richard de la Rokely, s. of Sir Richard (d. 1222) of South Okendon or Wokingdon, Essex, d. 1277. (Morant, *Essex* (1816), i. 99.)

FITZWILLIAM of Sprotborough

137. *Thomas le fitz Will'm mascle d'argent et de gules.*
(*a*) and (*b*) *Lozengy argent and gules.*

Cf. 133, —, —.

B II is in error in making Thomas bear the same arms as 136, i.e. *Lozengy ermine and gules.*

Sir Thomas Fitzwilliam of Elmley and Sprotborough, Yorks., living 1243–66, m. Agnes, dau. of Sir Roger Bertram of Mitford (B 144). His grandfather William FitzGodric was also ancestor of B 136. (Clay, *Extinct and Dormant Peerages*, 76; *Ancestor*, xii. 114; Hunter's *South Yorks.* (*Doncaster*), i. 334–5; ii. 93.)

FITZRANDOLPH

138. *Henry le Fitz Randolf d'azur frette d'or et le chief d'or.*
(*b*) 'Henry le Fitz Raulffe'.

Cf. 134, —, —.

This family was later known as FitzHugh.

Sir Henry FitzRandolf of Ravensworth, in Richmondshire, d. 1262. His s. Randolf Fitz-Henry d.s.p. (monument at Jervaulx Abbey—Lawrance, p. 17) and was succ. by his brother Sir Hugh FitzHenry *a quo* the Lords FitzHugh. (*CP* v. 416; cf. E 96; P 133; N 130.)

MERLAY

139. *Roger de Merlay barre d'argent et de gules od la bordure d'azur merlotz d'or en la bordure.*
(*a*) *Barry of six with eight martlets on the bordure.*
(*b*) *Eleven martlets on the bordure.*

Cf. 135, —, —.

Roger de Merlay III of Morpeth, Northumb., s. of Roger II, succ. 1239 and d. 1266 leaving three daughters and coh., one of whom, Isabel, m. Sir Robert de Somerville (d. 1304).

The arms are those of Stuteville (*Barry argent and gules*, see B 171) differenced, Roger, grandfather of this man, having m. Alice, dau. of Roger de Stuteville of Burton Agnes. The martlets, *merles*, are a canting emblem of Merlay. The first Roger sealed with a conventional tree on which four birds are perched, this Roger with a shield charged with three legless birds with open wings one above the other. (Hodgson, *Northumberland*, pt. 2, vol. ii, pp. 374–6; *Trans. of East Riding Antiquarian Society*, xxix. 32; Birch 11747.)

FITZRANULF of Middleham

140. *Rauf le Fitz Randolf d'or od le chief d'azur endente.*
(*b*) 'Raulfe fitz Raulffe or fitz Randolffe'.

Cf. 136, —, 105.

B IV substitutes Ralph's father 'Randolf FitzRobert de Midelham', who was s. of Robert Fitz-Ralph. Ralph FitzRanulf was s. of Ranulf FitzRobert who d. in 1252. (*EYC* v. 302.). His grandfather Robert FitzRalph m. Helewise dau. of Ranulf de Glanville.

The coat was borne not only by the Glanville and Middleham families but also by the Fitz-Randalls of Spennithorne (descendants of Ralph FitzRanulf's younger brother), and by several other families. (Wagner, *Historic Heraldry*, pp. 37–38.)

It may be noticed that though the chief is tricked here with three points, it has five points in B IV, and TJ 773 specifies that *Mons Randolf fitz Rauf de Midelham port dor a chief endentee dazure de cynk.*

Sir Ralph FitzRanulf was dead in 1270, leaving three daughters as coheirs—Joan, wife of Robert de Tateshal, Mary, wife of Robert de Neville, and Anastasia. (*VCH Yorks., North Riding*, i. 254.)

FITZALAN of Bedale

141. *Alein le fitz Brian, barre d'or et de gules.*
(*a*) *Barry of six pieces.*
(*b*) *Barry of eight, or and gules.*

Cf. 137, —, 136.

B IV substitutes Brian FitzAlan de Bedale, which may refer either to Alan's father or to his s. who d. 1306. It also specifies that the barry is of eight pieces. It is also to be noticed that it blazons the coat from the base upwards, *Barre de goules et d'or.*

Alan FitzBrian of Bedale, s. of Brian FitzAlan (living 1242), d. 1267. His seal, *c.* 1250, shows a barry shield (Birch 5942). (*CP* v. 393.)

ODINGSELES or DODDINGSELES

142. *Will'm de Oddyngeseles d'argent od la fesse de gules et deus estoilles de gules en le chief.*

(*a*) and (*b*) argent, a fess gules and in chief two pierced mullets gules.

Cf. 138, —, —: MP II. 57: C 157.

William de Odingseles of Solihull, Warws., was dead 1271: same person as William in MP II. 57.

FERRERS

143. *Hugh de Ferrers verree d'argent et d'asur.*

(*a*) *Vair (argent and azure).*
(*b*) *Vairy gules and or.*

Cf. 139, —, —: MP II. 10; VII. 1.

Sir Hugh de Ferrers, younger s. of William de Ferrers, Earl of Derby (MP II. 10), was dead 1257. The change of tincture from the usual gules and or (as tricked in (*b*)) to argent and azure was presumably a cadency difference: it makes the arms identical with Beauchamp of Hatch (B 95). (*CP* v., pedigree facing p. 320.)

BERTRAM

144. *Roger Bertram de gules od un faus escuchon d'or od croiselez d'or.*

Cf. 140, —, —.

Sir Roger Bertram of Mitford, Northumb., s. of Roger, was born 1225, succ. 1242, summ. to Parliament 1264, and d. 1272–3 leaving a dau. Agnes (see B 137). The arms are Balliol differenced, Roger's ancestor William Bertram having m. Hawise, dau. of Guy de Balliol. (*CP* ii. 159–60; Hodgson, *Northumberland*, pt. ii, vol. ii., p. 40; *Book of Seals*, 234; Birch 5706; Hunter Blair, *Seals of Northumberland and Durham*, no. 71; TJ 1083.)

MOUNTENEY

145. *Erneus de Mounteney d'azur od six merlotz d'or et une bende d'or.*

Cf. 141, —, —: MP IV. 82.

Arnold de Mounteney, d. 1252: same person as MP IV. 82.

BERNERS

146. *Johan de Berners esquartele d'or et de vert od un label de gules.*

Cf. 142, —, —: MP II. 78: C 149.

John de Berners of Streethall and Great Dunmow, Essex, fought against the king in 1264–5 and was dead 1270. (*Cal. Pat. Rolls*, 1266–72, p. 410; *Cal. Close Rolls*, 1268–72, p. 251.) His relationship to John de Berners of Nosterfield (MP II. 78) has not been found. This entry may refer to the same person as MP II. 78.

FURNIVAL

147. *Thomas Furnivall d'argent od six merlotz de gules et un bende de gules.*

Cf. 143, —, —: MP II. 45, 77: B 148, 149.

FURNIVAL

148. *Will'm Furnivall au tiel od label d'asur.*

(*b*) 'William Furnevall son of Thomas'.

FURNIVAL

149. *Gerard Furnivall d'or od six merlotz de gules et un bend de gules.*

148–9. Cf. 144–5, —, —: MP II. 45, 77: B 147.

The arms in these three entries (147–9) suggest that here we have a father and two sons. The pedigrees, however, do not support this but suggest that these are three brothers. Sir Gerard de Furnival (d. 1219) had three sons—Thomas, Gerard, and William (Clay, *Extinct and Dormant Peerages*, 81). Thomas was living 1238 (*CP* v. 580) but Matthew Paris states that he and his brother Gerard accompanied Simon de Montfort on a crusade in 1240 (*CM* v. 44) and records Gerard's death in 1241 (*CM* v. 175). No William son of Thomas has been found and B I (*b*) may be mistaken in naming him thus. The arms suggest a different relationship, label for an elder son, and a difference of tincture for another, but in this formative period of heraldry differencing was not so systematic as it became later.

HASTINGS

150. *Henry de Hastinges d'or ove une manche de gules.*

Cf. 146, —, 87.

Henry, s. of Sir Henry de Hastings of Ashill, Norfolk (d. 1250), by Ada, dau. of David, Earl of Huntingdon, d. 1269 leaving a s. John. (*CP* vi. 345.)

CRIOL or KYRIEL

151. *Bertram de Croyl d'or a deux cheverons de gules et un quartier de gules.*
(*a*) *A chevron and a half*, see Plate III.
(*b*) *Or, two chevrons and a canton gules.*

Cf. 147, —, —.

As often in medieval and Tudor rolls B I (*a*) suppresses the dexter limit of the upper chevron, but B I (*b*) shows the end of this projecting below the canton.

Bertram de Criol, or Kyriel, of Sarre, Kent, and Albury, Herts., s. of John de Criol, fl. 1225–47. His s. Sir Nicholas de Criol was dead 1274. (Dugd. *Bar.* i. 770; *Misc. Gen. et Her.* 5th s. vi. 254; *Cal. Inq.* ii, no. 87.)

PEYVRE

152. *Paulyn Peyvre d'azure [argent] ove un cheveron de gules od florettes d'or en la cheveron.*
(*a*) *Argent, on a chevron gules three fleurs-de-lis or.*
(*b*) *Paule Peyver: Azure, a fess gules fretty or.*

Cf. 148, —, —: MP IV. 78.

Paulyn Peyvre d. 1251: same person as MP IV. 78. B I (*a*) blazons the field azure, and the fact that B I (*b*) also makes it azure shows that it was so blazoned in 1253. Glover, however, corrected it to *Ar* in his trick. B II also makes the field silver and that is confirmed by MP IV. 78, TJ 680, and other rolls. Cooke's substitution of *fretty* for *florettes* in B I *b* is perhaps an attempt to get over the apparent anomaly of a red fess on a blue field.

B II names this 'William Peyver'. It is Peyvre in MP, i.e., Piper, a nickname, peppery.

QUINCY

153. *Robert Quency de gules od une quintefoill d'ermyne.*
(*a*) *and* (*b*) *A pierced cinquefoil.*

Cf. 149, —, —: MP I. 32, 34; II. 11; IV. 17: B 8.

Robert de Quincy, third but second surviving son of Saher de Quincy, Earl of Winchester (MP I. 32), and brother of Roger de Quincy, Earl of Winchester (MP II. 11: B 8), d.s.p.m. 1257. (Dugd. *Bar.* i. 687; *CP* iii. 170; xii (2) 751 n. (*e*).)

His mother was Margaret, dau. and coh. of Pernel, Countess of Leicester (d. 1212), and we may guess that the cinquefoil or pimpernel was Pernel's canting device. It appears on Margaret's seal (Birch 6700) and on that of her brother Robert FitzPernel, Earl of Leicester, who d.s.p. 1204 (*CP* vii. 535), and also on that of his brother Roger. (Birch 6346, &c.)

FITZNICHOL

154. *Rauf le fitz Nichol de gules od un quintefoill d'or od le scalops d'argent entour.*
(*a*) *A pierced cinquefoil in an orle of eight escallops.*
(*b*) *Gules semy of escallops argent, a pierced cinquefoil or.*

Cf. 150, —, —: MP II. 39.

B II's blazon *De goules ung quintefueil de or le champs pleyn des escallopes dargent*, fits B I (*b*)'s trick better than B I (*a*)'s blazon and trick. Ralph FitzNichol, the king's steward, d. 1257: same person as MP II. 39. (*CM* v. 616.)

LEXINGTON

155. *Joh'n de Lexington d'argent od une croix d'azure furchee au kauee [? kanee].*
(*a*) A blank shield.
(*b*) *Argent, a cross moline azure.*

Cf. 151, —, —: MP II. 59.

John de Lexington of Laxton, Notts., sometime Keeper of the Great Seal, d.s.p. 1257 (*DNB*; Dugd. *Bar.* i. 743): same person as MP II. 59.

The blazon of this coat is one of the outstanding problems of this roll. The trick in B I (*b*) of a moline cross would fit *furchee*, but seems to ignore the last two words of the blazon. Glover transcribed these as 'au Kanee' and they were so printed by Nicolas and Armytage. There seem to be two possible explanations. On the one hand, *Kanee* may be meant for *Cane* which Godefroi gives as an old word for tooth. On the other hand, it may be a misreading of coue, queue or tail. (J. G. Nichols, *Herald and Genealogist*, v. 476.) The blazon may therefore mean a forked cross either with a tooth or with a foil, either of which aptly describes the Lexington cross as it is drawn by Matthew Paris IV. 59, namely a moline cross, with a little point between the horns. Alternatively, *au* may be a misreading of ou (or), and *Kanee* or *Kouee* may be an adjective, in which case the blazon would mean either forked-or-toothed or forked-or-tailed. This, however, would not fit the drawing in Matthew Paris.

The College of Arms MS. Vincent 88, p. 56, and J. C. Brooke, Aspilogia, i. 66 draw Lexington seals with a cross paty, and Bishop Lexington is said by Browne Willis (cited in Bedford, *Blazon of Episcopacy*, p. 71) to have borne *Argent, a cross paty azure* charged with a gold mitre.

WALERAND

156. *Robert Walrand d'azur [argent] od un bend engrele de gules.*
(*a*) *Argent a bend of five lozenges gules.*
(*b*) Robert Wallerand' *azure a bend engrailed* (modern).

Cf. 152, —, —.

Again B I (*a*) and (*b*) misblazon the field *azure*. It is corrected in (*a*)'s trick and B II's blazon, and argent is confirmed by later rolls, as F 76 and TJ 324, both of which give *Argent, a bend of fusils gules*.

This possibly refers to Robert Waleran, Walerand, or Walrond, Lord of Kilpeck. He was s. of William Waleran by Isabel, dau. and coh. of Hugh de Kilpeck (sister of Philip Marmion's wife Joan; see B 57). He d. 1273 leaving as h. his nephew Robert. His seal in 1267 and 1269 shows a bend of five fusils. (*Book of Seals*, 94, 411; *DNB*; *Top. and Gen.* i. 29–30; Moor, v. 147.)

MULTON of Egremont

157. *Thomas de Multon d'argent od trois barres de gules.*

> Cf. 153, —, —: MP IV. 38: B 158.

Thomas de Multon of Egremont, d. 1294 leaving a s. and h. Thomas. He was s. of Lambert de Multon (d. 1246), by Amabel, elder dau. and coh. of Richard de Lucy of Egremont, and gds. of Thomas de Multon (MP IV. 38) by his first wife. (*CP* ix. 402; Birch 6245.)

MULTON of Gilsland

158. *Thomas de Multon 'Forst' au tiel od un label noir.*
(*b*) 'Thomas Multon Forester'.

> Cf. 154, —, —: MP IV. 38: B 157.

Thomas, elder s. of Thomas de Multon of Lincs. (MP IV. 38) gdfather of B 157 by his second wife, and h. to his mother Ada, dau. and coh. of Hugh de Morville, Forester of Cumberland, d. January 1271. Usually called 'the Forester' or 'of Gilsland' to distinguish him from his nephew (B 157). (*CP* ix. 405–6.)

FITZGERALD

159. *Warin le fitzGerard de gules od un leopard d'argent coronne d'argent.*

> Cf. 155, —, —.

Warin FitzGerald, s. of Henry (d. *c.* 1231) and gds. of Warin FitzGerald, Chamberlain of Henry II; d.s.p. His sister and h. m. Robert de Lisle *a quo* Lisle of Rougemont and Lisle of Kingston Lisle. (*CP* viii, pedigree opposite p. 48.)

OXTED

160. *Roland de Akstede d'[argent] od un kene de gules.*
(*a*) Blank shield.
(*b*) 'Roland de Akstede who bereth od la kene de gules.'

> Cf. 156, —, —.

As B I (*a*) and (*b*) and B II omit the field tincture it is obvious that this must have been omitted in 1253. Roland de 'Okestede' or 'Akstede' of Oxted, Surrey, d. 1270. (*Cal. Inq.* i, no. 741.) His son Roland d. 1291. (*VCH Surrey*, iv. 313.)

Both B I (*a*) and (*b*) failed to understand *kene* and left the shield blank. The name shows that it is a canting charge—an aik, or oak-tree, French *chêne*, and that is confirmed by FW 245 which gives for Roland de Okestede, *Argent, an oak-tree gules the acorn cups and stalks vert* (cf. A 246). The seal of Roland's gddau. Thomasina also displays an oak-tree. (*Proc. Soc. Ant.* 2nd s. v. 197.)

BRANCH

161. *Piers Branch d'ermyne frette de gules.*

> Cf. 157, —, —.

Sir Piers Branch of Oxford and of Gresham, Norfolk, occurs in the Patent Rolls from 1242 to 1257 and was dead by May 1259. (*Cal. Pat. Rolls*, 1232–47, pp. 334, 350; 1258–66, p. 52; Birch 7743.)

BRYAN

162. *Guy de Bryan dazur od trois peus d'or.*
(*a*) and (*b*) *Three piles meeting in base.*

> Cf. 158, —, —.

Guy de Bryan, s. of Guy de Bryan, d. *c.* 1307. (Dugd. *Bar.* ii. 150.)

BAUZAN

163. *Estiene Basan unde argent et de gules od un quartier noir.*
(*a*) *Barry wavy of six argent and gules a canton sable.*
(*b*) *Barry wavy of six or and gules a canton sable.*

Cf. 159, —, —.

B II agrees with B I (*a*) in making the metal silver.

Stephen Bauzan or Baucham occurs in the Patent Rolls from 1234 (*Cal. Pat. Rolls*, 1232–1247, p. 41) to 1257 (ibid., 1247–58, p. 586) and was dead by January 1258 (ibid., p. 615). He was probably a Gascon, and was steward first to Prince Edward and later to Prince Edmund in 1254.

SARREN

164. *Will'm de Sarren dazur od trois croix d'or.*
(*a*) A blank shield.
(*b*) 'Will'm Sarran azure iij crosses or'—shield blank.

Cf. 160, —, —.

B II agrees with B I. Neither version specifies the pattern of the crosses nor does the coat seem to occur elsewhere. Possibly *trois* is a mistake, *un* being misread as *iij*. (cf. B 197).

STRANGE

165. *Johan Lestrange d'argent od deus leons passants de gules.*

166. *Joh'n son fils au tiel od un label d'azur.*

165–6. Cf. 161–2, —, —.

John le Strange or Lestrange (B 165), s. of John le Strange (dead 1234), was dead by 1269. His s. John (B 166), Lord of Knockyn, m. Joan, dau. and coh. of Roger de Somery, Lord of Dudley (C 95) and coh. to her mother Nichole, dau. of William, Earl of Arundel; he d. 1276; their s. John d. 1309. (*CP* xii (1) 350–2.)

BERKELEY

167. *Morys de Berkele de gules od un cheveron d'argent.*

Cf. 163, —, —.

Maurice succ. as Lord of Berkeley in 1243 and d. 1281. He was s. of Thomas de Berkeley by Joan, dau. of Sir Ralph de Somery of Campden, Gloucs. His seal bears the chevron as here. (*CP* ii. 126–7; *Book of Seals*, 403.)

He was succ. by his second s. Thomas (Maurice the eldest s. d.v.p.), who sealed with the familiar chevron between ten crosses. (Seal 1301 Barons' Letter.)

LOVEL

168. *Richard Lovel d'or od un leon d'azur.*

Cf. 164, —, —.

Richard Lovel of Castle Cary, Som. (brother of Henry who d. 1216), d. *c.* 1253/4. His s. Henry (d. 1263) was succ. in turn by his sons Richard (d. 1264) and Hugh (d. 1291). The latter's s. Richard, summ. to Parliament 1348, d. 1351, sealed with *Crusuly a lion.* (*CP* viii. 199, 203, 205 n. (*c*).)

EURE or FITZJOHN

169. *Roger le fitz John de Eure esquartele d'or et de gules od un bend noir.*

Cf. 165, —, 116: MP I. 88; IV. 39.

The arms are the same in all three versions, but whereas B I and B II write Roger FitzJohn of Eure, B IV substitutes Robert FitzRoger of Clavering his s.

Roger Fitz John of Eure or Iver, Bucks., and of Clavering, Essex, and Warkworth, Northumb., was s. of John FitzRobert (d. 1240; MP IV. 39); d. 1249. (*CP* iii. 274-5. The arms are derived through Vere ultimately from Mandeville, Earl of Essex. Robert FitzRoger, gdfather of this man, was s. of Roger FitzRichard by Alice dau. of Aubrey de Vere and sister of Rohese, who was wife of Geoffrey de Mandeville, Earl of Essex (d. 1144).

TREHAMPTON

170. *Rauf de Trehamton' d'argent od un bende de gules.*

Cf. 166, —, 117.

Ralph de Trehampton (s. of Sir Roger) of Leymarsh, Lincs., fl. 1212-42. (Birch 6478; *Cal. Pat. Rolls*, 1225-32, p. 352; 1232-47, p. 323.)

STUTEVILLE

171. *Will'm Destutevill de la Marche burle d'argent et de gules od trois coks noirs.*
(*a*) *Buruly of fourteen pieces* (no cocks).
(*b*) *Barry of eight argent and gules, three cocks sable.*

Cf. 167, —, —: B 200.

The addition of *de la Marche* identifies this as the William de Stuteville who held the honour of Richard's Castle, Herefords., in right of his wife (m. 1230) Margery, dau. and h. of Hugh de Say, and widow of Hugh de Ferrers and Robert de Mortimer. He is probably identical with the William de Stuteville of Cowesby and Gressenhall in the North Riding, s. of Osmund (d. 1192) who d. 1259. His s. Robert d.s.p. 1275 and was succ. by his sister's s. Jordan Foliot (see B 172). (*EYC* ix. 35-37, 142; Eyton, *Shropshire*, iv. 310-16; *HKF* iii. 397.)

The original arms seem to have been *Buruly argent and gules* as on the seal of Joan, dau. and h. of Nicholas de Stuteville and wife successively of Hugh Wake (B 51) and Hugh Bigod (B 89) (see *EYC* ix, frontispiece and p. 130) and E 186, TJ 589, 1231, and cf. B 139. The Valmont line differenced with a sable lion (see B 200), and other branches added two (GA 21) or three sable lions (C 85; N 581). This version with the three cocks occurs also in 1441 as a quartering of 'John Cherowin' (Curwen), Constable of Portchester Castle, on a slab in Brading Church, Isle of Wight.

Sir George Sitwell (*Tales of My Native Village*, p. 75) points out that some of the family's English vassals took variants of the buruly coat, viz. Goushill, *Barry of six or and gules, a canton ermine* (S 476); Hathersage, *Paly or and gules, a chief argent* (see B 175); Longford, *Paly or and gules, a bend argent* (N 623).

FOLIOT

172. *Richard Foliott de gules od une bende d'argent.*

Cf. 168, —, —.

Sir Richard Foliot of Fenwick and Norton, Co. York, m. Margery, sister and in her issue h. of Sir Robert de Stuteville (see B 171), and d. 1299. (*CP* v. 538; Birch 9848-51.)

ROS of Wark

173. *Robert de Ros de Werk d'or od trois bouz noirs.*

Cf. 169, —, —: MP II. 55: B 66.

Robert de Ros, younger brother of William de Ros of Helmsley (B 66), obtained the lordship of Wark in Northumberland from his father; d. 1269. (*CP* xi. 119.)

BOLBEC

174. *Hugh' Bolebek vert ove un leon d'ermyne.*

Cf. 170, —, —.

B II adds a marginal trick of this coat, needlessly, as it seems.

Hugh de Bolbec, Sheriff of Northumberland 1245, s. of Hugh (d. *c.* 1240) by Margaret, sister and coh. of Richard de Montfichet, m. Theophania de Balliol and d. 1262 leaving four daughters as his coheiresses. (*NCH* xiii. 78, correcting vi. 234, &c.)

HATHERSAGE

175. *Matheu de Haydresegge pale dor et de gules od un chief d'argent.*
(*a*) and (*b*) *Paly of six pieces.*

Cf. 171, —, —.

Matthew de Hathersage of Hathersage and Whitwell, Derbys., d.s.p. 1259. His heirs were his sisters Maud, wife of Walter de Goushill, and Cecilia, wife of Nigel de Longford. He was s. of Matthew de Withington of Hathersage (d. *c.* 1218) by Emma de Meinill. (*Derbyshire Arch. Soc.* N.S. ii. 302, 307–10; J. P. Yeatman, *Feudal History of Derbyshire,* passim.) The Hathersages were vassals of the Stuteville family of whose arms theirs are a variant (see B 171).

SEGRAVE

176. [*Gilbart Segrave, sable, three garbs argent.*]

Cf. 172, —, —: MP I. 66; IV. 48: C 98.

B I (*a*) omits this but it occurs in B I (*b*) and B II.

Gilbert, Lord of Segrave, Leics., s. and h. of Stephen (MP I. 66; IV. 48), succ. 1241, d. 1254.

The garbs are derived from the arms of the earls of Chester (B 16) under whom Stephen de Segrave held Segrave before 1200. Gilbert's s. and h. Nicholas, however, left the garbs and bore *Sable, a lion argent crowned or* (K, line 120), though C 98 still gives the garbs for Geoffrey. It has been suggested that the lion was derived from Gilbert's wife Amabel, dau. and coh. of Robert de Chaucombe, but it is not known as arms of that family, and *c.* 1205 Hugh de Chaucombe sealed with *Fretty, on a chief a crescent between two stars.* (*CP* xi. 596, 601; Birch 13392, 13399; Nichols, *Leics.* iii. pt. i, pp. 240, 407.)

NEVILLE of Laceby

177. *Johan de Nevill cowe de rat mascle d'or et de gules od un quartier d'ermyne.*
(*b*) Omits 'cowe de rat'.

Cf. 173, —, —.

John de Neville of Laceby, Lincs., was s. of Geoffrey de Neville, s. of Alan de Neville, who was a brother of Gilbert de Neville whose gddau. Isabella m. Robert FitzMeldred from whom came the Nevilles of Raby. (*Genealogist,* N.S. xxvii. 1–7.)

'Cowe de rat' is presumably a nickname, which B II renders as 'cowerde'.

NEVILLE

178. *Johan de Nevill le Forster d'or od un bend de gules od croiseles noirs.*
(*a*) and (*b*) *A bend between six crosses crosslet.*
(*b*) 'John Nevile the Forrester.'

Cf. 174, —, —: MP IV. 69.

John de Neville, Chief Forester, d. 1246. (*Genealogist,* N.S. xxvii. 7.) Matthew gives him different arms, *Per fess indented gules and vert, a bend sable* (MP IV. 69).

BOTELER of Wem

179. *Rauf de Botellier de gules od une fesse eschekere d'argent [et de sable] od croisilles d'or.*
(*a*) *A fess countergobony between six crosses crosslet.*
(*b*) *Gules a fess 'checkye' argent and sable between six crosses crosslet argent.*

Cf. 175, —, —.

B I (*a*) omits 'et de sable', B I (*b*) and B II give the fess correctly *checky argent and sable*. B I (*b*) makes the crosslets silver.

Rauf Boteler of Oversley, Warws., m. Maud, dau. and h. of William Pantulf of Wem, Salop. He d. *c.* 1281. (*CP* ii. 230–1.)

FITZRALPH

180. *Hugh le fitz Rauf de gules od une fesse de veer.*

Cf. 176, —, —.

Hugh, s. of Ralph FitzHugh, Sheriff of Nottingham and Derby 1236–9, d. 1261. (*Book of Seals*, 353; Birch 9755; *HKF* i. 162; *Book of Fees*, 984.)

ST. OMER

181. *Will'm de St. Omer d'azur od un fesse d'or billettes d'or.*
(*a*) and (*b*) *A fess between six billets.*

Cf. 177, —, 118.

William de St. Omer, Sheriff of Herefordshire and Constable of the Castle, 14 October, 1252. (*Cal. Pat. Rolls*, 1247–58, p. 152.) He and his wife Pernel de Tony occur from 1256 to 1272. He held land at Britford, Wilts. (Ibid., p. 503; *Cal. Inq.* ii,, no. 74.)

BLANKMINSTER

182. *Reynaud de Blankmister dargent frette d'azur.*

Cf. 178, —, —.

Sir Reynold de Blankminster, Blankmouster, Blamuster, or de Albo Monasterio (now Oswestry, Salop), occurs from 1223 to 1257. He was Sheriff of Bedfordshire and Buckinghamshire in 1237. (*Cal. Pat. Rolls*, 1216–25, p. 407; 1232–47, pp. 165, 181; 1247–58, p. 601.)

BASKERVILLE

183. *Walter de Bacreville d'argent a trois molettes de gules od un cheveron de gules.*
(*a*) *A chevron between three roundels.*
(*b*) *Argent, a chevron between three pierced mullets gules.*

Cf. 179, —, —.

Here too, as in B 83, B I uses 'molettes' for roundels. B II emends the blazon to torteaux. The fact that B I (*b*) tricks mullets shows that Cooke worked from an original which had blazons only, without illustrations.

Sir Walter de Baskerville of Orcop in Archenfield, Herefords., and Pickthorn, Salop, succ. his father Walter 1244 and d. 1282. (*Cal. Inq.* i, no. 20; ii, no. 595; *Cal. Fine Rolls*, i. 168.)

FITZWARIN

184. *Fouk le FitzWaryn esquartele d'argent et de gules endente de l'un et del aultre.*
(*a*) *Quarterly per fess indented,* see plate III.
(*b*) *Quarterly indented both ways argent and gules.*

Cf. 180, —, —.

The version in B I (*a*) is correct (*Book of Seals*, 172; Birch 6022).

The arms seem to be a differenced version of the indented chief of Glanville (B 140). The family are supposed to spring from a shadowy or mythical Warin of Metz in Lorraine, whose s. Fulk, Baron of Whittington and Lord of Abberbury, Salop, d. in 1170 or 1171. His gds. Fulk m. firstly Maud, widow of Theobald Walter and dau. of Robert le Vavasour, and secondly Clarice Dauberville, both marriages connecting him with the Glanvilles. (Wagner, *Historic Heraldry*, pp. 31, 37–38.)

The entry may refer to Fulk, living 1250, or to his s. Fulk who d. 1264. (*CP* v. 495.)

TURBERVILLE

185. *Johan de Turberville.*

(*a*) Blank shield.

(*b*) The trick, *Argent, a chevron between three mullets gules*, is cancelled with pen-scrawls.

Cf. 181, —, —: MP I. 56.

Both B I (*a*) and B II omit the arms. The trick in B I (*b*) is not known as a Turberville coat; it is an accidental repetition of B 183.

John de Turberville of Dorset and Herefords., d. 1270. (*Cal. Pat. Rolls*, 1266–72, p. 493; *Book of Fees*, 811; Hutchins, *Dorset*, i. 138.) His s. and h. Richard, who bore *Checky or and azure a fess ermine* (E 350), held Acton Turville, Gloucs., and d. *c.* 1283. (*Cal. Inq.* ii, no. 521; *Cal. Gen.* 3421.) His relationship to Henry de Turberville (MP I. 56) has not been found.

FITZWALTER

186. *Walter le fitz Robert d'or od deus cheverons de gules od la fesse de gules.*

(*a*) and (*b*) A fess between two chevrons.

Cf. 182, —, 92: MP II. 32, 86; IV. 33.

B IV follows B I's blazon, but B II emends it to read 'ung fece entre deux chevrons'.

Sir Walter FitzRobert, s. of Robert (MP II. 32), succ. 1235 and d. 1258. (*CP* v. 427; xi. 381–2.)

LONGESPÉE

187. *Estienne Longespée d'azur od six leonceaux d'or od un label de gules.*

Cf. 183, —, —: MP I. 40, 90: B 22.

Stephen de Longespée, third s. of William, Earl of Salisbury (MP I. 40); seneschal of Gascony and Justiciar of Ireland 1259–60; d. 1260. His seal does not show a label. (*CP* xi. 381–2, n. (*k*); Birch 11462.)

BOHUN

188. *Humfrey de Bohun d'azur od six leonceux d'or od un bende blanche et deux cutices d'or a un label de gules.*

Cf. 184, —, —: MP I. 33, 35; II. 9: B 10, 189: C 123.

Sir Humphrey de Bohun, s. of Humphrey, Earl of Hereford and Essex (MP II. 9), d.v.p. 1265.

He is perhaps the same person as Humphrey de Bohun who sealed in 1260 with *A bend semy of fluers-de-lis*, but not coticed, *between six lions*. (Birch 7530; *CP* vi. 462.)

BOHUN

189. *Henry de Boun d'azure od six leonceux d'or a un bende de gules et deux cutices de gules.*

Cf. 185, —, —: MP I. 33, 35; II. 9: B 10, 188: C 123.

B II makes the bend argent coticed gules, but B I (*b*) follows (*a*) in making both the bend and the cotices gules: so too E 116. Whichever is correct it is an example of differencing by change of tincture, and is the more interesting as it ignores the supposed rule forbidding colour upon colour.

This entry may be intended for Henry de Bohun, uncle of B 188, though Dugdale (*Bar.* i. 180) states that he died in his youth, and his father Henry, Earl of Hereford, d. in 1220.

BOHUN of Midhurst

190. *Frank de Boun de gules od un cressant d'ermyne od merlots d'ermyne en lı urle.*

(*a*) *A crescent in an orle of martlets.*

(*b*) *Gules semy of martlets a crescent ermine.*

Cf. 186, —, —.

Sir Frank or Franco de Bohun, s. of Savary, of Midhurst, Sussex, d. 1273 leaving a s. John (d. 1284). (*CP* ii. 199; *Herald and Genealogist*, vii. 314; *Genealogist*, N.S. xxviii. 1 sqq.)

His father, Savary, sealed with *A crescent in a bordure* (Birch 7555). The family afterwards bore *Or, a cross azure* (E 625, &c.) and other variations are found.

SAVAGE

191. *Robert le Savage barre d'or et de gules.*

(*a*) *Barry of six pieces.*

(*b*) *Barry of ten pieces or and gules.*

Cf. 187, —, —.

Robert le Savage, sometime Sheriff of Norfolk and Suffolk, Bedfordshire and Buckinghamshire, occurs from 1227 and was dead by March 1258, leaving a s. Richard. (*Cal. Pat. Rolls*, 1225–32, p. 138; 1247–58, pp. 40, 234, 447, 448, 619.)

GORGES

192. *Rauf Gorges roele d'argent et d'azur.*

(*a*) and (*b*) A spiral whirlpool.

Cf. 188, —, —.

B II blazons as B I (*a*) but adds a marginal trick; B I (*b*), four concentric annulets argent. This fits the blazon 'roele' from the old French *roel* or *roele*, a wheel or disk, better than the spiral form, although the latter was preferred in later times. Both forms represent a whirlpool, Latin *gurges*.

CP vi. 13–15 n. shows that there were two brothers, both named Ralph, in 1253 and 1271 between whom it is virtually impossible to distinguish. One brother m. Ellen, dau. and coh. of Ives de Morville, and is dead 24 October 1271. The other m. a certain Joan. Heraldry may be of help in distinguishing between the brothers. Two distinct coats were borne by Gorges in the thirteenth century, (*a*) *Azure a gurge argent* of which the first appearance is here, and (*b*) *Lozengy or and azure.* The first coat appears in various rolls, temp. Edward I for Ralph de Gorges who d. 1297, and who may be the s. of Ralph de Gorges (d. 1271) by Ellen de Morville. But the second coat is borne by Ralph, Lord Gorges, thought to be his son. The entry G 135 for the lozengy coat may well be for Ralph (d. 1297). If it could be attributed to the Ralph who m. Joan, it would appear reasonable and tidy that one brother bore coat (*a*) and the other coat (*b*), but that would mean that Ralph, Lord Gorges, was descended from Ralph and Joan and not from Ralph and Ellen de Morville. It is more likely that the family used both arms and finally settled on coat (*b*). Cf. Mohun. (*CP* vi. 9–15; Raymond Gorges, *The Story of a Family through Eleven Centuries.*)

GOURNAY

193. *Robert de Gorney d'or od un leon rampant noir od la bordure de gules.*

Cf. 189, —, —.

Probably Robert de Gournay or Gurney of Englishcombe, Farringdon-Gurney and Harptree, Som. His parentage is uncertain. Dugdale says that he was the s. of Anselm de Gurney by Eve, sister and heir of Maurice de Gaunt. According to Smyth Eve was dau. of Hawise de Gurney by Robert FitzRobert FitzHarding of Berkeley. He says that she married a Gurney but does not give the Christian name. Daniel Gurney says that Eve was half-sister of Maurice de Gaunt and that she m. Thomas, s. of William de Harptree, by whom she bore Robert de Gurney. Dugdale says that Robert, s. of John de Harptree, was grandfather of Robert de Gurney, and presumably he meant maternal grandfather. It would seem that Dugdale knew of a Harptree connexion but was not certain of the details.

Robert de Gurney sealed temp. Henry III with *Three piles, on a chief a label* (4) (Birch 10334). The usual arms of the family were *Paly of six or and azure*, and it is safe to assume that piles and pales were the same in the thirteenth century. The label may be a difference borne during his mother's lifetime.

No explanation has been made for the arms attributed to him in this roll. (Dugd. *Bar.* i. 429–31; Smyth, *Lives of the Berkeleys*, i. 52–54; Daniel Gurney, *Record of the House of Gurney*, pt. iv, pp. 593, 614–21.)

LE FORT de Vivonne

194. *Will'm de Fortz de Vyvone dargent al chief de gules.*
(*b*) 'Walter le Fortz de Vyvone'.

Cf. 190, —, 89.

This is one of the cases where B II adds a superfluous trick.

William le Fort of Vivonne in Poitou and of Chewton, Som., d. 1259. He was the second husband of Maud (d. 1299), dau. of William Ferrers, Earl of Derby. Her first husband was Simon de Kyme (d. 1248) and her third Aimery, Vicomte de Rochechouart in Poitou. For the four daughters and coheiresses of her marriage to William le Fort see *CP* iv. 199.

B II also calls William 'de Vivonia', but B IV says 'de Coupland', apparently by confusion with the Forz, earls of Albermarle (see *EYC* vii. 19, &c.).

The family of Vivonne in Poitou bore *Ermine, a chief gules*. (*Nav.* 1291 for 'le Sire de Tors', 1375–8; *Berry* 1078.)

COLUMBERS

195. *Mathew de Colombers au tiel.*
(*a*) Chief.
(*b*) 'Mathew Columbers autiele'. Shield blank.

Cf. 191, —, —.

Matthew, s. of Michael de Columbers of Hants. and Wilts., living 1245, d. 1272 leaving a widow Maud and a brother and h. Michael (d. 1284). (*Cal. Charter Rolls*, i. 282, &c.; *Cal. Fine Rolls*, i. 163, 165; Dugd. *Bar.* i. 633.)

BEAUCHAMP of Bedford

196. *Geoffrey Bealchamp esquartele d'argent et de sable.*

Cf. 192, —, —: MP II. 28, 76: B 54.

Geoffrey, s. of Simon de Beauchamp of Bedford and younger brother of William (MP II. 28: B 54): same person as MP II. 76. (*Beds. Hist. Rec. Soc.* ii. 211.)

BIGOD

197. *Rauf Bygot d'or od trois* [*un*] *croix de gules od les eschalops d'argent en la croix.*
(*a*) Trick blank.
(*b*) *Or, on a cross gules five escallops argent.*

Cf. 193, —, —: MP I. 39; II. 12, 94: B 6, 89: C 91.

B I (*a*) writes *d'or od trois croix . . .*, an obviously faulty blazon which Glover did not attempt to trick. Cooke, however, in B I (*b*) and the unknown author of B II, both give the arms correctly.

Probably in taking the item from the 1240 collection the 1253 compiler misread *un* as *iij* and therefore wrote *trois*. A similar mistake may well account for William Sarren's unsatisfactory *trois croix* in B 164.

The entry presumably refers to Rauf Bigod of Settrington, Norfolk, fourth s. of Hugh, Earl of Norfolk (MP I. 39, d. 1225) and brother of MP II. 12 and B 89. He seems to have been succ. at Settrington by his nephew John (d. 1305) who was a younger s. of Earl Hugh's second s. Hugh Bigod, Justiciar of England (d. 1266), and who bears the same arms in E 463 and F 133. (*Yorks. Arch. Journ.* xxxii. 172, &c.; *CP* ix. 590; *DNB*.)

CORBET

198. *Thomas Corbet d'or od deux corbeux noirs.*
(*a*) and (*b*) *Two corbies in pale.*

Cf. 194, —, 122.

B IV paints the corbies side by side, but the usual arrangement is in pale.

Thomas, s. of Robert (d. 1221), Corbet of Caus, Salop, d. 1274. His s. Piers d. 1300. (*CP* iii. 417.)

ST. AMAND

199. *Amery de Seint Aymane d'argent frette de sable au chief de sable od trois myrrours d'or en le chief.*
(*a*) and (*b*) *Fretty and on a chief three bezants.*

Cf. 195, —, —.

Note the use of 'myrrours' to blazon the bezants; no other instance has been noticed. B II omits the bezants, probably by inadvertence.

Either Amaury de St. Amand, d. 1241, or his gds. (s. of Ralph, d. 1245) who did homage for his lands in 1256 and d. 1285. (*CP* xi. 295.)

STUTEVILLE

200. *Robert Lestouteville le Normant burle dargent et de gules od un leon noir.*
(*a*) *Buruly of fourteen pieces, a lion rampant.*
(*b*) *Barry of ten argent and gules, a lion rampant sable.*

Cf. 196, —, 109: B 171.

B IV's painting omits the lion although it is duly blazoned. The epithet 'le Normant' shows that Robert d'Estouteville (s. of John, d. 1258) of Valmont in Normandy is meant. He also held lands in Notts. and Derbys. and other English counties. He d. 1306 when Valmont passed to Robert his gds. by his first wife Joan (Talbot?), while the English lands were inherited by John (d. 1322), the s. of his second marriage to Eleanor de Genoure, widow of Alexander de Balliol of Bywell. (*EYC* ix. 37, 42, 57, &c.; *NCH* xii. 411; *CP* ii. 161; Sitwell, *Tales of my Native Village*, p. 74, &c.)

Robert, his father, and his s. John, sealed with these arms. (Birch 5901, 13715; Demay, *Sceaux de la Normandie*, 239; 2336; *NCH* vi. 190; Jeayes, *Derbyshire Charters*, no. 1095.)

FAUCONBERGE

201. *Walt' de Fauconberg noir od un quintefoill d'argent et les avoz d'argent entour.*
(*a*) *A pierced cinquefoil.*
(*b*) *Walter Foconbrege, Sable, a pierced cinquefoil between three birds argent.*

Cf. 197, —, —: C 90.

Whoever added the tricks in this version was unfamiliar with the arms, for B I (*a*) omits the *avoz* entirely and B I (*b*) draws three birds only although *entour* must mean that the birds are in *orle* or, as C 90 puts it, *bordeans*. Both B II and C 90 blazon martlets, though one would have expected falcons as a cant.

Sir Walter de Fauconberge of Rise and Withernwick in Holderness, Yorks., s. of Sir Piers (living 1230), d. 1304 leaving a s. Walter.

The family seem to have descended from the Chatelains of St. Omer, lords of Fauquembergue, who in MP I. 91 bore *Argent, a fess or*, and Sir Walter sealed the Barons' Letter in 1301 with *A fess and in chief three pallets*, which is blazoned in E 159 *Or, a fess azure, in chief three pallets gules* (see also Birch 5905, 9637). His s., however, assumed *Argent, a lion rampant azure* (N 133, 1079), being the arms of his mother Agnes, sister and coh. of B 48, Piers Brus of Skelton. (*CP* v. 267–70.)

The origin of the cinquefoil is not known.

MARTIN, FitzMartin

202. *Nichol le fitz Martin d'argent od deux barres de gules od un label d'azur.*

Cf. 198, —, —: B 65.

Nicholas Martin or FitzMartin, s. of William FitzMartin (d. *c.* 1216) of Kemys, Pembroke, and *iure uxoris* of Barnstaple, Devon; d. 1282. (*CP* viii. 533.)

MALTRAVERS

203. *Johan Mautravers noir frette d'or.*

Cf. 199, —, 108.

John Maltravers, s. of John Maltravers (d. *c.* 1220), held lands in Dorset, Glos., &c.; d. *c.* 1262. (*CP* viii. 578–9.)

BEAUCHAMP

204. *Johan de Beauchamp noir od un egle d'argent le bek et les pees d'or.*

Cf. 200, —, —: MP II. 27.

The same person as MP II. 27, whose identity is uncertain.

LINDSAY

205. *Walter de Lyndesey de gules od un faus escuchon veyr.*

Cf. 201, —, —.

Sir Walter Lindsay of Lamberton, co. Berwick, and of Molesworth, Hunts., was a gds. of Sir Walter Lindsay who was a younger brother of David Lindsay of Crawford; he was dead 1271. (Lindsay, *Lives of the Lindsays*, i. 28–31; *Cal. Inq.* i, no. 820.)

DE VALE of Pembrokeshire

206. *Gilbert de Val de la Marche d'argent ove une crois furche de gules.*

(*a*) Blank shield.

(*b*) *Argent, a cross moline gules.*

Cf. 202, —, —.

As in 171 la Marche means the Welsh Marches.

Sir Gilbert de Vale, seneschal of Pembroke 1241–6, though not a tenant in chief, held considerable lands in the Palatinate of Pembroke and Barony of Kemys, as well as in Ireland. He is, perhaps, the same who occurs in 1207 and again *c.* 1219 and *c.* 1229. The last male of the family, Sir Robert de Vale, d. shortly before 1303, when the lands were divided among his daughters.

Robert de Vale of Pembrokeshire sealed *c.* 1200–10 with a plain cross. The fourchy cross of this roll may be a cadency difference, but it is more likely that it merely shows the fluidity of arms at this time.

Post-Tudor Welsh armorials assign to the family *Argent, three oak-branches* or *leaves vert*, but there is no contemporary warrant for that coat. (*Ex inf.* Major Francis Jones citing *Cal. Fines* 9 John, p. 410; BM Add. ch. 8408, 8412–3; *Baronia de Kemes*, pp. 52–53; Poyston Deeds no. 1 in Nat. Lib. of Wales.)

RABAYNE

207. *Helys de Rableyne d'argent od trois escalopes de gules od la fesse de gules.*

Cf. 203, —, —.

Ellis de Rabayne, Constable of Corfe Castle in 1272, d. 1285 leaving a s. John. He held the manor of Thorisway, Lincs. His widow Maud, dau. and coh. of John de Bayeux, afterwards wife of Peter Mallore, sealed in 1317 with *Paly on a chief three escallops* (Hutchins, *Dorset,* i. 469, 495; ii. 619, &c.; iii. 420; *Book of Seals,* 266; Birch 12891.)

ROCHFORD

208. *Guy de Rochford le Peytevyn esquartele d'argent et de gules.*
(*b*) Omits 'le Peytevyn'.

Cf. 204, —, —: C 148.

Guy de Rocheford, a Poitevin, was banished from England in 1258. (*Book of Fees,* 1160; *CM* v. 725.)
   He is frequently confused with his contemporary Guy de Rochford of Rochford, Essex, who bore *Quarterly or and gules* (C 118; FW 183), but there is no need to assume that the compiler confused them or the arms. Charles de Rochfort in Poitou bore *Quarterly a label* (5) on his seal in 1269. (Ddq. 3413.)

GACELIN

209. *Geffrey Gacelin d'or billette de sable od un label de gules.*

Cf. 205, —, —.

Geoffrey Gacelyn, Gwacelyn, or Wascelin, occurs from 1242 and was dead 1282. (*Cal. Fine Rolls,* i. 166), holding lands in Wilts., Dorset, &c.

EVERMUE

210. *Walter de Quermui [Evermue] d'or od un quintefoille de gules.*
(*b*) *Walter Evermue, Or, a pierced cinquefoil gules.*

Cf. 206, —, —.

B I (*a*) writes 'Walter de Quermui'. B II writes 'Walter de Queryne', but Glover has added 'Evermue' in the margin, presumably to emend the text. Without doubt the 1253 manuscript also put Q for E.
   Walter de Evermue or Evermuth (rectius Envermeu), of Knayth, Lincs., and Runham, Norfolk, d. 1273 leaving as his coheirs the three daughters of Sir Jollan de Evermue of Huntington, Lincs. (*Cal. Inq.* ii, no. 32.) In 1227 he held Knayth (*Cal. Charter Rolls,* i. 28) and was appointed in 1230 Sheriff of Lincolnshire. (*Cal. Pat. Rolls,* 1225–32, p. 337.) Sir Jollan de Evermue sealed with a *Sexfoil and a label* (Birch 9542).

SACKVILLE of Fawley

211. *Bartholomew de Sakevyll d'ermyne od trois cheverons de gules.*

Cf. 207, —, —.

Bartholomew de Sackville occurs at Fawley, Bucks., from 1234 to 1250. He must have descended from Herbrand who held Fawley at Domesday and whom Round has shown to be the ancestor of the Sackvilles of Essex, but it is not possible to place him in the pedigree. Both Lipscombe and Phillips identify him with the Bartholomew, an idiot from the age of 18, s. of Jordan de Sackville by Maud de Normanville whose Irish interests were entrusted in 1290 to Jordan de Evermue and fifteen months later to Walter and John de Sackville and who was dead by September 1308 if not by 1304. That the Fawley Sackvilles had interests in Ireland is clear, but that identification is doubtful as no mention of Bartholomew has been found between 1250 and 1290. At the same time the reference to Jordan de Evermue is significant seeing that the immediately preceding entry on this roll is an Evermue. (Round, *Peerage and Pedigree*, i. 285–9; *Arch. Journ.* lxiv. 217, &c.; Lipscombe, *Bucks.* iii. 560; C. J. Phillips, *History of the Sackville Family*, i. 6, &c.)

None of the above sources give the arms of the Fawley and Irish Sackvilles. The coat here attributed to Bartholomew is clearly a variant of Clare (B 5). At Domesday Fawley was held of Walter Giffard and passed to Richard de Clare, Earl of Pembroke, 'Strongbow', gtgds. of Rohese, sister and in her issue h. of Walter Giffard. His dau. and h. Isabel de Clare m. William the Marshal. The Sackvilles held the manor of the Honour of Giffard. (*Book of Fees*, 467.)

MONTGOMERY

212. *Will'm Moungomery d'ermyne od la bordure de gules od les fers d'or en la bordure.*

Cf. 208, —, —.

William de Montgomery in 1242 held Ecton, Northants., Moreton, Staffs., Marston Montgomery and Cubley, Derbys., of William de Ferrers, Earl of Derby, whence the horseshoes. (*Book of Fees*, 934, 969, 993.)

F 108 gives this coat for William with the field argent. The Armorial du héraut Navarre, no. 160, *c.* 1370, attributes this coat to the sire de Ferrères in Normandy.

B I (*b*) has inadvertently exchanged the tricks of 212 and 213.

RICHMOND

213. *Rowaud le Conestable de Richemond de gules od le chief d'or od deux gymeus del un et del autre.*

(*a*) *Two gemel bars and a chief.*
(*b*) *Gules, three gemel bars and a chief or.*

Cf. 209, —, 145.

The blazon of both B I and B II seems to mean that one gemel is red on the gold chief and the other gold on the red field. But Roald's seal displays two gemels and a chief, like B I (*a*)'s trick and that is how the coat appears in B IV. 145 and in many later rolls, though TJ 551 gives *Gules, a fess double coticed or.*

Roald succ. his father Alan as Constable of Richmond and was dead in 1281, when he was succ. by his s. Roald. Their descendants took Benton and Richmond as surnames.

B I (*b*)'s version of the arms with three gemels is otherwise unknown. (*EYC* v (Richmond), 4, 91; *VCH North Riding*, i. 233–4.)

GERNON

214. *Will'm Gernon ounde de long d'argent et de gules.*

(*a*) The trick is something between *paly and pily of six pieces.*
(*b*) *Paly wavy of six pieces argent and gules.*

Cf. 210, —, —.

William Gernon, d. 1258 aged over 70. He was s. of Ralph (d. 1247), founder of Leigh Priory, Essex. (*Feudal Cambs.*, p. 218.)

The arms are perhaps intended as a pun on the name Gernons, whiskers or beard. They were variously drawn. No impression of William's seal has been found, but his s. Ralph (d. 1274) sealed with *Paly wavy of six pieces*, as in B I (*b*)'s trick (Birch 10072: cf. 10071, 10075–6–8), and Ralph's s. William sealed in B 1309 with *three narrow piles wavy.* (*Suffolk Inst. of Arch. Proc.* xxi. 29, seal 55.) Another seal used by Ralph Gernon of Essex, temp. Henry III, has *Paly wavy of ten pieces* (Birch 10073), but it does not appear whether that is a differenced version of the arms used by the above Ralph, v.p., or whether the seal belonged to another Ralph.

MORTEYN

215. *Will'm de Mortayne Breton d'ermyne od le chief de gules.*

Cf. 211, —, —.

Sir William de Morteyn of Derbys. and of Marston, Beds., s. of Eustace (d. 1224), d. 1283, his h. being his nephew Roger, s. of Roger de Morteyn. (*Derbys. Arch. Journ.* N.S. ii. 104–6; Birch 11948; *Cal. Inq.* ii. no. 508; cf. *VCH Beds.* iii. 433; *Genealogist,* N.S. xxxviii. 197, 203.)

B II gives the Christian name as Robert, meaning perhaps William's brother of that name. (*Beds. Hist. Rec. Soc.* ix. 5–22.) This is probably Robert de Morteyn who held Tickhill, Yorks., and Grave, Notts., and d. in 1299 leaving a s. Eustace. (*Cal. Inq.* iii. no. 497.)

Version II

SHAFTO

(II) 212. *Robert de Shaftowe goule sur ung bende d'argent trois moletes dazure.*

This and the six succeeding coats are additions made *c.* 1310. They are not in B I. It will be noticed that they all belong to Northumberland, Cumberland, or Durham.

NCH iv. 417 identifies Robert as a Shafto of Little Barington, but jumps from him to William de Schafthowe in 1300 and from him to the 1666 visitation even though the arms had been recorded in the 1552 visitation.

SWINBURNE

(II) 213. *Adam de Swyneburne de goules a trois testes de senglier d'argent.*

Adam de Swinburne of East Swinburn, Northumb., d. 1318. (*NCH* iv. 309.)

FITZMARMADUKE

(II) 214. *Richard le filz Marmaduke de goules ung fece et trois papegeyes dargent a ung baston dazure sur tout.*

Sir Richard fitz John FitzMarmaduke of Harden, Durham, seneschal of the Bishop of Durham, was slain on the Old Bridge at Durham in 1318 by his kinsman Robert Neville. He d.s.p. His sister and h. m. Robert de Lumley. (Surtees, *Durham,* i. 24–26; *CP* viii. 268; Birch 9742; N 1001.)

His father Sir John FitzMarmaduke, a banneret (N 142; E 622), d. 1310, and the fact that Richard's arms are differenced with a baston both here and in N 1001 suggests that this version was not copied until 1310 or later.

HERON

(II) 215. *Odinel Heron dazur a trois herons dargent.*

Odinel Heron living 1292, d. before 1312. He was a younger s. of William Heron of Ford, Northumb. (d. 1297). (*NCH* xi. 370, 378.)

KENDAL

(II) 216. *Edmond de Kendale argent ung bende cotisee dauncee vert.*

Sir Edmund de Kendal occurs from 1313 to 1336. He held land in Middlesex and Sussex, was granted Lyndon Manor, Rutland, in 1317, and was afterwards keeper of the peace and commissioner of assay in Hampshire. He is probably the Sir Edmund de Kendal of Northumb. and Cumb. who bears the same arms in N 994, where the blazon specifies that both the bend and the cotices are dancy.

LAMPLUGH

(II) **217.** *John Lamplowe argent ung crois sable florettee.*

Sir John de Lamplugh of Lamplugh, Cumb., s. of Robert de Lamplugh (d. 1285), d. 1330 leaving a s. Ralph. (*Cumb. and Westmorland Arch. Soc.*, N.S. xxxviii. 80, 82.) Later rolls make the field gold. (N 1003; G 190; S 381.)

REDMAN

(II) **218.** *Maheu de Redmain de goules a trois horielers d'or.*

The cushions or pillows are usually ermine with gold tassels. (N 1016; S 472, &c.)

Sir Matthew de Redman d. 1319, father of another Matthew. He was s. of Henry de Redman of Levens, Westm. (d. 1278). (W. Greenwood, *The Redmans of Levens and Harewood*, passim; *VCH Lancs.* viii. 175.)

Version III

SOMERI

(III) **20.** *Roger de Someri esquartele d'or e de gules.*

This is a conflation of two items. It should read: *Roger de Someri d'or deus leopartz d'azur* (see B I. 97) *Le Comte de Maundevill esquartele d'or e de gules* (see B I 19).

AUDLEY

(III) **34.** *James de Audedoyle de gul' frete de or.*

Henry de Aldethley (d. 1246) sealed in 1233 with *Fretty and on a canton a cross formy* (Birch 7017), but his s. James (d. 1271) and his heirs dropped the canton and cross and bore the coat given here, e.g. the seal of Sir James Audley, Justice of Chester in 1259 (Birch 7025).The fretty is derived from the arms of Verdun (B I. 90), overlords of the earlier Audleys. (*CP* i. 337–8.)

Version IV

BEAUCHAMP of Elmley

(IV) **81.** *William Beauchamp de Almeleye port de goules ove un fesse dor.*

(iv)81.

William de Beauchamp of Elmley, Worcs. (s. of Walter, d. 1235), d. 1268. He m. Isabel Mauduit in whose right their s. William Beauchamp succ. to the earldom of Warwick in 1268; as earl he quartered the old arms of Warwick (B I. 20), the field of his paternal coat being powdered with gold crosses. (*CP* xii (2) 368; Baker, *Northants.* ii. 218–9.)

APPENDIX I

MARMION

THE two Marmion entries in Glover's Roll do not seem to have attracted any attention in the past, and yet they are of great importance for the light which they throw on the arms. They are: 47. *Will'm Marmyon de veer od un fesse de gules*. 57. *Philip Marmyon de veer od la fesse de paile*. The latter coat is tricked in both copies of Version I as *Vair, a fesse gules fretty or*. As the roll was compiled about 1253, these must refer to Sir Philip Marmion of Tamworth, Scrivelsby, &c., the then head of the senior line of Marmion, and his cousin german, William Marmion of Winteringham, the head of the junior branch.

The Marmions were a Norman family, whose chief seat was at Fontenay-le-Marmion, in the department of Calvados. As Sir Charles Clay wrote in *The Complete Peerage* (viii, 505 et seqq.), there are few families whose origin has given rise to more erroneous speculation. Their pedigree was, however, examined with minute care by C. F. R. Palmer in *A History of the Baronial Family of Marmion* (Tamworth, 1875), and for the earlier generations reference should be made to that, to J. H. Round's *Feudal England*, p. 190, &c., and to Sir Charles Clay's article in *The Complete Peerage*. Here it will suffice to begin with Robert Marmion, King's Justice, who died in 1218. His two elder sons were both named Robert. Robert the elder, son of the Justice by his first wife, Maud de Beauchamp, died *c.* 1242, leaving a son and heir Philip (no. 57). The other, Robert the younger, was by the Justice's second wife, Philippa, and was father of no. 47.

Sir Philip, who succeeded his father as head of the senior line about 1242, died in 1291 s.p.m. His first wife was Joan, daughter and coheir of Hugh de Kilpeck. By her he had three daughters, Joan (d. 1295 s.p.), Mazera, whose daughter Joan de Cromwell married Alexander de Freville, and Maud, who married Ralph le Boteler. By a second wife, Mary, Sir Philip had one daughter, another Joan, who was married first to Thomas de Ludlow and afterwards to Henry Hillary; her granddaughter, Margaret Ludlow, married Sir John Dymoke, of whom more later. On Sir Philip's death his properties were divided among his four daughters or their heirs, Tamworth falling to Mazera and Scrivelsby to the younger Joan.

The younger cousin, William Marmion of Winteringham (no. 47), was hardly less prominent than Sir Philip. He was born *c.* 1230, was summoned to Parliament in 1264, married Lorette, daughter of Rohese de Douvres (see no. 82), and died in or before 1276 His son John was summoned to Parliament from 1313 to 1322.

Although this is a Norman family French sources are of no help as to their arms. Dr. Adam-Even could find no mention of them in any of the French rolls, and the only recorded armorial seal[1] is too damaged to be legible. La Roque[2] says (1) that the family originally bore vair plain, (2) that a cadet line added thereto a fess gules, and (3) that that in turn was differenced by the addition of a golden fretty on the fess. The statement that the arms were originally vair plain may or may not be correct; in the absence of any supporting evidence[3] one can only be sceptical, especially as the further statement

---

[1] Douët-d'Arcq, *Sceaux de l'Empire*, no. 2719.

[2] *Histoire généalogique de la Maison d'Harcourt*, Paris, 1662. I have to thank M. Robert Viel, of Paris, for drawing my attention to this and for searching other French sources for me.

[3] The fact that the family of Gouvis, neighbours and vassals of Marmion in Normandy, bore vair plain cannot be considered sufficient as evidence that the Marmions wore that coat.

that the fretty fess is a cadenced version of the plain red fess is certainly wrong; the exact contrary is the case. The fretty fess is a misrepresentation or simplification of the fess *paillé* which was borne by Sir Philip as head of the senior line, and which was changed by the younger line to the plain red fess which this roll gives for William (no. 47).

Sir Harris Nicolas in his edition of this roll translated *paile* as pal**y** (p. 31), but reference to Sir Philip's seal (see below) proves beyond all doubt that *paile* in this entry is the French *pailé* or *paillé*, Low Latin *palla* or *pallea*, a rich figured silk of oriental manufacture. Such fabrics, like the furs, were sometimes used in making display shields. As a term of blazon *paillé* seems to be unknown to English armory outside this roll, and in France it is confined to a handful of Norman families of whom the best known are Tesson or Taisson, and Clères. Both these families were apt to represent *paillé* as green or blue with a gold pattern of rings or ovals enclosing lions and eagles.[1] But these creatures were not an essential feature of the design,[2] nor is there any reason why the ground colour should always be green or blue. Indeed, in the case of Marmion, as the *paillé* is on a field of vair, the choice of red as ground colour was almost inevitable.

Sir Philip Marmion's own seal in 1265 represents the *paillé* by a row of five contiguous annulets enclosing small roses or cinquefoils.[3] Smallpece's Roll, no. 150, which seems to have been compiled soon after, if not even before, Sir Philip's death, makes the fess or fretty engrailed gules, while Peter Le Neve's Book, no. 928, paints the arms as quartered by Dymoke with the fess lozengy gules and or.[4] On the other hand, St. George's Roll (E 60), which is perhaps a little earlier than Smallpece's, *c.* 1285, makes Philip's fess gules fretty or like the tricks in this roll, and that version recurs in the mid-fifteenth-century Mandeville Roll for John Marmion (II. 92).[5] The latter, however, appears to be a mistake. John's mother Avice was great-granddaughter of no. 47 and his seal in 1372 bears the plain fess of the junior line.[6] The fess on his effigy in St. Nicholas's Church, West Tanfield, also appears to be plain.[7] Yet another variation appears in the early fifteenth-century blazoned version of St. George's Roll (E II. 60), which gives the arms of William (*sic*) Marmion as *Verre dargent et dasur une fece de gueules entre ij bareletz de gueules.* As the corresponding entry in the thirteenth-century painted version is for Philip Marmion with the fess gules fretty or (E I. 60), it is evident that all these variants are no more than attempts to rationalize the pattern of the unfamiliar *paillé*.

The Tesson family, above-mentioned, bore *Barry of six pieces paillé and ermine*, the ground of the *paillé* being either green or blue.[8] The Tessons and the Marmions were near neighbours in Normandy and may have sprung from a common stock. In any case, there

---

[1] The Fitzwilliam Roll blazons the arms of both these families with azure instead of *paillé* (nos. 562, 564), thus showing how little *paillé* was understood in England.

[2] See, for example, the Clères and Taisson coats in the *Armorial Equestre . . .*, pl. LXXIX, nos. 2, 3, 14, 15. These coats occur also in the *Armorial Wijnbergen*, nos. 370–1, 389, 390; the illustration, pl. V, does not permit the pattern of the *paillé* to be distinguished, but I saw the roll itself in 1950 and my recollection is that the pattern does not include either lions or eagles.

[3] B.M., Harl. ch. 53 D 4. Birch 11621–2 describes the fess as 'diapered', and *The Complete Peerage*, taking the 'diaper' to be mere artistic decoration, ignores the decoration and blazons a plain fess, although it does give the blazon from Glover's Roll.

[4] Sir John Dymoke married Margaret, great-granddaughter of Philip Marmion by his second marriage. This marriage carried Scrivelsby and the Championship to the Dymokes, as appears below.

[5] John Lord Grey of Rotherfield married as his second wife Avice, sister and coheir of Robert, third Lord Marmion of Winteringham (d. *c.* 1360 s.p.), and their son John (d. 1387 s.p.) took the name and arms of Marmion.

[6] *Arch.* xlvii (1883), 183–4, cf. 181, 185.   [7] McCall, *Richmondshire Churches*, p. 195.

[8] So on a seal of 1205. See A. de Tesson, 'Le Paillé et le diapré héraldique' in *Annuaire du Conseil héraldique de France*, xvi (1903) 133. Cf. *Armorial Wijnbergen*, no. 389, and other French armorials.

were several intermarriages and there can be no doubt but that the *paillé* in their respective arms was derived from a common source.

That Philip of the *paillé* fess was of the senior line is confirmed by the three swords which fill the spandrels of his seal, and which have the same significance as the shield, *Sable, a sword erect argent*, which is attributed to him in the Camden (215), Dering (174), and Heralds' (HE 118, FW 131) Rolls, and which was afterwards used with the tinctures reversed by his Dymoke descendants.[1] It has been suggested that this was the coat of Kilpeck, marshalled by Sir Philip for his first wife, Joan de Kilpeck,[2] but no Kilpeck seal has been found with these arms nor is the sword assigned to Kilpeck in any mediaeval roll. On the contrary, it is clear that the sword was in the nature of an official badge borne by Sir Philip in token of the Championship.

Of all the fables with which the Marmion pedigree has been bedevilled, perhaps the most glaring and persistent has been that which makes William the Conqueror confer Tamworth Castle on Robert Marmion, 'the Champion of Normandy', to hold by the service of Champion in England. No serious student would now accept that,[3] and yet it is impossible to doubt that Sir Philip held some part of his possessions by that service. The evidence was set out by Palmer, examined by Round, and summarized by Sir Charles Clay. It was found in Henry III's reign that the Marmions held both Tamworth and Scrivelsby of the king, but by what service was not then known. In 1328, however, it was found that Tamworth was held by the service of appearing armed in the royal arms and mounted on the king's best charger to make proof for the king against any who opposed his coronation, and that finding was confirmed on various occasions down to the death in 1339 of Joan, daughter of Sir Philip's second daughter Mazera, widow of Sir Alexander Freville. Unlike Tamworth, Scrivelsby passed to Sir Philip's youngest daughter Joan, and an inquisition of 1327/8 found that it was held by that same service. Thereafter the Championship was for some time in dispute between the holders of Tamworth and Scrivelsby, but in 1377 Sir John Dymoke, who had married Joan Marmion's granddaughter and heiress Margaret, produced 'more and better records and evidences' and thereby established his claim to the Championship *jure uxoris*. That right is not undisputed.[4]

Round's statement that in England the service of Champion cannot be traced any earlier than 1326[5] ignores the evidence of Sir Philip's seal. The fact that he set the sword on that seal, coupled with the later evidence outlined above, leaves no room to doubt that the Championship was held by the Marmions in 1265, though nothing conclusive has yet been found to show how or when it came to them.

It remains to consider the Marmion entry in Walford's Roll: 155. *Philip Marmion de veire un fesse de gules.*

Here we have the plain red fess of the Winteringham branch, but no head of that branch was named Philip. There was, however, a Philip Marmion who held Westbury Manor and other lands in Wiltshire. He died before March 1276 leaving as heir his grandson Roger, son of his deceased son Philip. He also had William, Eva, and Iseult.[6]

[1] Fenwick's Roll II. 944; cf. the Tudor MSS. L 1, p. 102 and L 10, p. 57*b*, both in the College of Arms. A similar shield, *Argent, a sword in bend sable*, is attributed to Pulverbatch, a family who took their name from one of the Marmion manors. (Starkey's Roll 1011; Letter E Roll 223; MS. L 9, p. 103*b*.)

[2] e.g. Parker's *Glossary of Heraldry*, 1892, p. 397 and pl. II, &c.

[3] Round pointed out that no evidence has ever been produced to show that the Marmions or anyone else held the office of Champion to the Norman dukes. (*Family Origins*, p. 117.)

[4] Palmer, op. cit., p. 108, &c.; Round, *The King's Serjeants*, p. 381, &c.; *CP* viii. 513 nn.

[5] *Family Origins*, p. 117.

[6] *CP*, p. 512, n. (*h*), citing an Inquisition of 1276 (*Cal. Inq.* ii. 103) and *Cal. Pat. Rolls*, 1258–66, p. 585; Moor, iii. 121 citing *Fine Roll* and *Inq.*

This Philip is not named in the *Complete Peerage* pedigree, but Palmer (p. 118) places him as fifth son of Robert the Justice and younger brother of the two Roberts above-named, elder and younger. Whether that placing is correct or not it is clear that Philip of Westbury had slight claim to the plain red fess of Winteringham without some difference mark. It is also clear that he was not a person of any prominence in his day, and on the whole it looks as though this item must be meant for Sir Philip of Tamworth, the unfamiliar, and no doubt puzzling, *paillé* fess of his arms being assimilated to the plain red fess of the younger line.

I have to thank Sir Charles Clay and Sir Anthony Wagner for reading the draft of this appendix and for several helpful suggestions.

APPENDIX II

DIAPER AND THE ARMS OF CHAMPAGNE

MANY besides myself must have wondered at the cotices potent which are such a distinctive feature in the arms of the county and province of Champagne. Many, too, will have wondered at the use of the term 'diaper' in the Walford's Roll blazon of those arms.[1]

The arms of Champagne appear in the elaborate blazon of modern French textbooks as: *D'azur a une bende d'argent accompagnée de deux doubles cotices potencées et contre potencées*, though earlier heralds were content with some simpler formula such as: *D'azur a une bende d'argent a ij fresteaux* [cotices] *d'or potenchiez*.[2] In English the usual blazon is: *Azure, a bend argent coticed potent-counterpotent or*. Dr. Adam-Even has, however, pointed out that that coat is not known to have been used until towards the end of the thirteenth century. Before that both the Counts of Champagne and their cadets, the Counts of Blois and Chartres, and the Counts of Sancerre, used on their seals either a plain bend or a bend coticed.[3] After 1234, when Count Theobald the Great (d. 1253) succeeded his maternal uncle as King of Navarre, the coticed bend was sometimes marshalled with the escarbuncle of Navarre, as, for example, in the Camden Roll, c. 1280, no. 10: *Le Rey de Navare l'escu parte de azur et de goules od demy charbocle d'or a une bende d'argent od deus cotices d'or*, that is: *Gules, an escarbuncle or dimidiating Azure, a bend argent coticed or*. Matthew Paris, however, only notes the coticed bend: *Regis Navarie scutum d'azuro benda alba utrobique lineata auro*.[4] Apart from that last reference the earliest allusion to the arms of Champagne in a roll of arms is to Count John I of Sancerre (d. 1270) in the Bigot Roll, c. 1254, no. 286: *L'escu d'azur papellonne d'or a une bende d'argent a iij* [sic] *listiau* [cotices] *d'or a une molette de geules en la bendee'*.[5] The Chifflet–Prinet Roll, which like the Camden Roll dates from about 1280, gives for Count Stephen of Sancerre (d. 1306): *Azure, a bend or coticed argent*. Dr. Adam-Even read this as the shield of Champagne differenced by inverting the tinctures of the bend and its cotices. Prinet, however, failed to notice this inversion in his edition of the roll and it is perhaps significant that Sir William Le Neve's Roll (temp.

---

[1] For particulars of this and other rolls mentioned herein see Sir Anthony Wagner, *Catalogue of English Medieval Rolls of Arms*, and Dr. Paul Adam-Even, 'Catalogue des armoriaux français imprimés', in *Nouvelle Revue Héraldique*, 1941, p. 19, &c. Convenient summaries of the dynastic history of Champagne will be found in *La Grande Encyclopédie* and in the *Encyclopaedia Britannica*. Fuller details will be found in Anselme, *Histoire généalogique des Pairs de France*, ii. 835, &c.

[2] Armorial du héraut Navarre, no. 603.

[3] Dr. Paul Adam-Even, 'A propos d'un sachet aux armes des comtes de Champagne', *Archives Héraldiques Suisses*, lxvii (1953) 50. See also Birch 17984; Ddq. 434–42, 568–86, 958–75, 3572–4, 11372–82; C.B (i.e. Auguste Coulon, *Inventaire des Sceaux de la Bourgogne*, 1912), 12, 13; GB (i.e. Gandilhon, *Les Sceaux du Berry*, 1933), 251–8. On the death of Count Henry III in 1274 his daughter and heiress, Jeanne, was only about 18 months old. A year or so later her mother, Blanche of Artois, was married to Edmund Earl of Lancaster, 'Crouchback', the second son of King Henry III of England. Edmund thereafter and for the rest of Jeanne's minority held the county of Champagne on her behalf and did homage to the King of France therefor. Eventually, as a consequence of Jeanne's marriage to Philip the Fair (King Philip IV, 1285–1314), Champagne was annexed to the Crown of France.

[4] M.P. II 60.

[5] The earliest known French roll of arms, edited by Dr. Adam-Even as 'Un Armorial français du milieu du XIIIᵉ siècle, le rôle d'armes Bigot, 1254', in *Archives Héraldiques Suisses*, 1949.

Edward I, no. 32) assigns the identical coat to the Count of Champagne, while the roll of a tournament held at Mons in 1310 gives the usual tinctures, *Bend argent coticed or*, for Sancerre (no. 123).

Slightly earlier than the Camden and Chifflet–Prinet Rolls are Walford's Roll, *c.* 1275, the Compiègne Tournament, *c.* 1278, and perhaps Smallpece's Roll, temp. Edward I. The entry in Walford's Roll no. 42 reads thus: *Le Counte Chaumpaine d'azur a une bende d'argent a custeces d'or diasprez.* The Roll of the Compiègne Tournament attributes to the King of Navarre a shield of Navarre dimidiating Champagne as in the Camden Roll but with the cotices potent-counterpotent, and Smallpece's Roll, no. 17, assigns the identical shield to Champagne. As these two rolls are only known from modern copies the entries may be regarded with some hesitation, but on the whole I am disposed to accept them. In any case the potency cotices were firmly established in the fourteenth century. They are given both for Champagne and for Sancerre in the Roll of the Herald Navarre, *c.* 1370 (603, 1396) and in other rolls too numerous to list.

On seals the earliest appearance of the potency cotices seems to be on that of Louis de Sancerre in 1280,[1] but it is I think significant that Theobald IV had used a seal with the Champagne cotices diapered some thirty years earlier[2] and that his son Theobald V used a similar seal in 1267–70, the cotices in this case being, in Douët d'Arcq's words, 'diaprées et non potencées'.[3] Moreover, an ornament of enamelled silver preserved at All Souls' College, Oxford, and dating from between 1297 and 1302, shows the arms of Champagne with the cotices dovetailed instead of potenty.[4]

Modern English heraldry books, and some French, explain diaper as a decoration, generally of arabesques or of some geometrical pattern, used by artists to break up and help the play of light on large surfaces of a single tincture or, in uncoloured work, to distinguish the different tinctures. They are unanimous that such diaper has no heraldic significance, and that it can be omitted or the pattern varied at the artist's pleasure. Such decorative patterning was certainly used in the thirteenth century,[5] but that was not the original meaning of the word diaper, and it is doubtful whether such patterns were called diapering before the end of the fifteenth century. Indeed, the *OED* gives no example of the term diaper used in heraldry in that sense before the nineteenth century.

The Low Latin *diasprus* or *diapretus*, from which diaper comes, meant some kind of rich and costly textile. In the fifteenth century the word was applied to a fabric of linen or cotton so woven that the threads formed a small and simple pattern, usually geometric in character. In earlier times the name was applied to richer and more costly stuffs imported from the Near East and apparently of silk damasked or brocaded with gold. It then meant much the same as *paille* (Low Latin *palla* or *pallea*), an old French term for a rich figured silk of oriental manufacture, which, like the furs, was sometimes used in covering the more elaborate shields used for mere display, *écus d'apparat*.[6]

---

[1] Ddq. 436; G.*B* 258.   [2] C.*B* 12.   [3] Ddq. 11377.

[4] *Proc. Soc. Ant.* 2nd s. xxx. 92, 94.

[5] For examples see Gevaert, *L'Héraldique, son esprit . . .*, 1923, fig. 296; Boutell, *Heraldry Historical and Popular*, 1863, pl. VI and VII; Hope, *Heraldry for Craftsmen and Designers*, p. 104, &c.

[6] According to the most reliable continental armorists, from the fifteenth-century manuscript treatise in the library at Carpentras, known as 'L'Ordre des Hérauts' to D. L. Galbreath's *Manuel du Blason* (Lausanne and Lyons, 1942, p. 89), *paille* represented an oriental brocaded silk with a gold pattern on a ground of green or blue. Its use in heraldry was a speciality of Normandy. The pattern consisted of a series of rings linked together in some way and enclosing lions and eagles, and it is interesting to notice that, with the substitution of fleurs-de-lis for the lions and eagles, this is in fact how Ferne depicts diaper (*The Blazon of Gentrie*, 1586, pt. 1, p. 189). Ferne describes diaper as 'a costly furniture of linnen' (not, be it noted, of silk) and he goes on to say that his use of the term differs from that which his interlocutor-pupil was taught 'by your first maister'.

English armorists divide the tinctures into metals, colours, and furs, the last-named comprising ermine and vair and their derivatives. French armorists make the same division, but some give *panne* or *penne* as an alternative term for *fourrure*, fur. This is a mistake, venial no doubt in view of the Low Latin use of *pannus* and *panna* in the sense of fur, but still a mistake. *Panne*, like the Latin *pannus* means cloth, woven material, and the *pannes* form a 4th class of tinctures. I say *pannes* advisedly. Although so far *paille* is the only *panne* which has been generally recognized as such, it is clear that diaper was originally a *panne*, and it is probable that papelonny and perhaps plumetty also should be so classed. But whereas the terms *paille*, papelonny, and plumetty were restricted to certain patterns or classes of pattern there is nothing to suggest that diaper was ever so restricted. In fact one might even say that *paille*, papelonny, and plumetty are special varieties of diaper.

In the light of these facts it is difficult to avoid the conclusion that the Champagne cotices were at one time, probably early in the thirteenth century, made of, or represented as though made of, gold brocade, the 'custeces diaprez' of Walford's Roll. The pattern was, doubtless, of a simple, geometric character, and after a few decades was stereotyped as the potent-counterpotent of the later blazons.

One last point—it will have been noticed that the Bigot Roll blazons the arms of John Count of Sancerre with the field *d'azur papellonne d'or*. On John's seal, however, the field is *crusuly*, as it is also on that of his son Count Stephen II and on that of his contemporary and namesake, John Count of Blois.[1] The seals of Count Theobald of Blois in 1213 and of Stephen of Sancerre in 1281 also display shields with patterned fields. In Theobald's case it is doubtful whether the pattern is a crusuly or mere arabesques. In Stephen's case the field is certainly traced with arabesques.[2] Dr. Adam-Eden took the papelonny of the Bigot Roll to indicate the same pattern which was afterwards so blazoned,[3] but in view of the crusuly and arabesqued fields of the above seals we cannot overlook the possibility that the papelonny, crusuly, and arabesques alike represented a field of diaper, that is of some rich fabric brocaded with gold.

The only other early example of the term diaper which I have met in blazon is, like the coat of Champagne, in Walford's Roll, no. 146: *Le Counte de le Ille gules treis barres d'or diaspres*. This coat is probably that of the earldom of Devon, or of the Isle (of Wight) as it was often called.

This shows that there was then some uncertainty as to the meaning of diaper among English armorists. It is probably an allusion to Gerard Legh who says that fretty engrailed is to be blazoned 'dyapre' (*Accedens of Armorie*, 1562, f. 93; cf. f. 111*b*). In this connexion it may be recalled that the arms of Philip Marmion, which Glover's Roll, *c.* 1225, blazons *De veer od la fesse de paile* (no. 57) are shown in the accompanying tricks and in other rolls with the fess gules fretty or.

[1] Ddq. 438, 439, 961; G.*B* 256.

[2] Ddq. 958, 3574. In the latter case the arms are differenced with a five-pointed label.

[3] He read it as a difference mark, but the red mullet on the bend seems to be difference enough without any change of the field.

V. WALFORD'S ROLL

THE EMPIRE

1. *L'Empereur de Almaine d'or ung egle espany a deux testes sable.*

Cf. 1, 1: MP I. 21.

Instead of *espany a* Hearne printed *peyr a*, but neither phrase is now to be seen in Leland's MS., the corner of the page having perished and gone. *Espany* has been supplied from C I. The tincture *sable* is omitted in Leland's MS. but is given in C I and C II (*b*).

In 1257 there was a split among the electors, one faction electing Richard, Earl of Cornwall, and the other choosing Alphonso of Castile. Richard dying in 1271 and Alphonso withdrawing, Rudolf of Habsburg was elected Emperor in 1273; he died in 1291. (*AVD* vii. 350–1.)

FRANCE

2. *Le Roy de France d'azure seme de floretes d'or.*

Cf. 5, 2: MP I. 8.

Or has been worn away, but it is given in the other manuscripts.

Philip III, 'le Hardi', s. of St. Louis by Margaret of Provence, succ. 1270, d. 1285.

ENGLAND

3. *Le roy d'engleter de goules a treys lepardes de or.*

Cf. 4, 3: MP I. 2, 19, &c.

SPAIN

4. *Le roy d'Espaine esquartile de argent e de goules, a deus chastelles de or en les quarters de goules, a deus liunceus d'azur en les quarters de argent.*

Cf. 6, 4: MP II. 72.

Alphonso the Wise, 1252–84.

The different methods of blazoning here and in C I may be noticed. C II (*b*)'s blazon is nearer to C I; it specifies that the lion is for Leon—both it and C I make the lion purple.

SICILY

5. *Le Roy de Cecyle d'azur poudre a florettes de or a un lambeu de goules.*

Cf. 8, 5.

Charles, Count of Anjou, s. of King Louis VIII and Blanche of Castile, King of Sicily 1266, titular King of Jerusalem 1278, d. 1285.

At first he bore France in a border of Castile, *Gules, semy of castles or* (Ddq. 340, dated 1253), but later he replaced the border by a label gules as here blazoned. (Ddq. 11765 A.D. 1271; *Bigot* 246; *Wijn.* 1261; *Nav.* 1255; D 8.) His s. Charles II d. 1309, and his gds. Robert d. 1343.

NAVARRE

6. *Le Roy de Navar de goules a un charbucle de or lesance* [sic] *d'or.*

Cf. 9, 6: MP II. 60: C 42.

Henry III, Count of Champagne and King of Navarre 1270–6.

Count Theobald IV of Champagne succ. to the throne of Navarre in 1234 on the death of his maternal uncle Sancho VII, and thereafter the arms of Navarre and Champagne were often dimidiated (e.g. FW 11; D 10). Theobald was succ. in turn by his sons Theobald V, 1253–70, and Henry III. (*AVD* vi. 496, &c.) (Cf. C 42.)

The charbocle should be bezanty but that word is garbled in both copies of C II (*lesance* and *lozence* respectively) and omitted in C I.

Dr. Adam-Even suggests that *lesance* may be a mistake for bezanty. The central boss was often pierced or jewelled and in RD I. 7, *c.* 1310, the piercing is lozenge-shaped, so it seems possible that *lesance* is really lozengy.

CASTILE

7. *Le Roy de Chastelle de goules a un chastel de or.*

Cf. —, 7: MP I. 97.

Alphonso the Wise, King of Castile 1252–84. (*AVD* vi. 58.)

This item is omitted from C I, perhaps because Alphonso had already appeared as King of Spain in C 44.

GERMANY

8. *Le Roy d'Almayne de or a un egle de sable.*

Cf. 3, 8: MP I. 21.

Richard, Earl of Cornwall, d. 1271, or Rudolf of Habsburg, elected 1273—see C 1.

In C II (*b*) a four- or five-letter word has been scrawled through after 's'. This may have been 'doubl' as, unlike C I and C II (*a*), C II (*b*) gives the single eagle to the Emperor—see C 1.

ARAGON

9. *Le Roy d'Arrogon pale de or et de goules.*

Cf. 7, 9: MP II. 44.

James I, King of Aragon, succ. 1213, d. 1276. His s. and h. Peter III d. 1285. (*AVD* vi. 525, &c.)

The Counts of Barcelona, whose arms these are, acquired Aragon by the marriage of Raymond Berengar IV (d. 1162) with Petronella (d. 1173), h. of Aragon. The arms are now usually given as *Or, four pales gules* (*Wijn.* 1262; *Nav.* 1253; Ddq. 11222, &c.), but originally the tinctures were reversed and the number of stripes varied (Pinoteau, vol. ii). FW 22 gives *Or, three pales gules*; *ZWR three paly of six*; and copy C II (*b*) of this Roll *paly of eight pieces*. See also the different versions given by Matthew and D 39 for the Counts of Provence.

BOHEMIA

10. *Le Roy de Boesme de argent a un lion de sable corone de or a un croyz d'or sur l'espaule.*

Cf. 10, 10.

C I omits the tincture of the cross.

Ottokar II the Victorious, King of Bohemia 1253, d. 1278. His s. and h. Wenceslaus IV d. 1304. (*AVD* viii. 19, &c.)

The arms are otherwise unknown. The arms of Bohemia from the time of Ottokar I, 1192–1230, were an eagle, which from the fourteenth century was sable surrounded with flames in a silver shield. But from 1264 onwards Ottokar II and his successors bore, either instead of or together with the eagle, the familiar shield *Gules, a lion with forked tail argent*, with or without a gold crown. (*ZWR* 25; P.*MA*; *Wijn.* 593, 1266; *Nav.* 1260.)

Clipearius 5 says nothing of the forked tail:

> 'Dumque Bohemie tibi rubeum clipeum fore ponam.
> Hic albus leo vult antepreferre coronam.'

HUNGARY

11. *Le Roy de Hongerye de or estenzele a deus [leons] passans d'azur.*

Cf. 12, 11.

Either Stephen, King of Hungary 1270–2, or his s. and h. Ladislaus III, d. 1290. (*AVD* vii. 424.)

The blazon is corrupt. All three copies omit *leons* and C II (*b*) writes *rormy* (sic) instead of *d'azur.*

Two coats have been borne for the kingdom of Hungary, *Barry* (usually of eight pieces) *argent and gules* (*Wijn.* 594, 1305; *ZWR* 26), and *Gules, a patriarchal cross argent*, which may or may not stand on a triple mount vert. The ends of the cross are usually slightly formy, and that may account for C II (*b*)'s *rormy*. The barry is the earlier coat. The cross appeared under Béla IV (1235–70), then disappeared, but reappeared under Sigismund III (1386–1437).

Hitherto it has been supposed that C's blazon was meant for the patriarchal cross though the tincturing is abnormal and no other instance has been found where the field is *étincelé*. Dr. Adam-Even has, however, suggested that the missing word must be *leons* and that the blazon is really that of Denmark. This is certainly correct, see C 18. It is not the only instance in which this roll has muddled a foreign coat. For a third coat attributed to Hungary see C 17.

CONSTANTINOPLE (Latin Empire)

12. *L'empereur de Constantinople de goules poudre a crosyle d'or a un croyz d'or passaunt a quatre roundeles d'or en quatre quarteres e en chekun roundelle un croysille.*

Cf. 2, 29.

Arms of the Latin Empire of Constantinople. (*Wijn.* 1273; MCh.)

C II (*b*) 29 blazons *iiij bessauntes . . . in cheschun bessaunt ung croshylle g*, but that version is otherwise unknown. On a seal (Ddq. 11829, but this merely says *armes de Jérusalem*, without blazoning) which Philip, Emperor of Constantinople 1273–4, used in 1263 during the lifetime of his father Baldwin II de Courtenay, the shield is *Crusuly with a cross between four annulets*. (Demay, *Flandre*, 48.) In later rolls this is commonly shown with five crosslets in each quarter, one being within the annulet. It would therefore seem that C II (*b*) is mistaken and that the roundels in C I and C II (*a*) are to be read as pierced roundels, i.e. annulets.

LLYWELYN AP GRUFFYDD, Wales

13. *Llewellin ap Griffith escartelle d'or et gules a [quatre] leparz de l'un et l'autre.*

Cf. 21, 30: MP IV. 59.

Llywelyn ap Gruffydd, Prince of Wales, s. of Gruffydd s. of Llewlyn ap Iorwerth (MP IV. 59), succ. 1246, slain December 1282. He m. Eleanor, dau. of Simon de Montfort, Earl of Leicester, and left a dau. Gwenllian (*DNB*).

In this version the attitude of the lions is not stated, but both copies of C II omit *quatre* though this is given in C I. C I blazons lions without specifying the posture, but C II (*a*) and (*b*) both say leopards, and leopards, i.e. lions passant gardant, are also given in D 28. MP IV. 59 and E 7, on the other hand, have lions passant but not gardant, and FW 27 has lions rampant gardant. *Wijn.* 1304 paints lions rampant, and lions rampant were borne by Owen Glendower a century later. (Wagner, *Historic Heraldry*, pp. 42, 56.) There can be little doubt that Sir Anthony Wagner is right in reading the arms as a differenced version of the royal arms, Llywelyn's stepmother Joan being an illegitimate dau. of King John, who before succeeding to the throne sealed with two lions passant (but not gardant—see *Ant. Journ.* xxxv. 224). That being so the variations in the posture of Llywelyn's lions go some way to show that the English royal beast was originally a lion and that its attitude was of no importance.

JERUSALEM (Latin Kingdom)

14. *Le roy d'Acre d'argent poudre a croysille d'or a une croyz d'or byllette.*

Cf. —, 31: MP I. 6, 101; II. 1.

C I omits this.

Arms of the Latin kingdom of Jerusalem, of which the capital was transferred to Acre after the loss of Jerusalem in 1239. (*Wijn.* 1259; *Nav.* 1256; FW 2; D 1.)

Hugh de Lusignan, 'le Grand', King of Cyprus, took the title of King of Jerusalem in 1269 and d. 1284. His s. and h. John I d. 1285. (*AVD* v. 127.)

Note the description of the cross as *billetty* instead of the later potent. P 11 calls the same cross *martellee*. *ZWR* 18 paints *Argent, a cross potent fitchy at the foot or charged with five roundels* (nail-heads) *gules*.

SCOTLAND

15. *Le roy d'Eschosce d'or a un lion de goules a un bordure d'or flurette de goules.*

Cf. 11, 32: MP I. 85.

Alexander III, 1249–86, s. of Alexander II (MP I. 85).

CYPRUS

16. *Le Roy de Chipre de vert besantee de goules a un croyz d'or passant.*

Cf. 13, 33.

C I makes the bezants gold.

This coat is otherwise unknown as arms of Cyprus. It seems to be a composition from a device found on some Cyprus coins, e.g. a *denier* of Guy de Lusignan, *c.* 1192–4, on which the reverse bears a formy cross between four roundels. (Sir G. Hill, *Hist. of Cyprus*, ii. 41.)

Hugh II de Lusignan, King of Cyprus 1253–67, like his predecessors of that family, bore the Lusignan buruly argent and azure (C 71) differenced with a gold-crowned red lion. (*Wijn.* 1276; FW 26.) His cousin and successor, Hugh III, 1267–84 (s. of his sister Isabel by Henry s. of Bohemund IV of Antioch), assumed the same arms, often marshalling therewith after 1269 the arms of Jerusalem, C. 14. (P. Adam-Even, *Contribution à l'Héraldique de l'Orient Latin*, privately printed, 1950.)

NORWAY

17. *Le Roy de Norwey de goules a un chevald d'or selle.*

Cf. 16, 34: MP I. 100.

Either Haakon IV, 1247–63, or Magnus IV, 1263–80.

The horse has not been found elsewhere as arms of Norway. These are *Gules, a lion rampant or holding an axe argent*; they go back at least to the latter half of the thirteenth century. (*Wijn.* 1275; *Nav.* 1262; FW 20; D 14; &c.)

The owner of the horse is uncertain. *Wijn.* 1296 paints *Gules, a horse rearing argent* for 'Le roy de Poulenne', and a similar coat is given in RD II. 12, P 18, &c. This is a canting attribution, for *poulain* in mediaeval French meant both a colt and a Pole; the word survives in the latter sense in the expression *chaussure à la poulaine*, i.e. *à la polonaise*. *Clipearius* 4 assigns the same coat to Hungary:

> 'Albus equus rubeo clipeo regis solet esse
> Ungarici. Nec equo frenum nec sella deesse.'

A similar coat but with the field azure was painted in the *Haus zum Loch*, where Merz and Hegi attribute it to Hungary and assume that it was the Hungarian beast or banner (*ZWR* l. 122). LM 16, temp. Edward I, attributes the horse to Pomerania, and WLN 34, *c.* 1500, to 'Lettowe'. This suggests that it is closely connected with the coat of Lithuania, *Gules, a mounted knight in full armour argent*, which is quartered by Poland in RH 63 and the KB 31, both temp. Henry VI.

In the case of Norway it is, however, also possible that the attribution is due to confusion with the white horse which is familiar as a pre-heraldic device of the Jute and Saxon settlers in this country, and more recently as the Hanoverian royal beast. *Gules, a white horse saddled and passant* is called the old arms of Brunswick in the *Wappenbuch von den Ersten* (ed. Hildebrandt and Seyler, Berlin, 1893, f. 28), and it occurs in the crest of the dukes of Brunswick some decades earlier. (See H. S. London, *Royal Beasts*, p. 54.)

A totally different coat is assigned to Haakon IV in MP I. 100.

DENMARK

18. *Le Roy de Denemark d'or a un beuf de goules.*

Cf. 15, 35.

Eric V, King of Denmark 1259–86. (*AVD* viii. 176.)

This is one of several coats invented for or attributed to the Kings of Denmark.

The modern arms of Denmark, *Or semy of hearts gules, three lions passant alias passant gardant azure*, appear on the seals of Knud VI, *c.* 1190, and Waldemar II (d. 1241), though some rolls omit the hearts and show only the three lions. The red powdering is now regularly blazoned as hearts, but originally leaves may have been intended. AS 18 calls the objects 'papmous de voces', whatever that may mean, and *Wijn.* 1268 paints red flames. *Nav.* 1261 makes the field *goutiché* (gutty) and makes the lions passant vert. Another variant appears above, C 11, where it is wrongly attributed to Hungary; there too the lions are passant but the field is *étincelé*, semy of sparks.

KING OF MAN

19. *Le Roy de Man de goules a treys gambes armes o tucte le guisses et chekun cornere seyt une pee.*

Cf. 17, 36.

FW 23, D 18, *Wijn.* 1277, and other rolls paint *Gules, three legs in mail armour argent joined mill-sailwise.*

Magnus, succ. 1252, d. November 1265, was the last King of Man, which King Magnus IV of Norway ceded to King Alexander III of Scotland (d. 1286) by the treaty of 2 July 1266. (*Handbook of British Chronology*, 1939, p. 61.)

We are indebted to Sir Anthony Wagner, who is himself indebted to Mr. Basil Megaw of the Manx Museum, for the following note on this item:

'H. R. Oswald writing in *Manx Society*, vol. 5, p. 8, in 1860 refers to the recent discovery by Dr. J. R. Oliver of two seals "among the Cottonian manuscripts in the British Museum" but "fast hastening to decay" attached to two charters of Harald King of Man of about 1246 and showing the device of a ship. The existence of such an early seal of the Kings of Man is also referred to by Camden in the *Britannia*, ed. 1607, p. 847. Now King Harald visited the Court of Henry III in 1246, and King Magnus did the same in 1256. I am inclined to associate the adoption of the three-leg coat, and indeed of a heraldic device at all, with the latter visit. At all events since Walford and the rolls mentioned above attribute the coat to the King of Man, I feel that it must belong to the period not later than 1265 when there was in fact a King of Man, not merely an English or Scottish suzerain with a Lord of Man under him.

'With regard to the source of the three-leg device, the fact that it was used on coins by the 10th-century Norse dynasty of York and Dublin (see Brooke, *English Coins*, ed. 1942, pl. IX, 15, 16), while Anlaf Sihtricson, one of these kings, may well have ruled the Isle of Man (see *Handbook of British Chronology*, p. 59, and A. W. Moore, *History of the Isle of Man*, vol. I, 1900, pp. 90–91) seems to me to indicate its probable origin.'

ARMENIA

20. *Le Roy d'Ermenye d'or a un lion rampant de goules a un bordure de goules endente.*

Cf. 14, 37.

Livon II, King of Armenia, succ. *c.* 1270, d. 1288 or 1289. (*AVD* v. 107.)

C I omits the field tincture, but both copies of C II make it gold. The indented border has not been found elsewhere. *Wijn.* 1269 makes the lion rampant gardant, and some later rolls vary the tinctures. *Wijn.* 1301 gives *Gules, a lion rampant gardant crowned or,* with a patriarchal cross gold rising from its back. (cf. *Gelre's Wapenboek,* ed. V. Bouton; Virgil Solis's *Wappenbüchlein,* 1555, p. 34.)

TEMPLE

21. *Le baucent del Temple d'argent al chef de sable a un croyz de goules passant.*

Cf. 19, 38: MP I. 62; VIII. 1.

C I has *auntient* instead of *baucent.* C II (*b*) has *baron,* which is probably a miscopying or mishearing of *bacon* or *baucan* and therefore comes to the same thing.

This blazon is a combination of the Templars' black and white banner (MP I. 62, &c.) with the red cross which they wore as badge or device and which was afterwards taken as their arms. The combination also occurs in the Armorial of the *Tournoi de Chauvency* of 1285. (Galbreath, *Manuel du blason,* 1942, pp. 208 and 331 n. 6 *bis.*)

THE HOSPITAL

22. *Le baucent del Hospitale de goules a un croyz d'argent fourme.*

Cf. 20, 39: MP I. 61; IV. 41.

As in C 21 C I substitutes *auntient* for *baucent.* All three copies blazon the cross *formy.* This seems to be the earliest occurrence of that term.

POITOU, Count of

23. *Le counte de Poyters party d'azur e de goules per le goules poudre a tureles d'or l'azur pudre o flurettes d'or.*

Cf. 22, 40.

Alphonse, Count of Poitou, b. 1220, d. 1271, sixth s. of King Louis VIII of France and Blanche of Castile. The arms might be blazoned as France and Castile impaled, the single castle of Castile being converted into a semy of towers for the sake of symmetry, cf. C 126. (*Les Armoiries des Comtes de Poitiers,* by P. Adam-Even, privately printed s.d. (*c.* 1950); P.*MA*; GWW 67; Ddq. 1077; Pinoteau, op. cit.)

BRITTANY

24. *Le counte de Bretaine eschekere d'or et d'azur a une kantelle d'ermin a un bordure de goules.*

Cf. 23, 41.

The arms are a cadenced version of those of the Counts of Dreux and Braine, C 26. Pierre de Dreux, dit 'Mauclerc' (d. 1250), second s. of Robert II, Count of Dreux and Braine, m. Alice, dau. and coh. of Guy de Thouars, Duke of Brittany, and became Duke of Brittany in her right in 1213. As a younger s. he differenced his paternal shield with an ermine canton. (Ddq. 534.) He was made Earl of Richmond in 1219. He was succ. in 1238 by his son John I, 'le Roux', (d. 1286), the duke here intended. (Ddq. 538.) The earldom of Richmond, which his father had forfeited, was restored to John in 1268. His s. and h. John II (d. 1305; *Wijn.* 922) m. King Henry III's dau. Beatrice, and their younger s. John differenced the above coat by charging the border with lions of England. In Brittany John II was succ. in turn by his s. Arthur (d. 1312) and his gds. John III (d. 1341). The latter quarrelled with his half-brother, John de Montfort (Arthur's s. by his second wife Yolande de Dreux), and *c.* 1318 he left the Dreux chekers and took ermine plain, which was retained thenceforward as the arms of the duchy. ('The Arms of the Earldom of Richmond', *Coat of Arms,* iii. 241.)

CHÂTILLON-BLOIS

25. *Le counte de Blaes pale de veyr e de goules al chef d'or.*

Cf. 24, 42.

John de Châtillon-sur-Marne, Count of Blois 1241–79, s. of Hugh I de Châtillon, Count of St. Pol, and Marie d'Avesnes, the h. of Blois. On his death Blois passed to his nephew Hugh, s. of Guy III de St. Pol. (*AVD* xi. 393; Du Chesne, *Histoire de la Maison de Chastillon-sur-Marue*; *Nav.* 1074; Ddq. 961. Cf. C 27.)

DREUX, Count of Braine

26. *Le Counte de Abrenes eschekere d'or et d'azur a une bordeur des goules.*

Cf. 25, 43.

Robert IV, Count of Dreux, Braine, and Montfort 1249–81. He was gds. of Robert III, elder brother of Pierre Mauclerc, Duke of Brittany. His dau. Yolande was the second wife of Arthur, Duke of Brittany. (*AVD* xi. 467; *Wijn.* 895; *Nav.* 17; Ddq. 730. Cf. C 24.)

The Dreux family are cadets of France, their founder being Robert, Count of Dreux, brother of Louis VII. The checkers appear on Count Robert's seal as early as 1184 (Pinoteau, op. cit.). The tinctures are those of the royal arms of France, but it is not known why Robert took the checkers. Smith Ellis (*Antiquities of Heraldry*, 179, 180) sought to derive them from Vermandois (cf. MP) on the ground that Count Robert's uncle Hugh m. the Vermandois h., but the argument is not convincing and Pinoteau says that the Vermandois became extinct in 1167 and that the checkers were therefore free when Robert assumed them.

CHÂTILLON-ST. POL

27. *Le Counte de S. Paule pale de veyr et de goules al chef d'or a une labeu d'azur.*

Cf. 26, 44.

C II (*b*) misblazons the label argent.

Guy III de Châtillon (d. 1289) succ. his father Hugh as Count of St. Pol-sur-Ternoise in the Pas de Calais in 1248, adding a label to distinguish his arms from those of his elder brother John, Count of Blois, C 25. In 1292 Hugh de Châtillon, who had succ. to the county of Blois on John's death in 1279, surrendered St. Pol to his younger brother Guy IV, Grand Butler to the King of France, d. 1317. Their sister Mary m. Aymer de Valence and founded Pembroke College, Cambridge, in 1347. As Count of Blois Hugh bore the plain chief while Guy differenced it with the blue label of St. Pol. (*AVD* xii. 397; *Nav.* 1075; Ddq. 362; de Raadt, i. 359.)

BRIENNE-EU

28. *Le Counte d'Eu d'azur billette d'or a un lion d'or.*

Cf. 27, 45.

Arms of Brienne. Alphonse de Brienne, dit d'Acre, m. Marie d'Issoudun, dau. and h. of Raoul de Lusignan and d'Issoudun, Count of Eu. Their s. Jean de Brienne succ. his mother as Count of Eu 1249 and d. 1294. His s. and h. Jean II perished at Courtrai in 1302, and was succ. by Raoul, Constable of France, who d. 1344. (*AVD* xii. 456–7; *P.MA*; *ChP* 1; *Wijn.* 320, cf. 321, 830.)

FLANDERS

29. *Le Counte de Flaundres d'or a une lion de sable raumpant.*

Cf. 28, 46: MP II. 37.

Guy de Dampierre, Count of Flanders in 1278 by grant of his mother Margaret of Flanders (d. 1280), at first bore the two lions passant gardant of Dampierre with a label. (Ddq. 1990.) Later he took the lion of Flanders with a baston gules for difference (*ex. inf.* P. A.-E.), dropping the baston on succeeding to the county. (Ddq. 629.) He died in 1305 aged 80 and was succ. by his s. Robert de Béthune who also bore the lion. (*Wijn.* 1232; *Nav.* 1163.)

The lion was also borne by John d'Avesnes, Count of Hainault (d. 1304), Margaret's s. by her first marriage, as claimant of Flanders. (Ddq. 625; *Wijn.* 1205.)

BAR

30. *Le Counte de Bar d'azur pudre a croisile d'or a deus bars de mere.*

Cf. 29, 47: MP I. 60.

The manuscript of C I has conflated C 30 and 31 thus: *Le Contee de Barre d'azure poudre a floretes d'or un labell gulez poudre circle d'or.*

    Thibaut II, Count of Bar-le-Duc (dépt. of Meuse) 1239–96, s. of Henry II (MP I. 60).
    The barbels should be gold. The crusuly is of crosses crosslet fitchy.

ARTOIS

31. *Le Counte d'Artoys d'azur pudre a florette d'or a une labeu de goules pudre a circle d'or.*

Cf. —, 48: MP I. 94.

In C I this is conflated with C 30. Both C I and C II (*a*) read *circle*, but it should be *chasteles*, castles. C II (*b*) has *c'eles* and the copyist of the other copies must have misread that or some similar contraction in the original manuscript.

    Robert II, Count of Artois 1250–1302. (*Wijn.* 760; FW 78; Demay, *Inventaire des Sceaux de l'Artois et de la Picardie*, 15.) He bore the same arms as his father Robert I, s. of King Louis VIII, who differenced the semy of France with a red label charged with gold castles for his mother Blanche of Castile.

    Robert II's s. Philip, d. 1298 v.p., charged the label with silver roundels and it was perhaps a knowledge of that fact which led to the misinterpretation of *c'eles* as *circle*. Robert was succ. in the county of Artois by his dau. Maud, wife of Otto of Burgundy, Philip's s. Robert III having migrated to England.

VAUDÉMONT

32. *Le Counte Waldemond burle de une grose burlure d'argent et de sable.*

Cf. 30, 49.

Henry I, Count of Vaudémont (dépt. of Meurthe et Moselle) 1246–79. His s. and h. Henry II d. 1299.

    De une grose burlure contrasts with the *menue burlure* of C 35, &c. C I omits the phrase. Though their arms are different the Vaudémonts were cadets of the House of Lorraine. The number of stripes on seals and coins varies from 8 to 12. In this roll the tinctures are silver and sable, but *Wijn.* 530 paints *barry of eight pieces argent and gules*, and FW 72 replaces the buruly by *a bendy of ten pieces argent and azure*. This suggests that the item was copied from an earlier document where *bende* was used in the sense of striped without directional connotation (see the Glossary). (*AVD* xiii. 454–5; *Wijn.* 530; Des Robert, *Sceaux de Lorraine*, 199.)

PIERREPONT-ROUCY

33. *Le Counte de Russye d'or un liun rampant d'azur.*

Cf. 31, 50.

The Counts of Roucy (dépt. of Aisne) of the family of Pierrepont at first bore a barry shield like Coucy with a canton for difference. (Ddq. 1022, A.D. 1227.) Count John III, 1250–82, sealed with that coat in 1260 (Ddq. 1023; the alternate bars are diapered), but in 1265 he used an equestrian seal with a lion on the shield, relegating the barry to the counterseal. (Ddq. 1024.) His s. John IV, 1282–1304, did likewise. (*T. de C.* 12; *Wijn.* 826; Ddq. 1025.)

VENDÔME

34. *Le Counte de Wandome d'argent al chef d'azur a une lion rampant de goules.*

Cf. 32, 12.

John V de Montoire, Count of Vendôme 1271–1318, s. of Bouchard V. (Ddq. 990.)

The Montoires succ. to the county of Vendôme in 1207 and took the arms which had been borne by their Preuilly predecessors, *a chief with a lion over all*. In other rolls the chief is gules and the lion azure, e.g. *Bigot* 264, *ChP* 76, Urfé, Gelre, and *Berry*. *Nav.* 765 attributes that coat to Johan de Vandosme de Fiellet who was of a cadet line.

GRANDPRÉ

35. *Le Counte de Grantpre a une menue burlure d'or et de goules.*

Cf. 33, 13.

Henry V, Count of Grandpré (dépt. of Ardennes) 1231–87. C I merely blazons buruly. The coat is usually drawn as barry of twelve pieces, but the stripes may be as many as twenty. (P.*MA*; *Wijn.* 853; seal in Archives Nationales, Paris.) *Nav.* 613, on the other hand, makes the barry of five pieces only.

AUVERGNE

36. *Le Counte d'Alverne d'or a un gunfanun de gules.*

Cf. 34, 14.

Robert V (s. of William X), Count of Auvergne 1247–77, inherited the county of Boulogne in 1260 through his mother Alice of Brabant, cousin and h. of Maud de Dammartin, Countess of Boulogne, wife successively of Philip of France and Alphonso of Portugal (C 126). His two sons and successors, William XI and Robert VI, d. in 1279 and 1314.

The gonfanon appears on seals of the counts of Auvergne from the twelfth century. It often has a green border. It is said to allude to the fact that the counts of Auvergne were Grand Gonfaloniers of the Church, but Galbreath does not mention them as such in his *Papal Heraldry*. (*AVD* x. 142; *Nav.* 1076; P.*MA*; *Wijn.* 1231.)

FOREZ

37. *Le Counte de Forest de goules a un dauffin de mer d'or.*

Cf. 35, 15.

Either Reynold, Count of Forez (in the Lyonnais) 1257–75, or his s. Guy VII 1275–87. They were of the same stock as the Dauphins of the Viennois who differenced the arms by changing the tinctures to blue on gold. (*AVD* x. 495; *Wijn.* 1164, cf. 1129; *ChP* 7; *Nav.* 609; Ddq. 677.)

Originally a personal name in Scandinavia Dauphin became the hereditary forename of the Counts of Vienne, thence their title, Dauphin du Viennois, and finally the name of the province, Dauphiné.

SOISSONS-NESLE

38. *Le Counte Sessons d'or a une liun rampant de goules a une bordure entere de goules.*

Cf. 36, 16.

John III de Nesle, Count of Soissons 1270–84. The line became extinct in 1306. (*AVD* xii. 263; cf. *ChP* 31.) In *Wijn.* 827 and *Nav.* 916 the lion is passant.

This is one of several cases where the capitals *S* and *M* have been confused, both C I and C II (*a*) writing *Messons*. In C II (*b*) the initial appears to be a *D* but it may be meant for *S*.

GUINES

39. *Le Counte de Gynes veyre d'or et d'azur.*

Cf. 37, 17.

Arnold III, Count of Guines from 1245, sold the county to King Philip III of France 'le Hardi' in 1283, but it was bought back by his gddau. Jeanne in 1295. (*AVD* xii. 424–5; *Nav.* 1077.) Vair appears on the seals of these counts as early as 1186, on the seal of Arnold II. (Ddq. 1071.)

Guines, a little south of Calais, was ceded to England by the Treaty of Bretigny in 1360. From the time of Edward IV until its recapture by France in 1558 it gave title to one of the English extraordinary or garrison pursuivants.

He was one of several foreign lords who received money-fiefs from Henry III on several occasions between 1233 and 1267. (Powicke, *The Thirteenth Century*, p. 544.)

HAINAULT

40. *Le Counte de Henaud cheverone d'or et de sable.*

Cf. 38, 18.

Margaret, Countess of Hainault and Flanders 1244–79. (*AVD* xiii. 370.)

These arms were borne by the Counts of Hainault at the end of the twelfth century, as on the seal and counterseal of Baldwin V 'le Courageux' in 1195, and on the counterseals of two husbands of Jeanne Countess of Flanders and Hainault (1206–44), Ferdinand of Portugal (1214–26), and Thomas of Savoy (1237).

Margaret's father, Baldwin VI, was s. of Count Baldwin V of Hainault (d. 1195) by Margaret d'Alsace, Countess of Flanders, and he sealed with the lion of Flanders with the Hainault chevrons as counterseal. In 1278 Margaret ceded Flanders to Guy de Dampierre (d. 1305), s. of her second husband (C 29). It was, nevertheless, claimed by John d'Avesnes (d. 1304), a gds. by her first marriage, and although he had succ. to the county of Hainault he left the chevrons and bore the lion. (*Wijn.* 1205.) John was Richard of Cornwall's chief representative in Germany. He had a money-fief of £200 from Henry III. (Bryce D. Lyon, 'The Money Fief under the English Kings', *EHR* lxvi (1951) 175.)

TOULOUSE

41. *Le Counte de Tolosa de goules a un croyz d'or pate et perse a une bordere d'or.*

Cf. 39, 19: MP II. 42.

Raymond VII, Count of Toulouse, d. 1249: same person as MP II. 42.

C I misblazons the cross argent. There should be no border. Even in the thirteenth century the cross was pommetty, a fact which the blazon omits. The modern French blazon of the cross is *clechée, vidée, et pommettée.*

CHAMPAGNE

42. *Le Counte Chaumpaine d'azur a une bende d'argent a custeces d'or diasprez.*

Cf. 40, 20: MP II. 60.

C I also blazons the cotices diapered. C II (*b*) writes *erasrer* (sic).

Henry III, King of Navarre and Count of Champagne (C 6), d. 1274, and in 1275 his widow Blanche of Artois m. Edmund Crouchback, second s. of King Henry III. Edmund thereupon assumed the title of Count of Champagne and Brie (*Wijn.* 824), and bore it until 1284 when the h., Count Henry's daughter Jeanne, m. Philip the Bold, King of France 1285–1314. (P.*MA*; *Wijn.* 824; Ganz, p. 141 n.)

On the arms of Champagne and the term 'diaper', see Appendix II above pp. 164–6.

RÉTHEL

43. *Le Counte de Restelle de goules a treis rastelles d'or.*

Cf. 41, 21.

Hugh IV, Count of Réthel, succ. 1273, d. *c.* 1276. His dau. Jeanne carried the domains to her husband Louis I, Count of Flanders. According to contemporary seals there should be only two rakes (Ddq. 581–4), though Palliot and later writers blazon three. They are generally drawn without handles. *T. de C.* 10 gives rakes. (*AVD* xi. 410–11; *P.MA.*)

JOIGNY

44. *Le Counte de Joeny de gules a une egle d'argent.*

Cf. 42, 22.

John I (d. 1283), s. of William III (d. 1255), Count of Joigny. (*AVD* xi. 310; Ddq. 521; *Nav.* 612; cf. *Berry* 759.)

In the manuscript of C I *Joeny* is underlined and *Polony* added in the margin, but Poland is C 79 below.

THURINGIA

45. *Le Counte de Rige d'azur a un liun raumpant barre d'argent et de goules coronee d'or.*

Cf. 43, 23: MP I. 81.

These arms were borne both by the Landgraves of Thuringia and by those of Hesse. The colouring of the lion may allude to the barry argent and gules of Hungary (C 11), Louis IV of Thuringia having m. St. Elizabeth (d. 1231), dau. of Andrew II of Hungary.

After the death in 1247 of Henry Raspe, Margrave of Thuringia and King of Germany (MP I. 81), his possessions were divided, Thuringia falling to his sister Jutta, wife of Dietrich, Margrave of Meißen, and Hesse to his niece Sophie (d. 1275), dau. of his brother Louis IV and wife of Henry II, Duke of Brabant (d. 1248). (Ströhl, *Deutsche Wappenrolle* (1897), 34, 37.) The reference here is probably to Sophie's s. Henry of Brabant, Landgrave of Thuringia, d. 1308 (*Bigot* 64 n.), but may perhaps be to Jutta's s. Henry the Illustrious (b. 1221, d. 1288). The latter, however, is not known to have used the Thuringian lion, although his son Albert certainly bore it. (*AVD* xv. 493–4; *Wijn.* 603; *ZWR* 310; *T. de C.* 325.)

Clipearius 28 makes the field sable:

> 'Thuringen nigro clipeo stat forma leonis
> Cujus pellem variam rubeo niveoque reponis.'

BRABANT

46. *Le Duke de Braban de sable a un lion rampant d'or.*

Cf. 73, 24: MP II. 43.

John I, Duke of Brabant 1261 and Limburg 1282, was gds. of Duke Henry II (MP II. 43), d. 1294. This are now the arms of Belgium. (GWW 31; *Bigot* 43; *Wijn* 1170; *AVD* xiv. 97–99.)

The coat attributed to Brabant in *Clipearius* 16 seems rather to be that of Limburg:

> 'Dux Brabante tuus clipeus rubet hunc ita pingam.
> Album quod caput hic auri diademate cingam.'

Gevaert's theory that the lion of Brabant was at first gules in a silver field (*Héraldique Provinces Belges*, pp. 37–8) will not bear examination.

AUSTRIA

47. *Le Duk d'Ostriche de goules a un fesse d'argent.*

Cf. 74, 25.

The fess appears on seals of the margraves and dukes of Austria of the Babenberg family from 1136. (*ZWR* 28.) *Clipearius* 14 blazons it:

> 'Dux tuus, Austria, vult clipeum praeferre rubentem
> Cui pars fert media zonam candore nitentem.

The Austrian eagle first appears *c.* 1156. (*ZWR* 28.)

From the death of Frederick II, the last of the Babenberg dynasty, in 1246, Austria was occupied by the King of Bohemia until 1282.

BAVARIA

48. *Le Duk de Bavaire macle de argent e d'azur.*

Cf. 75, 26.

C II (*b*) blazons this 'catele az. ar.', a term which is still to be explained.

Louis II von Wittelsbach 'the Austere', Duke of Bavaria 1255–94. He seems to have been the first to display this fusilly coat. It belonged to the county of Bogen and was inherited by Louis's father Otto the Illustrious in 1242. The arms have regularly been borne as fusilly bendways (e.g. *Wijn.* 595; *ZWR* 29).

As Counts Palatine of Bavaria the Wittelsbachs sealed with the imperial eagle at least from 1166 (cf. *Bigot* 10). In 1180 Otto IV was made Duke of Bavaria and in 1214 his s. Louis I (1183–1231) was granted the Palatinate of the Rhine and assumed its arms, *Sable, a lion rampant or crowned gules.* These are described twice in *Clipearius* 20, 40:

> 'Bavarici ducis est in nigro ferre leonem
> Gilvum sicque sui signi dare cognitionem.
> Ecce palatini Reni stat forma leonis
> Ex auro, nigrum tamen huic campum fore ponis.'

(*AVD* xv. 348–9, xvi. 125, &c.; Ganz 176–8; *ZWR* 29. xxviii; *Wijn.* 595.)

POLAND

49. *Le Duk de Poulane d'or a un egle de sable a une cressant en la petryne d'argent.*

Cf. 76, 27.

C II (*b*) has 'first' instead of 'petrine' (*poitrine*). This looks like a mis-hearing of breast or the German Brust.

Bolesław V succ. 1227, d. 1279. (*AVD* viii. 107.)

The arms of Poland are *Gules, an eagle argent crowned or.* (*Arm. Equestre*, pl. CVII; cf. C 45 and RD II. 14 for 'Rex de Cracou', i.e. Cracow, the then capital of Poland.) A canting coat attributed to Poland, *Gules, a colt (poulain) argent,* is considered under C 17 above.

The coat attributed to Poland both here and in AS 12, is that of Lower Silesia. The dukes or princes of Silesia were a branch of the Polish royal house of Piast, and differenced the Polish eagle by changing the tinctures. The crescent, which is usually ensigned with a cross, appears on the breast of the eagle in the twelfth century on a seal of Duke Bolesław I (d. 1201), Prince of Lower Silesia and Duke of Breslau, and elder s. of Władysław II by Agnes von Babenberg. He bore the eagle tinctured as here, whilst his younger brother, Mieszko, who had Upper Silesia, bore a gold eagle in blue sans crescent. (*ZWR* 311.)

LORRAINE

50. *Le Duke de Loreyne d'or a une bende de goules a treis egles d'argent en la bende.*

Cf. 77, 28.

Henry III, Duke of Lorraine 1251–1303, m. Margaret, dau. of Theobald of Champagne, King of Navarre. (GWW 30.)

It is to be noticed that the Lorraine birds are eagles. They are also blazoned as eagles in *ChP* 92, *c.* 1300, and in *Clipearius* 18:

> 'Lothoringus habet gilvum clipeum sed oportet
> Quod tres zona rubens albas aquilas ibi portet.'

Wijn. 517, on the other hand, shows the birds without feet. That, however, is probably due merely to the small scale of the drawings, for Prinet cites seals in the Archives Nationales as showing that the birds were then borne with beak and feet. (P.*MA.*)

LIMBURG

51. *Le Duk de Limeburg d'argent a un lion de goules rampant a la cowe croyze e coronee d'or.*

Cf. 78, 138.

Waleran, Duke of Limburg 1247–80, younger s. of Henry IV of Limburg (d. 1247) by Irmgarde, dau. and h. of Count Adolphe VI of Berg (d. 1218). On Irmgarde's death in 1248 Berg as the more important property fell to her elder s. Adolphe VII (d. 1259) while her second s. Waleran succ. as Duke of Limburg. As holder of the fief Waleran bore the undifferenced arms of Limburg, *Argent, a lion gules* (Bigot 22; FD 23; W 33), while Adolphe, instead of taking the two bars embattled, etc., emblazoned of Berg, differenced the lion with a label azure (Bigot 8). Waleran d. 1280 and his dau. and h. Irmgarde (wife of Count Reynold of Gueldres) d. 1283 s.p. Adolphe VIII, who had succ. to Berg in 1259 (C 116) thereupon dropped the label and bore the Limburg lion undifferenced although he disposed of his rights in that duchy to the Duke of Brabant. It is probably the Limburg lion which Clipearius assigns to Brabant (C 46). The Limburg lion seems at first to have been uncrowned and to have had a single tail. It is not clear when or why the crown was added and the tail forked.

WERD

52. *Le Counte de Guerd de gules a un bende d'argent a litte d'or fluretes.*

Cf. 44, 139.

Both copies of C II make the cotices *fluretes*, flory, though C I omits that. Usually both bend and cotices are silver and the cotices are flory on the outside only.

Henry Sigbert, Count of Werd or Wörth (dépt. of Bas-Rhin) and Landgrave of Lower Alsace 1238–78. The Emperor Henry VI granted Lower Alsace to Count Sigbert III of Werd in 1196, and his family arms have been kept as arms of the Landgravate, and of Lower Alsace after this was bought by the bishops of Straßburg. (*AVD* xiv. 44; P.*MA*; J. J. Waltz (Hansi), *Art Héraldique en Alsace*, p. 137.)

DILLINGEN

53. *Le Counte de Belingne d'azur a un bend d'or a deus liuncels d'or raumpantes.*

Cf. 45, 140.

Hartmann V (d. 1286), Count of Dillingen and Bishop of Augsburg, s. of Hartmann IV (d. 1258), gave the county to his bishopric. The arms, which are a cadenced version of Kyburg (C 117), appear in 1195 on the seal of Count Hartmann I. *Clipearius* 71 writes:

> 'Diligen clipeum de lasuro fore pones,
> Obliquam tabulam geminosque leones.'

Dillingen is on the Danube, in Swabia. (P.*MA*; *ZWR* 42; Ganz, 20, &c.)

The name is garbled in all three copies, Bologne in C I, Belingne in C II (*a*), Lilyngne in C II (*b*).

RAPPERSWIL

54. *Le Counte de Rampsvile d'or a treis rosers sur chekune roser une rose de goules chekune roser verte.*

Cf. 46, 141.

The blazon in C I is incomprehensible. C II is better though it omits the tincture of the roses. On seals and tombstones, *c.* 1233–70, the arms appear as three roses each with a short stalk but merely rudimentary leaves or none at all. In the *Haus zum Loch,* *c.* 1300, the roses are red with green barbs and gold seeds each having a short green stalk and two small leaves. (Ganz, 34, 133, pl. VII, no. 7, VIII, no. 13; *ZWR*, pl. XXIX, no. 6, XXXII, no. 156.)

Clipearius 33 says:

> 'Rapreswile rosas tres fert prestante rubore'.

The castle of Rapperswil is on the lake of Zürich in the canton of St. Gall. Its lords were avoués of Einsiedeln Abbey. Rudolf III took the title of Count in 1232. His s. and successor Rudolf IV, born posthumously in 1262, was the last of the line, dying without issue in 1283. (*AHS* 1892, p. 9, &c.)

LÜTZELSTEIN

55. *Le Counte de la Petite Pierre d'or al chef de gules a une chefrune d'argent sur le chef.*

Cf. 47, 142.

Hugh III, Count of Lützelstein 1266–99, s. of Hugh II (1243–74) by Elizabeth de Sarrebrück. (P. A.-E.; cf. Ddq. 10946.) Petite-Pierre or Lützelstein is in Alsace, dépt. of Bas-Rhin.

FROBURG

56. *Le Counte de Munjoy d'or a une egle de veyr.*

Cf. 48, 143.

Montjoie = Froh-berg, but the arms are those of the Counts of Froburg in the canton of Solothurn—cf. *ZWR* 48, *Haus zum Loch* 14 and *Clipearius* 52:

'De Froburg aquila varie fert pellis amictum
In clipeo, quem de gilvo dicam fore pictum.'

On the death of Count Herman II in the thirteenth century the family split into two branches, Zofingen and Waldenburg, and these soon after subdivided so that by the end of the thirteenth century there were four branches: Honberg, Zofingen, and Waldenburg senior and junior. (*ZWR*, loc. cit.; P. A.-E.)

C II (*a*) omits the tincture; C II (*b*) makes it *or* which is correct, but C I makes it *argent*.

LÖWENSTEIN

57. *Le Counte de Leonsteine d'argent a une lion de goules corone d'or estant sus une mote d'azur.*

Cf. 49, 144.

Sus is an old form of *sur*. C I has *rampant* instead of *estant*.

The Counts of Calw, Löwenstein (in Württemberg) and Vaihingen were of the same stock and bore the same arms. The *Clipearius* 68 says:

'Calwen fert gilvum clipeum sed rufus in illo
Vult leo stare super petre terreve pusillo.'

In *ZWR* 452 Vaihingen bears *Argent, a lion statant gules on an isolated mount of four coupeaux vert*, and Siebmacher (i. 16) gives the arms of Calw as *Argent, a lion gules crowned azure standing on a mount of three coupeaux azure*; cf. Spener, ii. 226.

Godfrey III, the last count of this line, sold Löwenstein in 1277 to the Bishop of Würzburg. The bishop in 1281 sold it to Rudolf of Habsburg and he gave it to his bastard son Albert of Schenkenberg who thereupon assumed the name and arms of the old Löwensteins.

NEVILLE of Hornby

58. *Geffrey de Neville d'argent a une sautour de goules.*

Cf. 79, 145.

Sir Geoffrey de Neville, Justice of Forests north of Trent in 1270, he held Hornby Castle and other lands in Lincs. *jure uxoris* Margaret, dau. and h. of John de Lungvillers, died 1285 leaving s. and h. John. The connexion with Neville of Raby is probable but unproved. (*CP* ix. 487, &c.)

FITZJOHN

59. *John le fiz John esquartere d'or e de gules a un bordure endente d'argent e de azur.*

Cf. 80, 146: B 28.

John FitzJohn, of Shere, Surrey, &c., summ. to a Council 1265, d. 1275 s.p., and was succ. by his brother Sir Richard. (*CP* v. 433–6.)

The border is also indented in C I. This must be a misreading of the border of vair which B 28 gives for John's father, John FitzGeoffrey, and which appears on his own seal. (Birch 9736.)

FORZ, AUMALE

60. *Le Counte de Albemarle de gules a une croyz de veyr.*

Cf. 50, 147: MP II. 38.

Thomas de Forz, Count of Aumale, succ. his father William (MP II. 38) in 1260 and was dead in 1269. His younger sister and sole h. Aveline marr. Henry III's s. Edmund, Earl of Lancaster, and d. 1274 s.p. (*CP* i. 356.)

    C I makes the cross *patee*, but that word is omitted from both copies of C II.

DUNBAR

61. *Le Counte Patriz de gules a une liun rampant d'argent.*

Cf. 51, 148.

Patrick de Dunbar, Earl of Dunbar, s. and h. of Patrick, succ. 1248, d. 1289. (*CP* iv. 506; *SP* iii. 257.)

    C I's blazon is the same as this, but C II (*b*) adds *a bourdour az* [sic, for ar.] *seme rossetetes g.* The border of roses seems to have been added by this earl. His predecessors, the fifth and sixth earls, and he himself in 1251 and 1279, sealed with the lion alone, whereas on another seal in 1261 and on those used by his successors the lion is enclosed by a rose-charged border. (Macdonald 778, &c.)

STRATHBOGIE, Earl of Athol

62. *Le Counte de Lascele pale d'or e de sable.*

Cf. 52, 149.

John de Strathbogie, Earl of Athol 1270–1306, s. of David de Strathbogie, Earl of Athol (d. 1270), by his second wife. He inherited Chilham Castle from his mother Isabel, dau. of Richard de Douvres (B 82) by Maud *suo jure* Countess of Athol. He swore fealty to Edward I in 1291, but rebelled and was hanged in 1306. (*CP* i. 305–6; *SP* i. 425.)

    The number of stripes varied and John's seal shows three pales. The arms are those of the old earls of Fife, John's ancestor David having got Strathbogie from his father Duncan, Earl of Fife (d. 1203), who bore paly. (Macdonald 925, &c., 2729; *DL* 42.)

MAR

63. *Le Counte de Marre d'azur bylete d'or a une bende d'or.*

Cf. 53, 150.

William, Earl of Mar, s. of Duncan, succ. *c.* 1243, d. 1281. (*CP* viii. 401; *SP* v. 574–7.)

BRECHIN

64. *William de Breguyn d'or a treys peuz de goules.*

Cf. 81, 151.

C I's original text is substantially the same as C II's, but *Guiliam de Breyuin* and *gules* were then underlined and *Guy de Bryen* and *azure* were superscribed. It is not clear whether this emendation was due to Glover or to an earlier scribe.

    Sir William de Brechin succ. 1245 and was dead in 1292. He was s. of Henry de Brechin, an illegitimate s. of David, Earl of Huntingdon (B 14). He is perhaps the same who sealed in 1286 with *Three piles meeting in base* (Birch 15851; *SP* ii. 216.)

CHESTER, Earl of

65. *Le Counte de Cestre d'azure a treys garbes d'or.*

Cf. 54, 152: MP I. 48: B 16.

LASSER

66. *Alein Lasser d'argent a chef de goules.*

Cf. Cf. —, 153.

This item is not in C I.

The name Lasser has not been found in any of the mediaeval rolls, nor in the *Book of Fees* and similar works. It might be a form of Lisours. John Lisours bears *Azure, a chief or* in SD 108 and TJ 815, and *Or, a chief azure* in E 135 and PO 282.

B 194 assigns *Argent, a chief gules* to William le Fort de Vivonne, while E 499 and F 364 assign it to Champaine. It was also borne by Montferrat.

HANSARD

67. *William Hansard d'azur a treys molettes d'argent.*

Cf. 82, 154.

Here *molettes, mullettes* or *meuletes* are the modern mullets, straight-rayed stars, the *estoilles* of B 75, and not roundels as in C 145 and in B 183.

In 1201 William Hansard held land at Kingston Bucy (Kingston by the Sea), Sussex (*HKF* 351), and in 1242-3 the same or a namesake held in North Tadworth and Little Bookham, Surrey. (*Book of Fees* 686, 690.)

ROS of Ingmanthorpe

68. *William de Ros d'azure a treys buz d'or.*

Cf. 83, 155: MP II. 55: B 173.

Sir William de Ros of Ingmanthorpe d. *c.* 1308–10. He was presumably third s. of Sir William (s. of Robert—MP II. 55) de Ros of Helmsley (d. *c.* 1264). (*CP* xi. 117.)

CHALON

69. *Le Counte Chaloun de goules a un bende d'or.*

Cf. 55, 156.

John de Chalon, Count of Auxerre, d. 1309, second s. of John 'le Sage' of Burgundy (d. 1267) and gds. of Count Stephen of Burgundy (d. 1241) by Beatrice of Chalon-sur-Saône. As Counts of Burgundy Stephen, John, and the latter's eldest s. Hugh (d. 1266) sealed with an eagle (Ddq. 502, &c.), but John de Chalon and his successors as Counts of Auxerre bore the Chalon bend as blazoned here (Ddq. 512; *Wijn.* 1086; *Nav.* 611), although his father had sold Chalon to the Duke of Burgundy. (P. A.-E.)

COMYN

70. *John Comyn de goules a treys garbes d'or.*

Cf. 84, 157.

Either Sir John, 'the Red Comyn', nephew of Alexander, Earl of Buchan, succ. to Badenoch 1258, d. between 1273 and 1278.

Or, his second s. Sir John, 'the Black Comyn', who succ. his father at Badenoch. He swore fealty to Edward I in 1296, was a competitor for the Crown of Scotland, and d. *c.* 1303. (*SP* i. 506–8.)

The arms are canting, three sheaves of cummin.

LUSIGNAN

71. *Le Counte de la March burle de une menue burlure d'argent et d'azur.*

Cf. 56, 158: MP I. 86; II. 64.

Hugh X de Lusignan 'le Brun', d. 1249: same person as MP I. 86.

LUSIGNAN-VALENCE

72. *Le Counte de Valence burle d'argente et d'azur a merloz de goules bordeand.*

Cf. 57, 159: MP I. 83: B 23.

No Count of Valence (dépt. of Vienne) bore these arms. The person meant is the s. of C 71, William de Lusignan, seigneur de Valence, commonly known as William de Valence: same person as MP I. 83.

CLARE

73. *Thomas de Clare d'or a treys cheverouns de gules a une labeu d'azur.*

Cf. 85, 160: MP I. 46: B 81.

A younger s. of Richard, Earl of Gloucester and Hertford (MP I. 76) and nephew of William de Clare (B 81); d. in Ireland 1278. On his seal in 1269 the label has four points. (*CP* v. 701 n.; *Book of Seals*, 411 and pl. VII.)

LEYBURN

74. *Roger de Leyburne d'azur a sis liuncels d'argent.*

Cf. 86, 161: B 34.

Probably identical with B 34.

LONGESPÉE

75. *Gul. Longespe d'azure a sis liuncels d'or.*

Cf. 87, 162: MP I. 40; II 8: B 22.

Sir William Longespée, s. and h. of B 22, d. 1250 (*Book of Seals*, 56) was succ. by his s. William who d. 1257 leaving dau. and h. Margaret aged about two. She m. *c.* 1256 Henry de Lacy, Earl of Lincoln, and d. between 1306 and 1310. (*CP* xi. 384.)

LONGESPÉE

76. *Soun frer au tel a une cauntel d'ermin.*

Cf. 88, 163: C 75.

Stephen de Longespée. d. 1260: same person as B 187.
  As in several other cases Leland's manuscript has a capital *M* (*Moun*) instead of *S*.

BARNAGE. LE WEEDE

77. *Hernoll de la Wede barre d'or e de goules frette d'argent.*

Cf. 89, 164.

C II (*b*)'s blazon, *Barre dor e de g a goules frette ar*, makes it clear that only the red bars are fretty, or as L'Espinoy blazons it charged with five saltires. (*Noblesse de Flandres*, pp. 227–8, 386–7.)
  The reference is probably to Aernoult de Barnaige or Baronaige, a noble family of Flanders, anciently called de le Weede, lords of Mouvre and of Beveren in West Flanders. (P.*MA*; de Raadt, i. 204.) Their war-cry was 'Bevres! Bevres! joyeulx Bernage!'. (Cornelius-Gailliard, *L'Anchienne Noblesse de la Contée de Flandres*, p. 95.)

BORNHEM

78. *Henry de Bernam les armes le Roy de Fraunce al chef pale d'argent e de gules.*

Cf. 90, 165.

The arms are those of Bornhem in the Low Countries. (*Ex. inf.* P. A.-E.)

MALDEGHEM. ISEGHEM

79. *Le Seyre de Segney d'argent un croiz sable a merlos de sable bordeanz.*

Cf. 91, 166.

C II *a* writes *Le Meyre* but that is presumably another instance of the confusion of *M* and *S* for C I writes *Le Sire*.

Roger I de Maldeghem, sire d'Iseghem or Ysenghien (near Ingelmunster in west Flanders) 1259–93. (*Wijn.* 1247.) The lords of Iseghem were a branch of the Maldeghem family; they cried 'Maldeghem' and bore the Maldeghem arms *Or a cross and an orle of martlets gules.* (*Wijn.* 1249; *Arm. Equestre*, lxxxiii) differenced by change of tinctures. (L'Espinoy, p. 117; Cornelius-Gailliard, *L'Anchienne Noblesse de la Contée de Flandres*, p. 91; de Raadt, ii. 138.)

GHISTELLE

80. *Gualtier de Gistelle a gules a un cheffron d'ermine.*

Cf. 92, 167.

The sires de Ghistelle, near Ostend, were hereditary chamberlains to the Counts of Flanders in 1207. By the marriage of John III de Ghistelle (fl. 1275–93) with Isabel, dau. and h. of Philip de Woestine, the Ghistelles acquired that lordship. (L'Espinoy, pp. 122–3; GWW 390; cf. *Arm. Equestre*, pls. 83, 84, 86.)

FURNIVAL

81. *Walter de Furnivalle d'argent un bende de gules a sis merloz de gules.*

Cf. 93, 168: MP II. 45: B 147.

Not identified. Walter must have been a cadet though he is given the undifferenced arms which were then borne by Sir Thomas Furnival (B 147).

GOURNAY

82. *John de Gurney d'argent a une croyz de goules engrale.*

Cf. 94, 169.

Sir John de Gournay I, living 1245–77, s. and h. of Sir William de Gournay (living 1234–43), of Harpley, Norfolk, &c. (D. Gurney, *House of Gournay*, pp. 286, 327, &c.)

PIGOT

83. *Perys Pigot d'azur a sis merlot d'or a une bende d'or engrale.*

Cf. 95, 170.

Sir Peter Pigot or Picot, b. *c.* 1227, succ. his father Thomas Pigot of Ratcliff, Notts., in 1255. (*Cal. Inq.*, i. no. 344.) Dead by 18 January 1286 leaving s. John (*Cal. Inq.* ii. no. 602.)

FITZNICHOL

84. *Richard FizNicol d'azur a un quintefoyl d'or as escalopes d'argent bordeauntz.*

Cf. 96, 171.

Not identified. B 154 assigns the same arms to Ralph FitzNichol.

C II (*a*) merely says *as escalopes bordeanntz*, i.e. with a border of escallops. C II (*b*) says *six escalops.*

STUTEVILLE. ESTOUTEVILLE

85. *Walter de Stotevile burle d'argent e de goules a iij cos sable.*

Cf. 97, 172: B 200.

Both copies of C II have *cos* (sic) which may be meant for lions as in C I, but which seems nearer to the cocks which B 171 attributes to William de Stuteville.

The only reference to Walter seems to be in the Close Roll on 9 February 1302 (*Cal. Close Rolls*, 1296–1302, p. 514) providing dower for his widow Maud and mentioning but not naming his h.

GAUNT

86. *Geffrey de Gaunt barre d'or e d'azur a un bende de gules.*

Cf. 125, 173: MP IV. 54: B 72.

Younger s. of MP IV. 54, (Clay, *Extinct and Dormant Peerages*, p. 84.)

MUNCHENSY

87. *Warin de Montchesy d'or a iij escochons barry de veyr et de gules.*

Cf. 126, 174: MP VI. 11: B 25.

Warin de Munchensy d. 1255: same person as MP VI. 11.

MONMOUTH

88. *John de Monemuth d'or a iij cheverons de gules a une fesse d'argent.*

Cf. 127, 175.

John de Monmouth of Lassindon and Bolley, Glos., hanged in 1279 for killing a chaplain in Wilts. His relationship to B 92 has not been found. (*Cal. Fine Rolls*, i. 115; *Cal. Close Rolls*, 1279–1288, p. 90.)

MORTIMER of Richard's Castle

89. *Robertus de Mortimer barrey d'or e de vert flurete del une e de aultre.*

Cf. 128, 176.

C I has a marginal trick of this coat.

Sir Robert de Mortimer of Richard's Castle, Herefords., d. 1287, s. and h. of Sir Hugh (d. 1274). (*CP* ix. 263.)

Mesire Guillaume de Mortemer bears these arms differenced with a baston gules in *ChP* 124 and *Wijn.* 443. Though like Mortimer of Wigmore (B 32) they took their name from Morte-mer-sur-Eaulne (Seine-Inf.), there is no reason to suppose that the two families were related. From the arms it would rather seem that the Richard's Castle Mortimers were of kin to those of Attleborough, Norf., who bore *Or semy of fleurs-de-lis sable.*

FAUCONBERGE

90. *Gualter de Falconberge de sable a une quintefoil d'argent a merlos de argent bordianz.*

Cf. 129, 177: B 201: same person as B 201.

BIGOD

91. *Hugh Bigot de goules a un leun d'or passant.*

Cf. 130, 101: B 89.

Hugh Bigod, Justiciar of England, d. 1266: same person as B 89.

BASSET of Drayton

92. *Rafe Basset pale d'or e de goulles a une cantel d'argent a une croys de sable patee en le cantelles.*

Cf. 131, 102.

Sir Ralph Basset of Drayton, d. 1265, s. and h. of B 128. His mother, Margaret de Somery, was sister of 138 below; or perhaps his s. and h. Ralph, who was summ. to Parliament 1295, and d. 31 December 1299. (*CP* ii. 2.)

HAY

93. *Rauf Delahaye d'argent a ruell de goules.*

Cf. 132, 103: B 87.

Ralph de la Hay, d. 1254: same person as B 87.

ZOUCHE

94. *Aleyn de la Zouch de sable besantie d'or.*

Cf. 133, 104: B 85.

Presumably the same person as B 85, although all three copies make the field *sable* and that tincture has not been found elsewhere. The addition *forse gules* after *sable* in C I must be Charles's emendation; it is supported by Glover's and other rolls.

SOMERY

95. *Roger de Somery d'or a deus leons d'azure.*

Cf. 134, 105.

S. & h. of B 97 and brother of 135's mother. In neither version is the posture of the lions blazoned, the compiler perhaps assuming that as there were only two they must be passant.

ENGAINE

96. *Hugh Dengayne de goules a iij rouelles d'or a une dans d'or en le chefe.*

Cf. 135, 106.

The blazon in all three copies appears to mean three pierced molets with a dance in chief, but such a coat is otherwise unknown.

All three copies write the surname with a capital *S*, but the name must be d'Engaine. That family bore a dance, often differenced by the addition of billets, crosslets, or other minor charges; the tinctures vary. (FW 669; J 42; H 65; K, line 317; N 57, 414; &c.)

A Hugh d'Engaine was living at the end of the twelfth century and was fined in 1202 for selling wine contrary to the assize. He seems to have held at Wootton, Beds., but it has not been possible to link him with the more important branches of the family. (*Bedf. Hist. Rec. Soc.* i. 247, xiii. 137, 146, 147, and n. 147.)

No later Hugh has been found.

TREGOZ of Blunts Hall, Essex

97. *Geffrey Tregoz d'or a un leparde de gules en le chef a ij gymeles de goules.*

Cf. 136, 107: B 113.

Geoffrey de Tregoz of Blunts Hall, Essex, d. 1254. He was gds. of Geoffrey de Tregoz (d. 1175), elder brother of Robert de Tregoz who m. Sibyl, dau. and h. of Robert d'Ewyas, and whose s. Robert appears in B 113. (*Sussex Arch. Coll.* xciii. 34–58.)

SEGRAVE

98. *Geffrey de Segrave de sable a treys garbes d'argent.*

Cf. 137, 108: MP I. 66: B 176.

The relationship of this man to Stephen (MP I. 66) and Gilbert (B 176) has not been found.

TATESHAL

99. *Robert de Tatishale eschekere d'or e de gules al chef armine.*

Cf. 138, 109: MP II. 61: B 50.

Both copies of C II write Robert, who may be the same as B 50, who d. 1273 (*Cal. Inq.* i, no. 145), or his s. Robert who d. 1303 (ibid. iv. 163). C I gives the name as Raffe Tattishalle. This may be a mistake. Ralph de Tateshale was ordered to provide corn from Norfolk and Suffolk in 1302 for the Scots war. (*Cal. Close Rolls*, 1302–7, p. 68.)

BOYVILL

100. *William de Boyvile esquartile d'or e de sable a une leun passant de goules en le cantel d'or.*

Cf. 140, 110.

Probably Sir William Boyvill of Peasenhall Manor, who sealed with *Quarterly* temp. Edward I (Birch 7687), and to whom N 485 assigns *Quarterly or and sable*. He was dead April 1320, leaving a widow, Joan. His s. William having died v.p., his h. was his niece Margaret, dau. of his brother John. (*Cal. Inq.* vi, no. 229.)

BREUSE

101. *John de Brusse d'or a treys cheverons de gules a une bordure d'azur endente.*

Cf. 141, 111.

C II (*a*) writes *bod* for bordure. C II (*b*) makes the border argent, but C I, as also E 337 and F 406, both of which paint it engrailed, confirm azure.

Sir John de Breuse, s. and h. of Robert (d. 1276), held lands in Hants., Glos., Surrey, Som., and Essex. (*Cal. Inq.* ii. 194.) He was dead by Whitsun 1284, when his heirs, minors, were found to be overlords of Spargrove Manor, Som. (Ibid. 526).

The arms are evidently a differenced version of Clare, but how they were acquired does not appear.

MORTIMER of Wigmore

102. *Roger de Mortymer barre d'or et d'azur al chef pale al chantel gerone a un esbochon d'argent.*

Cf. 142, 112: B 32.

Roger de Mortimer d. 1282: same person as B 32. (*CP* ix. 276–81.)

THWENG

103. *Marmaduke de Twenge d'argent e une fesse de gules a treys papagays.*

Cf. 143, 113: MP II. 70: B 133.

C II gives no tincture for the popinjays, which may mean that their colour was already conventionally fixed. C I blazons them *vert*. Marmaduke de Thweng d. *c.* 1282/3: same person as B 133.

BURGH

104. *John de Burgh macle de veyr et de goules.*

Cf. 144, 114: MP I. 73.

Sir John de Burgh, of Causton, Norfolk, s. and h. of Hubert de Burgh (MP I. 73) was dead November 1274 leaving s. and h. Sir John aged forty. He also held in Essex, Sussex, Northants., and Som. (*Cal. Inq.*, ii. nos. 82, 142.)

Between 1243 and 1251 he sealed with *Lozengy of [gules] and vair with a five-pointed label*, even though his father was already dead. (*Book of Seals* 112.) Later, in 1261 and 1269, he omitted the label. (Birch 5772, 7944.)

GIFFARD of Brimpsfield

105. *John Giffard de goules a 3 lions d'argent passantz.*

Cf. 145, 115.

Sir John Giffard of Brimpsfield, Glos., aged sixteen in 1247–8, s. and h. of Elias; d. at Boyton 1299, leaving John his s. and h., aged twelve. (*CP* v. 639.)

GENEVILLE

106. *Geffrey de Genevile d'azur al chef d'ermine a un leun recoupe de goules en l'azur iij bresses d'or.*

Cf. 146, 116: B 103.

Geoffrey de Geneville was summ. to Parliament 1299: same person as B 103.

CLIFFORD

107. *Robert de Clifford eschekere d'or et d'azur a une fesse de goules.*

Cf. 147, 117.

Though the arms are undifferenced this is perhaps the Robert de Clifford who in 1279 inherited lands in Ellingham, &c., Northumb., from his kinsman Sir Ralph de Gaugy. (*Cal. Inq.* ii, no. 321; *Cal. Fine Rolls*, i. 111.) His place in the Clifford pedigree has not been found. He is perhaps the same who held Hilton, Northumb., in 1242–4. (*Book of Fees*, 1119.)

The entry cannot refer to B 31's gds. and h. Robert as he was only born *c*. 1274.

CRESPIN

108. *William Crepyn d'argent a treys barres de goules engrelles.*

Cf. 148, 118.

William Crespin, seigneur of Bec-Crespin, Constable of Normandy, Marshal of France 1282, d. 1283. The arms were variously drawn as two or three bars of fusils or as lozengy argent and gules. (*Wijn.* 39–41; *ChP* 15–17.)

MEULAN

109. *Amary de Miland de sable a un liun d'argent raumpant a la cowe furche l'escue bylete d'argent.*

Cf. 149, 119.

Amaury II de Meulan accompanied St. Louis on the Crusade of 1270 and was still living in 1295. He was son of Amaury I, who was second s. of Waleran I (d. 1166), Count of Meulan, by Agnes, dau. of Amaury de Montfort. (Anselme, ii. 408–9.)

The Counts of Meulan bore *Sable, a lion with forked tail argent*, and both *Wijn.* 43 and *ChP* 14 give that coat for Amaury although he was a cadet, whence without doubt the billetty field of this roll.

CHEVREUSE

110. *Henry de Chevrouse d'argent a un croyz de gulez a quatre liuns rampant d'azur.*

Cf. 150, 120–1.

The surname in C II (*a*) is garbled and the spelling is uncertain; fourth and fifth letters might be either *n*, *u*, or *v* and *s* or *f* respectively. Apart from that this is perhaps the most puzzling item in the three rolls.

The entry in C I *a* 150 is almost identical with the above: *Henry de Cheverouse d'argent un crois gulez 4* or *iiij lions rampant d'azur.* C II (*b*), on the other hand, divides the item into two:

120. *Henry de Cheverouse ar a une crosse de g a iiij egles d'az.*

121. . . . *de Cheverouse ar a crosse g iiij lions rapt on the cross of the feld.*

The latter coat, with the lions on instead of beside the cross, is otherwise unknown.

At first sight it seemed obvious that C II (*b*) had preserved the original version, and that its two items had been conflated in C I and C II (*a*). But on closer consideration and for reasons set out in the foreword, we have concluded that that is not the case, that C II (*a*) has preserved the original version and that the splitting of the item in C II (*b*) is the C II (*b*) copyist's emendation. That conclusion is to some extent borne out by Prinet's remarks in his comments on the roll in *Le Moyen Âge.*

Prinet, who only knew Hearne's edition of C II (*a*), observed that the arms given there (and in the text above) are those of a cadet line, the senior line wearing the cross between four eagles (as in C II (*b*) 120). He also observed that no Henry de Chevreuse is known to have been living at the end of the thirteenth or beginning of the fourteenth century, and he opined that the entry was meant for Hervé de Chevreuse, Lord of Maincourt (near Rambouillet), younger s. of Guy III de Chevreuse,[1] and husband of Clemency d'Aulnois, or perhaps his s. of the same name who migrated to the kingdom of Naples. (Bibl. Nat., Paris, MS. 31911, f. 58; Moutie et Merlet, *Cartulaire de l'Abbaye des Vaux de Cerney,* ii. 199–201; P. Durrieu, *Les Archives angevines de Naples,* ii. 305; cf. *ChP* 20 and authorities there cited.)

Prinet also observed that a Hervé de Chevreuse, of the senior, eagle-bearing line, was living in 1263–78, and if one should agree that Henry is a mistake for Hervé it may be to him that C II (*b*) 120 refers.

In the junior, Maincourt, line Hervé above-named was succ. in 1262 by his s. Anseau, Marshal of Sicily, d. 1304. It might be thought that C II (*b*) 121 was meant for him, but that is improbable, for he bore the cross between four lions, not charged with lions. (*ChP* 20.)

Such are the particulars which we have been able to collect. Readers must draw their own conclusions from them and from such other details as they may be able to supply.

MONTMORENCY

111. *John de Mount Morency d'or poudre d'egle d'azur a une croyz de goules.*

Cf. 151, 122.

C II *a* inserts a superfluous *e* after *d'egle.*

This is the well-known coat of Montmorency, there being normally four eaglets in each canton. (*ChP* 10.)

Prinet pointed out that no head of the family was named John before 1305 and he suggested that the roll was not compiled until after that or that the entry is an interpolation. (*P.MA.*) But there are several instances in this roll of a cadet being assigned the undifferenced arms, and this may be meant for John de Montmorency, seigneur de Roissy, third s. of Matthew II 'le Grand', seigneur de Montmorency and Constable of France. John fl. 1226–36. (Anselme, iii. 569–70.)

BURGUNDY

112. *Le Duk de Burgoyn bende d'or e d'azur a une bordure de gules.*

Cf. 72, 123.

Robert II (s. of Hugh IV), Duke of Burgundy 1272 and titular King of Thessalonica, d. 1305. (*Wijn.* 1083.) He m. Agnes, dau. of Louis IX of France. (GWW 32.)

This coat, now known as Burgundy ancient, was borne by the dukes of the house of Capet until 1361, and was then taken by their successors of the house of Valois. (*P.MA; AVD* xi. 57.)

A similar coat without border, *Or, four bends gules,* is attributed to the Latin kingdom of Salonica or Thessalonica, which belonged to the dukes of Burgundy from 1266. (*Wijn.* 1291.)

---

[1] Guy de Cheneros' alias Goneros' [*sic*] knight, was given a safe-conduct in 1254 when going on pilgrimage to Santiago through Gascony. (Cal. Pat. Rolls, 1247–58, p. 385.)

CLEVES

113. *Le Counte de Cleve de goules a un escochon d'argent a une charbocle d'or flurte.*

Cf. 58, 124.

C I omits the tincture of the charbocle writing *de* instead of *d'or*.

Originally the charbocle (see Glossary) was no part of the arms. The earliest symbol of the Counts of Cleves was a lion, as on the seal of Count Dietrich in 1193, but by the middle of the thirteenth century they were using a scocheon. Conrad von Würzburg (d. 1287), in *Der Turney zu Nantheiz* (Ganz 167–8), tinctures this gules in an ermine field. It is doubtful whether those tinctures are correct for in 1254 *Bigot* 19 blazons *l'escu de geules a un escuchon d'argent*. That must be for Thierry VI, 1202–60, and he displayed the scocheon on his equestrian seal in 1247. Nevertheless, the counterseal which he used at the same time shows a charbocle overlying the scocheon, and *Wijn.* 632 paints the arms of Count Thierry VIII, 1275–1305, as *Gules, a charbocle or with a scocheon argent over all*. (Ströhl, *Deutsche Wappenrolle* 23; W. Ewald, 'Die Siegel der Grafen und Herzöge von Kleve' in *Veröffentlichungen des hist. Vereins für den Niederrhein*, t. ii, 1909, p. 276, &c.; *AVD* xiv. 395–6; de Raadt, ii. 220.)

LUXEMBURG

114. *Le Counte de Lucenburg burle d'argent e d'azur a une leun de gules rampant corone d'or.*

Cf. 59, 125.

Henry II, 'le Blondel', Count of Luxemburg (b. 1217, d. 1281), s. of Waleran Duke of Limburg (d. 1226) and Ermesinde de Namur, h. of Luxemburg (d. 1247). He m. Marguerite, dau. of Henry II, Count of Bar. He sealed at first with a lion in a plain field, but afterwards bore the red lion of Limburg (C 51) changing the silver field to buruly as here. (*Bigot* 17: cf. *Wijn.* 524, 629; *ZWR* 312.)

SAYN

115. *Le Counte de Musein de goules au lapard d'or raumpant a la cowe furche.*

Cf. 60, 126.

The arms show that the Counts of Sayn, near Coblenz, are meant. The name was probably written Su Sein and the initial *S* miscopied as *M* as in other cases. The name is also mishandled in *Wijn.* 622 where it appears as Le conte desne.

The old house of Sayn failed in the male line in 1240 on the death of Count Henry. Henry's sister, however, was m. to Count Godfrey von Spanheim, and their gds. Godfrey assumed the name and arms of Sayn. He became Count of Sayn in 1261 and d. 1283.

Wijn. 622 paints the lion rampant gardant with the tail forked and crossed in saltire.

BERG

116. *Le Counte du Monte d'argent a un lion rampant de goules a la cowe croyse corone d'or a une labeu d'azur.*

Cf. 61, 127.

C I misblazons the label *d'or*.

Adolphe VIII, Count of Berg 1259–96. (*Wijn.* 620.) He dropped the label after 1280.

The county of Berg, *Montensis comitatus*, a mountainous district round Düsseldorf, was made a duchy by the Emperor Wenceslaus in 1380. It came to the house of Limburg by the marriage of Adolphe's grandparents, Henry IV of Limburg (d. 1247) and Irmgarde, dau. of Adolphe VI of Berg (d. 1218). (C 51.)

De Raadt calls the lion on seals of 1265, 1276, and 1292 *courant* (i. 229).

KYBURG

117. *Le Counte de Kyburc de gules a un bend d'or a ij liuns rampant d'or.*

Cf. 62, 128.

Kyburg is in canton Zürich, to the south of Winterthur.

The counts of Kyburg were of the same stock as the Dillingen (C 53). The two branches divided about 1180, Hartman of Kyburg taking *Sable, a bend between two lions rampant or,* and his brother Adalbert zu Dillingen *Azure, a bend between four lions or.* The male line of Kyburg expired in 1264 on the death of Hartman IV. His dau. and h. Anna m. in 1271 Count Eberhardt von Halsburg-Laufenburg, whereupon their issue took the arms of Kyburg but altered the tinctures to *Gules, a bend between two lions or* as blazoned here and painted in *ZWR* 42. In the *Haus zum Loch,* 125, the tinctures are inverted. *Clipearius* 34 gives the old coat:

> 'Kiburg in nigro gilvam tabulam fore ponis
> Obliquansque duos gilvos secet illa leones.'

(P.*MA*; *ZWR*, loc. cit.; Ganz, *passim*; *AHS* 1887, p. 33, &c., 1924, 49, &c.)

FREIBURG im Breisgau

118. *Le Counte de Friburc d'or a un egle de gules a un bordure de veyr.*

Cf. 63, 129.

The shields of the Counts of Freiburg im Breisgau and of their cousins the Counts of Fürstenberg combine the eagle of Zähringen and the vair of Urach. Egon IV von Urach (d. 1230) m. Agnes von Zähringen, and their s. Egon V in 1218, on the death of his maternal uncle Berthold, the last Duke of Zähringen, acquired Freiburg and other Zähringen properties. Of his sons Conrad (succ. 1236, d. 1271) founded the line of Counts of Freiburg, and Henry (d. 1264) founded the Counts of Fürstenberg. Conrad's s. and h. d. 1316. Both these lines bore the arms given here. *Clipearius* 51 blazons them thus:

> 'De Friburg aquila rubet in gilvo, sed oportet
> Quod per circuitum quedam variamina portetur.'

ZWR 66 paints the same for Fürstenberg. Both there and in the *Haus zum Loch,* 127, the border is *Party orleways nebuly argent and azure*; as a result it has sometimes been blazoned as a border of clouds, but it was really vair.

The early symbol of the Counts of Urach was a lion passant, but from 1230 or before they bore *Per fess, in chief or a lion passant argent, in base vair.* (P.*MA*; Ganz 181 n.; *ZWR*, loc. cit.; *AVD* xiv. 61, &c.; *AHS* 1889, p. 322, &c.)

WÜRTTEMBERG

119. *Le Counte de Wirtenberg d'or a iij perche de deym de sable.*

Cf. 64, 130.

Ulrich II, Count of Württemberg 1205 *c.* to 1278, or his brother Eberhard I, d. 1325.

As arms of Württemberg the three antlers first appear on a seal of Count Conrad in 1228. But in 1238 Count Ulrich sealed with a canting coat, *Three watch-towers on a triple mount,* i.e. *drei Warttürme auf einem Berge.* The antlers came from the Counts of Veringen, Count Conrad's father, Hartmann I, having m. a Veringen h. *Clipearius* 46, 47 assigns the black antlers both to Württemberg and to Veringen:

> 'Wirtenberg cervina tria nigra cornua defert
> In clipeo, qui tincturam croceam tibi prefert,
> Veringen gilvo cervi tria cornua nigra
> Pretendit, nec in hoc, tibi sit mens credere pigra.

Later the Veringen antlers were changed to red, the gold field being retained. They are so painted in *ZWR* 46 and in the *Haus zum Loch,* 9, as well as on an embroidered purse dating from the end of the thirteenth century and now in the Swiss National Museum. The counts von Nellenburg, another related family, bore blue antlers in gold. (P.*MA*; Ganz 56, 107–9, 180, pl. I; *ZWR* 46, 47, 315; *Haus zum Loch,* 9, 26.)

TIERSTEIN

120. *Le Counte de Tresteyn d'or a un bys de gules.*

Cf. 65, 131.

The Counts of Tierstein took their name from a castle near Wittnau (canton Aarfau), but on inheriting possessions in Solothurn they built another castle there and called that Tierstein. The arms are canting, *ein rotes Tier* (hind) *auf grünem Stein*, or as *Clipearius* 37 puts it:

'Tierstein sit gilvus clipei color et bene cerva [serva]
Que [quod] supra lapidem vult stare ibi cerva.'

Neither this roll nor *Bigot* ever mentions the stone, but Count Rudolf sealed in 1208 with a hind on a triple mount, and the mount has been used regularly ever since, though the number of coupeaux varies.

This roll presumably refers to the Rudolf who succ. in 1262 and d. 1318.

Bigot 5 is almost unrecognizable, *Seclin de Wistesale l'escu d'or a une ouisse* [hind] *de gueules*, but Dr. Adam-Even identified it as referring to Rudolf's second s. Ulrich (d. 1330); he sealed in 1267 with the hind and mount. (P.*MA*; *ZWR* 505; *Wappenbuch d. Stadt Basel* by Staehelin and Roschet, part i (5).)

ÖTTINGEN

121. *Le Counte de Whitingwen veire d'or e de gules a une escuchon d'azur a un sautour d'argent.*

Cf. 66, 132.

Conrad, Count von Öttingen, living 1265, or his s. Ludwig VIII, d. in or after 1334. (Siebmacher I. iii, Div. 3, p. 190.)

Originally counts of Riesgau, they called themselves from the beginning of the twelfth century after their seat at Öttingen in Swabia. The arms as here blazoned appear *c.* 1200 on the seal of Ludwig II. Their earlier seal device was a stag.

Clipearius 61 seems to make the inescocheon green:

'Oetingen viret et gilvo rubeoque repingit
Limbum quos nivea cancellans linea stringit.'

ZWR, however, makes it blue as here. (P.*MA*; *ZWR* 58; Ganz 182.)

COLESTEYN

122. *Le Counte de Colesteyn d'or a un chief de sable.*

Cf. 67, 123.

C II *a* has *cherf* which might be meant for *cerf*, stag, but C II *b* writes *cheif* which agrees with C I.

Prinet suggested that this might be meant for the counts of Falkenstein, in the Taunus, near Königstein. As lords of Minzenberg and an offshoot of the counts of Bolanders they bore *Quarterly, 1 and 4, azure, a wheel argent*, for Bolanders; *2 and 3, or a chief gules*, for Minzenberg. That may or may not be correct. But his further statement that Beatrice, the third wife of Richard of Cornwall, King of the Romans (m. 1269—B 3, C 124), was a Falkenstein is mistaken. She was a dau. of Waleran de Fauquemont (Valkenberg or Falkenberg near Maastricht), and a niece of Archbishop Engelbert of Cologne. (*CP* iii. 431 citing Chron. Balduini Avennensis in *Monumenta Germanica Scriptores*, xxv. 462; cf. de Raadt, i. 442.) Waleran appears in *Bigot 30* as *Valeran de la Monjoie, l'escu d'argent* or *a j lion de geules rampant au lablel vert*; cf. FW 435 where the label is omitted and the lion's tail is forked.

BOHUN of Hereford

123. *Le Counte de Herford d'azur a sis liuncels d'or a un bende d'argent lyte d'or.*

Cf. 98, 134: MP I. 33: B 10.

Humphrey de Bohun, Earl of Hereford, s. of Henry de Bohun, Earl of Hereford (MP I. 33), d. 1275: same person as MP II 9.

CORNWALL, Earl of

124. *Le Count de Cornwale d'argent a un lion rampant de goules corone d'or a une bordure de sable besante d'or.*

Cf. 99, 135: MP I. 38: B 3.

This may refer either to Richard, Earl of Cornwall, d. 1272 (MP I. 38), or to his s. Edmund who d.s.p. 1308. (*CP* iii. 430, &c.)

QUINCY

125. *Le Counte de Winchestre de goules poudre a fause losenge d'or.*

Cf. 100, 136: MP I. 32: B 8.

Roger, the last Earl of Winchester, of the Quincy family, s. of Saher de Quincy, Earl of Winchester (MP I. 32) d. 1264 s.p.m., and thereafter the earldom was in the Crown until 1322. Saher de Quincy, his grandfather who d. 1217, bore on his seal *A fess and a label.* (Birch 6355.)

PORTUGAL

126. *Le Roy de Portugal de goules poudre a turelles d'or a une labeu d'azur.*

Cf. 18, 137.

Alphonso, younger s. of Alphonso II of Portugal (d. 1223) and Urraque of Castile; Regent of Portugal from 1245 owing to the insanity of his brother Sancho II; King of Portugal as Alphonso III 1261–79. In 1241 he sealed with a semy of castles (towers) for Castile impaling Dammartin-France, that is *Barry, semy of fleurs-de-lis,* for his wife Maud de Dammartin, h. of Boulogne, the counterseal showing a semy of France impaling *Barry of six in a border* for Dammartin. (Ddq. 1063; C 127.) The arms blazoned above are probably those which Alphonso used as Regent; they are a differenced version of Castile (C 7).

The historical arms of Portugal, the five *quinas,* i.e. *Argent, five shields in cross azure each charged with as many silver roundels in saltire,* appear in 1189 on seals of Sancho I and his sister Maud Countess of Flanders (Demay, *Inventaire des Sceaux de la Flandre* 142), and that coat with the addition of a border of Castile (*Gules, semy of towers or*) was borne by Alphonso after he took the royal title in 1261. (*Wijn.* 1264.) In FW 25 and some later rolls the shields are misrepresented as dice.

The coat described above as Dammartin–France is a combination of those two coats. In 1236, as Countess of Boulogne, Maud sealed with a semy of France with a label, and in 1239 she used two shields *accolés,* the dexter Dammartin, *Barry of six argent and azure in a border gules,* the sinister France with a label. (Ddq. 1060–1; cf. Alfonso's 1241 counterseal mentioned above.)

DAMMARTIN

127. *Counte de Danmartyn de Boleyngne barre d'argent et d'azur a une bordre de goules.*

Cf. 71, 51.

These are the arms of the old counts of Dammartin-en-Goële, near Meaux. They first appear in 1185 as four bars without the border on the seal of Aubrey de Dammartin, d. 1200. In the middle of the thirteenth century Alice, his dau. and h., carried both county and arms to her husband John, Lord of Trie (dépt. Oise) and Mouchy-le-Châtel (near Beauvais). Her s. Matthew de Trie, Count of Dammartin in 1259, d. 1272, sealed with the bend of Trie and on the counterseal shields of Trie and Dammartin, but his s. John, Count of Dammartin (d. in or after 1304) used in 1272 and 1298 Dammartin alone, and his s. Renaud differenced that v.p. with a sable bird. The county of Boulogne, which was held by Renaud de Dammartin (temp. Philip Augustus 1180–1223) and by his dau. Maud, passed on the latter's death in 1259 to the house of Auvergne (C 36). (Anselme, vi. 663; *AVD* xi. 438–41; P.*MA*; GWW 479; Ganz 14; *Wijn.* 2, 4; *ChP* 33.)

FW 77 assigns a similar coat, *Argent, three bars azure in a border gules* to Le Cunte de Puntif, i.e. Simon de Dammartin, Count of Ponthieu *jure uxoris* Mary, only dau. of William II, Count of Ponthieu (d. 1239).

TRIE dit BILLEBAULT

128. *Signeur de Bilebatia de Trie d'or a une bende gobone d'argent et d'azure.*

> Cf. 69, 52.
>
> C II *a* writes *Mi Mir Bilebatind* and C II *b mys' bileard.* C I's version of the name has been
> adopted above. The arms are a differenced version of Trie, *Or, a bend azure,* the gobony bend
> recalling the arms of Dammartin (C 127). John de Trie 'Billebault' (a nickname borne by
> several of the family) sealed with a gobony bend in 1263 during the lifetime of his father Matthew
> de Trie, Count of Dammartin (C 127). It was apparently this Billebault who gave his name to
> the hamlet of Le Plessis-Billebault or Le Plessier-Billebault (dépt. of Oise). (*P.MA.*)
>
> In *Wijn.* 6 and *ChP* 26 Renaud de Trie bears *Or, a bend of Dammartin (gobony argent and azure
> bordered gules).* Both Prinet and Dr. Adam-Even identify him as Renaud, seigneur de Plessis,
> gds. of Matthew above-named. He was slain at the battle of Courtrai in 1302 and was presumably
> s. of the above John 'Billebault'. The Tournoi de Chauvenci gives Renaud's arms in 1285
> as *D'or à celle bende troncenée d'argent et d'azur est listée à deux bastons vermaux en coste* (line 2208; de
> Raadt, iv. 56).

TRIE

129. *Reynalde de Trie d'or a un bende d'azure a un label de gules.*

> Cf. 70, 53.
>
> Presumably Renaud, s. of Philip (d.v.p.), eldest s. of Count Matthew (74). He is known from
> documents of 1277–98. The bend and label were borne by Philip in 1251 and by his brother
> Henry in 1282. They are attributed to the latter and the label gules in *Wijn.* 5 and to his brother
> Thibaud in FW 480 (but cf. *Wijn.* 59). (*P.MA*; GWW 480.)

VIENNE

130. *Le Counte de Vian de gules a une egle d'or.*

> Cf. 68, 54.
>
> C I specifies that the eagle is *espany,* displayed.
>
> Hugh, s. of Hugh d'Antigny, Lord of Pagny-le-Château (dépt. Côte d'Or) and Beatrice
> de Vienne, inherited from his uncle William (dead 1256) the county of Vienne and important
> domains in Burgundy. He sold Vienne in 1266 to the Archbishop of Vienne but still used the
> name and arms (the eagle) and transmitted them to his issue. He was dead 1277. His s. and h.
> d. 1312. (Anselme, vii. 795, viii. 426; *P.MA*; GWW 73.)
>
> An anonymous coat in *Wijn.* 1128 shows the eagle with no feet. The editors identify it as
> the coat of Philip d'Antigny, Count of Vienne 1261–96.

MOWBRAY

131. *Roger de Moubrey de gules a un leun rampant d'argent.*

> Cf. 104, 55: B 74.
>
> Roger, Lord Mowbray 1295, d. 1297, a minor at the death of his father Roger (B 174) in
> 1266. (*CP* ix. 376.)

ROS of Helmsley and Belvoir

132. *Robert de Ross de goules a treis buz d'argent.*

> Cf. 105, 56: MP II. 55: B 66, 67.
>
> Robert de Ros, s. of William de Ros (B 66), d. 1285: same person as B 67.

NEVILLE of Essex

133. *Hugo de Nevile d'azur a un leon rampant d'or.*

Cf. 106, 57.

Sir Hugh de Neville of Essex and Sussex, s. and h. of John; d. before 5 October 1269. His brother John (dead 1282) bears these arms in E 56 and TJ 54, and John's s. Hugh (b. 1276) bears them in N 113; both were of Essex. (*CP* ix. 482, &c.)

LUCY

134. *Geoffrey de Luscy de goules poudre a croisil d'or a treis luz d'or.*

Cf. 108, 58.

Geoffrey has not been identified with certainty. The arms were borne both by Lucy of Charlecote, Warws., and by Lucy of Dallington, Northants.

The former descended from Sir Walter de Charlecote, temp. Richard I, whose s. and h. Sir William was known as de Lucy, whence Dugdale supposes that Walter m. a lady of the Northumberland Lucys. (Dugd. *Warws.* i. 502.)

The Lucys of Dallington (CG 521; CKO 348) were cadets of Newington (B 112), Geoffrey de Lucy of Newington (d. 1251/2) having m. Juliana, dau. and h. of Aymery Despenser of Dallington. Their s. and h. Sir Geoffrey of Dallington d. 1272/3. (Baker, *Northants.* 1. 130.)

NEVILLE of Raby

135. *Robert de Nevile de goules a une sautor d'argent.*

Cf. 107, 59: B 59.

Robert de Neville d. 1282: same person as B 59.

BASSINGBOURN

136. *Garin de Bassingburn geroun d'or et d'azur.*

Cf. 109, 60: B 35.

Warin de Bassingbourn was dead 1269: same person as B 35.

BARDOLF

137. *Thomas Bardulf d'azur poudre a croisil d'or e treis quintefoiles d'or.*

Cf. 110, 61.

Younger brother of C 138—see B 70.

BARDOLF of Wormegay

138. *William sun frer d'azur a treys quintefoiles d'or.*

Cf. 111, 62.

William Bardolf (s. and h. of B 70), of Wormegay, Norfolk, and Shelford, Notts., m. Julian dau. and h. of Hugh de Gournay of Mapledurham; d. 1289. His s. and h. Hugh, Lord Bardolf, d. 1304. (*CP* i. 417; Birch 7132.)

KERDESTON

139. *Fouk de Kerdeston gulez un sautour engrelle d'argent.*

Cf. 112, 63: B 79.

Both copies of C II garble the name, Karketon and Barg'ron respectively: same person as B 79.

SANDFORD

140. *Nicolaus de Sanfort unde d'argent e de goules.*

Cf. 113, 64: MP IV 81: B 115–16.

Probably the same as Nicholas de Sandford (MP IV. 81) who d. 1252. All three copies write *Manford* instead of *Sanford*.

DE LA MORE

141. *Richard de la Moore esquartile d'argent et d'azure endente.*

Cf. 114, 65.

Sir Richard de la More, younger s. of Bartholomew, held half a knight's fee in Bitton Manor, Glos., 1260, was dead 1292 leaving his nephew Stephen (s. of Bartholomew) as h. (*Cal. Inq. Misc.* 1219–1307, no. 259; *Cal. Pat. Rolls*, 1258–66, p. 595; *Cal. Fine Rolls*, i. 310.)

BALLIOL of Red Castle and Tours

142. *Eustache de Bailiol de goules a un faut eskochin d'argent.*

Cf. 115, 75: B 38.

Eustace de Balliol of Red Castle and Tours, although B 38 differences the arms with a gold label: same person as B 38.

MARSHAL

143. *La Counte de Pennebrok party d'or et de vert a un lion rampant party de or e de gules en lunge.*

Cf. 101, 76: MP I. 29: B 17.

Both copies of C II make the lion party paleways or and gules; it should be all gules as in C I. The arms are those of Marshal, extinct in 1245.

WARWICK, Earl of

144. *Le Counte de Warwik eschekere d'or et d'azure a un cheveron d'ermine.*

Cf. 102, 77: MP I. 70: B 20.

These are the arms of the 'Newburgh' family of whom the last earl d.s.p. 1242. (See MP I. 70.)

PLESCY

145. *John de Plescy d'argent a treis molettes de goules perces.*

Cf. 116, 78.

C II *b* has *moulettes perceys*. C I reads *mullettes percees*, but the word *mullettes* is underlined and *anulettez* written in the margin; this is evidently a copyist's gloss. This is an instance of *meulette*, 'little millstone', used for a roundel.

It does not appear to whom this entry refers, cf. B 24.

REVIERS, Earl of Devon and the Isle of Wight

146. *Le Counte del Ille de goules a treis barres d'or diaspres.*

Cf. 103, 79: MP I. 75: B 12.

The fact that this item fellows two English earldoms in C II and five such in C I shows that another English earldom is meant, and that can only be the earldom of Devon, or of the Isle (of Wight) as it was often called. In 1275 this was in Isabel de Reviers, the sister of B 12, q.v. for further remarks on this item.

BEAUCHAMP

147. *Walter Belechaump equartile d'or e de goules a un bende de gules.*

Cf. 117, 80: MP II. 28: B 54.

Walter has not been placed in the pedigree.

ROCHFORD

148. *Guy de Rocheforte esquartile d'or et de gules.*

Cf. 118, 81: B 208.

Guy de Rochford of Rochford and Elsenham, Essex, d. 1274. (*Cal. Inq.* ii, no. 68.)

BERNERS

149. *John de Berner esquartile d'or et de verte a une labeu de gules.*

Cf. 119, 82: MP II. 78: B 146.

Probably the same person as B 146.

BEAUCHAMP

150. *Geffrey de Belchaump esquartile d'argent e de sable.*

Cf. 139, 83: MP II. 76: B 196.

S. of Simon de Beauchamp of Bedford and younger brother of William de Beauchamp of Bedford (MP II. 28): same person as MP II. 76.

CAMOYS

151. *Rafe de Camoys d'or al chef de goules a treis gastelles d'argent sur le chef.*

Cf. 120, 84.

Ralph de Camoys, s. and h. of B 64, Constable of Pevensey Castle 1264, was dead 1277 leaving John s. and h. (*CP* ii. 506.)

MAUDUIT

152. *Walter Maldust d'argent a deus barres de gules.*

Cf. 121, 85: MP II. 75: B 65.

Not identified. C II *b* has telescoped this and 126 giving Mauduit the coat of Boys.

BOYS

153. *Arnald de Boyis d'argent a deus barres de goules a une kantel de goules.*

Cf. 122, 85: MP II. 74; VII. 6, s. of Ernald de Boys (MP II. 74) d. 1277 (*CP* ii. 202).

MERCK

154. *Ingram del Merk de gules a un lion rampant d'argent.*

Cf. 123, 86.

Ingram or Ingelram de Merck was dead March 1259 holding in Dunmow and Steeple Bumpstead, Essex. His s. and h. Robert was dead April 1306 leaving s. and h. Ingram aged fourteen. (*Cal. Inq.* i. no. 441, iv. no. 345; *Cal. Gen.*, p. 84; *Cal. Close Roll*, 1256–9, p. 369.)

The Merck family were cadets of the vicomtes de Marck near Calais, and were already established in Essex at Domesday, but Ingram has not been placed in the pedigree. (Round, *Peerage and Family Origins*, p. 157; *HKF* iii. 211, 273; *Feud. Cambs.* pp. 225–7.)

In the *Armorial Equestre*, pl. lxxxvi, Mons de Marke bears *Gules, a lion with tail forked in saltire argent, crown, tongue, and claws gold.* So too in *L'Anchienne Noblesse de la Contée de Flandres* by Cornelius Gailliard who gives their cry as 'Lymbourg! Lymbourg!' (p. 127).

MARTELL

155. *Walter Martel de goules a treis martelles d'argent.*

Cf. 124, 87.

Walter Martell held land at Shepreth, Cambs., 1302–9. (*Feud. Cambs.* 232.)

    The three hammers in varying tinctures occur for Martell in E 576, F 212, and N 318 as well as in *ChP* 83, *Wijn.* 339, &c., and later rolls. But this seems to be their sole appearance in these tinctures before about 1460 in SK (750) and the MY (124) rolls. In the latter as also in Thomas Wall's Book, f. 132*b*, the family is placed in Essex, but Sir Adam in N 318 is of Berks.

FREVILLE

156. *Baudewin de Friville de veyr a une croiz passant de goules.*

Cf. 152, 88.

Baldwin de Freville, s. of Maud Devereux, d. 5 September 1289, and was succ. by his younger brother Sir Alexander. He held at Tatington and Wellingham, Herefords., and also in Norfolk. (*Cal. Gen.*, p. 400; *Cal. Inq.* ii, no. 709; *Cal. Fine Roll*, 1272–1307, pp. 264–5.)

    The arms are variously blazoned. Here they are *Vair, a plain cross gules* (cf. Birch 9958). E 254 and F 146 paint *Or, a cross lozengy vair and gules*, and E 583 for an unspecified Freville paints *Or, a cross patonce lozengy gules and vair*. Sir Alexander changed the cross to a saltire and bore *Or, a saltire lozengy vair and gules* (E 540; F 152), but on succeeding his brother he resumed the cross. (N 873.)

ODINGSELES

157. *William Dodingceles d'argent a une fesse de gules a deus roueles de gulez en le chef.*

Cf. 153, 89: MP II. 57: B 142.

C II *a*'s blazon with this, but C II *b* gives only one rowel in chief: same person as MP II. 57.

AGUILLON

158. *Robert Angevyn de gules a une florette d'or.*

Cf. 154, 90: B 63.

C II gives the surname as *Angevyn*, but in C II *b* the word is underlined and *Launcelyn* super-scribed by the same hand. The arms are those of Aguillon with the fleur-de-lis tinctured gold instead of silver as in B and other rolls: same person as B 63.

MARMION

159. *Philip Marmion de veyr a une fesse de gules.*

Cf. 155, 91: B 57.

The arms with the plain red fess are those of the younger branch as they were borne by William Marmion of Winteringham (B 47) and presumably by his father Robert the younger. Neverthe-less, this entry is probably meant for Sir Philip Marmion of Tamworth and Scrivelsby, the head of the senior line and a prominent man in his day—see Appendix I, last paragraph.

PAVELEY

160. *Edwarde de Paveley d'azure a un croys d'or rescersele.*

Cf. 157, 92.

Recercele applied to a cross is synonymous with moline. C II *b*'s term *recrossele* is more suggestive of a cross crosslet or *recroisetée*. The Paveley cross is generally given either as patonce or as flory at the ends. On Sir Walter Paveley's Garter Stall-Plate it is patonce.

    Edward is otherwise unknown, and it is possible that the variation in the cross is a difference.

HUSSEY or HOSE

161. *Hugh de Huse barre d'ermine e de goules.*

Cf. 158, 93: MP II. 56.

Perhaps Hugh Hose who held Penkridge Manor, Staffs., in 1212, being then the king's ward. (*Book of Fees*, 143.) This Hugh was possibly a brother of Henry Hose, the father of Matthew (MP II. 56). The identification of this Hugh is very conjectural.

FITZWARIN

162. *Philip le FizWarine ebartile d'argent e de goules endente.*

Cf. 156, 94.

Younger brother of B 124. Both copies of C I write FitzWarine which is evidently correct. C II has Philip de (or le) fitz Marmion. That is evidently a case where the scribe has carried the Marmion on from a preceding entry, and it suggests that version C I, where the two entries are contiguous, may give the original order rather than C II where there are two intervening items. On the other hand, it is possible that the copyist of C II skipped the entry and when he noticed the omission he put it in out of order and with the name mistaken.

ST. JOHN of Basing

163. *John de Sein John d'argent a chef de goules a deus roueles d'or al cheif.*

Cf. 159, 95.

Sir John de St. John of Basing, s. of B 111, was dead 1302. His widow Alice was dau. of Reynold FitzPiers. His s. and h. Sir John was summ. as Lord St. John in 1299, and d. 1329. (*CP* xi. 323; Barons' Letter.)

VAUX of Caterlen

164. *Robert de Vausse eschekere d'argent et de gules.*

Cf. 160, 96.

Robert de Vaux of Catterlen and Tryermain, Cumb., was overlord of Newland by Sowerby, Cumb., in 1278 and was still living in 1305. (*Cal. Inq.* ii, no. 246, iv., no. 322.)

    The Vaux of Caterlen were cadets of Gilsland (B 33), though Robert is here given the undifferenced arms.

PECCHE

165. *Bawdewin Peche veyre d'or e de gules.*

Cf. 161, 97.

Not identified unless Baldwin is a mistake for Bartholomew (cf. C 166), Bartholomew de Pecche held lands of the Earl of Salisbury in Wilts. d. in 1242–3. (*Book of Fees*, 720; *Book of Seals*, 318.) The arms, however, are those of Ferrers and are otherwise unknown as a Pecche coat.

CREKE

166. *Bawdewin de Creyke d'azur a une manche d'ermine.*

Cf. —, 98.

C I omits this, the copyist having apparently jumped a line owing to the identity of the Christian names in this and 165.

    No Baldwin de Creke has been found. The name may be a mistake for Bartholomew as already suggested for C165. Geoffrey, eldest s. of Bartholomew de Creke and Margery..., of Helmingham, Suffolk, sealed with a maunch in the thirteenth century. (Birch 9061; cf. Banks, *Baronies in Fee*, ii. 145.) Bartholomew de Creke, d. *c.* 1250, acquired Groton, Suffolk *jure uxoris*, and was succ. there by his gds. Bartholomew. (Copinger, *Suffolk Manors*, i. 111.)

MAUCLERK

167. *Peres de Meuclerk d'azur a treys quintefoiles d'argent.*

Cf. 162, 99.

Arms otherwise unknown for Mauclerk. The only Piers Mauclerk who has been found is Pierre de Dreux, dit 'Mauclerc', Earl of Richmond, but he bore quite different arms.

ST. JOHN of Nashenden

168. *Walter de Sein John d'azur a treis fermaulx d'or.*

Cf. 163, 100.

Walter de St. John of Nashenden Manor, near Rochester, Kent, and Great Wakering, Essex, dead August 1260 leaving Margaret sister and h. (*Cal. Inq.* i, no. 467.) He was doubtless of the same family as the Robert de St. John who *c.* 1200 sealed a charter confirming certain lands to Cumbwell Priory; the seal displays three buckles, two round and one hexagonal with concave sides. (*Arch. Cant.* vi. 208.) Three buckles are not otherwise known as a St. John coat. Both copies of C II write *Main* for *Sein*.

BURGH

169. *Walter de Burg eskartile d'argent et de gules a une croyz de gules passant.*

Cf. 164, 66.

In 1272 Walter de Burgh was granted a market and fair at Burgh Manor, Norfolk. (*Cal. Charter Rolls*, ii. 184.) His wife Euphemia, dau. and coh. of Joland de Evermue and coh. of Walter de Evermue, held lands in Knaith and Kexby, Lincs. (*Cal. Close Rolls*, 1272–9, p. 60; *Cal. Gen.* p. 201.) Walter was still living in 1280 (*Cal. Close Rolls*, 1279–88, p. 60.) He is perhaps the same who in 1242–3 held of Gilbert de Gaunt in Beckingham, &c., Lincs. (*Book of Fees*, p. 1039.)

The arms are otherwise unknown in England. They may be derived from the *Or, a cross gules*, which was borne by Bigod, Earl of Norfolk, and by Burgh, Earl of Ulster

HESLINGTON

170. *Richard de Haselington d'argent a treis crescant de sable.*

Cf. 165, 67.

Not identified. The arms have not been found in any early roll. They are assigned to Lenyngton or Levyngton in SHY 203 (late fifteenth century), and Wriothesley attributes them to Hagelinton. (LH 74, 800.)

Both C I and C II *b* blazon three crescents but there is no *treis* in C II *a*.

FITZGERALD

171. *Morice le Fiz Gerald d'argent a un sautour de goules.*

Cf. 166, 68.

Sir Maurice FitzGerald, called 'Mael' the Bald, second s. of Maurice, second Baron of Offaly (d. 1257), succ. to his father's lands in Tyrconnell, Fermanagh, and Connaught. Justice of Ireland 1272; m. Emeline, Countess of Ulster, dau. of Stephen de Longespée. He was dead at Ross, co. Wexford, 1286, Emeline surviving him. (*CP* vii. 200.)

TALBOT

172. *Richard Talbot d'or a un leon de goules a une color d'or a une borde de vert besante d'or.*

Cf. 167, 69.

Richard has not been identified nor have the arms been found elsewhere. They appear to be connected with those borne by Sir Richard Talbot of Eccleswall, Herefords., in 1301, *Gules, a lion in a bordure engrailed or.*

HARCOURT

173. *John de Harcourte de gules a deus barres d'or.*

Cf. 168, 70.

John I, Lord of Harcourt in Normandy, s. and h. of Richard, succ. 1242, d. 1288. (*Wijn.* 322; FW 552; Anselme, v. 128.) He is perhaps the John de Harcourt who with his wife Joan had suit about the manors of Hengham, Banham, and Messingham in 1278 (*Close Roll*, 6 Edward I, m. 11*d*, 1278), and who with the said Joan nominated attorneys in 1282. (*Cal. Pat. Rolls*, 1281–92, p. 10.)

His son, John II 'le Preux' (*Wijn.* 323; FW 553; *ChP* 88; Anselme, v. 129) is perhaps the Sir John de Harecurt whom Edward I promised in 1299 to indemnify for losses in the exchange of prisoners between England and France. (*Cal. Pat. Rolls*, 1292–1301, p. 428.) He was Marshal of France 1285–1302 and d. 1304.

PARTHENAY, dit l'Archevêque

174. *Hugh l'Archevesk burle de une menue burlure d'argent et d'azure a une bende de gules.*

Cf. 169, 71.

Hugh III (s. of William III), Lord of Parthenay, &c., in Poitou, d. 1271. One of his sons and a gds. were named Hugh. The nickname l'Archevêque came from Hugh II, Archbishop of Bordeaux in 1205. The family were said to be cadets of Lusignan (C 72) and the arms support that idea. (La Chenaye, xv. 480.)

The Lord of 'Parteneye' is one of those whom Edward I promised to indemnify for losses in the exchange of prisoners in 1299 (*Cal. Pat. Rolls*, 1292–1301, p. 428), but that is perhaps the Robert de Parteneye who was sent to Ireland in 1305. (Ibid. 1301–7, p. 337.)

SERGINES

175. *Geffry de Sergynes de gules a une fesse d'or et une danse d'or en cheife.*

Cf. 170, 72.

All three copies write Mergines. C II *a* has *dazur* for *danse*.

Geoffrey de Sergines (near Sens), seneschal and bailiff of Jerusalem, *c.* 1267, d. 1297. He is mentioned repeatedly by Joinville. (P.*MA*; *Wijn.* 857, 1118; Ddq. 11806.)

CRESÈCQUES

176. *Robert de Creseques d'azur al chef d'or a treis gemelles d'or.*

Cf. 171, 73.

Cresèques, now Crecques, is near Péronne in the Pas-de-Calais. C I misspells the name Cresignes.

A Robert de Cresècques, seneschal of the kingdom of Jerusalem, was killed in 1269 near Acre. Another Robert was summ. to serve against the English in 1294. (P.*MA*.)

From seals it appears that the family bore three tierces and a chief, not three gemels. (Demay, 272; Clairambault 2990–1); *Sceaux de l'Artois*. La Chenaye (vi. 491) blazons the arms *à deux tierces ou cresèques d'or*. This suggests that cresèque is a synonym of tierce, but it has not been found as such elsewhere.

BAUCEY

177. *Hugh de Baucey le labiau verte d'or a une croyz de goules recersele a une labeu de sable.*

Cf. 172, 74: MP II. 49.

In the Ordinary appended to the *Archaeologia* edition of this Roll Walford translated this coat as *Quarterly vert and or, a cross* . . ., but the note 'Ingham's cote' in the margin of C I suggests that Charles thought the field should be per pale or and vert. (Cf. CG 29, *Monsire Oliver de Ingham port parte d'or et vert a une crois recercele gules.*) This, however, is beside the point. *Le labiau* (*labyn* in C I) *vert* must be a note correcting the tincture of the label incorporated in the text by a mistake of an earlier copyist.

Baussy-le-Noble is in the dépt. of Vienne. Hugh de Baucey succ. his father Pierre *c.* 1270 and was dead 1309. Pierre (s. of MP II. 49) bears *Or, a cross moline gules* in *Bigot* 248, and Hugh bears the same in *ChP* 126. The addition of the label may perhaps point to a younger Hugh, but more probably means that the entry was written in Pierre's lifetime.

ST. MARD

178. *Launcelot de Sein Mark d'argent a un bende de gules engralle a une labeu d'azur.*

Cf. 173, —.

This and the following seven items are missing from C II *b*. They should have followed no. 74.

Lancelot de St. Mard, Marshal of France 1270–98. He sealed with a bend of lozenges and a label in 1269 and 1276. In *Wijn.* 114 he bears a bend of fusils and a label of four pendants.

St. Mard is a hamlet near Dammartin-en-Goële (dépt. Seine et Marne). (P.*MA*; Anselme, vi. 631.)

MONTREUIL dit Eschalas

179. *Eschelard de Mont Tyrelle d'argent a une bende de gules engralle a sis escalopes d'azur.*

Cf. 174, —.

C I writes 'Eschalard de Monsyrolle'; Montreuil is meant.

In 1267 one 'Robertus Eschallas versus Vernonem' (Vernon near Evreux) is mentioned as newly knighted. In 1290 William Eschalas de Montreuil held at Boissy-sans-Avoir and at Le Bois-Nivard (both near Montfort-l'Amaury), and in 1291 Pierre dit Eschalas de Montreuil, knight, and Jeanne de la Boissière his wife, sold their house at Boissy-sans-Avoir and land at Bois-Nivard. (P.*MA*.)

In *Wijn.* 115 Guillaume Eschalaz de Monstreu, banneret, bears *Argent, a bend of five fusils gules and a label of four pendants azure bezanty.*

The person here was perhaps a cadet of the house of Montreuil-Bellay who bore *Argent, a bend of fusils gules between six fleurs-de-lis azure* (Spener, iii. 519–20), the fleurs-de-lis being changed to escallops (perhaps canting) as a difference. (CBB.)

COUCY

180. *Thomas de Coscy barre de veyr e de gules et une bende d'or.*

Cf. 175, —.

Raoul sire de Coucy sealed with a barry shield as early as 1190. Later this became *Barry of vair and gules* as in *Wijn.* 876 and *ChP* 65 for Enguerran IV, sire de Coucy 1250, d. 1311 s.p. The gold bend or baston was the difference of the Coucy–Vervins branch, of whom Thomas II was dead in 1276 and Thomas III d. 1302. (*Wijn.* 877.) The Coucy–Pinon branch differenced with a gold quarter instead of the bend. (*Wijn.* 878; *ChP* 66; FW 466.) Coucy is near Laon (dépt. Aisne). (P.*MA*; GWW 455.)

A Thomas de Coucy was in attendance on Queen Mary of Scotland in 1250–1. (*Cal. Pat. Rolls*, 1247–58, pp. 63, 109.)

CHÂTILLON-BAZOCHES

181. *Robert de Basseges pale de veyr et de gules al chef d'or a une flurette de sable recoupe.*

Cf. 176, —.

The lords of Bazoches (dépt. Aisne) were cadets of Châtillon (C 26), whose arms they differenced with a fleur-de-lis issuant on the chief.

Robert was Lord of Bazoches 1234–71, in succession to his brother Nicholas III. Another Robert, a cadet, occurs in 1272. (P.*MA*; GWW 380; du Chesne, *Maison de Chastillon sur Marne*, 691.)

In A 315 this coat is assigned to the Sire de Basipes. In *Wijn.* 883 it is unnamed, but the editors assign it to James II, sire de Montchâlons and Château–Porcien, equating it witn FW 449, *Jakes de Monkablon, Vert, three pales vair and on a chief or a demi-fleur de lis sable*, and with *ChP* 79, *Mesire Gobiert de Monsablon, Gules, three pales vairy argent and vert and a chief or*. In *Wijn.* 874 and *ChP* 109 Hugh III de Bazoches, Vidame de Chalons, d. 1279, bears *Gules, three pales vair and on a chief or two lions passant face to face sable* (cf. du Chesne, p. 701, &c.).

In England a William de Basoges was summ. to serve against the Scots in 1296 (Parl. Writs); he is probably the same to whom D 232 assigns *Gules, three pales argent* (sic, for *vair*) *and on a chief or a lion passant gules*. A Ralph de Besages, clerk, was employed by the king in various capacities in 1275–7. (*Cal. Pat. Rolls*, 1272–81, pp. 97, 227.)

CHAUVIGNY

182. *William de Chavegn d'argent a une fesse de goules engralle a une labeau de sable.*

Cf. 177, —.

William II de Chauvigny, s. of William I (d. 1233), Baron of Châteauroux, by Maud d'Issoudun. He accompanied St. Louis on the 1248 Crusade and d. at Palermo in 1272. (*Bigot* 290.) His s. William III, 'Dent de May', d. 1322. (P.*MA*; GWW 508.) The latter is one of those whom Edward I promised to indemnify for losses in the exchange of prisoners in 1299. (*Cal. Pat. Rolls*, Edward I, 1292–1301, p. 427.)

William II's wife, Agatha de Lusignan, was a dau. of King John's widow Isabel of Angoulême by her second husband Hugh de Lusignan. She is called the king's sister in a patent granting her and her husband two hundred marks a year in 1254. (*Cal. Pat. Rolls*, 1247–58, p. 283.)

MONTFORT

183. *Philip de Mountfort de goulez a un leon d'argent a la cowe furche a une labeu d'azure.*

Cf. 178, —.

C I writes *leon* correctly, but C II *a* has *bende*.

Philip de Montfort, Lord of Castres and Count of Squillace in Calabria, d. in the Holy Land 1270. He was s. of Guy de Montfort, younger brother of Simon, 1st earl of Leicester (MP I. 30). (*AVD* xi. 485; *Wijn.* 91–92; P.*MA*.)

BAUTERSEM

184. *Henry de Bausterseyn de vert a iij fause losenges d'argent al chef pale d'or e de goules.*

Cf. 179, —.

A sketch of this coat is in the margin of C I. In *Wijn.* 1178 the arms are *Per fess, the chief or with three pales gules, the base vert with three voided lozenges argent.*

Henry, sire de Bautersem (near Louvain, in Brabant), seneschal of Brabant, d. before 1290. He was s. of Henry III and gds. of Henry II. The last-named sealed with three voided lozenges but this Henry sealed with the lozenges and a paly chief in 1266 and 1273. The chief presumably alludes to an alliance with the Berthouts of Malines (C 185). D 44 garbles both name and arms. (*Bigot* 45; *Wijn.* 1178; de Raadt, i. 210; cf. FW 434.)

BERTHOUT

185. *Gauter Bertaut pale d'or et de gules a une cauntel d'azur a une rouel d'argent,*

Cf. 180, —.

Not identified. C II gives the surname correctly as Bertaut.

Gauthier Berthout V, avoué de Malines, d. 1285, bore *Or, three pales gules*. (*Wijn.* 1173; FW 430; de Raadt, i. 245.) His s. Gauthier VI, d. 1299, differenced by adding a canton of Brabant for his grandmother Alice of Brabant. (*Wijn.* 1172; FW 431; de Raadt, ibid.) Gilles sire de Humbeke 1268–1303, a younger s., differenced with a canton argent charged with a molet sable. (*Wijn.* 118.) The canton tinctured as here was borne by Henry Berthout, dit Bebbeken, 1283–1303, a nephew of Gauthier VI. (*Wijn.* 1187; de Raadt, i. 246.)

A 'Walter Bertaus' was envoy of John, Duke of Brabant, in 1275. (*Cal. Pat. Rolls*, 1272–81, p. 106.)

ORDINARY OF THE THREE ROLLS

PLAIN

Brown probably The Oriflamme
                MP VIII. 17 (*b*)

Gules The Oriflamme   MP IV. 43

Sable, dimidiated by England
    Henry the young King   MP III. 13

ANNULET

*Per fess or and azure, two an-
nulets argent in pale*
    The Genoese   MP VIII. 18 (*c*) and (*d*)

Brown, two annulets argent
    Guisnes, Baldwin de   MP VIII. 15 (*b*)

*Per fess or and vert two annulets
gules, with bordure or and a
small band of or between the or
and the vert*
    The Pisans   MP VIII. 18 (*a*) and (*b*)

Argent, six annulets gules
    Plescy, John de   B 24

Gules, six annulets or
    Vipont, John de   B 99

Argent, semy of annulets gules
    Boulogne, Reynold de
                MP VIII. 7 (*c*)

ANTLER

Or, three antlers sable
    Württemberg, Count of   C 119

AXE

Or, an axe proper
    Denmark, Sweyn, King of
                MP VIII. 21

Two axes
    Denmark, Sweyn, King of
                MP VIII. 21

Azure, three axes argent
    Denmark, Sweyn, King of
                MP VIII. 24

Gules, three axes argent
    Norway, Harold Hardra-
     da, King of   MP VIII. 27 (*g*)

BAR

Argent, two bars gules
    Mauduit, Walter   C 152
        William   MP II. 75: B 65

Gules, two bars or
    Harcourt, John de   C 173

Or, two bars gules
    Harcourt, Richard de   B 69

*Per pale the dexter checky or and
azure and the sinister vert,
over all two bars argent*
    Courtenay, John de   B 109

Argent, two bars gules bezanty or
    Welle, Robert de   B 53

*Argent, two bars and a canton
gules*
    Boys, Ernald de
       MP II. 74; VII. 6: B 105: C 153

*Argent, two bars gules and a
label azure*
    Martin, Nicholas fitz   B 202

*Argent, two bars in chief three
mullets sable*
                       B 108

*Argent, two bars in chief three
roundels gules*
    Moels, Nicholas de   B 83

*Or, two bars gules in chief three
roundels argent*
    Wake, Hugh   MP IV. 50

*Or, two bars gules in chief three
roundels gules*
    Wake, Hugh   B 51

*Argent, two bars gules and on a
canton gules a lion passant
gardant or*
    Lancaster, William de
              MP II. 74: B 49

*Semy of martlets sable, two bars
vert cotised gules*
    Edmund Ironside   MP VIII. 22

BAR (*cont.*)

Vert, with a narrow edge of white at top and bottom, two bars between two cinquefoils argent
   Breauté, Fawkes de   MP VIII. 12

Argent, three bars azure
   Grey, Richard de   MP II. 68: B 42

Argent, three bars gules
   Multon, Thomas de   MP IV. 38
   — Thomas de   B 157

Gules, three bars or diapered
   Reviers, Earl of Devon   C 146

Ermine, three bars gules
   Giffard   MP II. 56, 113
   Hussey   MP II. 56, 113

Or, three bars engrailed gules
   Crespin, William   C 108

Argent, three bars gules and a label sable
   Multon, Thomas de   B 158

Or, three bars azure and a bend gules
   Gaunt, Gilbert de   MP IV. 49

Barry argent and azure
   Grey, Richard de   MP II. 68: B 42
   Lusignan, Hugh le Brun, seigneur de, Count de la Marche   MP I. 86; II. 63: C 71

Barry argent and gules
   Chaworth, Patrick de   B 56

Barry argent and sable
   Vaudémont, Henry I, Count of   C 32

Barry (eight) argent and vairy of gules and argent
   Coucy, Enguerrand de   MP I. 95

Barry or and gules
   Fitzalan of Bedale, Alan   B 141
   Grandpré, Henry Count of   C 35
   Savage, Robert le   B 191

Barry or and gules fretty argent
   Barnage le Weede   C 77

Barry or and vert fleuretty counterchanged
   Mortimer of Richard's Castle   C 89

Barry ermine and gules
   Hussey, Hugh de   C 161

Barry wavy argent and gules
   Sandford, Nicholas de   MP IV. 81: B 116: C 140
   — William de   B 115

Barry wavy or and gules
   Basset, Gilbert   MP II. 34; IV. 44
   — Philip   B 93

Barry wavy argent and gules, a canton sable
   Bauzan, Stephen de   B 163

Barry argent and azure, a label gules
   Grey, John de   B 43

Barry azure and argent, a label gules on each point three lions passant gardant or
   Lusignan, William de, Seigneur de Valence   MP I. 83; II. 64; IV. 72

Barry argent and gules, in chief three roundels azure
   Wake, Baldwin   MP IV. 50

Barry argent and azure, an orle of martlets gules
   Lusignan, William de, Seigneur de Valence   B 23; C 72

Barry argent and gules, a bordure azure semy of martlets or
   Merlay, Roger de   B 139

Gules, two bars gemel and a chief or
   Richmond, Roald, Constable of   B 213

Gules, two bars gemel in chief a lion passant or
   Tregoz, Geoffrey de   C 97
   — Robert de   B 113

Azure, three bars gemel or and a chief or
   Cresecques, Robert de   C 176
   Meinill, Stephen de   B 125

BEASTS

Or, a bull gules
   Denmark, Eric V, King of   C 18

Or, a hind gules
   Tierstein, Count of   C 120

BEASTS (*cont.*)

Gules, a horse saddled or
Norway   C 17

Gules, a lion passant or
Bigod, Hugh   C 91

A lion rampant
Sweyn, son of Rigan   MP VIII. 3

Argent, a lion rampant azure
Bruce, Piers de   B 48

Argent, a lion rampant azure,
quartered by Castile
Leon, Alphonso X, King
of Castile   C 4

Argent, a lion rampant gules
Montfort, Simon de, Earl
of Leicester   MP II. 91; IV. 15

Argent a lion rampant or,
quartered by Castile
Leon, Alphonso X, King
of Castile   MP IV. 83

Argent, a lion rampant purpure,
quartered by [Castile]
Leon, Ferdinand IV, King
of Castile   MP II. 72

Argent, a lion rampant sable
Geneva, Peter de   MP I. 87 (*b*)

Azure, a lion rampant argent
Mohaut, Roger le   B 98

Azure, a lion rampant gules,
dimidiating Or, a cross re-
cercely sable
Barres, John de   MP I. 89

Azure, a lion rampant or
Harold, King of England   MP III. 1
Neville, Hugh de   C 133

Gules, a lion rampant argent
Boulogne, Count of   MP I. 93
d'Aubigny   MP II. 102
Dunbar, Patrick, Earl of   C 61
Mareys, Geoffrey de   MP I. 68
Merck, Ingram de   C 154
Mowbray, Roger de   B 74: C 131

Gules, a lion rampant or
Bigot, Hugh   B 89
d'Aubigny, Hugh, Earl of
Arundel
MP I. 72; II. 5; IV. 57: B 18

— William, Earl of   MP IV. 18
Fitzalan, John   B 88

Or, a lion rampant azure
Lovel, Richard   B 168
Pierrepoint-Roucy, John
III, Count of   C 33
Reviers, Baldwin de, Earl
of Devon
MP II. 17; IV. 35, 60: B 12

Or, a lion rampant gules
Holland, William, Count
of   MP I. 82 (*a*); II. 89

Or, a lion rampant sable
Flanders, Count of   MP II. 79
— Guy de Dampierre,
Count of   C 29
Mareys, William de   MP I. 67

Sable, a lion rampant argent
Geneva, Ebles de   B 104
— Peter de   MP I. 87 (*a*)

Sable, a lion rampant or
Brabant, Henry, Duke of   MP II. 43
— John, Duke of   C 46
Flanders, Thomas, Count
of   MP II. 37; VII. 11

Vert, a lion rampant ermine
Bolbec, Hugh   B 174

Azure, billety a lion rampant or
Brienne-Eu, Alphonse de   C 28

Azure, crusuly a lion rampant or
Brewes, William de   B 55

Barry argent and gules, a lion
rampant sable
Stuteville, Robert   B 200

Party per pale or and gules, a
lion rampant party gules and or
Marshal   C 143

Party per pale or and vert, a lion
rampant argent
Marshal, Gilbert, Earl   MP IV. 47

Party per pale or and vert, a lion
rampant gules
Marshal   B 17
— Anselm, Earl   MP IV. 67
— Gilbert, Earl   MP I. 65; II. 18
— Walter, Earl   MP IV. 66; V. 2
— William, Earl
MP I. 47; IV. 14, 30

BEASTS (*cont.*)

Or, a lion rampant gules, a label azure

Brabant, Count of	MP II. 80
Savoy, Peter of	MP II. 81

Or, a lion rampant sable, a bordure gules

Gournay, Robert de	B 193
Soissons-Nesle, John III, Count of	C 38

Or, a lion rampant gules, a bordure flory counter flory gules

Scotland, Alexander II, King of	MP I. 85

Or, a lion rampant gules, a bordure or flory gules

Scotland, Alexander III, King of	C 15

Or, a lion rampant, a bordure indented gules

Armenia, Livon II, King of	C 20

Or, a lion rampant gules, a single tressure flory gules

Scotland, Alexander II, King of	MP II. 48; IV. 80

BEASTS, two or more

Argent, two lions passant gules

Strange, John le	B 165

Or, two lions passant azure

Somery, Roger de	C 95

Or, étincelé two lions passant azure

Hungary, Stephen V, King of	C 11

Gules, two lions passant gardant or

Douvres, Richard de	B 82

Or, two lions passant gardant azure

Somery, Roger de	B 97

Vert, two lions passant gardant tinted pink, the upper lion crowned

Offa, King	MP VIII. 33 (*c*)

Gules, three dogs argent

Kennet, Nicholas de	MP II. 50

Gules, three lions passant argent

Giffard of Brimpsfield	C 105

Vert, three lions passant gules

Offa, King	MP VIII. 34 (*a*)

Gules, three lions passant gardant or

England	C 3
Henry I	MP I. 5, 10; III. 7, 8; VI. 2
Henry II	MP I. 14, 18; III. 10; IV. 1
Henry, s. of	MP I. 17
Henry III	MP I. 28, 99; II. 2, 98; IV. 13; VIII. 2, 13, 20: B 1
John	MP I. 23, 27; IV. 4, 12; VI. 5
Richard	MP I. 19, 22; IV. 2, 3; VI. 4
Stephen	MP I. 11, 13; III. 9, 10
William I	MP I. 2, 3; III. 3, 4
William II	MP I. 4; III. 5, 6; VI. 1

Gules, three lions passant gardant or dimidiating sable

England: Henry 'the young young King', s. of Henry II	MP III. 13

Gules, three lions passant gardant dimidiating the Empire

Henry s. of Frederick II	MP VI. 7
Otto IV	MP I. 21; IV. 5

Or, three lions passant gardant argent

England, Henry III	MP VIII. 12

Party per pale, gules and sable, three lions passant gardant or

Henry 'the young King', s. of Henry II	MP III. 11

Gules, three lions rampant or

FitzPiers, Reynold	B 77

Party per pale, gules and azure, three lions rampant or

FitzMathew, Herbert	MP I. 74

Party per pale, gules and azure étincelé or, three lions rampant or

FitzMathew, Herbert	MP II. 71; IV. 61

Gules, three lions passant gardant or, a label azure

Edward, s. of Henry III	B 2

Or, three lions passant gardant argent alternately with two bars gemel

England, Henry III (?)	MP VIII. 9

BEASTS, two or more (*cont.*)
Four beasts

Quarterly or and gules four lions passant counterchanged
Wales, David, Prince of — MP IV. 68
— Gruffydd, s. of Llywelyn, Prince of — MP IV. 59
—Llywelyn ap Gruffydd, Prince of — C 13

Six beasts

Azure, six lions rampant argent
Leyburn, Roger de — B 34; C 74

Azure, six lions rampant or
Longespée — MP II. 99
— William de, Earl of Salisbury — MP I. 40: B 22
— William de, s. of — MP I. 90; II 8: C 75

Azure six lions rampant or, a canton ermine
Longespée, Stephen de — C 76

Azure, six lions rampant or, a label gules
Longespée, Stephen de — B 187

BEAST, modified

Or, a lion rampant gules collared or and a bordure vert bezanty
Talbot, Richard — C 172

Gules, a lion passant gardant argent crowned argent
FitzGerald, Warin le — B 159

Azure, a lion rampant barry argent and gules crowned or
Thuringia, Louis IV, Landgrave of — C 45

Barry argent and azure, a lion rampant gules crowned or
Luxemburg, Henry, Count of — C 114

Argent, a lion rampant gules crowned or on a mount azure
Löwenstein, Count of — C 57

Argent, a lion rampant sable crowned or charged on the shoulder with a cross or
Bohemia, Ottokar II, King of — C 10

C 137

Argent, a lion rampant gules crowned or, a bordure sable bezanty
Cornwall — MP II. 97
Richard, Earl of — MP II. 3: B 3: C 124

Argent, a lion rampant queue fourchée gules
Montfort, Guy de — MP I. 31
— Simon de — MP I. 30; II. 6

Azure, a lion rampant queue fourchée or
Harold — MP I. 1

Gules, a lion rampant queue fourchée argent
Montfort, Simon de, Earl of Leicester — B 4

Gules, a lion rampant queue fourchée or
d'Aubigny, William, Earl of Arundel — MP I. 36

Or, a lion rampant queue fourchée azure
Reviers, Baldwin de, Earl of Devon — MP I. 75

Or, a lion rampant queue fourchée gules
Holland, William of, King of Germany — MP VII. 8

Sable, a lion rampant queue fourchée argent
Geneva, Peter de — MP II. 82

Party per pale gules and vert, a lion rampant queue fourchée argent
Marshal, Anselm, Earl — MP I. 79
— Walter, Earl — MP I. 78

Party per pale or and vert, a lion rampant queue fourchée gules
Marshal, Gilbert, Earl — MP I. 51
— Richard, Earl — MP I. 50; IV. 32
— William, Earl — MP I. 29

Sable, billety argent a lion rampant queue fourchée argent
Meulan, Amaury de — C 109

Gules, a lion rampant queue fourchée argent, a label azure
Montfort, Philip de — C 183

P

BEAST, modified (*cont.*)

Argent, a lion rampant queue fourchée crowned or
    Limburg, Waleran, Duke of   C 51

Argent, a lion rampant gules queue fourchée crowned or, a label azure
    Berg, Adolphe, Count of   C 116

Argent, a lion rampant queue fourchée gules, crowned or, a bordure sable bezanty
    Cornwall, Richard, Earl of   MP I. 38

BEND

Argent, a bend gules
    Trehampton, Ralph de   B 170

Gules, a bend argent
    Foliot, Richard   B 172

Gules, a bend or
    Chalon, Count de   C 69

Or, a bend gobony argent and azure
    Trie dit Billebault   C 128

Barry argent and azure, a bend gules
    Gaunt, Gilbert de   B 72
    Parthenay dit l'Arche-
        vêque   C 174

Barry or and azure, a bend gules
    Gaunt, Geoffrey de   C 86

Barry vair and gules, a bend or
    Coucy, Thomas de   C 180

Azure billety, a bend or
    Mar, William, Earl of   C 63

Checky azure and or, a bend argent
    Warwick   MP II. 104

Checky azure and or, a bend ermine
    Warwick, Thomas, Earl of
        MP I. 70; II. 13; IV. 54

Checky or and azure, a bend gules
    Clifford, Walter de   B 30

Paly or and gules, a bend sable
    Scot, John le, Earl of Huntington   B 14

Per fess indented gules and vert, a bend or
    Neville, Hugh de   MP IV. 19

Per fess indented gules and vert, a bend sable
    Neville, John de   MP IV. 69

Quarterly or and gules, a bend gules
    Beauchamp, William de
        MP II. 28: B 54
    — Walter de   C 147

Quarterly or and gules, a bend sable
    Eure, Roger FitzJohn de   B 169
    Fitz Robert of Clavering, John   MP IV. 39

Quarterly argent and gules fretty or, a bend sable
    Despenser, Hugh   MP II. 58: B 114

Quarterly indented both ways gules and vert, a bend or
    Neville, Hugh de   MP II. 31

Or, a bend azure and a label gules
    Trie, Renaud de   C 129

Quarterly or and gules, a bend sable and a label argent
    Lacy   MP II. 90
    — Edmund de, Earl of Lincoln   B 9
    — John de, Earl of Lincoln   MP I. 63; II. 20; IV. 37

Azure, a bend between two lions rampant or
    Dillingen, Hartmann V, Count of   C 53

Gules, a bend between two lions rampant or
    Kyburg, Count of   C 117

Azure, a bend argent between six lions rampant or
    Bohun   MP II. 95
    — Henry de, Earl of Hereford   MP I. 33
    — Humphrey de, Earl of Hereford, s. of   MP II. 9

BEND (*cont.*)

Argent, a bend between six martlets gules
Furnival   MP II. 45; 77
—Thomas de   B 147
—Walter de   C 81

Azure, a bend between six martlets or
Mounteney, Arnold de
MP IV. 82: B 145

Or, a bend between six martlets gules
Furnival, Gerard de   B 149

Or, a bend gules between six crosses sable
Neville, John de   B 178

Azure, a bend argent cotised or
Champagne
— Theobald, Count of, and King of Navarre   MP II. 60

Azure, a bend cotised or diapered
Champagne,
Henry III, Count of, and King of Navarre   C 42

Or, a bend gules cotised sable
Bohun Henry de, Earl of Hereford   MP IV. 16

Gules, a bend argent between two cotises fleury or
Werd, Henry Sigbert, Count of   C 52

Azure, a bend cotised gules between six lions rampant or
Bohun, Henry de   B 189

Azure, a bend argent cotised or between six lions rampant or
Bohun, Humphrey de   B 10: C 123

Argent, a bend between six martlets gules a label azure
Furnival, William de   B 148

Azure, a bend argent cotised or, between six lions rampant or, a label gules
Bohun, Humphrey de   B 188

Argent, a bend between five martlets gules, on a chief gules a lion passant gardant or
Bassingbourne, John de   MP II. 29

Argent, a bend engrailed gules
Walerand, Robert   B 156

Argent, a bend engrailed gules a label azure
St. Mard, Lancelot   C 178

Azure, a bend engrailed between six martlets or
Pigot, Peter   C 83

Argent, a bend engrailed gules between six escallops azure
Montreuil, dit Eschalas, Robert   C 179

Argent, a bend dancy cotised dancy vert
Kendale, Edmund de   B II. 216

Or, on a bend gules three eagles argent
Lorraine, Henry III, Duke of   C 50

Gules, on a bend argent three mullets azure
Shafto, Robert de   B II. 212

Gules, three bends or
Grelley, Thomas de   B 73

Bendy or and azure
Montfort, Piers de   B 117

Quarterly or fretty sable and argent, a bend sinister sable
Despenser, Geoffrey   MP IV. 79

BILLETS

Or, billetty sable a label gules
Gasselin, Geoffrey   B 209

BIRD

Azure, an eagle or
Thuringia Henry Raspe, Landgrave of   MP I. 81 (*b*)

Argent, an eagle sable
Beauchamp, John de
MP II. 27

Gules, an eagle argent
Joigny, John I, Count of   C 44

Gules, an eagle or
Vienne, Hugh, Count of   C 130

Gules, an eagle sable
Harold (?)   MP VIII. 29 (*p*)

BIRD (cont.)

Or, an eagle vair
Froburg, Count of   C 56

Sable, an eagle argent
Beauchamp, John de   B 204

Or, a double eagle sable
Empire   C 1
— Frederick II   MP I. 96; II. 46;
           IV. 26, 76
— Otto IV   MP IV. 5 (a)

Party per pale or and vert a double eagle sable
Enzio, King of Sardinia   MP I. 84
Henry fitz Emperor   MP IV. 51

Or, a double eagle sable dimidiating Gules, a cross recercly argent
Henry fitz Emperor   MP I. 69

Or, a double eagle sable dimidiated by (England)
Henry fitz Emperor   MP VI. 7
— Otto IV   MP I. 21; IV. 5 (b)

Or, two corbies sable
Corbet, Thomas   B 198

Azure, three herons argent
Heron, Odinel   B II. 215

Barry argent and gules, three cocks sable
Stuteville, Walter de   C 85
— William de   B 171

Sable, three eagles or
Barantine, Dru de   B 84

Azure, three sparrow-hawks or
Muschet, Robert   MP II. 41

Or, an eagle gules, a bordure vair
Freiburg im Breisgau, Count of   C 118

Or, an eagle displayed sable, charged on the breast with a crescent argent
Poland, Bolesław, Duke of   C 49

Or, a double eagle sable and a crescent in chief enclosing a roundel gules
Conrad, King of Sicily
    MP VI. 8; VII. 3

Or, a double eagle sable and over all a fess argent
Manfred, bastard of Frederick II   MP VI. 9; VII. 4

Barry argent and azure, an orle of martlets gules
Lusignan, William de, Seigneur de Valence   B 23: C 72

BORDURE

Vert, a bordure or
Lacy, Hugh de   MP IV. 56

Barry argent and azure, a bordure gules
Dammartin, Count of   C 127

Bendy or and azure, a bordure gules
Burgundy, Duke of   C 112

Checky or and azure, a bordure gules
Dreux, Robert IV, Count of   C 26

Party per pale gules and or, a bordure vert
Burgh, Richard de   MP IV. 55

Quarterly or and gules, a bordure vair
FitzGeoffrey, John le   B 28

Quarterly or and gules, a bordure indented argent and azure
FitzJohn, John le   C 59

Ermine, a bordure gules semy of horseshoes or
Montgomery, William de   B 212

Gules a bordure or, over all two ships argent with sails azure
Canute   MP VIII. 4

BOUGET

Azure, three bougets or
Ros of Ingmanthorpe, William de   C 68

Gules, three bougets argent
Ros, Robert de   MP II. 55: C 132
— William de   B 66

Or, three bougets sable
Ros, Robert de   B 173

BOUGET (cont.)

*Gules, three bougets argent, a
label azure*
    Ros, Robert de   B 67

BRAY

*Azure, three horse-brays or, on a
chief ermine a demi-lion rampant
gules*
    Geneville, Geoffrey de   B 103: C 106

*Sable, three horse-brays or on a
chief argent a demi-lion rampant
gules*
    Geneville, Simon de   B 102

BUCKLE

Azure, three buckles or
    St. John of Nashenden,
    Walter de   C 168

CANTON

*Checky or and azure, a canton
ermine and a bordure gules*
    Brittany, John, Duke of   C 24

*Argent, fretty gules on a canton
gules a lion passant gardant or*
    Dunstanville, Walter de   B 58

*Quarterly or and sable, on a
canton or a lion passant gules*
    Boyville, William de   C 100

*Paly or and gules, on a canton
azure a pierced mullet argent*
    Berthout, Walter   C 185

CASTLE

*Gules, a triple-towered castle
argent*
    Castile, Ferdinand III,
    King of   MP I. 97

Gules, a castle or
    Castile, Alphonso, King of   C 7

*Gules, a triple-towered castle
or, quartering Argent, a lion
rampant or*
    Alphonso X, King of
    Castile and Leon   MP IV. 83

*Gules, a triple-towered castle or,
quartering Argent, a lion rampant purpure*

Castile, Ferdinand IV,
    King of, quartering
    [Leon]   MP II. 72
  — Alphonso VII, King
    of, quartering [Leon]   C 4

*Gules, semy of towers or a
label azure*
    Portugal, Alphonso, King of   C 126

CHECKY

Checky argent and gules
    Vaux, John de   B 33
  — Robert de   C 164

Checky azure and or
    Warenne, William de,
    Earl   MP I. 64; IV. 36

Checky or and azure
    Warenne   MP II. 92
  — John de, Earl of Surrey   B 7
  — William de, Earl of   MP II. 7

*Per pale the dexter checky or and
azure the sinister vert, over all
two bars argent*
    Courtenay, John de   B 109

Checky or and gules
    Tateshale, Robert de   MP II. 61

CHEVRON

Gules, a chevron argent
    Berkeley, Maurice de   B 167

Gules, a chevron ermine
    Ghistelle, Walter de   C 80

*Checky or and azure, a chevron
ermine*
    Warwick, Thomas, Earl of   B 20: C 144

Argent, a chevron gules bezanty or
    Stafford, Robert de   B 52

*Or, a chevron gules and a bordure
sable*
    Kyme, William de   B 127

*Or, a chevron gules and a bordure
sable bezanty*
    Kyme, Philip de   MP IV. 52

*A chevron between three roundels
azure*
    One of Sweyn's men   MP VIII. 24 (c)

*Argent, a chevron between three
roundels gules*
    Baskerville, Walter de   B 183

CHEVRON (cont.)

Argent, on a chevron gules three
fleurs-de-lis or
    Peyvre, Paulyn   MP IV. 78: B 152

Or, two chevrons and a canton
gules
    Criol, Bertram de   B 151

Or, two chevrons and a bordure
gules
    Daubeney of Belvoir,
      William   MP I. 52; II. 21
    — William   B 68

Or, two chevrons gules and a
bordure gules bezanty
    Daubeney   MP II. 107

Argent, three chevrons gules
    Clare   MP II. 96

Or, three chevrons gules
    Clare, Gilbert de, Earl of
      Gloucester   MP I. 46; IV. 29
    — Richard de, Earl of
      Gloucester
        MP I. 76; II. 4; IV. 63: B 5

Ermine, three chevrons gules
    Sackville, Bartholomew de   B 211

Gules, three chevrons azure, a
label
    Montfichet   MP II. 105

Or, three chevrons gules, a label
azure
    Clare, Thomas de   C 73
    — William de   B 81
    Montfichet, Richard de
        MP II. 24: B 80

Or, three chevrons gules and a
fess argent over all
    Monmouth, John de   C 88

Or, three chevrons gules and a
fess azure over all
    Monmouth, John de   B 92

Or, three chevrons gules and a
bordure gules bezanty
    Daubeney of Belvoir   MP II. 107

Or, three chevrons gules and a
bordure indented azure
    Breuse, John de   C 101

Chevronny or and sable
    Hainault, Margaret,
      Countess of   C 40

CHIEF

Argent, a chief gules
    Columbers, Matthew de   B 195
    Fort de Vivonne, William
      le   B 194
    Lasser, Alan   C 66

Argent, a chief sable
    The Temple
      MP I. 62; IV. 42; VIII. 1, 5, 19

Gules, a chief vair
    Castro Novo, Fulk de
        MP I. 80; IV. 70

Or, a chief sable
    Colesteyn, Count of   C 122

Sable, a chief ermine
    Castellan de Ghent   MP I. 92

Ermine, a chief gules
    Morteyn, William de   B 215

Checky or and gules, a chief
ermine
    Tateshal, Robert de   B 50; C 99

Azure fretty or, a chief or
    FitzRandolph, Henry le   B 138

Paly or and gules, a chief argent
    Hathersage, Matthew de   B 175

Paly vair and gules, a chief or
    Châtillon-Blois,   John,
      Count of   C 25

Azure semy de lis or, a chief paly
argent and gules
    Bornhem, Henry de   C 78

Azure, on a chief gules a demi-
lion issuant rampant or
    Holland, William, Count
      of   MP I. 82 (b)

Gules, on a chief sable, a demi-
lion rampant queue fourchée or
    Turberville, Henry de   MP I. 56

Or, on a chief gules a chevron
argent
    Lützelstein,   Hugh III,
      Count of   C 55

Argent, on a chief sable a cross
patonce gules
    The Temple   C 21

CHIEF (*cont.*)

Paly vair and gules, on a chief or a fleur-de-lis issuant sable
Châtillon-Bazoches,
Robert de — C 181

Paly vair and gules, on a chief or a label azure
Châtillon-St. Pol,
Guy III de — C 27

Argent, on a chief gules two mullets or
St. John — B 110
— Sir John de — C 163
— Sir Robert de — B 111

Or, on a chief gules three roundels argent
Camoys, Ralph de — B 64: C 151

Argent fretty sable, on a chief sable three bezants
St. Amand, Amaury de — B 199

Argent, a chief azure over all a lion rampant gules
Vendôme, John V, Count of — C 34

Or, a chief indented azure
Fitz Randolph, Ralph — B 140

CRESCENT

Gules, a crescent ermine in an orle of martlets ermine
Bohun, Frank de — B 190

Argent, three crescents sable
Heslington, Richard de — C 170

Or, three crescents gules
Cressy, Roger de — MP II. 30

CROSS

A cross
Bigod, Hugh, Earl of Norfolk — MP I. 39

A cross sable
Upsale(?) — B 106

Argent, a cross gules
Vere, Robert de — B 132

Gules, a cross argent
Hospitallers — MP I. 61
Savoy, Peter of — MP IV. 40: B 101

Gules, a cross vair
Forz, Thomas de, Earl of Aumale — C 60

Or, a cross argent
Jerusalem, Baldwin I, King of — MP I. 7
— Fulk, King of — MP I. 12
— Godfrey of Bouillon — MP I. 6
— Henry of Champagne — MP I. 20
— John de Brienne — MP I. 53

Or, a cross gules
Bigod — MP II. 94
Bigod, Roger, Earl of Norfolk — MP II. 12: B 6

Or crusuly argent, a cross argent
Jerusalem, John de Brienne, King of — MP I. 101; II. 1

Or semy of eagles azure, a cross gules
Montmorency, John de — C 111

Argent crusuly, a cross billetty (potent) or
Jerusalem, Hugh de Lusignan, King of — C 14

Argent, a cross engrailed gules
Gurney, John de — C 82

Argent, a cross floretty sable
Lamplugh, John — B II. 217

Gules, a cross formy argent
Hospitallers — MP IV. 41: C 22

Gules, a cross formy fitchy at the foot argent
Vesci, William de — MP II. 35

Gules, a cross vair (the perpendiculars formy, the horizontals paty)
Forz, William de, Earl of Aumale — MP II. 38

Argent, a cross fourchy gules
Vale, Gilbert de — B 206

Gules, a cross fourchy argent
Vescy, William de — B 76

Argent, a cross fourchy 'au kanee'
Lexington, John de — B 155

Or, a cross moline gules
Baucey, Hugh de — MP II. 49
Moels, Nicholas de: arms wrongly attributed to — MP II. 49

CROSS (cont.)

Gules, a cross moline argent
Vescy, William de   MP I. 102; IV. 84

Argent, a cross patonce azure
Lexington, John de   MP II. 59

Gules, a cross patonce argent
Vescy   MP II. 106
Vescy, Eustace de   MP I. 26; IV. 11

Gules, a cross patonce vair
Forz   MP II. 103
— William de, Count of
Aumale   B 13

Vair, a cross patonce gules
Freville, Baldwin de   C 156

Quarterly argent and gules, a
cross patonce gules
Burgh, Walter de   C 169

Vert, semy of roundels gules, a
cross patonce or
Cyprus, Hugh de Lusi-
gnan, King of   C 16

Azure, a cross recercely or
Paveley, Edward de   C 160

Gules, a cross recercely argent
dimidiated by the Empire
Henry fitz Emperor   MP I. 69

Gules, a cross recercely or
Barres, John de   MP I. 59

Or, a cross recercely sable dimidiated by Azure a lion gules
Barres, John de   MP I. 89

Gules, a Toulouse cross or
Toulouse, Raymond VII,
Count of   MP II. 42

Or, a cross gules voided throughout
Crevequer, Hamo de   MP II. 66: B 61

Or, a cross recercely gules a
label vert
Baussay, Hugh de   C 177

Argent, a cross gules between
four lions rampant azure
Chevreuse, Henry de   C 110

Azure a cross between four
lions rampant or
Dakeny, Baldwin   B 46

Argent, a cross sable and a
bordure of martlets sable
Maldeghem, Roger de   C 79

Gules, crusuly or a cross patonce or between four roundels
each charged with a cross
Constantinople   C 12

Sable, a cross patonce between
four roundels argent
Siward, Richard   MP IV. 75

Gules, a cross patonce voided
and a bordure or
Toulouse, Raymond VII,
Count of   C 41

Sable, a cross recercely between
four roundels argent
Siward, Richard   MP II. 69

Azure, a cross moline sable
over all a lion rampant or
Harold   MP III. 2

Or, a cross gules charged with
escallops argent
Bigod, Ralph   B 197

Azure, three crosses or
Sarren, William de   B 164

Argent, semy of crosses pommy
gules
Edmund Ironside   MP VIII. 4 (a)

CUP

Gules, three covered cups argent
Argentine, Richard de   MP II. 36

CUSHION

Gules, three cushions or
Redman, Matthew de   B II. 218

DANCE

Azure billetty, a dance or
Deincourt, John   B 107

ESCALLOP

Gules, three escallops or
Chamberlain, Herbert   B 26
— Martin   B 39

ESCARBUNCLE

Gules, an escarbuncle or
Navarre, Henry III, King
of   C 6

ESCUTCHEON

Barry or and azure, a chief paly corners gyronny or and azure, an escutcheon argent
    Mortimer, Roger de   B 32; C 102

Gules on an escutcheon argent an escarbuncle flory or
    Cleves, Count of   C 113

Vairy or and gules, on an escutcheon azure a saltire argent
    Oettingen, Conrad Count of   C 121

Or, three escutcheons vair
    Munchensy, Warin de
        MP VI. 11; VII. 7

Or, three escutcheons barry vair and gules
    Munchensy, Warin de   B 25; C 87

VOIDED ESCUTCHEON

Gules, a voided escutcheon argent
    Balliol, Eustace de   C 142
    — John de   MP II. 53, 67: B 36
    — Roger de   MP I. 88

Gules, a voided escutcheon vair
    Lindsay, Walter de   B 205

Azure, crusuly a voided escutcheon or
    Balliol, Eustace de   MP II. 54, 112

Gules, crusuly or a voided escutcheon or
    Bertram, Roger   B 144

Gules, a voided escutcheon argent, on an escutcheon azure in dexter chief a lion rampant argent crowned or
    Balliol, Hugh   B 37

Gules, a voided escutcheon argent, a label or
    Balliol, Eustace de   B 38

FESS

Azure, a fess or
    St. Omer   MP I. 91

Gules, a fess argent
    Austria, Duke of   C 47

Gules, a fess or
    Beauchamp, William   B IV. 81

Gules, a fess vair
    FitzRalph, Hugh le   B 180

Or, a fess gules
    Coleville, Walter de   B 129
    Lacy, Walter de   MP IV. 46

Vair, a fess gules
    Marmion, Philip   C 159
    — William   B 47

Vair, a fess paillé
    Marmion, Philip   B 57

Checky or and azure, a fess gules
    Clifford, Robert de   C 107
    — Roger de   B 31

Azure fretty argent, a fess gules
    Amundeville, Richard de   B 130

Azure billety, a fess or
    St. Omer, William de   B 181

Gules billety or, a fess argent
    Lovaine, Matthew de   B 120

Argent, a fess of three fusils gules
    Montagu, William de   B 44

Azure, a fess of five fusils argent
    Percy, Richard de   MP II. 52, 85

Azure, a fess engrailed or
    Percy, Henry de   B 41

Gules, a fess engrailed argent
    Daubeney, Ralph   B 135

Gules, a fess engrailed or
    Newmarch, Adam de   B 121

Or, a fess engrailed azure
    Percy, Piers de   B 119

Argent, a fess between three popinjays gules
    Thweng, Marmaduke de   C 103

Argent, a fess gules between three popinjays vert
    Thweng, Marmaduke de   B 133
    — Robert de   MP II. 70

Argent, a fess between two chevrons gules
    Pecche, Hamo   MP II. 33
    — Gilbert, s. of   B 60

Or, a fess between two chevrons gules   MP II. 86
    FitzWalter, Robert
        MP II. 32; IV. 33
    — Walter le fitz Robert   B 186

FESS (*cont.*)

Argent, a fess between three escallops gules
Rabayne, Ellis de — B 207

Gules, a fess and in chief a dance or
Sergines, Geoffrey de — C 175

Gules, a fess checky argent and sable between crosses or
Neville, John — B 179

Argent, a fess and in chief two mullets gules
Dodingseles, Gerard — MP II. 57
— William — MP II. 57
— William — B 142

Argent, a fess gules in chief two pierced mullets gules
Doddingseles, William — C 157

Argent, a fess in chief three mullets gules
Doddingseles — MP II. 109

Gules, a fess and in chief three roundels argent
Devereux, William — B 45

Per fess gules and vert, a fess between two roundels in chief and a crescent in base argent
Mareys, Geoffrey de — MP IV. 64

Gules, a fess between three popinjays argent, over all a bend azure
FitzMarmaduke, Richard le — B II. 214

Or floretty gules, on a fess gules two fleurs-de-lis or
Deiville, John de — B 123

Or, on a fess gules three roundels argent
Huntingfield, Roger de
— MP II. 23: B 131

Argent, a fess engrailed gules and a label sable
Chauvigny, William de — C 182

Azure billety or, a dance or
Deincourt, John de — B 107

FISH

Azure, a fish hauriant or
Brienne, John de, King of Jerusalem — MP I. 53 (*b*)

Gules, a dolphin or
Forez, Reynold, Count of, or Guy — C 37

Azure, two barbels addorsed or
Bar, Henry II, Count of — MP I. 60

Azure crusuly or, two barbels or
Bar, Thibaut II, Count of — C 30

Gules, three herrings hauriant argent
Herring, Robert — MP II. 40

Gules, three luces or
Lucy, Geoffrey de — B 112

Gules crusuly, three luces or
Lucy, Geoffrey de — C 134

FLEUR-DE-LIS

Gules, a fleur-de-lis argent
Aguillon, Robert — B 63

Gules, a fleur-de-lis or
Aguillon, Robert — C 158

Azure, three fleurs-de-lis or
France, Louis IX — MP I. 98; IV. 22

Gules, three fleurs-de-lis or
Cauntelo — MP II. 87
— William de — MP I. 54
— William de, s. of
— MP II. 26; IV. 77; VI. 10; VII. 5
— William de, s. of — B 27

Vert, three fleurs-de-lis or
France, Philip II — MP VIII. 7 (*a*)

Azure, six fleurs-de-lis or
France, Louis VIII — MP I. 41
— Louis IX — MP I. 42, 98; II. 47
— Philip II — MP III. 12

Azure, semy de lis or
France, Louis VII — MP I. 16
— Louis VIII — MP IV. 21
— Philip I — MP I. 8
— Philip, associate King — MP I. 9
— Philip II — MP I. 15, 37; IV. 20
— Philip III — C 2

Azure, six fleurs-de-lis and a label (seven) gules
Artois, Robert of — MP I. 94

FLEUR-DE-LIS (cont.)

Azure semy de lis or, a label gules
    Sicily, Charles, King of   C 5

Azure semy of fleurs-de-lis or, a label gules semy of castles or
    Artois, Robert II, Count of   C 31

Barry or and vert, semy of fleurs-de-lis counterchanged
    Mortimer, Robert de   C 89

Azure, semy of fleurs-de-lis or, a chief paly argent and gules
    Bornhem, Henry de   C 78

Party azure and gules, the azure semy of fleurs-de-lis or, the gules semy of towers or
    Poitou, Alphonse, Count of   C 23

FLOWER

Argent, a quatrefoil in an orle of rings gules
    Boves, Hugh de   MP VIII. 7 (*b*)

Semy of quatrefoils (some barbed vert) and small rings gules
    Boves, Hugh de   MP VIII. 7 (*b*)

Gules, a cinquefoil argent
    Breauté, Fawkes de   MP IV. 23

Gules, a cinquefoil ermine
    Quincy, Robert de   B 153

Or, a cinquefoil gules
    Evermue, Walter de   B 210

Azure, three cinquefoils argent
    Mauclerk, Piers de   C 167

Azure, three cinquefoils or
    Bardolf, William   B 70; C 138

Azure crusuly, three cinquefoils or
    Bardolf, Thomas   B 71; C 137

Gules, three sixfoils ermine
    Vere, Simon de   B 134

Argent, three roses gules
    Darcy, Philip   B 118

Or, three rose branches vert with roses gules
    Rapperswil, Rudolf IV, Count of   C 54

Azure, a cinquefoil or and a bordure or
    Neville, John de   MP V. 4

Gules, a cinquefoil or and a bordure azure
    Umfraville, Gilbert de   MP II. 51

Or, a cinquefoil gules and a bordure azure semy of horseshoes argent
    Umfraville, Gilbert de   MP IV. 62: B 122

Sable, a cinquefoil and an orle of birds argent
    Fauconberge, Walter de   B 201

Sable, a cinquefoil and an orle of martlets argent
    Fauconberge, Walter de   C 90

Azure, a cinquefoil or and an orle of escallops argent
    FitzNichol, Richard   C 84

Gules, a cinquefoil or and an orle of escallops argent
    FitzNichol, Ralph   MP II. 39: B 154

FRETTY

Argent, fretty azure
    Blankminster, Reynard de   B 182

Gules, fretty argent
    Beauchamp, William de   B 96

Gules, fretty or
    Audley, James de   B III. 34

Sable, fretty or
    Maltravers, John   B 203

Or, fretty gules
    Verdon, John de   B 90

Ermine, fretty gules
    Branch, Piers   B 161

GARB

Azure, three garbs or
    Chester   MP II. 100: C 65
    — Blundeville, Ralph de, Earl of
         MP I. 48; II. 14; IV. 31: B 16
    Chester and Huntingdon, John le Scot, Earl of   MP IV. 34

Gules, three garbs or
    Comyn, John   C 70
    Segrave, Stephen de   MP I. 66

GARB (*cont.*)

Sable, three garbs argent
Segrave, Geoffrey de — C 98
— Gilbert de — B 176

Sable, three garbs or, bands and ears gules
Segrave, Stephen de — MP IV. 48

Per fess gules and azure, three garbs or
Brewes, William de, Constable of Chester — MP IV. 7

Per pale gules and azure, three garbs or
Lacy, Roger de, Constable of Chester — MP IV. 6

GONFANON

Or, a gonfanon gules
Auvergne, Robert V, Count of — C 36

GURGE

A gurge argent and azure
Gorges, Ralph — B 192

GYRONNY

Gyronny
Brut, s. of Rigan — MP VIII. 3

Gyronny or and azure
Bassingbourne, Warin de — B 35: C 136

Gyronny or and azure, a roundel in an orle of six smaller roundels gules all with white rims
Raspe, Henry, Landgrave of Thuringia — MP I. 81; IV. 71

HAMMER

Argent (? or), a hammer sable
Marshal, William, Earl — MP VIII. 15 (*a*)

Argent, three hammers gules
Marshal, Richard, Earl — MP VIII. 16

Gules, three hammers argent
Martel, Walter — C 155

Argent, semy of hammers gules
Marshal — MP VIII. 8

HEAD

Gules, three boars' heads argent
Swinburne, Adam de — B II. 213

LABEL

Quarterly or and vert, a label gules
Berners, John de — B 146: C 149
— Ralph de — MP II. 78

LEG

Gules, three legs armed argent
Man, Magnus, King of — C 19

LOZENGE

Fusilly argent and azure
Bavaria, Louis, Duke of — C 48

Lozengy argent and gules
FitzWilliam, Thomas — B 137

Lozengy gules and vair
Burgh, Hubert de, Earl of Kent — MP II. 83; IV. 58: B 21
— Raymond de — MP I. 45; IV. 28

Lozengy or and sable
Blount, William le — B 94

Lozengy ermine and gules
Rokely, Richard de la — B 136

Lozengy vair and gules
Burgh, Hubert de, Earl of Kent — MP I. 73; II. 16
— John de — C 104
— Richard de — MP I. 71

Lozengy or and gules, a canton ermine
Neville, John de — B 177

Gules, seven voided lozenges or
Quincy, Robert de — MP I. 34
— Roger de, Earl of Winchester — MP II. 11: B 8
— Saher de, Earl of Winchester — MP I. 32; IV. 17

Gules, semy of voided lozenges or
Quincy, Roger de, Earl of Winchester — C 125

Vert, three voided lozenges argent a chief paly or and gules
Bautersem, Henry de — C 184

MAUNCH

Argent, a maunch gules
Tony, Ralph de — MP I. 57: B 91
— Roger de, brother of — MP IV. 25

Azure, a maunch ermine
Creke, Baldwin — C 166

MAUNCH (*cont.*)

Gules, a maunch ermine
Mohun, Reynold de   B 62

Or, a maunch gules
Hastings, Henry de   B 150
Tony, Ralph de   MP II. 25

Vair, a maunch gules
Mauley, Piers de   B 124

MULLET

Quarterly gules and or, a mullet argent in dexter chief
Vere   MP II. 88
— Hugh de, Earl of Oxford   MP II. 15: B 11

Quarterly or and gules, a mullet argent in dexter chief
Vere, Hugh de, Earl of Oxford   B 11

Argent, a pierced mullet gules
Hay, Ralph de la   C 93

Azure, three mullets argent
Beneteby, Nicholas de   B 126
Hansard, William   C 67

Argent, three pierced mullets gules
Plescy, John de   C 145

Gules, three mullets argent
Hansard, Gilbert   B 75

Gules, three pierced mullets with dance in chief or
Engaine, Hugh   C 96

ORLE

Barry argent and azure, an orle of martlets gules
Valence, William de   B 23: C 72

PALE

Party per pale indented argent and gules
Montfort, Simon de, Earl of Leicester   B 4

Party per pale indented gules and azure
Brewes, William de   MP I. 44

Gules, three pales or
Provence, Raymond, Count of
     MP II. 73; IV. 65; V. 1

Or, four pales gules
Provence, Raymond, Count of   MP I. 77

Paly (eight) gules and or
Aragon or Provence   MP II. 44

Paly or and gules
Aragon   MP II. 84
— James I   C 9

Paly or and sable
Strathbogie, John de, Earl of Athol   C 62

Paly wavy argent and gules
Gernon, William   B 214

Paly or and gules, on a canton a cross patonce sable
Basset of Drayton, Ralph   C 92

Paly or and gules, on a canton azure, a pierced mullet argent
Berthout, Walter   C 185

Gules, three pales or and on a chief sable a lion passant gardant or
William, Bishop of Valentia   MP I. 55

PILE

Azure, three piles or
Bryan, Guy de   B 162

Or, three piles gules
Brechin, William de   C 64
Huntingdon, John le Scot, Earl of   MP II. 19

Gules, four piles or
Brewes, William de   MP IV. 27

Or, three piles gules, a canton ermine
Basset, Philip   B 128

QUARTERLY

Quarterly argent and gules
Rochford, Guy de   B 208

Quarterly argent and sable
Beauchamp, Geoffrey de
     MP II. 76: B 196: C 150

Quarterly azure and gules
Mandeville   MP II. 101

QUARTERLY (cont.)

Quarterly gules and or
Mandeville, Geoffrey de   MP I. 25
— Geoffrey de   MP IV. 10
— William de, Earl of
Essex   MP IV. 24

Quarterly or and gules
Mandeville, William de,
Earl of Essex   MP I. 43; II. 22 : B 19
Rochford, Guy de   C 148
Someri, Roger de   B III. 20
Say, William de   B 29

Quarterly indented argent and
azure
More, Richard de la   C 141

Quarterly indented argent and
gules
Fitzwarin, Philip le   C 162

Quarterly argent and gules per
fess indented
Fitzwarin, Fulk le   B 184

RAKE

Gules, three rakes or
Rethel, Hugh IV, Coun
of   C 43

ROUNDEL

Or, three roundels in pale gules
Courtenay, Robert de
    MP VIII. 10 (e)

Or, on a chief gules three
roundels argent
Camoys, Ralph de   B 64

Azure ten bezants
Biset, John   MP IV. 45

Azure bezanty
Zouche, William la   B 86

Gules bezanty
Zouche, Alan la   B 85

Sable bezanty
Zouche, Alan de la   C 94

Gyronny of six, a roundel in an
orle of smaller roundels gules
edged argent
Henry Raspe   MP I. 81 (a); IV. 71

Or, three roundels vert, on a
chief dancetty vert a lion
passant sable
Wales, David, Prince of   MP V. 3

SALTIRE

Argent, a saltire gules
Fitzgerald, Maurice le   C 171
Neville, Geoffrey de   C 58

Gules, a saltire argent
Neville, Robert de   B 59; C 135

Gules, a saltire engrailed argent
Kerdeston, Fulk de   B 79: C 139

Or, a saltire gules and a chief
gules
Bruce, Robert   B 100

SHIP

Gules, a bordure or over all two
ships argent with sails azure
Canute   MP VIII. 4 (b)

Gules, three galleys or
Norway, Haakon IV,
King of   MP IV. 73

Gules, three galleys or, above the
first a cross formy argent
Norway, Haakon IV,
King of   MP I. 100

SUN

Argent, a sun gules
Hay, Ralph de la   B 87: C 93

TREE

Argent, an oak-tree gules
Oxted, Roland de   B 160

TRINITY

The Trinity symbol
Scutum Fidei   MP IV. 8
Scutum Anime   MP IV. 9

TRUMPET

Gules, two trumpets in pile or
Dareines   MP I. 58

VAIR

Vair
Beauchamp, Robert de   B 95
Ferrers, Hugh de   B 143

Vairy gules and argent
Ferrers   MP II. 108

VAIR (*cont.*)

Vairy gules and or
Ferrers   MP II. 93

Vairy or and azure
Guines, Arnold III,
Count of   C 39

Vairy or and gules
Ferrers, William de, Earl
of Derby
       MP II. 10, 62; IV. 74: B 15
— William de, s. of
       MP VII. 1; VI. 6: B 15
Pecche, Baldwin   C 165

ORDINARY OF QUASI-HERALDIC ARMS AND THOSE NOT ATTRIBUTED TO ANY NAMED PERSON IN MP VIII

THE arms in this section are for the most part difficult to blazon in the normal way. The fields are frequently of a pale wash and it would be misleading to blazon a field azure because there were faint touches of blue. Some of the coats fall within the ordinary heraldic custom. They are placed here because, although they are not attributed to any named person, they nevertheless have some significance. Those coats which are given to named persons, e.g. Edmund Ironside, are found in the first general ordinary.

PLAIN

Gules

Englishman	MP VIII. 27 (*a*)
Banner	MP VIII. 28 (*h*)

ANNULETS

Pale wash between two pairs of thin lines two annulets gules

Banner	MP VIII. 29 (*i*)

BARS

Gules, two wide bars vert

French banner	MP VIII. 10 (*c*)

Barry (six) argent and sable

Norwegian	MP VIII. 26 (*a*)

Barry of (six) gules and pale wash

Englishman	MP VIII. 26 (*h*)

Pale wash, three bars gemel gules

Shield on Danish ship	MP VIII. 25 (*e*)

Pale wash, three bars gemel sable

Shield on Danish ship	MP VIII. 25 (*b*)

Vert, with edge of white at top and bottom, two bars between two cinquefoils argent

	MP VIII. 12

Pale wash three bars sable (?) *with very small cotises sable*

Englishman	MP VIII. 26 (*e*)

BEASTS

Azure, a beast uncoloured

Norwegian	MP VIII. 26 (*c*)

Green wash, a lion passant

Soldier	MP VIII. 31 (*c*)

Vert, a lion passant gardant gules

Follower of Offa	MP VIII. 33 (*a*)

Azure, a lion rampant argent

Norwegian	MP VIII. 27 (*k*)

Pale blue, a lion rampant uncoloured

Follower of Sweyn	MP VIII. 24 (*b*)

Brown, a lion rampant uncoloured

Norman banner	MP VIII. 28 (*g*)

Brown, a lion rampant or

Christian knight	MP VIII. 6

Pale brown wash, a lion rampant or

Dane	MP VIII. 25 (*f*)

Gules, a lion rampant argent

Norwegian	MP VIII. 26 (*d*)

BEASTS (*cont.*)

Pale wash, a lion rampant azure
Dane MP VIII. 25 (*c*)

Pale wash, a lion rampant sable
Dane MP VIII. 25 (*g*)

Brown, a boar passant un-coloured between three roundels argent
Englishman MP VIII. 26 (*f*)

Azure, a lion rampant un-coloured and a bordure vert
Pagan warrior MP VIII. 32 (*d*)

Pale wash, two lions rampant in pale gules
Banner MP VIII. 29 (*o*)

Pale wash, three lions rampant gules
Knight MP VIII. 29 (*f*)

Vert, three lions passant gules, and a bordure or
Knight MP VIII. 33 (*b*)

Pale wash semy of lions rampant gules
Horse trappers MP VIII. 29 (*f*)

DEMI-LION

Azure, a demi-lion argent and below in pale two lions heads couped argent
Norwegian MP VIII. 27 (*j*)

BENDS

Azure, on a bend gules a bend sable
Banner MP VIII. 29 (*h*)

Bendy argent and sable
Shield on Norwegian ship
MP VIII. 26 (*b*)

Bendy pale wash and azure
Shield on Danish ship
MP VIII. 25 (*d*)

Gules with lines bendy sinister
Norman MP VIII. 28 (*f*)

BORDURE

Brown wash, a bordure vert
Pagan soldier MP VIII. 34 (*b*)

A bordure engrailed gules within a bordure gules
Christian knight MP VIII. 11 (*c*)

C 137

CHEVRONS

Green wash, a chevron brown and in base a roundel brown
Norman MP VIII. 28 (*c*)

Pale green wash, a chevron azure with a bulbous point between three birds gules
Shield on Danish ship
MP VIII. 25 (*a*)

Gules, a chevron between in chief two sixfoils and a septfoil in base argent
Follower of Sweyn
MP VIII. 24 (*a*)

A chevron between three roundels azure
Follower of Sweyn
MP VIII. 24 (*c*)

Chevrons
Norman banner MP VIII. 28 (*d*)

CHIEF

Or, a chief gules
Banner on French ship
MP VIII. 10 (*a*)

Orange wash, on a chief azure two chevrons one sable, one gules and in base a sixfoil azure pierced gules
Banner MP VIII. 29 (*a*)

CRESCENTS

Or, three crescents gules
Banner on French ship
MP VIII. 10 (*b*)

Pale wash, semy of crescents with dots between the horns gules
Trapper MP VIII. 29 (*l*)

Uncoloured, semy of crescents with dots between the horns gules and semy of small annulets gules
Pagan soldier MP VIII. 32 (*c*)

CROSS

Shield edged pale red, a cross azure
Knight MP VIII. 23

A cross recercly gules and a bordure vert
Knight MP VIII. 14

Q

CROSS (cont.)

Or, a cross flory gules and a
bordure marked by a thin line
    Saracen   MP VIII. 11 (a)

A cross with elaborate floriated
ends gules, the centre a lozenge-
shaped boss vert, a bordure gules
    Pagan soldier   MP VIII. 32 (b)

Azure, a cross argent between
four roundels gules
    Banner   MP VIII. 29 (s)

Faint touches of blue, a cross
outlined gules between [four]
roundels gules
    Shield   MP VIII. 29 (r)

Argent, a cross recercly gules
between four roundels azure
    Knight   MP VIII. 7 (d)

Argent, two crosses pommy or
    Soldier   MP VIII. 9

FESS

Vert, a fess or fimbriated gules
    Banner on French ship
                  MP VIII. 10 (d)

Brown, a fess between two
chevrons uncoloured
    Back of saddle   MP VIII. 30 (b)

Vert, a broad fess sable semy of
white dots between two dots
gules
    Banner   MP VIII. 29 (b)

Gules, a fess and in chief a
chevron argent (the triangle
formed by the fess and
chevron is vert with a white
dot in the middle, in sinister
chief is a white dot and
another below the fess)
    Norwegian   MP VIII. 27 (h)

Per fess argent and azure, in
chief a fess gules between two
dots gules and in base a chevron
between five dots sable
    Banner   MP VIII. 29 (e)

Brown, a fess vert between three
roundels uncoloured
    Norman   MP VIII. 28 (b)

Gules, a fess between three
roundels argent
    Englishman   MP VIII. 27 (d)

Pale wash, a fess gules and in
base a crescent gules   MP VIII. 29 (g)

On a fess gules billets (?) *sable,*
on a chief vert two roundels un-
coloured each charged with a fess
gules and in base a similar
roundel   MP VIII. 29 (j)

Vert, on a broad fess checky
argent and sable a fess gules
                  MP VIII. 29 (m)

FLOWERS, FOILS

Azure, [three] cinquefoils argent
    Englishman   MP VIII. 27 (b)

Gules, five flowers of varying
number of petals argent
    Englishman   MP VIII. 27 (f)

FRETTY

Gules fretty argent
    Englishman   MP VIII. 26 (g)

Pale wash fretty azure
    Shield on Danish ship
                  MP VIII. 25 (h)

HAMMERS

White, two hammers gules
          MP VIII. 31 (b), 32 (a)

Semy of hammers
    Follower of Offa   MP VIII. 3

Argent semy, of hammers gules
    Minion of King John   MP VIII. 8

Three hammers and three small
crosses gules
    Christian   MP VIII. 32 (a)

Vert, [three] hammers a bordure
    Soldier   MP VIII. 31 (a)

LABEL

Pale wash, a label (5) *gules* MP VIII. 29 (c)

LOZENGES

Brown, voided lozenges un-
coloured
    Soldier   MP VIII. 30 (a)

Five voided lozenges gules, a
bordure vert
    Christian knight   MP VIII. 11 (b)

MONSTER

Azure, a mermaid argent
   Englishman   MP VIII. 27 (*e*)

PALES

Gules, two pales argent over all
two bars sable   MP VIII. 29 (*q*)

PILES

Pale brown wash, two piles
charged with annulets
   Englishman   MP VIII. 27 (*c*)

QUARTERLY

Quarterly vert and or
   French banner   MP VIII. 17 (*a*)

ROSACE

Red wash, an elaborate rosace,
outer line sable, inner part white
with azure centre with an eight

pointed device sable with black
dots between each point
   Banner   MP VIII. 29 (*k*)

ROUNDELS

Three roundels
   Norman banner   MP VIII. 28 (*a*)
Argent semy of roundels gules
   Soldier   MP VIII. 10 (*f*)

SALTIRE

A saltire between four roundels
   Follower of Offa   MP VIII. 3

UNCLASSIFIED

Gules, an elongated indeter-
minate device coloured dark
   Banner   MP VIII. 29 (*d*)

WINGS

Gules, a pair of wings argent
   Norwegian   MP VIII. 27 (*i*)

GLOSSARY

THIS is not a full list of all the heraldic terms used in the three manuscripts but only a list with their modern equivalents of those terms in Latin or Norman French with which some readers may not be familiar. After some of them the Latin word, distinguished by L. in front, or the French word distinguished by F., from which the term is derived or to which it is equivalent, is given in brackets.

Al croisel = crusuly   B 40.

a litte, *see* Litte.

Au kanee, *see* B 155.

Au tiel (L. *talis*) = the same   B 2, 29, 31, 37, 38, 43, 67, 81, 89, 111, 148, 158, 166, 195.

Avoz (L. *avis*) = birds   B 201.

Bars de mere = barbels   C 30.

Bastons = bars   B 49, 53, 105.

Baucent (F.) = piebald and hence applied to the black and white banner of the Temple   C 21, 22.

Benda = bar   MP II. 56, 113.   = fess   MP II. 23, 86.

Blank = argent   B 4, 44, 87.

Bordeand, bordeantz, bordeanz = in a orle   C 72, 79, 84, 90.

Bordeantz, *see* Bordeand.

Bordeanz, *see* Bordeand.

Bouz, buz (F. **bout**) = bougets   B 66, 173: C 68.

Bresses (F. *broie*) = brays   C 106.

Burlure a une menue, de une menue (F. *burele*) = barry of narrow bars   C 35, 71, 174.

— de une grose = barry of wide bars   C 32.

Bys (F. *biche*) = hind   C 120.

Caniculi (L. *canicula*) = dogs MP II. 50.

Charbocle, charbucle (F. *charboucle*) = escarbuncle   C 6, 113.

Cornere (F. *cornée*) = canton or dexter chief   B 37. = corner   C 19.

Cos = cocks   C 85.

Croix passant = cross patonce   C 12, 16, 21, 156, 169.

Croyz byllette = cross potent   C 14.

Dauffin (F. *dauphin*) = C 37.

Ebartile (F. *escarteler*) = quarterly   C 162.

En beliff = obliqueways   B 73.

Enermyne = ermined   B 50.

Entere = around   C 38.

Entour = in orle   B 154, 201.

Espany (F. *épanoui*) = displayed, spread   C 1.

Estenzele (F. *étincelé*) = étincelé   C 11.

Faulses losenges = voided lozenges   B 8: C 125.

Fauses roueles = annulets   B 24, 99.

Faux croix = cross voided   B 61.

Fermaulx (F. *fermail*) = buckles   C 168.

Fesse = bar   MP II. 28.   MP II. 68.

Floretes, floretts, florettes, flurett = fleur-de-lis   B 27, 123, 152: C 2, 5, 23, 158, 181.

Fluretes = flory   C 52.

Gastelles, gasteus (F. *gâteau*) = roundels   MP II. 23: C 151.

Gymeus = gemel bars   B 213.

Kanee, *see* B 155.

Kene (F. *chêne*) = oak-tree   B 160.

Lesance = lozengy   C 6.

Leunces = lions   B 46.

Litte, a (F. *liste*), strip = cotised   C 52.

Luz = luces   C 134.

Lyte (F. *liste*), strip, possibly an adjective = cotised   C 123.

Merlos, merlots, merlotz, merloz (F. *merlette*) = martlets   B 23, 139, 145, 147, 190: C 72, 79, 81, 83, 90.

Merlots, *see* Merlos.

Merlotz, *see* Merlos.

Merloz, *see* Merlos.

Moeles (F. *meule*), millstone = roundels   B 83.

Molettes = mullets   C 67.
  = roundels   B 183: C 145.
Mote (F. *motte*) = mound   C 57.
Muschet   (F.   *mouchet*) = sparrow   hawk
  MP II. 41.
Myrrours d'or = bezants   B 199.

Paile, fesse de, *see* Appendix I.
Peces = piles   B 162.
Perche de deym (F. *perchant*) = antlers   C
  119.
Peus, peuz (F. *pièce*) = piles   B 128: C 64.

Rastel (F. *râteau*), rake = label   MP II. 24,
  80, 81.
  = rake   C 43.
Recoupe, une flurette = a demi-fleur-de-lis
  C 181.
— un lion = a demi-lion.   C 106.
Reptans (L. *repto*), creeping = rampant   MP
  II. 48.

Rey de soleil = sun   B 87.
Roele, rouel, rouelles, ruell, ruelle
  = pierced mullets   C 96, 157.
  = sun   C 93.
  = whirlpool   B 192.
Rouel, *see* Roele.
Rouelles, *see* Roele.
Ruell, ruelle, *see* Roele.

Scintillatum auro = semy of sparks, étincelé
  MP II. 71.

Torteus   (F.   *tortel*),   little   cake = roundels
  B 131.
Tucte, treys gambes armes = toute   C 19.
Turelles = little towers   C 23, 126.
Turteaux, turtelli, turteux (F. *tortel*), little
  cake = roundels   MP II. 75: B 45, 51,
  64.

Vastellis, i.e. gastellis = roundels   MP II. 69.

INDEX OF PROPER NAMES

The Index references in italic type are to persons mentioned in the commentary

— Louis VIII, 21, *34*, 63, *81*, *172*, *174*.
— Louis IX, 21, 35, 45, 63, *167*.
— Mahaut, wife of Philip Hurpel, *see* Dammartin.
— Margaret, wife of Louis IX, *see* Provence.
— Mary, wife of Henry, Count of Champagne, dau. of Louis VII, *15*.
— Peter of, *81*.
— Philip I, 12, *27*.
— Philip II, Augustus, *12*, 14, 20, *21*, *34*, 59, 63, 80.
— Philip III, 167.
— Philip IV, *32*, *164*, *176*.
— Philip, s. of Louis VI, 13.
France, The Oriflamme, 67, 82.
Freiburg, in Breisgau, Count of, 191.
— Conrad, *191*.
Freville, Alexander de, *160*, *162*, *198*.
— Baldwin de, 198.
— Joan, wife of Alexander, *see* Cromwell.
— Mazera, wife of Alexander, *see* Marmion.
Froburg, Count of, 180.
— Herman II, *180*.
Froburg-Honberg, *180*.
— -Waldenburg, *180*.
— -Zofingen, *180*.
Furnival, Gerard de, *74*, *112* (*n.*).
— Gerard de, 144.
— Maud, wife of Gerard de, *see* Lovetot.
— Thomas de, 143, *144*, *184*.
— Walter de, 184.
— William de, 143, *144*.
Fürstenberg, Henry, Count of, *191*.

Gacelin, Geoffrey, 156.
Gaddesden, 135, *see also* Gatesden.
Gage, *131*.
Galloway, *112*.
— Alan, Lord of, *46*.
— Devorguilla, wife of John de Balliol, dau. of Alan, *122*.
— Margaret, wife of Alan, *see* Huntingdon.
Gatesden, John de, *135*.
— Margaret de, *135*,
Gaugy, Ralph de, *188*.
Gaunt, Eve, sister of Maurice de, *152*, *153*.
— Geoffrey de, *95*, 185.
— Gilbert de, 69, *92*, *128*, *200*.
— Gilbert de, *94*, 128.
— Maurice de, *153*.
— William de, *94*, *128*.
Geneva, *66*.
— Agnes, wife of Humbert, *see* Savoy.
— Ebal de, *32*, 135.
— Humbert de, *32*.
— Maud, wife of Peter, *see* Lacy.

— Peter de, 32, 53, *135*.
— Radolphe, *32*.
— William, Count of, *32*.
Geneville, *92*, *108*, *109*, *112*, *131*.
— Geoffrey de, *91*.
— Geoffrey de, *32*, 134, 135, 188.
— Maud, wife of Geoffrey, *see* Lacy.
— Simon de, 134, 135.
Genoese, the, 82.
Genoure, Eleanor, wife of Alexander de Balliol and of Robert Stuteville, *154*.
Gerberoy, Marguerite, wife of Gerard de, *see* Clermont-en-Beauvaisis.
Germany, King of, 168.
— Henry Raspe, Landgrave of Thuringia, King of, 30, 72.
— Richard, Earl of Cornwall, 168.
— Rudolf of Habsburg, King of, *167*, 168, *180*.
Gernon, *108*.
— Ralph, *157*.
— Ralph, *157*.
— William, 157.
Ghent, Hugh, Lord of Heusden, Castellan of, 33.
Ghistelle, Isabel, wife of John de, *see* Woestine.
— John de, *184*.
— Walter de, 184.
Giffard, *8*, *10*, 47, 57.
— Elias, of Brimpsfield, *188*.
— John, of Brimpsfield, 188.
— John, of Brimpsfield, *188*.
— Osbern, of Winterbourne Houghton, *47*.
— Osbern, s. of, *47*.
— Osbern, natural s. of King John, *47*.
— Rohese, *157*.
— Walter, *157*.
— of Yester, *47*.
Glanville, Helewise, wife of Robert FitzRalph, dau. of Ranulf de, *142*.
— Ranulf de, *142*.
Glendower, Owen, *169*.
Gloucester, Earl of, *100*.
— Amice, wife of Richard de Clare, dau. of William, Earl of, *22*.
— William, Earl of, *22*.
— *See also* Clare.
Gorges, Ellen, wife of Ralph de, *see* Morville.
— Joan, wife of Ralph de, *152*.
— Ralph de, *93*, *94*, *108*, 152.
— Ralph de, *152*.
— Ralph, Lord, *152*.
Gournay, Anselm de, *152*.
— Daniel, *153*.
— Eve de, *152*, *153*, *see also* FitzHarding, Harptree, Gaunt.
— Hawise, wife of Robert FitzHarding, *153*.
— Hugh de, *195*.

ADDITIONS AND CORRECTIONS
TO THE *CATALOGUE OF*
ENGLISH MEDIAEVAL ROLLS OF ARMS

INTRODUCTION

In my introduction to the *Catalogue* published in 1950 I tried to make clear my sense of its imperfections. I was sure that new texts would come to light—and they have; I expected that some which had been lost sight of would reappear—and they have; and I thought it likely that editors, studying the texts far more closely than I as a mere cataloguer could do, would correct some of my descriptions and conclusions—and so they have. These processes, I hope, will continue, but the opportunity to bring the *Catalogue* up to date, which the publication, after seventeen years, of this second volume of *Aspilogia* affords, is not to be missed.

The reappearance of the lost originals of Willement's Roll (p. 270) and the English version of the Rous Roll (p. 277) and the appearance of the hitherto unknown roll which I have acquired and named Wagner's Roll (p. 278) owe nothing to the students of the rolls. These rolls emerged from their hiding places independently. Other texts, however, came to light because, as I hoped in 1950 the existence of the *Catalogue* made it easier for their custodians or others to identify them. Professor Francis Wormald and Dr. Cyril Wright have been active in this field and have brought to light much new information referred to hereafter.

The editorial activity which has thrown a flood of fresh light on the nature and detail of many texts, both those known in 1950 and those found since, is predominantly the work of my ever regretted friend and colleague Hugh Stanford London (1884–1959), Norfolk Herald Extraordinary. For the new *Dictionary of British Arms* all the rolls had to be indexed. For most of the earlier rolls this was done, at least in the first instance, from texts prepared in the first quarter of the century by Oswald Barron. For some of the earlier and most of the later rolls in my *Catalogue*, however, there were no satisfactory texts in existence, and this gap London set himself to fill. At the same time he and I planned together the *Aspilogia* series to comprise a complete corpus of editions of all the rolls, and these, we decided, ought to follow the chronological order of the originals. Of this plan the present volume is the first fruit. It was, of course, intended that the texts of the later rolls made primarily for indexing for the *Dictionary* should ultimately form the basis of editions in the *Aspilogia* series, and this is still the intention. Some are bare texts, but some, including such important ones as Bruges' Garter Book and Sir Thomas Holme's Book, have been more or less fully edited. I have not tried to incorporate here all the conclusions reached by London in the course of this work, but where his findings revealed errors or serious omissions in my *Catalogue* I have said so. To this very extensive work London devoted a large proportion of his time in the years of his retirement, and the *Aspilogia* series should in due course reveal the extent of our debt to him.

The texts he worked on were not confined to those here catalogued for, whereas the date limit here is 1500, his was 1530, that of the projected mediaeval volume of the *Dictionary*. He did not, however, attempt completeness between 1500 and

1530 but concentrated on the remarkable and important group of heraldic manuscripts which issued from the studio of Sir Thomas Wriothesley, Garter King
of Arms 1505–34. Some armorials of the period 1500–30 have a miscellaneous
antiquarian character which links them rather to the products of Elizabeth I's
reign than to the mediaeval rolls; but Wriothesley's products constitute a link
between the rolls and the Heralds' Visitations, in a way which calls for mention
here.

Sir Thomas's father, John Writhe, Garter King of Arms 1478–1504, had been
responsible for the preparation of at least two large and important heraldic manuscripts, Writhe's Book of Knights (*CEMRA*, pp. 120–1) and Writhe's Garter Book
(ibid., pp. 122–4), and he was the owner of others (ibid., p. 156). Both as owner and
compiler, however, his son far surpassed him. On becoming Garter in 1505 he
built a great house called Garter House in Red Cross Street, Cripplegate, and here,
probably, his scriveners and artists did their work. That there were several of these
is evident from the different hands discernible in the manuscripts, and closer
study may make it possible to distinguish them more clearly and to determine
their several periods of operation.

The most splendid products of the Wriothesley studio are the great roll of the
Westminster Tournament of 1511, which depicts the procession to the joust, the
joust itself, and the return procession[1] and the Processional Roll of the Parliament of 1512.[2] These, as works of figure drawing, stand apart from the other
productions, yet they follow the tradition of John Writhe's record of the ceremony
of knighthood of the Bath (Writhe's Garter Book, Part III, *CEMRA*, p. 123), and
have a minor parallel in certain figure drawings in Prince Arthur's Book.[3]

The main bulk of the Wriothesley heraldic products falls into three classes, (*a*)
copies of earlier material, (*b*) digests of such material, and (*c*) new productions.
The first class comprises both the written copies of early texts in College of Arms
MS. M 14 (*CEMRA*, pp. 129–30), the plain tricked copy of part of Fenwick's
Roll (ibid., p. 82) and such painted copies as the Everard Green Roll (ibid.,
p. 13), Willement's Roll (*infra*, p. 270) and Creswick's Book (*infra*, p. 276).

The digests, which we have placed in class (*b*), begin with the *Registrum armorum
Th. WR Thomas Wriothesley als gartier Regis armorum anglicorum* (*CEMRA*, p. 97
and p. 279 *infra*), an index of names with references to rolls referred to by such
titles as 'Rot. E. primi' and 'In Rot. milit. H. VII'. Some of these have been and
others probably could be identified.

This may have been the basis from which Wriothesley moved on to a far more
ambitious project, nothing less than a painted Armory and Ordinary of all English
Arms. The place of this in Wriothesley's plans for extending and imposing his
jurisdiction[4] is obvious. Whether the project was ever completed is uncertain.
Enough survives, however, to show that a large proportion was. Moreover, the
dispersal of the Wriothesley manuscripts in the sixteenth and seventeenth cen-

---

[1] *Heralds' Commemorative Exhibition 1484–1934, Illustrated Catalogue*, 1936, pp. 40–42; Wagner,
The Records and Collections of the College of Arms, 1952, p. 15.

[2] Trinity College, Cambridge, MS. o. 3. 59g reproduced and described by C. W. Scott-Giles
in *Archaeologia*, vol. 101, pp. 142–51.

[3] Vincent MS. 152, ff. 90 and 178, *Heralds' Commemorative Exhibition Catalogue*, plates X and XI.

[4] Wagner, *Heralds and Heraldry in the Middle Ages*, ch. ix.

turies[1] has spread them through so many collections that others may still come to light.

Of the painted Armory sections for the letters A to D are in College of Arms MS. L. 10.[2] Membranes of a Letter E Roll are bound up in Sir Thomas Holme's Book (p. 273 *infra*). An Armory of names beginning with G is in College of Arms MS. Vincent 153 and one of names with H is in Society of Antiquaries MS. 176. Letters I to P are in College of Arms MS. L. 9,[3] while the letters R and S are in Society of Antiquaries MS. 176. The sources of the material are indicated here and there by such references as 'Liber Mydelsex', 'Lib' Northum' ', 'Brutus', and 'E. iij^cii'.

Sections of the corresponding Ordinary are similarly scattered. Bends and Fesses are in Holme's Book, Eagles in L. 10, Lions, Saltires, and Chevrons in Society of Antiquaries MS. 176, and Crosses, Saltires, Fesses, Crescents, Lions, and other beasts in College of Arms MS. Vincent 152, which has been named Prince Arthur's Book. This book was begun about 1520, when Katherine of Aragon was Henry VIII's queen, and their combined arms were painted at the beginning. At some date after 1527, when Henry began negotiations for the divorce, the painting was altered so as to suggest that it referred to Katherine's marriage to Prince Arthur, Henry's elder brother, and thus the book acquired its name.

Interspersed among these sections of the Armory and Ordinary are collections of Crests and Badges, of the arms of Saints, Religious Houses, Abbots, Priors, Bishops, Knights of the Garter, and others, and accounts of ceremonies and miscellaneous matters. We are thus led on to class (*c*), Wriothesley's new productions. These are for the most current records or products of official activity. When Peers and Knights of the Garter were created, Garter King of Arms had special duties to perform and fees to draw. At other knights' creations and at the funerals of the nobility and gentry he shared duties and fees with the other heralds. With the other Kings of Arms he had a somewhat disputed share in the right to grant arms and consequent fees and he disputed with them the right to make heraldic visitations and record arms and pedigrees thereat.[4]

Wriothesley manuscripts connected with all these activities survive. An unknown number of original patents of arms issued by him survives. There are manuscripts recording patents issued by him alone or in conjunction with Clarenceux or Norroy.[5] There is a collection of Standards,[6] a book of Funeral Banners,[7] Rolls of Arms of Peers,[8] and volumes of pedigrees,[9] as well as sections dealing with such matters in the manuscripts mentioned above. In all probability there is other Wriothesley material not yet noted and the whole subject would repay more detailed study. It is, however, already clear that Wriothesley's work constitutes an essential link—if not *the* essential link—between the heraldry of the Middle Ages and the heraldry of the College of Arms.

---

[1] Pp. 271–4, 276, 279–80 *infra* and Wagner, *The Records and Collections of the College of Arms*, pp. 10–11.   [2] *Heralds Commemorative Exhibition Catalogue*, no. 109.

[3] Ibid., no. 107.   [4] Wagner, *Heralds and Heraldry in the Middle Ages*, ch. ix.

[5] Society of Antiquaries MS. 443 and College of Arms MS. 2nd G 4, see Wagner, *Heralds and Heraldry*, pp. 90–91, 152.

[6] College of Arms MS. I 2, see *Heralds' Commemorative Exhibition Catalogue*, p. 64.

[7] BM MS. Add. 45131.

[8] *Heralds' Commemorative Exhibition Catalogue*, pp. 33–37.

[9] See Wagner, *English Genealogy*, pp. 309, 313; BM MSS. Harl. 1417, Add. 5530, and manuscripts in my own possession.

A REVISED REFERENCE LIST OF THE ROLLS OF ARMS

THE page references in the first column are to *CEMRA* and those in brackets are to the present volume. To the letter references in the second column have been added a number of new ones assigned by H. S. London; Oswald Barron's references are in the third column.

1 (266)	MP	I	Matthew Paris Shields	
			1. *Historia Anglorum*	c. 1250–9
			2. Nero D I shields	c. 1244
			3. *Chronica Majora I*	c. 1245–51
			4. *Chronica Majora II*	
			5. *Flores Historiarum*	1250+
			6. *Abbreviatio Chronicorum*	1255+
			7. *Chronica Majora III*	1254–9
3	B	II	Glover's Roll	
			I. Cooke's Version	c. 1253
			II. Harvy's Version	c. 1253
			III. St. George's Version	c. 1258
7	C	IV	Walford's Roll	c. 1275
9 (266)	HE		Herald's Roll	c. 1270–80
		VII (A)	I. Heralds' Version	
	FW	VII (B)	II. Fitzwilliam Version	
14 (266)	A	VII (D)	Dering Roll	c. 1275
16 (266)	D	VI	Camden Roll	c. 1280
18	G	VIII	Segar's Roll	c. 1282
19 (266)	E	V	St. George's Roll	c. 1285
21 (266)	F	V (a)	Charles' Roll	c. 1285
24 (266)	Q		Collins' Roll	c. 1295
25 (266)	J	IX	Guillim's Roll	c. 1295–1305
27 (267)	H	XI	Falkirk Roll	1298
29 (267)	K	XII	Caerlaverock Poem	1300
34	GA		Galloway Roll	1300
35 (267)	M	XIII	Nativity Roll	c. 1300
36	ST		Stirling Roll	1304
37	SP		Smalepece's Roll	temp. Edward I
37	FF		Fife Roll	temp. Edward I
37	WNR		Sir William Le Neve's Roll	temp. Edward I
38	LM		The Lord Marshal's Roll	c. 1310
38 (267)	LMS		Raine–Dunn Pt. I (The Lord Marshal's Roll Old, Pt. II)	c. 1310
39 (268)	L	XV	First Dunstable Roll	1308
40 (268)	I	X	Holland's Roll	c. 1310
44 (268)	N	XVI	Parliamentary Roll	c. 1312

50	O	XVII	Boroughbridge Roll	1322
51 (268)	PE		Peterborough Roll	*c.* 1321–9
52 (268)	HA	XIV	Harleian Roll	temp. Edward II
52	WNS		Sir William Le Neve's Second Roll	temp. Edward II
53	PV		Povey's Roll	temp. Edward II
53	CK		Cooke's Book	temp. Edward II
54	BL		Balliol Roll	*c.* 1332
54 (269)	CA		Carlisle Roll	1334
56	SD	XVIII	Second Dunstable Roll	1334
57	AS		Ashmolean Roll	*c.* 1334
58 (269)	CKO		Cooke's Ordinary	*c.* 1340
60 (269)	CG		Cotgrave's Ordinary	*c.* 1340
61	CL		[Third] Calais Roll	*c.* 1348
61	PO		Powell's Roll	*c.* 1350
62	P	III	Grimaldi's Roll	*c.* 1350
63	AN	XIX	Antiquaries' Roll	*c.* 1360
63 (269)	CV		Calveley's Book	
63	BM		1. Becket's Murderers Roll	*c.* 1350
63	CVL		2. Lancashire Roll	temp. Henry IV
64	CVC		3. Cheshire Roll	*c.* 1450
65	CVK		4. Kent Roll	13th and 14th cent.
65	CVM		5. Miscellanea	14th cent.
66 (269)	BS		Bruce Roll	*c.* 1370
66	NB		['Sixth'] Nobility Roll	temp. Edward III
67	R		Styward's (2nd Calais or Sir Symonds D'Ewes') Roll	temp. Edward III
68	CY		County Roll	temp. Richard II
69 (270)	WJ		William Jenyns' Ordinary	*c.* 1380
71	BG		Basynges' Book	*c.* 1395
71 (270)	S	XX	Willement's Roll	*c.* 1395
72	SM		Sherborne Missal Shields	*c.* 1400
73	NS		Norfolk and Suffolk Roll	*c.* 1400
73 (270)	TJ		Thomas Jenyns' Book	*c.* 1410
78 (270)	T		Rouen Roll	*c.* 1410
80 (270)	LC		Duchy of Lancaster Coucher Book	*c.* 1405
80 (270)	FC		Furness Coucher Book	*c.* 1412
81 (271)	LMO		Raine–Dunn Roll Pt. II (The LordMarshal's Roll Old Pt. I)	*c.* 1420
81 (271)	FK		Fenwick's Roll	
			Pt. I	temp. Henry V
			Pt. II	late 15th cent.
83	U		Ulster's Roll	temp. Henry V
83 (271)	BB		Bruges' Garter Book	*c.* 1430
86	RB		Red Book Roll	temp. Henry VI
86 (271)	ME		Merton's Roll ⎱	temp. Henry VI
	LY		Lucy's Roll ⎰	
87	CN		Clarence Roll	temp. Henry VI
87	AK		Atkinson's Roll	temp. Henry VI
88 (271)	BR		Bradfer-Lawrence's Roll	1445–6

90	PCL		Portcullis' Book	*c.* 1440
91 (271)	BW		Bowyer's Book	*c.* 1440
91	TB		Talbot Banners	*c.* 1442
92 (271)			Sir Thomas Holme's Book	
93	LP		2. Legh's Princes	*c.* 1446
93	MY		3. Legh's Shires (Military Roll)	*c.* 1446
94	LMA		4. Legh's Men of Arms Parliamentary Roll I. B)	
94	LD		10. Lords' Roll	*c.* 1495
95	SC		12. Scots Roll	*c.* 1490–1500
95	FLD		13. Flodden Standards	
96 (273)	LV		16. Legh's Visitations of London (Aldermen of London Roll)	1446–7
97	KB		Kings of Britain Roll	temp. Henry VI
98 (274)	DB		Dublin Roll	temp. Henry VI
98	CT		Cottonian Roll	15th cent.
98	CR		Clare Roll	1456
99	SES		2nd Segar Roll	*c.* 1460
100 (274)	FB		Friar Brackley's Book	*c.* 1440–60
100	PT		Portington's Roll	temp. Henry VI
101 (274)	ML		Mandeville Roll and Strangway's Roll	*c.* 1450
101	RH		Randle Holme's Book	temp. Henry VI
103	SK		Starkey's Roll	*c.* 1460
103 (275)	SA		Salisbury Roll	*c.* 1460
105	TZ		Tregoz Roll	15th cent.
105 (275)	LO		London Roll	*c.* 1470
105	DV		Domville Roll	*c.* 1470
106	CC		Domville, Copy A (Colour on Colour Roll)	
06	WSG		Wriothesley's St. George Roll	
106	FN		Sir John Fenn's Book of Badges	*c.* 1470
107	BN		Barnard's Roll of Badges	1475
108	RL		Rawlinson Roll	15th cent.
108	WB		Writhe's Book	*c.* 1480
109	PLN		Peter le Neve's Book	*c.* 1480–1500
110	CB		Collingborne's Book	late 15th cent.
110			Creswick's Book	
110 (276)	LQ	I	Le Neve's Equestrian Roll	*c.* 1470
	[CRK	II	Creswick's Book	*c.* 1510]
111	GY		Gentry Roll	*c.* 1480
111 (276)	BA		Ballard's Book	*c.* 1465–90
116 (277)	RW		Warwick or Rous Roll	1477–91
(278)	W		Wagner's Roll	*c.* 1480–90
120	WLN		Sir William le Neve's Book	*c.* 1500
120 (278)	WK		Writhe's Book of Knights	temp. Henry VII
122 (278)	WGA		Writhe's Garter Book	*c.* 1488
124	MK		Meyrick's Roll	temp. Henry VII
125	SHY		Shirley's Roll	15th cent.

Index of reference letters

ADDITIONS & CORRECTIONS TO *CEMRA*

pp. 1–9. THE MATTHEW PARIS SHIELDS; GLOVER'S ROLL; WALFORD'S ROLL
The descriptions are superseded by the editions in the present volume.

p. 12. HERALDS' ROLL
III. A. This contains 705 shields.

p. 15. DERING ROLL
B. Ashmole MS. 1120. 'ff. 171–4ᵇ'.

p. 16. *I. Harl. 6137.* Amend date '1607' to '1605' (cf. dating of other items in manuscript based on the date 1605 at f. 61).

p. 16. CAMDEN ROLL
Original. Dr. C. E. Wright and Professor Francis Wormald inform me that the writing on the dorse is in an early fourteenth century hand.

p. 17 (*Edition II*). For 'British Archaeological Society' read 'British Archaeological Association'.

p. 19. ST. GEORGE'S ROLL
I. Owners. For 'Tresswell' read 'Treswell'.
C. Harl. 6137. For 'ff. 73–89' read 'ff. 72ᵇ–89ᵇ'.
D. For 'headed' read 'with the following memorandum on f. 14ᵇ'.

p. 23. CHARLES' ROLL
Having collated II. A and B with I, H. S. London found that of the first 415 entries in II only two (27 and 324) do not appear in I, but that of the remaining 97 in II only 14 are in I. These are what I have called the *Additions*, but London suggests that they may rather represent an original ending lost from I.
The omission of certain small charges and errors in certain tinctures in II. A and B suggests to London that their original was already old and worn in the 1580's and so perhaps of fourteenth century date.
Version II. B. Vincent MS. 164 ff. 150–7ᵇ. For 'Leony' read 'Jeoūn'.

p. 24. COLLINS' ROLL
Versions I. B and II. A are copies by Richard Scarlett.

p. 26. GUILLIM'S ROLL
Version I. B. For '1607' read '1607?'.
Version II. A. H. S. London notes that MS. Laud 649 contains the autograph and notes in the hand of W. Waad, who must be Sir William Waad, 1546–1623 (see *DNB*) who bore *Azure a saltire between four escallops or.* These arms are at the foot of f. 53ᵇ. They occur again drawn by the same hand on the second flyleaf with quarterings—see *Burke's General Armory*, s.v. Wade, and *The Genealogist*, N.S. xxviii. 234.

p. 28. FALKIRK ROLL

Version I (Edition II). H. S. London notes that this confuses two texts.

p. 29 (*Version II*), l. 9, at end. For 'I. 35' read 'I. 87'.
Editions substitute:
1. *Scotland in 1298*, ed. Henry Gough 1888. After '1888' add 'd.p. 129–57'.
2. From A (and I. B parallel) text printed in proof only for Sir W. St. John Hope and Oswald Barron by Constable, *c*. 1903.

My thanks are due to Mr. N. Denholm-Young for drawing my attention to the excellent editions of both versions (from I. B and II. A), with introduction and notes by Henry Gough in his *Scotland in 1298. Documents relating to the campaign of King Edward the First in that Year, and especially to the Battle of Falkirk*, 1888, pp. 129–59.

Mr. Denholm-Young has also pointed out to me the evidence, cited on pp. 17 and 31 of the same book, for the presence in Scotland on 8 Jan. 1297/8 and 28 May 1298 (when letters of protection were issued for him), in the retinue of Henry de Percy, of Walter le Rey Marchys, who must be the Walter le Marchis, King of Heralds, who at Christmas 1300 was paid forty shillings for making a proclamation before the King at Northampton (*Heralds and Heraldry in the Middle Ages*, 2nd ed., 1956, p. 160). Was he, perhaps, the compiler of the roll?

p. 30. CAERLAVEROCK POEM

Version I. British Museum Cotton Caligula A. xviii ff. 23ᵇ–30ᵇ. A copy of this, said to be by John Anstis, Garter, in the Tixall Library sale, Sotheby's 6 November 1899, lot 119.

Version II. A. The manuscript from which Glover made this transcript is said to have belonged to Mr. Harvy of Leicestershire who also owned Glover II, see *Herald and Genealogist*, ii. 378; v. 475.

p. 34. *Version II P*. For '1606' read '1607?'.

p. 36. NATIVITY ROLL

Edition I. Mr. P. S. Spokes, F.S.A., has Greenstreet's MS. copy endorsed 'Collated with the original (at the Inner Temple Library) by me, James Greenstreet, this 21st December 1878.'

pp. 38 and 81. THE LORD MARSHAL'S ROLL OLD

In October 1955 H. S. London identified Cambridge Fitzwilliam Museum MS. 282 as a longer version of this roll. This manuscript was mentioned briefly by Professor Francis Wormald and Miss Phyllis Giles in 1952 in their *Handlist of Additional MSS. in the Fitzwilliam Museum*. It belonged at one time to Canon James Raine of Durham (1791–1858) and later to George Dunn of Wolley Hall near Maidenhead (see p. 142), and has therefore been named by London The Raine–Dunn Roll.

London printed a description of the roll in the *Coat of Arms*, vol. iv, no. 29 (Jan. 1957), pp. 196–8. From comparison of the Fitzwilliam MS. 282 with the Society of Antiquaries' MS. 664, Roll VI, London reached the conclusion that both represented a lost roll of uncertain length of *c*. 1310, recopied and augmented *c*. 1420 by a painter of the same school as the painter of Thomas Jenyns I (p. 73) and Grimaldi (p. 63). Each of the two copies, however, omits some items which the other gives.

On this basis London established a hypothetical original text:

Part I. c. 1310. Painted shields about 1¾ by 2 inches in rows of three with names and contemporary French blazons below each row.

Part II. c. 1420. Painted shields about 1⅜ by 1⅝ inches in rows of four with names only below each row.

Copies
    (*a*) *Fitzwilliam Museum MS. 282 (Handlist no. 82).*
        Art. 3, ff. 22–26ᵇ copies *c.* 1600: 92 shields in I, 26 in II.
    (*b*) *The Lord Marshal's Roll Old.*
See *Aspilogia I*, pp. 38 and 81.

p. 39. FIRST DUNSTABLE ROLL

In a note in the *Antiquaries' Journal*, xxxii (1952) 202–3, on 'A Dunstable Tournament, 1308–9', Mr. F. B. Stitt cited an account roll of the Manor of Wymondley, Herts., recording the provision of fodder in 1308–9 for the war horses of the Lord and Sir Giles d'Argenteyn, going to the Tournament at Dunstable, as evidence of the correctness of the headnote of the roll. He pointed out further that the names of those present suggest that the tournament was connected with the baronial opposition to Edward II and concluded that it may have been held at Easter 1309 as a prelude to the April Parliament of that year and must have taken place between Michaelmas 1308 and June 1309.

p. 42. HOLLAND'S ROLL

Version I. G. The heading should read 'Memo: in. the. olde. Rolle. sett in the olde Booke of Armes'.

p. 43. PARLIAMENTARY ROLL

Notice. N. Denholm-Young, *Collected Papers on Thirteenth Century Subjects*, 1946, p. 62, regards this roll as not far from a complete census of the knights then existing. See also F. M. Powicke, *The Thirteenth Century*, p. 552.

p. 44. *I. B.* Seven figures of knights in Writhe's Garter Book (see p. 123), pp. 160–3, are of identical pattern. Their surcoats are plain, their banners bear arms; cf. p. 160, The See of Chichester and the See of Salisbury; p. 161, St. George and St. Edmund; p. 162, St. Edward and England; p. 163 (blank).

p. 45. *Version I. R.* For 'ff. 1–31ᵇ' read 'ff. 1–31'.

I. S. After 'Roger Kemyss' delete '*c.*' before 1609 (the date is on f. 2).

p. 46. *I. X* δ. Dr. Wright considers that the hand of the inscriptions and tricking of ff. 42–45 is certainly that of Nicholas Charles—it was so identified by Wanley (see his description of the manuscript in the Harl. Cat.).

I. X ε. After 'Add. 18011' add 'ff. 244–50ᵇ'. There are 277 coats. The volume is a Glover volume and is related in contents in part at least to Harl. 1088—in both manuscripts the Yorks. church notes follow the roll.

p. 50 (*Edition II*). For 'O' read 'P'. The language of this version is slightly more modern than that of B or Edition I.

p. 51. PETERBOROUGH ROLL

I. Copy A. *College of Arms MS. Vincent 92, pp. 7–8.*

p. 52. HARLEIAN ROLL

The names are written below not over. H. S. London notes that there were 196 shields, but the last 5 on ff. 28ᵇ–31ᵇ are blank and nameless, while some of the earlier ones have been cut out and others lost when the top corner of the pages was eaten or torn away. When Greenstreet and Barron prepared their text the pages in question were out of order. They have now been rearranged so that the order of the shields now differs materially from that shown in those editions. The text in both editions is, however, generally—though not invariably—accurate.

p. 56. CARLISLE ROLL

In the preface of his unpublished edition of this roll London suggests that certain alterations in the text of the roll were made in the seventeenth century by a member of the Halse family who owned it.

p. 59. COOKE'S ORDINARY
l. 18. Read '29–98 lions; 99–112 eagles'.
l. 19. For 'Torteaux' read 'roundels'.
l. 30. For '598–644 various, plus 2', read '598–648 various'.

p. 60. COTGRAVE'S ORDINARY
Owner. 1562 Hugh Fitzwilliam of Sprotborough, co. York.

p. 63. SIR GEORGE CALVELEY'S BOOK

In 1955 Mr. J. A. Goodall drew attention to an interesting degree of correspondence between certain shields in Calveley's Book and the British Museum MS. Harl. 2116, ff. 13–18, a paper roll of six sheets pasted end to end but now separated and bound up, containing 120 shields rather crudely painted in 40 rows of 3 with names over. Their order differs considerably from that of Calveley's Book.

Part I. Becket's Murderers' Roll. In February 1951 S. C. Kaines-Smith told me of a vellum book of arms of Cheshire Gentry painted in the reign of Elizabeth I belonging to Lord Leigh at Stoneleigh Abbey, Warwickshire, which has on f. 32ᵇ a coloured drawing of a window formerly in the church at Brereton, Cheshire, depicting Becket and his murderers. Below is written 'lest this moniment in glasse being in the upper window of the northe syde the chauncell of Brereton churche shoulde be broken, I, Sir William Brereton, Knight, to the end hit may remayne in memorie to the posteretie, have caused the same to be hear purtred the xxvth of Marche 1608.' Kaines-Smith suggested that the Breretons may have claimed descent from Sir Roger Brito and their arms were, in fact, *Argent two bars sable* and those assigned to him *Or two bars gules.* However, I have seen no pedigree which makes this claim.

Original. This was on paper, not vellum, which increases the possibility that the leaves in Harl. MS. 2116 may belong to it.

p. 65. Copies D and E differ in order from A, B, and C.
Part IV. Kent Roll. *Copy B. Brit. Mus. MS. Harl. 6137, ff. 98–99.*

Sixty shields drawn in outline with names over, no tinctures, tricked, and many shields blank. The order differs considerably from A, and each copy contains many shields not in the other, printed by Greenstreet as the 'Kent Roll' in *Notes and Queries*, 5th s. iii (1 May 1875) 344–5.

p. 66. BRUCE ROLL

This should not be included in the present catalogue for it is not in any sense an English roll, but the Scottish section of a continental roll. This latter, the Mowbray Roll, is dated *c.* 1365–70 by Dr. Paul Adam-Even. It is a general roll of French compilation, remarkable for the absence of names, the display of the arms on banners (otherwise unknown in French armorials), and the numerous differenced coats.

p. 70. WILLIAM JENYNS' ORDINARY
l. 24. For 'often' read 'usually'.

p. 71. WILLEMENT'S ROLL
This roll, which had been lost to sight since 1834, reappeared in a sale at Christie's of manuscripts belonging to the Earl of Derby on the 24th of March 1954. It was bought for £120 by the British Museum and is now Brit. Mus. MS. Egerton 3713.

It is a vellum roll about 30 feet long of 13 membranes of which the first 9 are an original roll of Escheat of 10 Henry IV on the dorse of which Willement's Roll was painted in Sir Thomas Wriothesley's studio in the reign of Henry VIII. The last four membranes are vellum of Wriothesley's time. It belonged in the mid seventeenth century to Henry Davy.

It is described by Dr. C. E. Wright in the *British Museum Quarterly*, vol. xix, no. 3 (1954), p. 49, where plate 17 illustrates shields 21–37.

A complete text with foreword has been prepared by H. S. London who points out that Willement's edition is marred by misreading of the legends and tinctures and by the complete omission of three items. Nevertheless, Willement's dating appears sound.

p. 73. THOMAS JENYNS' BOOK
Last line. For 'under' read 'over'.

p. 74. *Date.* Dr. C. E. Wright dates the execution of this *c.* 1440, but the painting of Queen Margaret's arms later and the inscription thereto temp. Henry VII.

p. 75. Copy D is a very close copy of Add. 40851.

p. 78. Copy H ends with Amondevile. 'Blazon'd in French by William Flower Esqr. Norroy King of Armes in the tyme of Queen Elizabeth carefully preserved and thus bound up together [with a collection of pedigrees by Wm. Jenyns, Lancaster] by Tho. Penson Armes-Painter.'

Copy L should follow copy K.

p. 79. 'ROUEN' ROLL
Copy A. For 'ff. 171–4^b' read 'ff. 175–6'.

p. 80. THE GREAT COUCHER BOOK OF THE DUCHY OF LANCASTER
Sir Robert Somerville reproduces the arms of the Duchy from this book as the frontispiece of his *History of the Duchy of Lancaster*, vol. i, 1953, and dates its execution between 1402 and 1407.

p. 80. FURNESS COUCHER BOOK
Owners. Ralph Palmer died s.p. 1755, Lord Verney (d. 1791) was his cousin, see the *Genealogists' Magazine*, ii. 71.

Copy A. After 'Brit. Mus. Harl. 5019' add 'ff. 20–31^b'. And for 'Sampson Erdeswicke' read 'Sir Richard St. George' (the whole volume appears to be in his hand, his signatures as Norroy are at ff. 133, 134, and the compilation seems to be after 1586 (cf. ff. 12, 12^b); an engraving of the St. George coat of arms is at the beginning of the volume).

Copy C. For 'ff. 193–208' read 'ff. 193–208^b'; add '? by Robert Glover'; no date. Madden points out in a note at the beginning of Otho D IV that the collection is in the same hand as Claudius C VIII, which is said to be Glover's.

p. 81. THE EARL MARSHAL'S ROLL OLD and RAINE–DUNNE ROLL
See p. 267 *supra*.

FENWICK'S ROLL
Part I. For '9 ft. 6 inches' read '9½ inches'.

p. 82. *Copy A*. Cancel from 'ff. 180–6' to 'Garter', and substitute 'ff. 92ᵇ–95ᵇ and 137–49ᵇ' (180–6 and 187–212 in William Smith's pagination).

Copy in trick of 594 items extracted *passim* but in the original order. The omissions are mostly either (*a*) well-known coats like Nevile, &c., or (*b*) anonymous coats, or (*c*) cadenced versions of coats already entered. The copy supplies certain names and details and even a few complete items lacking from the other copies. Copy made for Sir Thomas Wriothesley, Garter, 1505–34.

p. 83. BRUGES' GARTER BOOK
Owners. Anstis mentions his purchase of this book in his *Register of the Garter*, i. 54–55.

p. 84. *Contents*. In the opinion of H. S. London the painter of Bruges' Garter Book also painted the Aldermen in Add. MS. 45133 (p. 96, no. 16), 'The Judges' in Coll. Arm. MS. A. 17 (see Wagner, *Heralds and Heraldry in the Middle Ages*, p. 117), 'Legh's Princes', i.e. the figures of kings at the beginning of Sir Thomas Holme's book Harl. MS. 4205, ff. 1–8 (p. 272), and perhaps the figures in Add. MS. 45133, ff. 6–7 (p. 273).

p. 86. *Notices*. 6. The late Mr. London's book of William Bruges is to be published by the Harleian Society in its Visitation Series.

p. 86. LUCY'S ROLL
Footnote 1. Mr. Wilfred Merton's Roll, since sold by him, was apparently executed in the reign of Henry VI and may well be a fragment of the lost original of Lucy's Roll.

p. 88. BRADFER-LAWRENCE'S ROLL
Section II can be dated between the 5th of April 1445 when Henry Beauchamp was created Duke of Warwick and his death on the 11th of June 1446.

p. 89. *ff. 41–45*. The English blazon of these excerpts includes many uncommon terms.

p. 91. BOWYER'S BOOK
Mr. London notes that the names and blazons are neatly and carefully written in marked contrast to the poor and amateurish draftsmanship of the shields. This suggests a student's exercise like the Carlisle Roll (see p. 56).

p. 92. SIR THOMAS HOLME'S BOOK
Closer study and fresh discoveries since 1950, instead of solving the problem presented by this book's links on the one hand with Wriothesley and on the other with Benolt, have revealed the following fresh difficulties.
(*1*) My suggestion of 1939 that item [4] of Benolt's Inventory (*Heralds and Heraldry in the Middle Ages*, 2nd ed., 1956, p. 150) might be identified with parts of this book has been confirmed by the discovery of Benolt's Inventory mark ⵋ at the top of Harl. 4305, f. 2. In the light of this London convincingly suggested that the Inventory [4] description was of four distinct items: (*a*) a 'Visitation of many Shires' i.e. the Military Roll, (*b*) 'London', i.e. section 16 of this roll, Roger Legh's 'Visitation' of London Aldermen in 1446–7, (*c*) 'princes', i.e. the drawings

of Kings of England in section 2 of this roll, and (*d*) painted 'men of armes', i.e. section 4 of this roll, being MS. Harl. 4205, ff. 41–112, Version I. B of the Parliamentary Roll.

(*2*) In the light of detailed stylistic comparison Mr. London reached the conclusion in agreement with Mr. A. J. Collins and Dr. C. E. Wright of the British Museum Manuscript Department, that the same artist was responsible for (*a*) the drawings of Knights of the Garter in Bruges' Garter Book (p. 271), (*b*) those of Kings of England in section 2 of this roll, (*c*) those of Aldermen of London in section 16, (*d*) a series of figures of Judges in Coll. Arm. MS. A. 17, which is item [5] in Benolt's Inventory (*Heralds and Heraldry*, 2nd ed., pp. 117, 150). Mr. London attributes section 4 of this roll to another painter of the same school. He suggests that the painter of (*a*), (*b*), (*c*), and (*d*) was employed by William Bruges and by his permission worked also for Legh.

(*3*) Item [55] of Benolt's Inventory, 'A booke of armes of divers gentilmen of Scotland, painted', might be the Scots Roll, section 12 of this roll.

(*4*) To the sections of II already noted as linked with Wriothesley by internal evidence must be added (15) which is a portion of his Salisbury Roll (see pp. 103 and 122). Furthermore both I and II were owned *c.* 1718 by the Rev. William Smith, Rector of Melsonby, Yorks., who owned other Wriothesley MSS., such as Brit. Mus. MSS. Add. 45131, 45132 (Funeral Banners), and 46354. Thomas Dawes, Rouge Croix 1570–*c.* 1580, the anagram of whose name was written in 1564 on f. 57[b] (p. 120), was servant to Sir Gilbert Dethick, Garter. Sir Gilbert or his son Sir William may well have owned this manuscript in 1564. According to Noble (*A History of the College of Arms*, 1805, p. 175), Charles Wriothesley, Windsor (d. 1562), sold many books which had been his father's to Sir William Dethick and it can be shown that Dethick in fact owned manuscripts which had been Sir Thomas Wriothesley's (Wagner, *Records and Collections of the College of Arms*, 1952, pp. 10–11: Coll. Arm. MS. Vincent 152, 'Prince Arthur's Book', is a Wriothesley manuscript and has the Dethick arms inserted on p. 147). After Sir William Dethick's death in 1612 his books were acquired by Jacob Chaloner (1586–1631), the herald painter, from whom ten were bought in 1616 by Sir Robert Cotton. His list of these in Add. 35213, f. 33, includes 'A larg booke in foll. paper having many tiltings and armes about H 6 time and Ed. 4'. If Cotton subsequently sold or gave this away, it could be Holme's Book.

The upshot of all this is to link large sections of the book (and of both its parts) *more* firmly than before *both* with Wriothesley *and* with Benolt. I can suggest only one explanation. Benolt in 1530 complained that Wriothesley had in his personal possession books which belonged to the Office of Arms (*Heralds and Heraldry*, p. 94). Following the King's decision in Benolt's favour, books claimed to be in this category may have been disgorged by Wriothesley, and at the time of Benolt's death may have been in his possession and thus included in the inventory of his books which Thomas Wall, Windsor, completed on 30 June 1534 (ibid., p. 110). Wriothesley, who survived till 24 November 1534, may then have pointed out that these particular books were not Benolt's property but 'office books' and have resumed possession on that footing.

p. 93. Harl. 4205 was bought by Harley in 1720 from Christopher Bateman, a London bookseller.

The drawing on f. 1[b] is of William the Conqueror (see Strangways' Book, Harl. MS. 2259, f. 95[b]). The series of drawings of kings dates from after Henry VI's marriage in 1445. Copies made by Thomas Willement in 1839 of Harl. 4205, ff. 1[b]–8, &c. were lot 60 in Sotheby's sale of 12 April 1954.

3. Military Roll. Date. For '*c.* 1480' read 'before 1448 when Sir Richard Wydville was created Lord Rivers'.

4. Parliamentary Roll I. B. Identified as Legh's *Men of Arms*, probably painted 1440.

p. 94. Add. MS. 45133 is noticed in the *British Museum Quarterly*, vol. xii, no. 3 (1938), pp. 83–84, where plate XXXII illustrates the figures of Edmund d'Arundell and Sibyl, daughter of William, Earl of Salisbury, from the Salisbury Roll. It belonged in 1718 to the Rev. William Smith, Rector of Melsonby, Yorks.

6. ff. 6–7 were transferred to the Guildhall in 1938 with the Aldermen (section 16).
10. ff. 33^b–34^b Shields of Lords now entitled the Lords' Roll.

p. 96. The description of *16. The Aldermen of London* should read as follows:

'16. ff. 61–72 (pp. 134–40, 143–4, —, 148^a, 149^a, 148^b, 149^b, 150–5). This section was, by arrangement, detached from Clumber MS. 189, when the British Museum acquired this, and transferred to the Guildhall Library to be reunited to III, *infra*; 20 full page figures of Aldermen of London, the first (fo. 62^b/134) of *Dominus Thomas Pomeray prior Ecclesie Sancte Trinitatis Londinii*, holding a banner of the Trinity and supporting a frame containing 12 blank shields with that of London (uncoloured) above and at the foot *Alderman. Warde. de Portsoken extra Aldgate. London.* [1445/81].

'fo. 63/135. *Johes Olney Maior* [1446–7]: Alderman for Coleman Street Ward 1435–58 with his shield and crest and a like frame of blank shields and so for each ward, the blank shields intended to be filled in with the successors' arms (which has in some cases been done). Walbrook Ward has 8, the last . . . *Salkeld*. The names are:

fo. 63^b/136^a	*Bassingeshaw*	Henricus Frowik Ald.	[1424–57]
fo. 64/137^b	*Langebornne*	Johes Pattesle Ald.*	[1437–51]
fo. 64^b/138	*Lymstrete*	Robertus Clopton	[1434–48]
fo. 65/139	*Quenehithe*	Johes Hatherle	[1437–60]
fo. 65^b/140	*Towre*	Thos. Catworth*	[1435–51]
fo. 66/143	*Cordwanerstrete*	Wills Grigory*	[1435–61]
fo. 66^b/144	*Walbrooke*	Wetenhale	[1446–51]
fo. 67/147	*Farygdon [extra]*	Wills Cowntes	[1437–51]
fo. 67^b/148^a	*Aldryschegate*	Johse Sutton	[1437–50]
fo. 68/149^a	*The Bryge*	Robertus Horn	[1444–56]
fo. 68^b/148^b	*Bred Strete*	Stephs Forseter*	[1444–58]
fo. 69/149^b	*Candelwykstrete*	Johes Derby	[1444–54]
fo. 69^b/150	*Algate*	Thos Canynges	[1445–61]
fo. 70/151	*Faryngedon infra*	Galfrid Feldyng	[1446–60]
fo. 70^b/152	*Dowgate*	Thos Scott	[1446–51]
fo. 71/153	*Ventre*	Wills Abraham*	[1446–56]
fo. 71^b/154	*Crepulgate*	Wills Cantlow	[1446–61]
fo. 72/155			
fo. 72^b/blank			

* No arms given.

'This Visitation of London evidently belongs to the Mayoralty of John Olney, 1446–7. This section has now been detached from the rest of the book and is in the Guildhall library together with the three leaves of III (q.v.) which originally formed part of it.

'The rest of the book (157–287) contains a voluminous index covering *inter alia* "Lib. North" by T. Wriothesley, and has a number of vellum membranes of rolls by his painter bound in. They include sections of "Letter E Roll", 157, 159, 161, 163, an Ordinary Roll of Bends only, 165, 168, 171, 173, 175, 177, 179, 180, 183, 186, 188, 190, 192,

194, 196. Part of a French Roll, 175, 177. From 206 is an alphabetical index "Registrum Armorum" by Th. WR. with page references to rolls of arms which research might identify.'

p. 97. *18. Registrum Armorum Th. WR.* (7). A Roll entitled by Wriothesley 'Saint George' is in Soc. Ant. MS. 476 (formerly Anstis's MS. I. 9), pp. 77–127. It is closely related to the Domville Roll.

(9) The mark ✗ is referred to also in the following places; (*a*) on p. 21 of Writhe's Garter Book, see p. 122. (*b*) At the foot of M. 3, f. 25, following an account of the jousts at the marriage of Prince Arthur, 1501, where there is a note 'querite plus in ij do folio ad tale signed ✗'. (*c*) W. H. Black's *Catalogue of the Ashmolean MSS.*, p. 655, MS. 858, f. 23. 'Abstract of seven documents contained "in a Visitacion of the North made by Norroy Tonge in E: marked thus ✗"'.

III. Correct as follows:

'[136^b] *Belynsgate Ward   Stephs Broun Al.* [1445–60]
'[137^a] *Cornhille Warde   Johes Gedney Alderm.* [1435–49]
'137^a. A note above "After Gedeney William Marowe the yere M^l cc XLIX^ti" and his shield below; Marowe followed Eyre in Broad Street Ward in 1449.'

p. 98. DUBLIN ROLL

I. Dublin, Genealogical Office (former Office of Arms) MS. 7, ff. 28–57^b.

For the Latin narrative of the Rulers of Britain, see Upton, *De Militari Officio*, ed. Bysshe, 1654, pp. 126–31.

p. 100. FRIAR BRACKLEY'S BOOK

This is now *Norwich Library MS. 38.*

Paper. Leaves of average measurement 5·8 by 4·2 inches bound in original sheepskin.

Pages 1–71 and 74–75 contain the shields, most with the names either over or under in a fifteenth century hand, with further names in two eighteenth century hands, perhaps those of Thomas Martin and Stephen Dale or Francis Blomefield.

Pages 115–22 and 126–32 contain a pedigree of Anne Barrey, memoranda, and Paston obits. Information from Mr. J. A. Goodall, 1956.

p. 101. MANDEVILLE ROLL and STRANGWAYS' ROLL, *c. 1450*

H. S. London points out that with the knowledge which we now possess the roll to which I gave the name Mandeville Roll in 1950 should have been named Strangways' Roll, since the most important version occurs in the manuscript written by Sir Richard Strangways (d. 1488), Brit. Mus. MS. Harl. 2259, which London noticed in 1951. He concluded, however, that it is now convenient to retain the name Mandeville Roll for the series originally so called, as described below, while reserving the name Strangways' Roll for a further series of 588 shields which occur scattered through Strangways' Book (Harl. 2259).

The main content of Strangways' Book is a series of notes on blazon, written in the 1450s, when Strangways was a student of the Inner Temple and probably in connexion with his studies there. It has important links with some of the early heraldic treatises discussed by London in the *Antiquaries' Journal*, xxxiii (1953) 169–83, and especially with Antwerp, Plantin–Moretus Museum, MS. O.B. 5. 6, which was noticed by Professor R. A. B. Mynors in 1949 and is referred to in the Addenda on p. 160 of this *CEMRA*. This volume to which London has given the name Patrick's Book, contains a version of the Mandeville Roll and some shields from Strangways' Roll.

The following description is taken from London's notes.

I. *Strangways' Version, c.* 1447–9. 108 coats in contemporary blazon, partly French and partly English.

1–76   'Les Armez de roy et seigneurs d'Engleterre plus auceynx.'

77–108   'Les Armez de plus noblez chivalers d'Engleterre.'

A   Harl. MS. 2259 (Strangways' Book), pp. 76ᵈ–77ᵈ and 185ᵈ–186; copies, perhaps compiled, by Richard Strangways of the Inner Temple.

B   Plantin–Moretus Museum, Antwerp, MS. O. B. 5. 6 (Patrick's Book— see *CEMRA*, p. 160), ff. 30ᵈ–33ᵈ. This adds 3 more items 109–11, copied from other parts of Strangways' Book.

II. *Povey's Version. College of Arms MS. B. 19, ff. 26–29* comprised in Povey's Extracts on Heraldry. 133 painted shields, 5 rows of 4 to a page, with names over, headed 'The ancient armes of the noble men of England'. Temp. Edward VI and Mary. F. 26, 1–64, English lords, beginning *Duke of Aumerle*; *The erle of Glocester*; *The erle of Cornewall*; *The erle of Warren*; 64 *Earle of Kildare*; 65 *The Armes of Cawen*; 66–101 English knights, begins *Sir Thōs Molton*; ends *Sir John Mandevill perigrinator* (sic); 102–33 sovereigns, worthies, and others, begins *Empour of Rome*; ends (*two lions combatant rere regardant*). Of these 92 items are in Mandeville I, 38 are imported from other parts of Strangways' Book, 2 are in no other version of these tracts and 1 is blank.

The Strangways' Roll consists of 588 painted shields, most of them accompanied by blazons, and names, a miscellaneous selection and set down in no order, of fabulous figures, kings, lords, cities, knights, and others, some noted as seen in specified places. London has described them and collated them with material elsewhere.

p. 103. SALISBURY ROLL

This must be the roll referred to as follows in the Inventory, now in Brit. Mus. Lansdowne MS. 75, taken 12 October 1593, of the Library of Robert Cooke, Clarenceux, '109 Item A Rowle of parchemente/of the descente of the Earle of Salisbury in Personages'.

London conjectured that John Waters, who was Warwick Pursuivant in the 1440's, Warwick Herald about 1455, and Chester Herald by 1463, and his successor David Griffith who became Warwick Pursuivant about 1455 and was Warwick Herald by 1463, or earlier, and dead by May 1480, may have been associated with the compilation.

p. 104. Substitute for U. 34–35:

The figures of Richard III and his Queen are reproduced in 'The Plantagenets' by John Harvey, 1948, fig. 74. The figures of Edmund d'Arundel and Sibyl, daughter of William, Earl of Salisbury, from Brit. Mus. Add. MS. 45133 are reproduced in the *British Museum Quarterly*, xii, no. 3 (1938), pl. XXXII.

pp. 104–5.

The Devereux Roll should be omitted. London found when he examined it that, though it incorporates some fifteenth century material, it is of late sixteenth or early seventeenth century compilation.

p. 106. DOMVILLE ROLL

The description of Copy A should read 'Trick, *c.* 1575, without heading. 513 shields comprising many sequences which occur in the Domville Roll, but interrupted and in different order. Begins *Gloucester*; *Halsham*; *de Gras*; *Malorye*; 476 *Keysyng*; 477 (Lytton), 478 *Argent fretty sable on a chief sable two mullets or*, 478–80 blank, 481 *Rex Anglie*; 482–510 are Domville 1, 761–82, and 1784–90, 511 *Cornwaile*, 512 *Bradschawe*, 513 *Moungomery* (Domville 1682). Vincent 164 is by Richard Scarlett.'

This roll was sold at Sotheby's in 1958 by Sir Sydney Cockerell and was bought for £220 by the College of Arms.

London noted the close connexion between this Roll and one which he named *Wriothesley's Saint George Roll* in Society of Antiquaries MS. 476 (formerly Anstis' MS. I. 9), pp. 77–127. This was written and partly tricked, partly painted, partly by and partly for Sir Thomas Wriothesley, Garter 1505–34. It contains 1,014 shields comprising many sequences which occur in the Domville Roll, though interrupted and in different order.

pp. 110–11. LE NEVE'S EQUESTRIAN BOOK

The owner, Mr. H. R. Creswick, who was Bodley's Librarian 1945–7, has been Cambridge University Librarian since 1949.

London, having examined and transcribed this book by kind permission of Mr. Creswick, made the following note in November 1952.

As the equestrian section is such a small part of this MS. the volume should be renamed CRESWICK'S BOOK, the two sections being called 'Le Neve's Equestrian Roll' (LQ) and 'Creswick's Roll' (CRK) respectively. The two sections are totally unrelated, but they were already united in Le Neve's day as is shown by the foliation in his hand.

LQ now contains 88 figures, 4 to the page, but leaves 25–28 and 37 have been cut out since Le Neve foliated the volume; 25–28 certainly belonged to this and 37 may have done so, so the roll must originally have comprised at least 120 figures. Of the 88 survivors 59 are certainly Irish, and it is probable that the whole roll is really Irish, the only medieval collection of Irish arms yet found. It can be dated between 1461 when Sir Thomas Waldegrave (107) was knighted and 1478 when Syr Robert Preston lord of Gormanston (118) became Viscount Gormanston. Such date fits the handwriting and the paper of which Briquet dates the watermark *c.* 1450–80. At least two more recent hands have added names and notes.

The figures are poorly drawn and the discrepancies between arms and blazons show that painter and scribe were different persons. The blazons suggest that their author was trying to follow the elaborate style which some fifteenth century armorists (see, e.g., Strangways' Book) were seeking to impose, but that he had forgotten or failed to grasp his mentor's teachings. Both blazons and paintings may be dubbed amateur immature.

The arrangement of this roll with 2 pairs of knights facing each other on each page, at once recalls Roger Legh's Military Roll (pp. 93/3, 94/9), and the same paper was used for both rolls. Was the compiler or painter of LQ an apprentice in Legh's studio?

CRK is a product of the Wriothesley studio and dates from early in the sixteenth century. It is a copy of an earlier collection compiled apparently between the marriage of Henry VI and Margaret of Anjou (1395) in 1445 and the death of Garter Bruges (309) in 1450. The fact that the Bruges coat is named 'Garter' is the more significant seeing that the arms of 'Smerte' appear later (911) with no mention that he was an officer of Arms.

p. 112. BALLARD'S BOOK

l. 3. For '1469' read '1460'.

p. 113. First line. For 'in 1477' read 'on 22 January 1477/8'.

l. 27. At the foot of f. 25 is a note in small writing 'querite plus in ijdo folio ad tale signed ⚔'.

p. 114. ll. 21–22. Omit 'by Wriothesley'.

p. 115. *Copy C.* For 'Egmont MS. 197' read 'Brit. Mus. MS. Add. 47171'.

p. 117. WARWICK OR ROUS ROLL
I. Latin Version. Copies. Read as follows:

'17TH CENTURY
'A. *Sir William Dugdale, Bt., Merevale Hall, co. Warwick.*
'By William Dugdale.
'B. *Oxford, Bodleian MS. Dugdale 14 (G. 2) [S.C. 6504], pp. 6–144.*
'By William Dugdale, 1636. He refers to Arden's loan of the roll to him between June and October 1636 in letters to Sir Symon Archer (*The Life, Diary and Correspondence of Sir William Dugdale*, ed. William Hamper, 1837, pp. 155–7, 159).
'C. *Stratford on Avon, co. Warwick: Shakespeare's Birthplace Museum. Deposited by the Earl of Plymouth.*
'Copy by Sir Simon Archer made in 1636, "The rolle itself remayning in the custody of Robt. Arden of Parkhall. . . being a very fayre peece of Antiquitye" (information from Sir Thomas Kendrick).'

p. 118. *Notices.* Add:
'14. Sir Anthony Wagner, "English Genealogy", 1960, pp. 307–8, discussed John Rous's collection of more than fifty genealogies inscribed on the face and dorse of this roll. The former give the ancestry on male and female lines of the Kings and the Earls of Warwick, the latter more extensive pedigrees of the Kings of Britain, France, England, and Scotland and the English earls, while the last is of his own family.'
II. English Version. This Roll was still at Kimbolton in 1869 (Hist. MSS. Comm. 1st Rep. 1870, App., p. 13). It was then lost sight of but in October 1955 was bought by the British Museum from Messrs. Robinson of Pall Mall, in whose cellars it had lain unrecognized for some years, for £2,500. It is described by Dr. C. E. Wright in the *British Museum Quarterly*, vol. xx, no. 4 (1956), pp. 77–81.

Two lines of argument suggest that the Latin version was Rous's original, from which he made the English version as a fair copy. First the execution in the former of both text and drawings is more spontaneous, but in the latter more finished. Secondly, the Latin text contains some learned passages, which the English translation omits while adding certain lighter touches. Perhaps Rous made the latter as a gift for Anne, Countess of Warwick (d. 1492).

The inventory of the books of Robert Cooke, Clarenceux, taken 12 October 1593, now in Brit. Mus. MS. Lansdowne 75 has '110. Item a Rowle of the Auncient Earles of Warwicke in Parchemente', and since Cooke's library was acquired by the College of Arms, which in 1640 possessed the English version, this probably refers to it.

p. 119. *Copies.*
A. *British Museum MS. Lansdowne 882, ff. 6–23ᵇ, 67, 67ᵇ.*
Copy of the text with watercolour copies of the drawings belonging to Thomas Ward of Warwick 1729 (cf. memorandum on f. 1).
B. *Oxford, Bodleian MS. Ashmole 839, ff. 8–31.*
Incomplete transcript by Robert Glover, Somerset (d. 1588), headed 'This roll was laboured and finished by Mr. John Rows of Warrewyke'. (This is derived from the inscription on dorse of the original, Brit. Mus. Add. 48976); arms 1–55 from the dorse of the Roll occupy ff. 30–31, at the foot of the last mentioned leaf occurring the phrase, 'The resydue of the Armes contyned in the roll of the Earles of Warwyk, do follow after

the Latyne story of the said Erles, here next ensuenge this leaf'. In fact the rest of the arms do not occur in Ashmole 839. It is to be noted that at the top of f. 2 is the date '1572' (ff. 2–86 formed originally a separate volume), i.e. the English Roll was presumably available to Glover in 1572. This note was kindly furnished by Dr. C. E. Wright.

C. *Stratford on Avon, co. Warwick, Shakespeare's Birthplace Museum. Deposited by the Earl of Plymouth.*

p. 119. WAGNER'S ROLL, *c.* 1490

Sir Anthony R. Wagner, Garter King of Arms, College of Arms, London

Vellum Roll of eight membranes 20 ft. 3 in. × 11 in. the face painted with 445 shields in 89 rows of 5, some with names over, but many without. The rows numbered on the left in Roman figures i–xc, but Rows 35 to 74 are misnumbered 34 to 73 and Rows 84 to 89 are misnumbered 85 to 90.

Owners. The Revd. David Thomas Powell (1763–1848) whose name is at the foot with the date 1817. This may have been Lot 454 in his Sale, Puttick and Simpson, 31 July 1848 ('An ancient roll of arms upon vellum, the Arms in colours'). It was acquired by Sir Thomas Phillipps, Bt., by whom, however, it was never catalogued, and passed with the rest of the remainder of the Phillipps Library to the Robinson Trust, by whom it was sold at Sotheby's 29 November 1966, Lot 76, and was there purchased by the writer.

Contents. Begins [*Cong*]*herst*; (?) *Boyton*; Azure three escallops within a bordure engrailed or; (?) *Baronby*; ends; Per bend joggled gules and argent an escutcheon counterchanged; *Wyt.*

Many of the coats occur also in Writhe's book, and Peter le Neve's book, and the painter appears to be the same as the painter of these and of the studio of John Writhe, Garter, while the arms of Writhe are painted as No. 421 with the name above in a later (Wriothesley) hand *Wryothesley Greckelade.* Furthermore, the names over the shields are in two or more distinct hands, which occur on other work of the Writhe and Wriothesley studio, with which this roll can therefore be associated.

Interspersed with familiar coats are a number of strange and unknown coats, regrettably unnamed, but possibly chosen for record here by Garter Writhe for their very strangeness.

Date. c. 1480–90.

Notice. Sotheby's Catalogue *Bibliotheca Phillippica Medieval Manuscripts: New Series: Second Part.* Sale: Tuesday, 29 November 1966. Lot. 76, p. 98. Plate 25 reproduces Nos. 156–85.

p. 120. WRITHE'S BOOK OF KNIGHTS

Owners. Ralph Thoresby, in a letter of 5 December 1720 to John Anstis (Brit. Mus. MS. Stowe. 749, f. 135), says that Francis Layton (d. 1661) had been of the Jewel House to Charles I and 'was really a Royalist, but when in these miserable times the King's Library was deplumed I presume he took what care he could to secure some', and had 'one of your predecessor (Wriothsley Garter)'.

Four other manuscripts in the British Museum contain the handwriting of the Rev. William Smith, the Rector of Melsonby (d. 1735). Of these Harl. 4205 (Sir Thomas Holme's Book I, see p. 94) was bought for Harley from Christopher Bateman, a London bookseller, 24 May 1720. The others, Add. 45131, 45132 (Sir Thomas Wriothesley's 'Funeral Banners'), and 45133 (Sir Thomas Holme's Book II, see p. 94) belonged to Sir George Nayler, Garter (d. 1831), were then bought by the Duke of Newcastle and were acquired for the British Museum at the Clumber sale of 1938.

p. 121. *Contents. Part II, 1. and 2.* Mrs. E. L. James prints from Brit. Mus. MS. Harl. 78, f. 31 in the *Coat of Arms*, iv (1956) 136–8), extracts from these sections translated into blazon by gems. H. S. London comments thereon ibid., pp. 248–50.

p. 122. WRITHE'S GARTER BOOK

Owners. Like other manuscripts of Sir Thomas Wriothesley this appears to have been owned later by Sir William Dethick, Garter (d. 1612), for Brit. Mus. Add. MS. 35213, f. 33, 'A Catalogue of such Books as Sir Robert Cotton had of on Jacob Chaloner. . . .' 'All other Sir William Dethick books as Sir Robert Cotton supposes in the hands of the said Jacob Challoner', mentions 'An other book in foll having the Ceremony of the Knights of the Bath in paynting'. 'An other book in parchment foll bound and bossed conteyning many Scrutinys [? scutcheons] of the Garter and ther Arms in Coller', while Harl. MS. 6018, f. 166, is a receipt of 1616 from Challoner for 'an old book of Tiltes and Turneys and a book of the Knights of the Bath in colours', returned to him by Cotton.

Like others of Dethick's manuscripts it was then acquired by Sir William Le Neve, Clarenceux (d. 1661), for Dugdale, *Antiquities of Warwickshire*, ed. 1656, p. 531, ed. 1765, p. 494, reprints Bysshe's plates of the Knighthood of the Bath 'delineated from a fair Book, in which they were drawn in much larger Proportions and in Colours, about K. Edw. the ivth Time'; 'Penès Guil. le Neve eq. aur. Claren. R. Arm.' Bysshe, *In Nicholaum Upton Notae*, 1654, p. 20, refers to the manuscript as in 'Bibliotheca Naeviana'. The plates precede the notes.

It was used by, and may have belonged to, Elias Ashmole, Windsor Herald (d. 1692), for engravings by Hollar of the paintings of the Officers of the Order of the Garter on pp. 11 and 15 appear in his *History of the Garter*, facing p. 234.

It was acquired by Henry Mordaunt, Earl of Peterborough (d. 1697), for Bernard, *Catalogi Librorum Manuscriptorum Angliae et Hiberniae*, 1697, tom. ii, p. 196. describes it among the manuscripts of Henry Mordaunt, Earl of Peterborough (d. 1697). Large folios.

6326. 1. 'A book of Honour and Armes containing the Armes, Crests and supporters of the Soveraigns of the Order of the Garter from King Edward III, to King Henry the VIII, inclusively, together with the Armes of most, if not all, of the Companions of the Order, to the Reign of King Edward VI, drawn in Colours, together with some Notes interspersedly upon the Soveraigns, and many of the Knights Companions. Then follow Limned in Colours his first Supper, Shaving, Bathing, etc., through the whole formality, all in the Habits of the Age. Then some Pedigrees of the Kings of Spain.

'After this several Figures drawn at length Limned in Water Colours, two upon the side of each leafe; beginning with King Edward the I and his Queen in their Robes. Then a Knight in very ancient fashioned Armes, and his Lady, with the Inscription of Ricardus de Monte Hermerii Comes Gloucestriae, & Joanna de Dores. On the next page Thomas de Monte Hermerii & Edvardus de Monte Hermerii in Armour. Then on the next Joannes de Monte Aouto, & the next Joannes Comes Sarum, & Matilda Comitissa Sarum. Then Thomas Comes Sarum, & Elionara Comitissa. Then Ricardus Nevil Comes Warwici & Anna filia Ricardi de Bellocampo. Then Ricardus III, Rex Angliae, & Anna filia Domini Comitis Warwici. Then Will. dom. de Ferrars de Groby & Margareta Uxor. All these noblemen are in very Ancient and differently fashioned Armour and Helmets, and upon these Helmets their peculiar Crests. Then two Knights in compleat Armour holding banners in their hands erected perpendicularly. Then follow several other Draughts of Armes, and Constitutions belonging to the Knights of the Garter, and the Computus Mri. Oweni Oglethorp Thesaurarii Ordinis Garterii. After which, or before them, two large sheets, pasted upon Cloth, with the Armes delineated, of the Companions of the Garter, in several Circles and Descriptions of them. Lastly to the end of the Book Travelling Scutcheons, of the Sovereign and Knights Companions, in K. Charles the II time with the titles only printed in French, but no Arms printed except the Kings of Sweden and Dukes of Saxony.'

I owe this information to Professor Francis Wormald.

John Montagu, second Duke of Montagu (d. 1749), then acquired it and would have had a double interest in it, both from its inclusion of the Salisbury Roll, which contains paintings of many whom he claimed as ancestors, and from the paintings of the Creation of Knights of the Bath, since he was made Great Master of the Order of the Bath on its reconstruction in 1725. From him the volume has descended to its present owner, the Duke of Buccleuch.

Anstis writes of this in his *Observations Introductory to an Historical Essay upon the Knighthood of the Bath*, 1725, p. 86. 'Bysshe, and Dugdale in his Warwickshire, have severally exhibited in Sculpture, the Method of conferring this Degree; the original Drawings, from whence these Sculptures were taken, are now in the possession of His Grace the Duke of Montagu: in them, several of the Esquires, as there represented, have, about their Necks, a collar of white Roses with a white Lyon pendent to it, which I have observed in another Place, was the Collar, and Badge used by the Domesticks of Edward the Fourth. But, if Henry VII permitted his Queen Consort to give her Servants that Badge used by her Father Edward IV, then this Sculpture may be the picture referred to in the Appendix, which represented the Manner of Creating Knights of the Bath, at her Coronation.'

The reference is to a statement in Cotton MS. Julius B. 12, p. 33 that K.B.s were created at her Coronation 'in manner and fourme as the picture thereof made, sheweth'.

Contents. Part I. H. S. London concluded that this was in the hand, not of Sir Thomas Wriothesley himself, but of an amanuensis who copied other documents of a non-armorial nature, e.g. Bruges' petition in Soc. Ant. MS. 476 (Anstis's MS. I. 9); it is annotated by Sir T. W. and on p. 30 in the margin is written by him Th. Wr. Greck. and on pp. 19 and 27 ⚔ cf. p. 97.

Part II. p. 81. These shields are from Strangways' Book, ff. 165^d–169^d, Strangways' Roll 516–526. Other shields from this are on pp. 164–9.

p. 123. *pp. 100–1*. At the top of p. 101 is written 'Th. W^r'.

Part V. pp. 160–3. These seven figures are identical with Legh's *Men of Arms* (Parliamentary V.B., see p. 64). The last is unfinished. The others have emblazoned banners, but plain surcoats. The banners are Sees of Chichester and Salisbury, SS. George, Edmund, Edward, and Quarterly France modern and England.

pp. 164–9. These shields are from Strangways' Book, see the note to p. 81 *supra*.

p. 124. *Copy B*. It was H. S. London who noticed that this was not a fifteenth–sixteenth century original and, on calling the attention of Professor Francis Wormald to it in 1948, the latter recognized it as a Hatton–Dugdale facsimile.

Notices, This volume was exhibited at the Birmingham Heraldic Exhibition 1936, no. 541.

p. 126. Under 'Harley 246' add 'ff. 6–14^b. [1st Calais II. D.]'

p. 127. Correct 'Harley 1405' to 'Harley 1408'.

p. 128. Under Harley 6137 for 'ff. 73–89' read 'ff. 72^b–89^b'.

HARLEY 6589

Contents and suggested dates

The flyleaf bears the date 1606.

Folios	Subject	Date
3–8	Parliamentary I. Q ⎫	? 1606
4	Parliamentary I. Y ⎭	
8ᵇ	1st Dunstable N	
9–9ᵇ	Falkirk I. B	1606
10	Nativity Roll	[? 1606]
11	Styward H	[? 1606]
11ᵇ	Glover III. B	1607
12–12ᵇ	Walford I. A	1607
13ᵇ	Caerlaverock IV. M	[? 1607]
15–20	St. George D	1607
21–34ᵇ	Thomas Jenyns II. F	1607
37–40	Thomas Jenyns II. F	[? 1607]
41–43ᵇ	1st Dunstable M	[? 1607]
44–45	Guillim I. B	[? 1607]
46–47ᵇ	Thomas Jenyns III. 1	[? 1607]
48–48	Thomas Jenyns III. J	? early 17th cent.
49–49ᵇ	2nd Dunstable D	? early 17th cent.
50–50ᵇ	Caerlaverock IV. P	[? 1607]
50ᵇ–51	Holland II. A	[? 1607]
51ᵇ	Calais I	[? 1607]

Under Lansdowne 860 A for 'ff. 257–61ᵇ' read '11–11ᵇ' (the 2nd Dunstable Roll: cf. p. 56).

Under Lansdowne 882 for 'Pt. 4' read 'ff. 6–23ᵇ, 67, 67ᵇ'.

p. 160. Under D correct 'Harl. 24ᵇ' to 'Harl. 246'. Between E and F insert heading '17TH CENTURY'.

The Harleian Society

———

FOUNDED 1869. INCORPORATED 1902.

Report for the Year 1961

The Council has to report that the Society has thirteen new subscribers, of whom eight subscribe to the Register Section and three are Libraries. There have been two resignations and two deaths, including that of the Secretary, Mr. R. H. D'Elboux, which having occurred early in 1961 was mentioned in the last Report.

The Visitation of London 1568, should be published in the summer of 1962, and the appearance of *The Register of St. Margaret's, Westminster*, may be expected shortly.

The Annual Accounts, duly audited, are appended.

By order of the Council,

CLITHEROE
Chairman

The Harleian Society

FOUNDED 1869 INCORPORATED 1902

INCOME AND EXPENDITURE ACCOUNT FOR THE YEAR ENDING 31ST DECEMBER, 1961

ORDINARY SECTION

£		£ s. d.	£		£ s. d.
297	Printing and Agents' charges	335 9 9	340	Subscriptions	342 13 4
40	Secretary and Treasurer's expenses (1960 and 1961)	80 0 0	—	Sale of surplus books	44 14 6
10	Other expenses	38 10 10	94	Interest received	103 0 8
63	Decrease in market value of 3½% War Stock	73 10 0	—	Deficit for year, carried to Accumulated Fund	37 2 1
24	Surplus for year, carried to Accumulated Fund	— —		*Note:* Printing and Agents' charges include £300 for a publication in preparation	
£434		£527 10 7	£434		£527 10 7

REGISTER SECTION

£		£ s. d.	£		£ s. d.
—	Printing and Agents' charges	108 18 9	249	Subscriptions	228 1 1
35	Secretary and Treasurer's expenses (1960 and 1961)	70 0 0	—	Sale of surplus books	9 9 0
4	Other expenses	12 0 5		*Note:* Printing and Agents' charges include £100 for a publication in preparation	
210	Surplus for year, carried to Accumulated Fund	46 10 11			
	Note: There was no publication in 1961				
£249		£237 10 1	£249		£237 10 1

BALANCE SHEET

31st December, 1961

	£	Accumulated Fund	£ s. d.	£ s. d.		£		£ s. d.
		Ordinary Section				£	DEBTORS—Subscriptions in arrear ...	113 0 5
	2,806	Balance at 31st December, 1960	2,830 10 3			—	£1,050 3½% WAR STOCK at market value	551 5 0
	(24)	Deficit (Surplus) from Income and Expenditure Account	37 2 1			625	553 NATIONAL SAVINGS CERTIFICATES (ninth issue)	511 10 6
				2,793 8 2		493	POST OFFICE SAVINGS BANK DEPOSIT	754 1 10
	£2,830					735	WESTMINSTER BANK LIMITED Current and Deposit accounts ...	1,410 8 4
	£	**Register Section**	£ s. d.	£ s. d.		1,466		
	279	Balance at 31st December, 1960	488 16 6					
	210	Surplus from Income and Expenditure Account	46 10 11					
	£489			535 7 5				
		Creditors						
	—	Subscriptions received in advance ...		11 10 6				
	£3,319			£3,340 6 1		£3,319		£3,340 6 1

CLITHEROE
A. R. WAGNER } Members of the Council

REPORT OF THE AUDITORS TO THE MEMBERS OF THE HARLEIAN SOCIETY

We have examined the above Balance Sheet and annexed Income and Expenditure Accounts and have obtained all the information and explanations which we considered necessary. In our opinion, proper books of account have been kept by the Society and the Balance Sheet and Income and Expenditure Accounts which are in agreement therewith comply with the Companies Act, 1948, and respectively give a true and fair view of the state of the Society's affairs at 31st December, 1961 and of the results for the year ended on that date.

5, London Wall Buildings,
LONDON, E.C.2.
14th March, 1962.

DELOITTE, PLENDER, GRIFFITHS & CO.,
Chartered Accountants

The Harleian Society

FOUNDED 1869   INCORPORATED 1902

INSTITUTED FOR THE

Publication of Inedited Manuscripts

RELATING TO

GENEALOGY, FAMILY HISTORY AND HERALDRY

Registered Office and Council Room:

79, DUKE STREET, GROSVENOR SQUARE, LONDON, W.I

Council

SIR ANTHONY WAGNER, K.C.V.O., M.A., D.LITT., F.S.A.,
GARTER PRINCIPAL KING OF ARMS (*Chairman*)
SIR CHARLES CLAY, KT., C.B., M.A., LITT.D., F.B.A., F.S.A. (*Vice-Chairman*)
THE LORD CLITHEROE, P.C., D.L., J.P., M.A., F.S.A.
WILFRID J. HEMP, ESQ., M.A., F.S.A.
G. D. SQUIBB, ESQ., Q.C., J.P., M.A., B.C.L., F.S.A., NORFOLK HERALD
EXTRAORDINARY
JAMES A. FRERE, ESQ., F.S.A.
G. H. WHITE, ESQ., O.B.E., M.A., F.S.A.
LESLIE DOW, ESQ., F.S.A.
A. C. COLE, ESQ., M.A., B.C.L., F.S.A., PORTCULLIS PURSUIVANT
MICHAEL MACLAGAN, ESQ., M.A., F.S.A., SLAINS PURSUIVANT
T. D. TREMLETT, ESQ., M.A.
R. O. DENNYS, ESQ., O.B.E., F.S.A., ROUGE CROIX PURSUIVANT
WALTER GOODWIN DAVIS, ESQ., B.A., LL.B., F.S.A.
C. F. H. EVANS, ESQ., M.A., F.S.A.

Hon. Secretary and Treasurer

*N. H. MACMICHAEL, ESQ., F.S.A.

c/o The Muniment Room and Library, Westminster Abbey, London, S.W.I.

Bankers

THE WESTMINSTER BANK LIMITED

21, Lombard Street, E.C.3.

Hon. Auditors

DELOITTE, PLENDER, GRIFFITHS & Co.

Agents

MESSRS. B. F. STEVENS & BROWN, LTD.,

79, Duke Street, Grosvenor Square, London, W.I

*To whom all Subscriptions should be paid and all Communications addressed

Report for the Year 1962

The Council has to report that the Society has six new subscribers, of whom three subscribe to the Register Section and two are Libraries. There have been two resignations.

The Council has also to report with deep regret the death of Mr. W. J. Hemp, a subscriber since 1930 and a Council member since 1937. The resignation of Lord Clitheroe as Chairman was received with regret and the Council were unanimous in electing Sir Anthony Wagner in his place and Sir Charles Clay as Vice-Chairman.

Further unexpected difficulties delayed the publication of *The Visitation of London 1568*, and *The Register of St. Margaret's, Westminster*. Both these books are expected to appear in 1963.

The Annual Accounts, duly audited, are appended.

By order of the Council,

ANTHONY R. WAGNER
Chairman

The Harleian Society

FOUNDED 1869   INCORPORATED 1902

Income and Expenditure Account for the Year ended 31st December, 1962

ORDINARY SECTION

£		£	s.	d.		£		£	s.	d.
335	Printing charges	394	2	4	Subscriptions	342	222	6	1
80 (Two)(yrs.)	Secretary and Treasurer's expenses ..	40	0	0	Sale of surplus books ...	45	46	3	9
39	Other expenses	28	1	7	Interest received	103	98	4	5
73	Decrease in market value of 3½% War Stock				Increase in market value of 3½% War Stock		94	10	0
					Deficit for year, carried to Accumulated Fund	37		19	8
£527		£462	3	11		£527	£462	3	11

Note: There was no publication in 1962 and the printing charges are on account of an intended publication

REGISTER SECTION

£		£	s.	d.		£		£	s.	d.
109	Printing charges	100	0	0	Subscriptions	229	162	16	0
70 (Two)(yrs.)	Secretary and Treasurer's expenses ..	35	0	0	Sale of surplus books	9	25	8	3
12	Other expenses	3	6	1					
47	Surplus for year carried to Accumulated Fund	49	18	2					
£238		£188	4	3		£238	£188	4	3

Note: There was no publication in 1962 and the printing charges are in respect of an intended publication

BALANCE SHEET

31st December, 1962

1961 £		£ s. d.	£ s. d.
	Ordinary Section		
	Accumulated Fund		
2,830	Balance at 31st December, 1961	2,793 8 2	
37	Deficit from Income and Expenditure Account	19 8	
£2,793			2,792 8 6
	Register Section		
488	Balance at 31st December, 1961	535 7 5	
47	Surplus from Income and Expenditure Account	49 18 2	
£535			585 5 7
	Creditors		
12	Subscriptions received in advance		13 0 1
£3,340			£3,390 14 2

1961 £		£ s. d.	£ s. d.
113	DEBTORS—Subscription in arrear (since received)		65 7 3
551	£1,050 3½% WAR STOCK at market value		645 15 0
512	553 NATIONAL SAVINGS CERTIFICATES (ninth issue)		531 5 3
754	POST OFFICE SAVINGS BANK DEPOSIT		772 18 10
1,410	WESTMINSTER BANK LIMITED Current and Deposit Accounts ...		1,375 7 10
£3,340			£3,390 14 2

ANTHONY R. WAGNER
RODNEY DENNYS } Members of the Council

REPORT OF THE AUDITORS TO THE MEMBERS OF THE HARLEIAN SOCIETY

We have examined the above Balance Sheet and annexed Income and Expenditure Account and have obtained all the information and explanations which we considered necessary. In our opinion, proper books of account have been kept by the Society and the Balance Sheet and Income and Expenditure Account which are in agreement therewith comply with the Companies Act, 1948, and respectively give a true and fair view of the state of the Society's affairs at 31st December, 1962 and of the results for the year ended on that date.

5, London Wall Buildings,
London, E.C.2.
1st April, 1963.

DELOITTE, PLENDER, GRIFFITHS & CO.,
Chartered Accountants